The Redemption

The Redemption

An Interdisciplinary Symposium on Christ as Redeemer

Edited by

Stephen T. Davis
Daniel Kendall, SJ
Gerald O'Collins, SJ

OXFORD
UNIVERSITY PRESS

OXFORD

UNIVERSITY PRESS

Great Clarendon Street, Oxford OX2 6DP

Oxford University Press is a department of the University of Oxford.
It furthers the University's objective of excellence in research, scholarship,
and education by publishing worldwide in

Oxford New York

Auckland Bangkok Buenos Aires Cape Town Chennai
Dar es Salaam Delhi Hong Kong Istanbul Karachi Kolkata
Kuala Lumpur Madrid Melbourne Mexico City Mumbai Nairobi
São Paulo Shanghai Taipei Tokyo Toronto

Oxford is a registered trade mark of Oxford University Press
in the UK and in certain other countries

Published in the United States
by Oxford University Press Inc., New York

British Library Cataloguing in Publication Data

Data available

Library of Congress Cataloging in Publication Data

Data available

ISBN 0-19-927145-3

1 3 5 7 9 10 8 6 4 2

Typeset by
Kolam Information Services Pvt. Ltd, Pondicherry, India
Printed in Great Britain
on acid-free paper by
Biddles Ltd., King's Lynn.

Preface

From the beginning until the end of the twentieth century many individual authors published important studies on redemption, or God's activity through Jesus Christ and the Holy Spirit in delivering human beings from the bondage of sin and evil, purifying them from guilt, and bringing them into a new relationship of covenanted love. Expositions of this central Christian doctrine early in the century by Gustaf Aulén, Karl Barth, Emil Brunner, James Denney, Peter Forsyth, Robert Campbell Moberly, Hastings Rashdall, and Jean Rivière proved landmarks. The century closed with important studies on redemption and related themes from such scholars as Godfrey Ashby, Ian Bradley, Jacques Dupuis, Paul Fiddes, Colin Gunton, Alan Hultgren, John McIntyre, Bernard Sesboüé, Raymund Schwager, Jon Sobrino, Richard Swinburne, Michael Winter, and Frances Young.

Theological reflection on redemption (or atonement and salvation, as it is often called) could be enhanced by more symposia, especially by those of an interdisciplinary character. An interdisciplinary work written by teachers (plus one research student) at the University of Durham and edited by Stephen Sykes, *Sacrifice and Redemption* (Cambridge: Cambridge University Press, 1991), concentrated on one important issue (the complexity of themes in the metaphor of sacrifice) and consisted of essays that had been commissioned and did not emerge from a meeting involving the contributors. More than a decade later, at the start of the third millennium, it seemed worthwhile gathering experts in a variety of disciplines (biblical studies, ancient Christian writers, ancient Jewish writers, theology, philosophy, preaching, literature, and the fine arts) from three continents to explore collaboratively the redemption. Hence we brought together eighteen specialists, many of whom have already published studies on different aspects of belief in human redemption. We managed to secure papers, sometimes more than one paper, in all the fields just mentioned.

To promote advance discussion and establish stronger connecting threads between the different contributions, we encouraged those presenting papers to circulate them in advance to all members of the symposium. In every case drafts had been sent out (and often made available by e-mail) for feedback before we met at Dunwoodie, New York (20–3 April 2003) for the Redemption Summit itself. Three earlier interdisciplinary 'summit' meetings held at Dunwoodie treated issues of Christ 'in himself': his personal resurrection from the dead (1996), his eternal life within the Trinity of Father, Son, and Holy Spirit (1998), and his incarnation (2000). The proceedings of all three 'summits' have been published by Oxford University Press: *The Resurrection* (1997), *The Trinity* (1999), and *The Incarnation* (2002). The fourth 'summit' focused on Christ 'for us' or Christ as the unique redeemer of all humanity and the whole created universe.

After a critical survey of the issues (O'Collins), this collection moves from biblical questions (Seitz, Fee, Wright, Aletti, and Ochs), through some classical teaching and reflection on redemption (Daley and Bynum), and on to theological and philosophical debates (Stump, Davis, and Evans). It ends with some 'practical' applications of redemption faith to literature, art, and preaching (Kiely, Brown, and Shuster). This volume proposes approaching redemption faith in an organized and coherent way: namely, by reflecting on biblical, historical, foundational, systematic, and practical data and questions. What now follows in the preface will unfold the movement of the book as a whole and the interrelationship between the particular papers. To achieve even more unity, Chapter 1 will also point out links with later chapters and their place in the landscape of redemption studies. That chapter, along with those to follow, recognizes how various issues connected with the redemption cannot be solved with relative ease. Here, as elsewhere, orthodox Christian faith must face serious and difficult challenges.

In Chapter 1, Gerald O'Collins selects and outlines seven key questions for any theology of the redemption: its nature as deliverance, expiation, and saving love; the appropriate language for redemption; the role of Christ as divine–human redeemer in his incarnation, ministry, death, and resurrection (with the coming of the Holy Spirit); the universal need for redemption; Christ the unique and universal redeemer; the link between creation and redemption;

the appropriation of redemption through justification, along with the Church's subordinate role in mediating redemption. O'Collins ends by recognizing some further significant questions which could be raised about redemption.

In Chapter 2, Christopher Seitz argues against Tom Wright that, as regards the reconciling work of Christ, using some 'extra-apostolic' categories to capture the 'self-understanding' of Jesus runs at least two serious risks: the displacement of the plain sense witness of the apostolic record by varieties of historical redescription; the generation of a category which drives christology away from concern with obedience and enactment (Hans Frei) towards Jesus' knowledge and self-awareness. This makes it difficult to reattach densely theological statements about Christ's identity with the Father to descriptions of Christ the reconciler. Moreover, these theological statements find their logic in relationship to the OT witness, a witness which is easily distorted by efforts at describing how it might have been heard by Jesus.

In his exposition of Isaiah 53 and the suffering servant, Seitz opens up the issue of whether and to what extent Christian convictions about the redemption are rooted in the historical Jesus' sense of his own redemptive mission. Can a critical examination of the Gospels establish that he already understood and interpreted both his ministry and his passion as redemptive—even if he did not necessarily apply to himself Isaiah 53? Or are theologies of the redemption, which became deeply coloured by the suffering servant theme, simply created by Paul and subsequent Christian writers? Some of the chapters that follow—in particular, those by Gerald O'Collins and Tom Wright—indicate that, whatever we decide about the particular issue of Isaiah 53, Pauline theology of redemption is to some extent continuous with the intentions of Jesus himself, even though that theology was radically transformed by the new situation brought by the resurrection of the crucified Jesus and the coming of the Holy Spirit.

Various items constitute this continuity between Jesus' view of redemption and that of Paul. First, Paul resembled Jesus in construing the plight of sinful human beings. God's law was not being observed and the wrong people were running the Temple. Second, the parable of the prodigal son reveals how Jesus understood sin as self-imposed exile. Paul, so Wright continues to argue, thought of Israel as an unredeemed people still living in exile. Third, both Jesus and Paul knew that the problem facing Israel was the problem facing the whole of humanity. All people should die to sin so that they could come alive to the new world of the kingdom (Jesus) or to the new exodus that had taken place in the death and resurrection of Jesus the Messiah (Paul). In fact, through his own public acts and words Jesus already gave an exodus-shaped meaning to his ministry, death, and resurrection. He opened his ministry by coming through the waters of baptism and spending forty days in the desert (Mark 1: 9–13). At the end he chose the setting of the Passover, a feast which more than any other recalled the original exodus, to indicate through the words and prophetic gestures with which he instituted the Eucharist the saving significance of his imminent death and resurrection (Mark 14: 12–25).

Fourth, Jesus persistently implied that God's redeeming promises to Israel and through Israel to the world had been fulfilled in his own person and activity (e.g. Luke 10: 23–4; Matt. 13: 16–17). For Paul the long story of the creator and covenant God had come to its climax in Jesus, the Jewish Messiah—as Wright's chapter abundantly illustrates. Fifth, the present/future balance in Jesus' preaching of the kingdom (i.e. salvation from God) opened the way for the present/future balance in Paul's elaborated theology of redemption. Thus Jesus interpreted his imminent death in terms of the forgiveness of sins and the coming kingdom (Matt. 26: 28–9; Mark 14: 25), just as Paul was to preach Jesus as delivering us from the evil age and for the age to come (e.g. Gal. 1: 4; Rom. 5: 21). Sixth, for Jesus to accept his saving offer of the kingdom meant becoming his disciple and following him; for Paul the redeeming call of God meant allowing oneself to be defined by the crucified and risen Messiah Jesus.

The last point introduces the essential shift entailed by the resurrection of Jesus and the gift of the Holy Spirit. With that turning point, redemption emerged as involving the new life of baptism and hope for the coming life of resurrection (e.g. Rom. 6: 3–11). Paul's understanding of redemption continued the basic themes of Jesus' preaching, but it was creatively transformed by what happened at the first Easter, with the resurrection and the outpouring of the Holy Spirit.

These reflections on Jesus' own redemptive intentions will be further elaborated in the chapter by O'Collins. We can turn now to three contributions on Paul.

In Chapter 3, Gordon Fee maintains that for Paul 'salvation in Christ' is the work of the Trinity and has as its goal 'a people for God's name'. The means of salvation is the death of Christ on the cross, an event of such moment that Paul expresses it through a variety of metaphors, no one of which is the whole. Which metaphor appears at any point in his letters depends on the perspective of human downfall that he has in view. This chapter examines in turn 'redemption' from slavery to sin and the law with its concomitant adoption as God's children and heirs, by Christ's being set forth as a 'hilasterion' (place/means of atonement) on our behalf, by God 'reconciling' his enemies to himself, and 'justifying' the ungodly, not reckoning their trespasses against them but instead offering them forgiveness and pardon. All these effects come through the Spirit.

In Chapter 4, Tom Wright examines the 'new perspective on Paul' launched by Ed Sanders in 1977 which has become a storm centre; but Sanders never really set out the implications of his work for a detailed Pauline theology of redemption, of the cross, of justification. Before doing this, Wright factors in other recent and equally important movements: the narrative readings of Paul, and the 'fresh perspective' of a political reading in which Paul affirms that Jesus is Lord and Caesar is not. Wright also recognizes the meaning of redemption as the new exodus, the historical moment when God finally liberates his people from the ultimate slavery and so brings his justice and freedom to the world. This enables Wright to see, in several dimensions, seven of the overlapping stories (there are probably many more) which go to make up Paul's thought world: the stories of creation, of Israel, of Torah, of the human race, of the apostolic ministry, of the powers, and of God himself. In each of these the cross plays a central role; by analysing these different roles Wright gets a more rounded picture of what Paul thought redemption was all about, how the cross effects it, and what 'justification' might mean. Several traditional theories prove their worth within a larger framework which prevents any single one from dominating the horizon.

In Chapter 5, Jean-Noël Aletti presents 2 Corinthians 5: 21 ('God made Christ to be sin') within its literary context and deals with two main readings, the sacrificial one (God made Christ to be a sin offering) and the one which sees Christ identified with the mortal effects of sin. The second is preferable, but even that reading cannot account for the paradoxical formulation. Since Paul does not justify his affirmations, all exegesis is to some extent conjectural. When Paul uses such a paradox, he wants to insist that God's ways cannot be mentally digested and that it is only through the rhetoric of exaggeration that Christ's death can be announced.

In Chapter 6, Peter Ochs asks: shall we say that the people Israel refers to the Redeemer only by referring to the One whose coming in the distant future leads us to the end of salvation history? He suggests that the rabbinic prayer book, the *siddur*, is the primary teacher in the ways of Israel's Redeemer, and that the lesson of the *siddur* is not only about the One for whom we wait, and wait. The *siddur* also teaches Jewish worshippers to pray, in this world, for the One who will redeem Israel tomorrow from what she suffers today. Ochs examines four primary sections of the Morning Prayer Service, the *shacharit*. He suggests that each section may (but without doctrinal implications) be read as awakening attentiveness to a certain level of ensoulment, such that all four levels prepare the way not only to encounter intimately the God who redeems, but also to be engaged by that God as agent of redemption and not merely as petitioner. The first section, Morning Blessings, awakens one to that animated soul without whose corporeal movements no redemption can be sought, let alone found. The second section, Verses of Praise, awakens to that relational soul which stirs up the voice that seeks 'redemption'. The third section, Sh'ma, calls into being that corporate soul of souls through which alone the petitioning voice can articulate its needs clearly, but as corporate and not merely individual subject. The fourth section, the Amidah, awakens that divine image through which Israel (naming now both individual and people) is now received no longer as mere petitioning subject but as agent of the One who redeems.

Beginning with Chapter 7, the book moves to the Patristic and medieval periods with the contributions of Brian Daley and Caroline Walker Bynum. In Chapter 7, Brian Daley faces one of the difficult theological questions for Christian believers: why—given the alienation of humanity from God through its own history of sin—we can be redeemed from sin and reconciled with God only through a Saviour who is both divine and human. If we regard redemption as a 'work', as something Jesus has accomplished for us through his death and resurrection, it is hard to see why he could not be simply a holy creature, delegated by God to fulfil a crucially important task in history. This chapter argues that the broad tradition of Patristic theology, in both East and West, did not think of redemption so much in terms of 'what Jesus did' as in terms of 'who Jesus is'. Surveying early Christian theologians from the second to the seventh century, this chapter offers a rough typology of the images and categories in which they conceive redemption, and argues that in all of them, the real reconciliation between God and humanity achieved by Christ begins in his own person, in the unity of natures and the transformation of humanity into the perfection of God's image. The chapter concludes by observing that christology, soteriology, and the theology of grace are really inseparable from one another in the Patristic period; it also suggests that the reason theologians moved from this approach to a transactional mode of redemption in the medieval West is probably connected with the replacement of typological or figural thinking by a more analytical or logical model, claiming the figural approach to scripture and to the theology of redemption may help us understand better how our own fundamental welfare as creatures in need of salvation is decisively rooted not only in the actions of Jesus but also in his very identity.

In Chapter 8, Caroline Bynum offers a historian's view of redemption theology in the later Middle Ages and argues four points. First, there are not, as the textbooks claim, two theologies of the atonement in the later Middle Ages—satisfaction theory and exemplarism—but only one. Second, this theology emphasizes blood and suffering, even where the shedding of Christ's blood is not seen as making satisfaction or proving an example of moral response. Third, medieval ideas of the redemption provided by Christ (which was relatively little discussed) cannot be understood unless they are placed in the context of the much more widely discussed theologies of purgatory and the eucharist. They must also be understood against the background of lived piety and not seen simply as the theories of university theologians. Fourth, the influence of late medieval piety has been profound, so much so that it is often hard for modern theologians to avoid making some very medieval assumptions. Bynum discusses three legacies of medieval ideas: the idea that pain itself is redemptive, the stress on body (and bodily difference) as central to understandings of personhood, and the idea of the Saviour as 'representing' humankind (which in medieval theology means something very different from the way the idea is often used today).

In Chapter 9, the book begins to take up foundational and systematic issues. Eleonore Stump examines one form of the problem of evil:

namely, that having to do with horrendous evil. She considers whether there is anything that can redeem the suffering even of those whose lives include the perpetration of great evil. She explores this question in a way unusual for a contemporary philosopher— that is, through a study of narrative rather than simply through analytic philosophy. In particular, she explores a biblical narrative of horrendous evil, in which it is the sufferer's own doing that his life is wrecked: the story of Samson. Stump contends that one way to understand Samson's suffering is that his suffering is redeemed by his repentance—in his letting go of his self-protective isolation, in his willingness to be open to God, and in his drawing near to God. In this condition, he accepts what God gives him as a gift, and in using that gift for the purpose for which God gives it, he in effect accepts the giver with the gift. And so Samson's suffering is redeemed in relationship with God, in his being present to God and God's being present to him. This reading of the narrative thus provides a defence, a possible morally sufficient reason for God's allowing suffering that accompanies the perpetration of a horrendous evil.

In Chapter 10, Stephen Davis defines and analyses philosophically two systems of salvation, karma and grace. He does so at an entirely theoretical level: that is to say, no application is made to actual religions of the world. Criticisms of both systems are discussed, as well as possible defences against those criticisms. The conclusion is that, at a purely philosophical level, grace is a superior system of salvation. The editors invited an expert in Buddhism to contribute a chapter on redemption according to non-theistic traditions, but he eventually had to withdraw. Davis did not intend to make up for that gap. His essay is a contribution to the philosophy of religion, not to the history of religions.

In Chapter 11, Stephen Evans addresses the question: how should Protestants and Catholics view their remaining disagreements over the doctrine of justification? He argues in support of the view of Cardinal Avery Dulles that Christians can regard other Christians as genuinely so, even when they have serious disagreements over such a doctrine as justification. Evans defends this view by appealing to a 'critical realist' account of theology, in which theological affirmations must be seen as approximative in character and as having a pragmatic as well as cognitive value. Claims of Nicholas Wolterstorff and Merold Westphal support the view that Christians can recognize the views of other Christians that they believe to be mistaken as nevertheless views that those Christians ought to hold as part of their authentic Christian commitment. This general principle is then applied to specific issues about the doctrine of justification. Evans suggests ways in which Catholic–Protestant differences can be narrowed, and then argues that remaining disagreements should be understood in the manner outlined above.

The fourth and concluding section of the book ('The Redemption Practised and Proclaimed') begins, in Chapter 12, with Robert Kiely's argument that the concept of 'redemption', in both its secular and religious connotations, has persisted in literature as a dialectic between faith and scepticism. Beginning with passages from the Book of Job and Matthew's Gospel, this chapter demonstrates that foundational texts from scripture include mockery as well as hope for a deliverance from suffering. Before addressing four American texts, Kiely looks at contextual definitions of redemption in two secular plays of Shakespeare and a religious sermon from John Dunne, which serve as literary bridges to English language works of a later period. In the American narratives, Henry David Thoreau's *A Week on the Concord and Merrimac Rivers*, Herman Melville's *Billy Budd*, Toni Morrison's *Beloved*, and Flannery O'Connor's 'Parker's Back', a secular American emphasis on self-reliance, an achievable goal, and repudiation of the past appears to take precedence over the need for a redeemer who will deliver human beings from past sins and death. Yet, somewhat surprisingly, even in the most ironical and irreverent of the American stories, allusions to the scripture coupled with the realization of the limits of self-reliance leave a narrow opening for a hope not unlike that expressed in the opening passages from Job and Matthew.

In Chapter 13, David Brown focuses on three images that appear in liturgical contexts (Lamb of God, descent into hell, and the Prodigal Son), and examines the various techniques employed by artists and composers to help the believer appropriate relevant aspects of the gospel of redemption. With the Agnus Dei the two principal artistic images considered are those by the van Eych brothers and Zurburán; in music Mozart and Bach for more traditional settings, and Haydn, Beethoven, Britten, and Macmillan for war contexts. Grünewald and Raphael, and Bach and Stainer, are then used to contrast the two quite different understandings that have been assigned in Christian history to the phrase 'descent into hell'. Finally, Rembrandt's approach to the Prodigal Son is contrasted with those of Steen and

Murillo, while Prokofiev and Britten are used as the two main musical examples. Numerous theological issues are raised in this chapter, including the development of images beyond their original biblical setting, alternative ways of interpreting penitence and peace, the limits of representation, and rival conceptions of grace.

In Chapter 14, Marguerite Shuster's analysis of fifty sermons (four classic and forty-six contemporary) on Romans 8: 18–25 provides the opportunity to explore how, if at all, preachers see human redemption as linked to the redemption of the whole created order. If we do not see the creation as having a future, or if we see its future as unrelated to our own, we will have little motivation apart from sheer sentimentality to care for it. These sermons take up exceedingly diverse themes, with only a minority dealing seriously with the redemption of creation. There is, moreover, a significant correlation between sermons that make no mention of the resurrection of the body and those that fail to suggest any hope for the rest of creation. Long-standing anxieties about bodiliness and about materiality generally still remain. Shuster also detects a dismaying reluctance on the part of the majority of the preachers to come to any robust conclusions about the worth of this creation that is destined one day to be set free by God.

As the summaries offered above indicate, this volume contains fourteen presentations from the Redemption Summit. In fact, each of the presentations was followed by a response that initiated the discussion of the particular paper. To avoid making this volume too long, we did not include the responses. In publishing this book, we are aware that it is not a precisely crafted systematic theology of redemption. The great systematic theologies of redemption in the twentieth century have come from individual authors like Karl Barth (d. 1968) and Karl Rahner (d. 1984). Yet we believe that our joint volume, which examines the major sources and issues for such a theology of redemption, can prepare the ground for some theologian of the twenty-first century to undertake such a systematic project.

We are most grateful to the McCarthy Family Foundation and, specifically, to Dr Eugene and the late Maureen McCarthy for their most generous and prayerful support of all our 'summits', down to the Redemption Summit of Easter 2003. Our special thanks go to Monsignor Peter Finn, Rector of St Joseph's Seminary, Dunwoodie (Yonkers, NY), for his gracious hospitality and help. We wish to thank warmly the Catholic Archbishop of New York, Edward

Cardinal Egan, for his continuing encouragement. We also want to thank John Allen, Tracy Early, Robert Blair Kaiser, Claudia McDonnell, Gary Stern, John Thavis, Cindy Wooden, Kenneth Woodward, and other members of the media for their vivid interest and sincere support. Lastly, we are particularly grateful to Hilary O'Shea, Lucy Qureshi, Jenny Wagstaffe, and Enid Barker of Oxford University Press, to all the scholars who participated in and contributed to our symposium, to those who shared in the open seminar on 24 April which followed the Redemption Summit, and to Caroline Walker Bynum who joined us in running that seminar.

As the human race continues to be torn apart by violence and to need reconciliation more than ever, we offer the results of this interdisciplinary and international symposium to all who seek justice, peace, and deliverance from evil and who know that in doing so they want something that no mere human being can give them. We dedicate our book with great affection to Fr Gerard F. Rafferty and all the Dunwoodie staff, who provided us with extraordinarily efficient assistance over four 'summits'. We end by endorsing the prayer of David Gascoyne in 'Ecce Homo': that 'from the tree of human pain' God may redeem 'our human misery', so that humanity's 'long journey through the night | May not have been in vain'.

STEPHEN T. DAVIS, DANIEL KENDALL, SJ,
and GERALD O'COLLINS, SJ
16 June 2003

Contents

List of Plates

Abbreviations

An Bib	Analecta Biblica
ANF	Ante-Nicene Fathers
BAGD	W. Bauer, W. F. Arndt, F. W. Gingrich, and F. W. Danker, *Greek–English Lexicon of the New Testament and Other Early Christian Literature*, (3rd edn., Chicago: University of Chicago Press, 2000).
BCE	Before Common Era
BETL	Bibliotheca Ephemeridum Theologicarum Lovaniensium
Bib.	*Biblica*
BibNotiz	*Biblische Notizen*
BibTrans	*Bible Translator*
CCG	Corpus Christianorum, Series Graeca
CE	Common Era
ET	English Translation
GNB	Good News Bible
GNO	*Gregorii Nysseni Opera*
HKAT	Göttinger Handkommentar zum Alten Testament
JSNT	*Journal for the Study of the New Testament*
JSOT	*Journal for the Study of the Old Testament*
JTS	*Journal of Theological Studies*
KJV	King James Version
LXX	Septuagint
NIB	New International Bible
NorTT	*Norsk Teologisk Tidsskrift*
NovT	*Novum Testamentum*
NPNF	Nicene and Post-Nicene Fathers
NSRV	New Revised Standard Version
NT	New Testament
OT	Old Testament
PG	Patrologia Graeca (J.-P. Migne)
PL	Patrologia Latina (J.-P. Migne)

SC	Sources Chrétiennes
ST	*Summa Theologiae*
TNIV	Today's New International Version
WA TR	*Weimar Ausgabe Tischreden* (volumes of Martin Luther's *Table Talk*)
WUNT	Wissenschaftliche Untersuchungen zum Neuen Testament

Participants in the Redemption Summit
(Easter, 2003, New York)

JEAN-NOËL ALETTI   Born in Groslay, France, he received his master's in philosophy and mathematics (Paris, Sorbonne); licentiates in theology at the Seminaire des Missions (Lyon) in 1973 and scripture at the Pontifical Biblical Institute (Rome) in 1975; and a doctorate in scripture (Pontifical Biblical Institute) in 1981. Currently he is Professor of New Testament Exegesis at the Pontifical Biblical Institute. Recent publications include: 'Romans 8: The Incarnation and its Redemptive Impact', in S. T. Davis, D. Kendall, and G. O'Collins, *The Incarnation* (Oxford: Oxford University Press, 2001), *Saint Paul Épître aux Éphésiens* (Paris: Gabalda, 2001), *Israël et la Loi dans la lettre aux Romains* (Paris: Cerf, 1998), *Il racconto come teologia: Studio narrativo del terzo Vangelo e del libro degli Atti degli Apostoli* (Rome: Dehoniane, 1996), and *Jésus Christ fait-il l'unité du Nouveau Testament?* (Paris: Desclée, 1994).

DAVID BROWN   Born in Galashiels, Scotland, he obtained an MA (in classics) at Edinburgh and a second MA (in philosophy and theology) at Oxford, and his Ph.D. (in moral philosophy) from Cambridge. Formerly a Fellow of Oriel College, Oxford, he is currently Van Mildert Professor of Divinity in the University of Durham. He was elected a Fellow of the British Academy in 2002. Publications by him include: (with David Fuller) *Signs of Grace: Sacraments in Poetry and Prose* (London: Continuum, 2000), *Discipleship and Imagination: Christian Tradition and Truth* (Oxford: Oxford University Press, 2000), and *Tradition and Imagination: Revelation and Change* (Oxford: Oxford University Press, 1999).

CAROLINE WALKER BYNUM   Born in Atlanta, Ga., she received her BA from the University of Michigan in 1962 and her Ph.D. from Harvard University in 1969. She is Professor of Medieval European History at the Institute for Advanced Study in Princeton and University Professor emerita at Columbia University. Recent publications include: *Metamorphosis and Identity* (New York: Zone Books, 2001), (co-ed.) *Last Things: Death and the Apocalypse in the Middle Ages* (Philadelphia: University of Pennsylvania Press, 2000), *The Resurrection of the Body in Western Christianity, 200–1336* (New York: Columbia University Press, 1995), and *Fragmentation and Redemption: Essays on Gender and the Human Body in Medieval Religion* (New York: Zone Books, 1991).

SARAH COAKLEY   Born in London, she obtained her undergraduate degree (1973) as well as her doctoral degree (1982) from the University of Cambridge. Currently she is Edward Mallinckrodt, Jr., Professor of Divinity, Harvard University. Writings by her include: *God, Sexuality and the Self: an Essay 'On the Trinity'* (Cambridge: Cambridge University Press, 2004), (ed.) *Re-Thinking Gregory of Nyssa* (Oxford; Blackwell, 2003), *Powers and Submissions: Spirituality, Philosophy and Gender* (Oxford, Blackwell, 2002), (ed.) *Religion and the Body* (Cambridge: Cambridge University Press, 1997), (co-ed.) *The Making and Remaking of Christian Doctrine: Essays in Honour of Maurice Wiles* (Oxford: Clarendon Press, 1993), and *Christ Without Absolutes: A Study of the Christology of Ernst Troeltsch* (Oxford: Oxford University Press, 1988).

BRIAN DALEY   Born in Orange, NJ, he obtained his bachelor's degree at Fordham University in 1961, and a BA (MA) in classics and philosophy at Merton College, Oxford, in 1964. After entering the Society of Jesus in that year, he obtained a Ph.L. at Loyola Seminary, Shrub Oak, NY, in 1966, and an STL at the Hochschule Sankt Georgen, Frankfurt-am-Main, in 1972. He received a D.Phil. in theology from Oxford University in 1978. He is currently the Catherine F. Huisking Professor of Theology at the University of Notre Dame. Books by him include *Gregory of Nazianzus: A Translation of Selected Works, with Introduction* (New York: Routledge, 2003), a translation and revision of Hans Urs von Balthasar's *Cosmic Liturgy: The Universe According to Maximus the Confessor* (San Francisco: Ignatius Press, 2002), *The Dormition of Mary: Early Greek Homilies* (Yonkers, NY: St Vladimir's Press, 1998), and *The Hope of the Early Church: A Handbook of Patristic Eschatology* (Cambridge and New York: Cambridge University Press, 1991).

STEPHEN T. DAVIS   Born in Lincoln, Neb., he obtained his bachelor's degree from Whitworth College in 1962, his M.Div. from

Princeton Theological Seminary in 1965, and his Ph.D. from the Claremont Graduate University in philosophy in 1970. Currently he is Professor of Philosophy of Religion at Claremont McKenna College. Books by him include: *God, Reason, and Theistic Proofs* (Edinburgh: Edinburgh University Press, 1997), *Risen Indeed: Making Sense of the Resurrection* (Grand Rapids, Mich.: Eerdmans, 1993), *Death and Afterlife* (New York: St Martin's Press, 1989), and *Encountering Jesus* (Atlanta: John Knox Press, 1988).

C. STEPHEN EVANS   Born in Atlanta, Ga., he received his bachelor's degree from Wheaton College in 1969 and his Ph.D. from Yale University in philosophy in 1974. He is currently University Professor of Philosophy and Humanities at Baylor University. His published works include: *Faith Beyond Reason* (Edinburgh: Edinburgh University Press, 1998), *The Historical Christ and the Jesus of Faith: The Incarnational Narrative as History* (Oxford: Oxford University Press, 1996), and *Passionate Reason: Making Sense of Kierkegaard's Philosophical Fragments* (Bloomington, Ind.: Indiana University Press, 1992).

GORDON FEE   Born in Ashland, Or., he received his BA and MA from Seattle Pacific University (1956, 1958) and his Ph.D. from the University of Southern California in 1966. He is currently Professor Emeritus of New Testament Studies at Regent College, Vancouver, British Columbia. Books by him include: *Paul, the Spirit and the People of God* (Peabody, Mass.: Hendrickson, 1996), *Paul's Letter to the Philippians* (Grand Rapids, Mich.: Eerdmans, 1995), *God's Empowering Presence* (Peabody, Mass.: Hendrickson, 1994), and *Commentary on the First Epistle to the Corinthians* (Grand Rapids, Mich.: Eerdmans, 1987).

DANIEL KENDALL   Born in Miami, Ariz., he obtained his bachelor's degree from Gonzaga University in 1962, his STM from Santa Clara University in 1971, and his STD from the Gregorian University in Rome in 1975. Currently he teaches theology at the University of San Francisco. Publications by him include: (with Gerald O'Collins) *In Many and Diverse Ways: A Festschrift Honoring Jacques Dupuis, SJ* (Maryknoll, NY: Orbis, 2003), (ed. with Stephen Davis and Gerald O'Collins) *Incarnation* (Oxford: Oxford University Press, 2001), (ed. with Stephen Davis) *The Convergence of Theology: A Festschrift Honoring Gerald O'Collins, SJ* (Mahwah, NJ: Paulist, 2001), (ed. with Stephen Davis and Gerald O'Collins) *Trinity* (Oxford: Oxford University Press, 1999), and (ed. with Stephen Davis and Gerald O'Collins) *Resurrection* (Oxford: Oxford University Press, 1997).

ROBERT KIELY   Born in New York City, he obtained his bachelor's degree from Amherst College and his Ph.D. in English and American Literature from Harvard University in 1962. Currently he is Loker Professor of English and American Literature and Harvard College Professor at Harvard University. His books include: *Still Learning: Spiritual Sketches from a Professor's Life* (Tucson, Ariz.: Medio Media, 1999), *Postmodernism and the Nineteenth Century Novel* (Cambridge: Harvard University Press, 1992), *Beyond Egotism: The Fiction of James Joyce, Virginia Woolf, and D. H. Lawrence* (Cambridge; Harvard University Press, 1980), and *The Romantic Novel in England* (Cambridge: Harvard University Press, 1973).

MICHAEL C. McCARTHY   Born in San Francisco, Calif., he received his BA from Santa Clara University in 1987, his BA/MA (literae humaniores) from Oxford University in 1991, his M.Div. from the Jesuit School of Theology at Berkeley in 1992, and his Ph.D. from the University of Notre Dame in 2003. Currently he is Edmund Campion Fellow and assistant professor in the Religious Studies and Classics Departments at Santa Clara University, California.

CAREY NEWMAN   Born in Florida, he earned degrees from the University of South Florida (BA, 1980), Southwestern Baptist Seminary, M.Div., 1983), the University of Aberdeen (M.Th., 1985), and Baylor University (Ph.D., 1989). He is currently the Executive Director of the Institute for the Study of Christian Origins at Baylor University. Recent publications include: (ed.) *The Jewish Roots of Christological Monotheism: Papers from the St. Andrews Conference on the Historical Origins of the Worship of Jesus* (Leiden: E. J. Brill, 2000), (ed.) *Jesus and the Victory of God: An Assessment with Responses* (Downers Grove, Ill.: InterVarsity Press, 1999), 'Resurrection as Glory: Divine Presence and Christian Origins' (in *Resurrection*, Oxford: Oxford University Press, 1997), and *Paul's Glory-Christology* (Leiden: E. J. Brill, 1992).

PETER OCHS   Born in Boston, he earned degrees at Yale (BA, 1971, Ph.D. 1979) and Jewish Theological Seminary (MA, 1974). Currently he is Edgar Bronfman Professor of Modern Judaic Studies at the University of Virginia. He is co-editor, with Stanley Hauerwas, of the series *Radical Traditions: Theology in a Postcritical Key* (for Westview Press/Perseus). His publications include: *Peirce, Pragmatism and the Logic of Scripture* (Cambridge: Cambridge University Press, 1998), *Reviewing The Covenant: Eugene Borowitz and the Postmodern Renewal of Theology* (Albany: State University of New York Press, 2000), (with Robert Gibbs and Steven Kepnes) *Reasoning after Revelation: Dialogues in Postmodern Jewish Philosophy* (Boulder, Colo.: Westview Press, 1998), (ed.) *The Return to Scripture in Judaism and Christianity* (New York: Paulist, 1993), (ed.) *Understanding the Rabbinic Mind* (Atlanta, Ga.: Scholar's Press, 1990), (co-ed.) *Christianity in Jewish Terms* (Boulder, Colo.: Westview, 2000), and (co-ed.) *Textual Reasonings* (London and Grand Rapids, Mich.: SCM/Eerdmans, 2002).

GERALD O'COLLINS   Born in Melbourne, Australia, he obtained his bachelor's degree from Melbourne University in 1957 and his Ph.D. from Cambridge University in 1968. Since 1974 he has taught theology at the Gregorian University in Rome. Publications by him include: (with Mario Farrugia) *Catholicism* (Oxford: Oxford University Press, 2003), *Easter Faith: Believing in the Risen Jesus* (London: Darton, Longman & Todd, 2003), (co-ed.) *The Incarnation* (Oxford: Oxford University Press, 2002), *Incarnation* (London and New York: Continuum, 2002) *The Tripersonal God* (Mahwah, NJ: Paulist Press, 1999), and (co-ed.) *The Trinity* (Oxford: Oxford University Press, 1999).

ALAN PADGETT   Born in Washington, DC, he earned his BA from Southern California College (1977), M.Div. from Drew University (1981), and D.Phil. from Oxford University (1990). Currently he is Professor of Systematic Theology at Luther Seminary (Minn.). Books by him include: *Science and the Study of God* (Grand Rapids, Mich.: Eerdmans, 2003), (co-author) *God and Time: Four Views* (Downers Grove, Ill., InterVarsity Press, 2001), (co-author) *Christianity and Western Thought*, ii (Downers Grove, Ill.: InterVarsity Press, 2000), *God, Eternity and the Nature of Time* (paperback edn.: Eugene, Or.: Wipf & Stock, 2000), and (ed.) *Reason and the Christian Religion: Essays in Honour of Richard Swinburne* (Oxford: Oxford University Press, 1994).

GERARD F. RAFFERTY   A native of New York, he received his bachelor's degree from Columbia University in 1974. He attended Harvard Divinity School before entering St Joseph's Seminary, Dunwoodie. In 1979 he was ordained as a priest for the Archdiocese of New York. He received his SSL degree from the Pontifical Biblical Institute in Rome in 1987. Since then he has served both as a parish priest and as an instructor of sacred scripture at St Joseph's Semin-ary, where he currently holds the John Cardinal O'Connor Distin-guished Chair in Hebrew and Scripture. He has been the on-site coordinator of all four 'summit' meetings which met at St. Joseph's, Easter 1996, 1998, 2000, and 2003.

ALAN SEGAL   Born in Worcester, Mass., he earned his bachelor's degree at Amherst College in 1967 and his Ph.D. at Yale University in 1975. Currently he is the Ingeborg Rennert Professor of Jewish Studies and Professor of Religion at Barnard College, Columbia Uni-versity. Publications by him include *Charting the Hereafter: The After-life in Western Religions* (Garden City, NY: Anchor Doubleday, 2003), *The Messiah: Developments in Earliest Judaism and Christianity* (Minne-apolis: Fortress, 1992), *Paul the Convert: The Apostleship and Apostasy of Paul the Pharisee* (New Haven: Yale University Press, 1990), and *Rebecca's Children* (Cambridge: Harvard University Press, 1988).

CHRISTOPHER R. SEITZ   Born in Blowing Rock, NC, he obtained BA with honours from the University of North Carolina at Chapel Hill in 1976, MTS from Virginia Theological Seminary in 1979, and, after a year of study at the University of Munich, an STM from Yale Divinity School in 1981. He received from Yale University an MA in 1982, M.Phil. in 1984, and Ph.D. in 1986. He was Professor of Old Testament at Yale University 1987–98. Currently he is Professor of Old Testament and Theological Studies, the University of St Andrews. His publications include: *Figured Out* (Louisville, Ky.: West-minster/John Knox, 2001), 'Isaiah 40–66', in *The New Interpreter's Bible*, vi (Nashville, Tenn.: Abingdon, 2001), (ed.) *Nicene Christianity: The Future for a New Ecumenism* (Grand Rapids, Mich.: Brazos, 2001), *Word Without End* (Grand Rapids, Mich.: Eerdmans, 1998), *Isaiah 1–39* (Louisville, Ky.: Westminster/John Knox, 1993), and *Theology in Conflict* (Berlin: De Gruyter, 1989).

MARGUERITE SHUSTER   Born in Santa Paula, Calif., she obtained her bachelor's degree at Stanford in 1968, M.Div. from Fuller Theo-logical Seminary in 1975, and her Ph.D. from the Fuller Theological Seminary Graduate School of Psychology in 1977. She served as a Presbyterian pastor for nearly twelve years. Currently she is Profes-sor of Preaching at Fuller Theological Seminary. Her publications include *The Fall and Sin* (Grand Rapids, Mich.: Eerdmans, 2003), (ed.) *Who We Are: Our Dignity as Human* (Grand Rapids, Mich.: Eerdmans, 1996), (co-ed.) *Perspectives on Christology: Essays in Honor of Paul*

K. Jewett (Grand Rapids, Mich.: Zondervan, 1991), and doctrinal sermons in *God, Creation, and Revelation* (Grand Rapids, Mich.: Eerdmans, 1991).

ELEONORE STUMP   Born in Germany, she received her BA in classical languages from Grinnell College, where she was valedictorian of her class in 1969, and she was awarded her Ph.D. in medieval studies and medieval philosophy from Cornell University in 1975. She has taught at Oberlin College, Virginia Tech., and the University of Notre Dame; since 1992 she has been the Robert J. Henle Professor of Philosophy at St. Louis University. She has held grants from the American Association of University Women, the Mellon Foundation, the Pew Charitable Trusts, the National Endowment for the Humanities, the Center for Philosophy of Religion at Notre Dame, and the National Humanities Center. She has been President of the Society of Christian Philosophers and of the American Catholic Philosophical Association, and in 2003 she gave the Gifford Lectures. Her writings include: *Thomas Aquinas* (London and New York: Routledge, 2003), (ed. with N. Kretzmann) *Augustine* (in the series Cambridge Companions to Philosophy) (Cambridge: Cambridge University Press, 1999), (ed.) *Reasoned Faith* (Ithaca, NY: Cornell University Press, 1993), (ed. with N. Kretzmann) *Aquinas* (in the series Cambridge Companions to Philosophy (Cambridge: Cambridge University Press, 1993), *Dialectic and its Place in the Development of Medieval Logic* (Ithaca, NY: Cornell University Press, 1989), *Boethius's In Ciceronis Topica* (Ithaca, NY: Cornell University Press, 1988), and *Boethius's De topicis differentiis* (Ithaca, NY: Cornell University Press, 1978, repr. 1989).

N. T. WRIGHT   Born in Morpeth, Northumberland, he received his BA from Exeter College, Oxford, 1971, his MA from Exeter College, Oxford, 1975, his D.Phil. from Exeter College, Oxford, 1981, and his Oxford DD in 2000. After serving as canon theologian at Westminster Abbey, he was appointed Bishop of Durham in 2003. Recent publications include: *The Resurrection of the Son of God* (London: SPCK; Minneapolis: Fortress, 2003), a series of popular guides to the New Testament, beginning with *Mark for Everyone* (London: SPCK, 2001), *Romans*, in the *New Interpreter's Bible*, x (Nashville, Tenn.: Abingdon, 2002), *The Challenge of Jesus* (Downers Grove, Ill.: InterVarsity Press, 1999), *The Way of the Lord* (Grand Rapids, Mich.: Eerdmans, 1999), *The Millennium Myth* (Louisville, Ky.: Westminster John Knox, 1999), (with Marcus J. Borg) *The Meaning of Jesus: Two*

Visions (San Francisco: HarperSanFrancisco, 1999), and *Jesus and the Victory of God* (Philadelphia: Fortress, 1996).

Note: Sarah Coakley, Daniel Kendall, Michael McCarthy, Carey Newman, Alan Padgett, Gerard Rafferty, and Alan Segal were all active and valuable participants in the Redemption Summit, but this volume does not include contributions from them.

1

Redemption: Some Crucial Issues

GERALD O'COLLINS, SJ

> Love bade me welcome: yet my soul drew back,
> Guilty of dust and sin.
>
> (George Herbert, 'Love (III)')

> It is our universal duty as human beings to elevate ourselves to
> this idea of moral perfection [found in the Son of God as] the
> personified idea of the good principle.
>
> (Immanuel Kant, *Religion within the Limits of Reason Alone*, 2. 1)

Three earlier 'summit' meetings held in New York treated issues concerning Christ 'in himself': his personal resurrection from the dead (1996), his eternal life within the Trinity of Father, Son, and Holy Spirit (1998), and his incarnation (2000). The fourth 'summit' of Easter 2003 focused on Christ 'for us' or Christ as the unique redeemer for all humanity and the whole created universe. Between our third and fourth 'summits' the terrorist attacks in the United States of 11 September 2001, the new wars in Afghanistan and Iraq, and the continuing wars in the Congo, the Sudan, and elsewhere violently tore humanity apart and showed more than ever the need for reconciliation on a world scale.

Even more than at the previous 'summits', the issues that could have been raised seemed endless. The vast amount of material on redemption from the scriptures and the entire Christian tradition, not to mention current theological discussion and official teaching, raises question after question. Since, however, my brief is to compose an introductory chapter and not a complete book, I have selected seven overlapping questions which serve to map some important features of the present landscape of studies on the redemption and which can introduce the chapters that follow. First of all, I take up the seemingly endless evil from which the whole of humanity and the universe itself needs to be redeemed.

UNIVERSAL NEED FOR REDEMPTION

Christian faith has always considered redemption to be necessary for all human beings. The all-pervading presence of evil and sin established this universal need for redemption.[1] Human beings were understood to be enslaved by hostile powers (e.g. 1 Cor. 15: 24–5; Eph. 1: 22–3; 2: 1–2), to suffer in exile, and to live under the shadow of death. Although the scriptures can think of death as the natural, normal end of a long and fruitful life (e.g. Gen. 25: 7–11) and even a friend (e.g. Phil. 1: 21–3), they also present death as the effect and sign of sin (e.g. Rom. 5: 12) and as an enemy to be overcome (e.g. 1 Cor. 15: 26). The heart of evil, however, is human sin, a condition which affects all people (e.g. Rom. 3: 23) and proves a tyrannical master enslaving human beings (c.g. Rom. 6: 12 7: 25). At times the Bible also portrays our sinful condition as that of those who are defiled and need cleansing (e.g. Ps. 51: 2, 7; 1 Cor. 6: 9–11), or those who lack affection and compassion (e.g. Luke 16: 19–31; Rom. 1: 31).

Through St Augustine of Hippo (d. 430), Paul's teaching on the inherited need for redemption (Rom. 5: 12–19) became articulated as 'original sin', a doctrine often accompanied by speculations

---

[1] Some expect that, along with 'the pervading presence of evil and sin', I should stress the universal 'wrath of God against all evil and sin' (Rom. 1: 18). Certainly we should not ignore Paul here, but we need to watch our language and that of the NT carefully. Whereas the theme of divine judgement recurs in the NT explicit reference to God's 'anger' is largely confined to the Pauline letters and Revelation. Furthermore, 'anger' for Paul is mostly eschatological or something to come (e.g. 1 Thess. 1: 10) and, as in this example, has, as it were, a life of its own and is not called the anger of 'God'. Translations are prone to add 'of God' to such texts as Rom. 5: 9 where the Greek original simply speaks of 'being saved from the anger'. Within the course of history, 'anger' expresses the permissive will of God who 'hands sinners over'—in the sense of allowing them to experience the self-destructive alienation from God which they have chosen for themselves (see Rom. 1: 24, 26, 28). 'Anger' designates God's judgement on sin and abhorrence of sin. In the context of this chapter, it is important to insist that the NT never invokes God's anger in connection with the sufferings and death of Christ.

about a state of original justice (graced by 'natural', 'supernatural', and 'preternatural' gifts), which Adam and Eve lost by falling into sin. The theory of evolution and other challenges to the view that all human beings are descended from one pair of ancestors have led many Christian thinkers to revise their account of the human race and its fall into sin. The heart of Paul's teaching concerns, however, an inherited solidarity in sin which personal sins express and endorse, and which found abundant confirmation from horrendous human behaviour in the twentieth century. In their own secular way, the novels of Albert Camus (d. 1960) depict our universal lack of innocence (e.g. *The Fall*). E. L. Doctorow's recent novel, *City of God* (2000), uses a broad range of characters to set out the omnipresent human suffering which prompts a hunger for meaning and salvation. The fictional works of Flannery O'Connor (d. 1964) spell out even more vividly the ubiquitous reality of sin and evil that goes back to human origins.

In the Genesis story, although offered the creator's friendship, Adam and Eve substitute themselves for God by independently deciding on good and evil and determining their destiny for themselves. Alienated from God, 'the man and his wife' become alienated from one another (Gen. 3: 16) and see their world spiralling out of control into murder and vengeful violence (Gen. 4: 24). Adam and Eve symbolize not only the dignity of human beings made in the divine image and likeness (Gen. 1: 26–7) but also their solidarity in sin from which the Redeemer will deliver them.

At the start of the third millennium, any belief about the universal need for redemption faces at least three challenges. First, a Pelagian-style self-redemption has assumed a new face in the modern world. 'The best and the brightest' often pursue success, aspire to self-improvement, and simply shake their heads over any suggestion that they are somehow enslaved, defiled, and in need of redemption. Poles apart from King David, who after committing adultery and murder, confesses 'I have sinned against the Lord' (2 Sam. 12: 13), self-sufficient moderns will only allow 'I made a little mistake'. Sometimes they will not admit even that, but talk more vaguely: 'Mistakes were made'. Selfishness is sometimes so smoothly distributed over every aspect of their life that they can continue for years without appreciating their radical need for redemption.

Sadly, some Christian writers and leaders in the Western world even champion the idea of self-redemption. They seem to endorse the notion, 'whatever our spiritual problems, we humans can deal with and solve them'. Let me give just one example, Bishop Richard Holloway. When he reinterprets the grace of justification, it becomes self-justification, the 'moment of self-acceptance' when we change, and accept ourselves 'utterly' and 'unconditionally'.[2] In place of our being reconciled to God through the mission of the Son and the Holy Spirit and so receiving peace (Rom. 5: 1–11; Col. 1: 20), Holloway's version of redemption is reduced to our making peace with ourselves or to the creed of self-redemption propagated, as Robert Kiely illustrates below, by Ralph Waldo Emerson (d. 1882) and other notable writers. Holloway's account converges with the 'karmic' traditions criticized below by Stephen Davis, who defends 'grace' and the faith that human beings are radically incapable of saving themselves.

Second, many Christians (and others) have come to acknowledge that redemption is needed not only because of personal sin but also because of sinful 'structures', deep faults in cultures and societies that institutionalize enslavement to evil, pervasive corruption, and selfish unconcern for the sufferings of masses of people. Sins are primarily personal, but they also create and preserve evil structures which seem to enjoy a life of their own in keeping whole populations indentured to evil.

Third, more and more believers have become aware that the scope of redemption extends beyond individuals and societies to the environment. In the face of rising, global-warmed seas and polluted atmosphere, the NT teaching about the whole universe hoping for reconciliation with God has assumed a new urgency (e.g. Rom. 8: 18–23; Col. 1: 20). A novel like Doctorow's *City of God* expresses and reinforces the widespread sense that humanity and its universe needs God's redemptive action if we are to survive and flourish. But how should we describe, albeit haltingly, what redemption is like?

---

[2] *Doubts and Loves: What is Left of Christianity* (Edinburgh: Canongate, 2001), 124–6.

The Nature of Redemption

When questioned on the nature of redemption[3] (or, what are often its equivalent terms, atonement and salvation[4]), one might answer by pointing to the goal of redemption, those finally redeemed and at home with God and the redeemed universe to come, 'the new heaven' and 'the new earth' promised in the scriptures (e.g. 2 Pet. 3: 13; Rev. 21: 1). Resurrected from the dead, the redeemed will be delivered from all the forces of evil and, purified from sin, will enjoy the utterly fulfilling happiness of God's loving company. Ancient and modern Christian witnesses have depicted the passage to final salvation as (*a*) a victorious liberation from evil, (*b*) the expiation of sins, and (*c*) the saving power of divine love.

Apropos of (*a*), NT and post-NT Christians understood redemption to break the curse of death and the power of sin, so that death has now been transformed into a passage from the dominion of sin into eternal, utterly satisfying life. The viciously cruel crucifixion of Jesus, while symbolizing the weakness and failure of suffering, became the means of human redemption. By dying and rising, Jesus overcame sin, evil, and their tragic consequences, and effected a new exodus from bondage. To celebrate this deliverance, Christian liturgies took over songs with which Moses and Miriam led the Jewish people in

---

[3] See F. W. Dillistone, *The Christian Understanding of Atonement* (London: Nisbet, 1968); The Doctrine Commission of the General Synod of the Church of England, *The Mystery of Salvation* (London: Church House Publishing, 1989); C. E. Gunton, *The Actuality of the Atonement* (Edinburgh: T. & T. Clark, 1988); M. Hengel, *The Atonement* (London: SCM Press, 1981); A. J. Hultgren, *Christ and his Benefits: Christology and Redemption in the New Testament* (Philadelphia: Fortress, 1987); J. McIntyre, *The Shape of Soteriology* (Edinburgh: T. & T. Clark, 1992); G. O'Collins, 'Salvation', in D. N. Freedman (ed.), *Anchor Bible Dictionary*, 6 vols. (New York: Doubleday, 1992), v. 907–14; B. Sesboüé, *Jésus-Christ l'unique médiateur: Essai sur la rédemption et le salut*, 2 vols. (Paris: Desclée, 1988–91); R. Schwager, *Jesus in the Drama of Salvation: Toward a Biblical Doctrine of Redemption* (New York: Crossroad, 1999); R. Swinburne, *Responsibility and Atonement* (Oxford: Clarendon Press, 1989).

[4] Usually 'atonement' is used more narrowly than 'redemption' or 'salvation', and expresses the means of redemption or salvation. Christians declare: 'it is through the atoning death of Jesus that we are redeemed/saved from our sins'. One may speak of coming (and complete) redemption or salvation for human kind and the created world but not of their coming atonement. Both salvation and redemption point to an entire programme which has been, is being, and will be accomplished, and which entails explaining all that being saved/redeemed from and being saved/redeemed for includes.

praising God for their victorious liberation from slavery (Exod. 15: 1–21). While the story of the exodus from Egypt was the prototype *par excellence* of such redemptive deliverance and the new life of freedom, from the earliest times Christian writers and artists found other precedents in such OT stories as Noah and his family being delivered from the flood, Daniel from the lions' den, the three youths from the fiery furnace, Jonah from the great fish, and Susannah from the two wicked elders. So much, briefly, about (*a*); I return below to (*b*) and (*c*), two other major ways of interpreting the passage to salvation.

The whole process of salvation has often been summarized, especially in Eastern Christianity, as 'deification', understood to be a sharing, not in the divine substance, but in the divine life or the loving relationship of the Son to the Father in the Holy Spirit. St Athanasius (d. 373) and other ancient writers interpreted in that way the bold language of 2 Peter 1: 4. Thus the ultimate *eudaimonia* of the redeemed will be seeing God 'face to face', a 'flourishing' that goes beyond the highest happiness imagined by Aristotle or any of the other remarkable thinkers of human history.[5] Final redemption will complete the being made 'in the image and likeness' of God (Gen. 1: 26–7). This becoming 'like God' will make redeemed men and women perfectly good, with the qualification that in this 'deification' such properties will belong to them contingently and not essentially.

With all that said about those finally redeemed, we are frustrated by our lack of direct access to their condition. We cannot answer the question: what does it feel like to be definitively redeemed and with God? At best we may point to shining examples of heroic men and women, whose lives reveal to some degree what it is like to be delivered from evil, purified from sin, and taken into the loving company of the tripersonal God. The lives of such saintly persons indicate partially and in advance what, through the whole process of redemption, we are saved from and what we are to be saved for.

---

[5] See A. Kenny, *Aristotle on the Perfect Life* (Oxford: Clarendon Press, 1992); id., *Essays on the Aristotelian Tradition* (Oxford: Clarendon Press, 2001), 17–46. Thomas Aquinas relates some of Aristotle's texts to the Christian doctrine of the everlasting happiness of the blessed in heaven (*ST* II–II, 2. 7). Aristotle deserved the 'compliment': in the *Eudemian Ethics* and *Nicomachean Ethics* he had linked perfect happiness to friendship and, even more, to the contemplative life of the intellect. He held that the life of the mind is the highest of which we human beings are capable.

The experience of full redemption eludes our grasp, and the tentative language we use calls for close scrutiny. Unlike the doctrine of, and terminology for, the one person of the Son of God in two natures (i.e. Christ 'in himself'), the redemption (i.e. Christ 'for us') did not provoke theological debate and teaching from the first seven general councils of the church. All parties simply took for granted that it was only through Christ that human beings could be saved, and that the purpose of everything from his incarnation to his final coming was, as the creeds stated, 'for us and for our salvation'. One enduring result of this lopsided development has been that, whereas theology and official teaching have tended to watch carefully talk about Christ 'in himself', talk about Christ 'for us' has at times suffered from harmful imprecision. Let us take some examples: first 'redemption' itself, then 'satisfaction', 'propitiation', 'sacrifice', and 'love'.[6]

THE LANGUAGE OF REDEMPTION

Two OT terms had a special role in creating a background for the NT and post-NT language of 'redemption' or 'buying back': *padhah* (to ransom or to free slaves by payment) and *ga'al* (to play the role of a relative or vindicator; to fulfil a promise or pledge). In his chapter below, Tom Wright correctly insists that the divine rescue of the Israelites from the slave-market of Egypt gave a specifically Jewish meaning to the language of redemption when used by Paul. The manumission of slaves and the ransoming of prisoners of war (out of captivity by a purchasing agent) also helped to shape the cultural setting in which NT Christians proclaimed Christ as 'redeeming', 'buying', 'ransoming', 'freeing', or 'liberating' 'us', 'you', 'his people', 'Israel', 'many', or 'all'. In a fictitious purchase by some divinity, owners would come with slaves to a temple, sell them to a god, and from the temple treasury receive money which the slaves had

---

[6] On 'redemption', 'sacrifice', and 'love', see A. Hastings, A. Mason, and H. Pyper (eds.), *The Oxford Companion to Christian Thought* (Oxford: Oxford University Press, 2000). Ibid. for such related terms as 'anger', 'atonement, theories of', 'covenant', 'creation', 'cross and crucifixion', 'death', 'devil', 'evil, problem of', 'fall', 'grace', 'Holy Spirit', 'humanity', 'justification', 'priesthood', 'punishment', 'reconciliation', 'resurrection', 'sacrifice', 'salvation', 'sanctification', and 'sin'. See also two issues of *Interpretation*: 'Atonement and Scripture', 52/1 (1998) and 'Atonement and the Church', 53/1 (1999).

previously deposited there out of their savings. Freed from their previous masters, the slaves became the 'property' of the god. At the temple of Apollo in Delphi and elsewhere inscriptions record how 'so and so [the slave being named] was sold to Apollo at the price of [the sum being specified] for freedom'. Christians knew themselves to be redeemed *from* the slavery of sin and purchased *for* God, so that they might become his 'slaves' or free children.

This kind of language could still have provided a lively image in the thought world of such early Christian communities as that in Corinth, while being more or less a dead metaphor in centres where few or no slaves and/or ex-slaves belonged to the community. St Paul writes of the human race being, along with the whole creation, 'in bondage to decay' and 'groaning' for 'redemption' (Rom. 8: 18–23), of Jews being slaves to the law (Gal. 4: 1–7; 5: 1), and of Gentiles being enslaved to 'gods' and 'elemental spirits' (Gal. 4: 8, 9). Christ has actually and not just fictitiously 'redeemed' or 'bought' us (Gal. 3: 13; 4: 4). At times the New Testament authors speak of Christ 'buying' us at 'a price' (1 Cor. 6: 20; 7: 23), 'ransoming' us with his 'precious blood' (1 Pet. 1: 18–19), 'giving himself to ransom/free us' (Tit. 2: 14), and 'giving his life as a ransom (*lutron* or *antilutron*) for many' (Mark 10: 45; 1 Tim. 2: 6). But nowhere does the NT speak of this 'price' or 'ransom' being paid to someone (e.g. God) or to something (e.g. the law).

In the first millennium and later, some Christians expanded the content of this metaphor[7], taking 'ransom' as if it described literally some kind of transaction, even a specific price paid to someone. They correctly recognized the hopelessly enslaved situation of sinful human beings, who were set free only by Christ's atrocious death. But in treating the metaphor literally and failing to observe its limits, they even spoke of human beings as being in the possession of devil, whose 'rights' of ownership were 'respected' by the price of Jesus'

---

[7] As Gordon Fee illustrates in his chapter, along with the primary language of 'redemption' Paul uses other such metaphors as expiation and self-sacrificing love to express the saving effects of the Christ-event; for a full list of Paul's version of these effects, see J. A. Fitzmyer, *Romans* (The Anchor Bible, 33; New York: Doubleday, 1993), 116–24. The use of metaphorical language suggests how problematic it is to express redemption in literal speech; the use of a plurality of metaphors indicates how no metaphor by itself is even minimally adequate. The role of paradoxes in Paul's letters (see J.-N. Aletti's chapter below) reveals the difficulty the Apostle felt in stating God's redemptive activity in any speech.

blood being paid to release them from bondage.[8] For the NT, however, the act of redemption was 'costly', in the sense that it cost Christ his life. The beneficiaries of this redeeming action became 'free' (e.g. Gal. 5: 1) or, by coming under Christ's sovereignty, 'slaves' to him (e.g. Rom. 1: 1; 1 Cor. 7: 22). Nowhere does the NT accept or imply that Satan has any rights over human beings. The metaphor of 'redemption' represents Christ as effecting a deliverance but not as literally paying a price to anyone. In developing his logically structured theory or fully worked out understanding of redemption, St Anselm of Canterbury (d. 1109) vigorously opposed any talk of the devil's 'rights'. Through *Cur Deus Homo?* Anselm established 'satisfaction' as an enduringly standard term for Christ's redemptive work when understood as expiation.

'Every sin,' Anselm argues, 'must be followed either by satisfaction or by punishment' (*Cur Deus Homo?*, 1. 15). God does not wish to punish but to see the good project of creation 'completed' (2. 5). Satisfaction, Anselm insists, requires from human beings not only that they should stop sinning and seek pardon but also that they do something over and above existing obligations: namely, a work of supererogation that will satisfy for the offence. However, since all sin offends the honour of the infinite God, the reparation must have infinite value—something of which finite human beings are incapable. Moreover, they have nothing extra to offer God, since they already owe God everything. Thus Anselm concludes to the 'necessity' of the incarnation. Only the *God*-man can offer something of infinite value; the hypostatic union confers such value on the human acts of Christ. Only the God-*man* has something to offer; being without sin, Christ is exempt from the need to undergo death and hence can freely offer the gift of his life as a work of reparation for the whole human race.

Anselm laid a fresh stress on the humanity and human freedom of Christ, who spontaneously acts as our representative and in no way is to be construed as a penal substitute who passively endured sufferings to appease the anger of a 'vindictive' God. Anselm's theology of satisfaction has often been criticized for being juridical and 'Roman'. In fact, its cultural roots were found rather in monasticism

---

[8] St Gregory of Nazianzus vigorously protested against the whole idea of divine redemption as a ransom paid to the devil (*Oratio* 45. 22), but his protests failed to carry the day.

and the feudal society of northern Europe. So far from being a legal or private matter, the 'honourable' service owed by monks to their abbots and vassals to their lords was a religious and social factor that guaranteed order, peace, and freedom. Denying the honour due to superiors meant chaos. Anselm's thoroughly logical version of redemption may be vulnerable on other grounds,[9] and one may prefer other language for interpreting the 'expiatory' aspect of redemption. But such preferences can never be an excuse for misrepresenting his theology of satisfaction, which still retains its grandeur and fascination.[10]

The expiatory dimension of redemption has, from the start of Christianity, been expressed in terms of Christ the great high priest and victim offering a unique *sacrifice* that once and for all expiated sins (Heb. 2: 17–18) and brought a new and final covenant relationship between God and human beings. Some Christians, especially from the late Middle Ages, have interpreted this to mean that Jesus was a *penal substitute* who was personally burdened with the sins of humanity, judged, condemned, and deservedly punished in our placc: through his death he satisfied the divine justice and *propitiated* an angry God. Anselm's theory about Jesus offering satisfaction to meet the requirements of commutative justice and set right a moral order damaged by sin acquired, quite contrary to Anselm's explicit statements, elements of punishment and vindictive justice. Such penal additions to Anselm's theology of satisfaction turn up in the Council of Trent's teaching on the sacrifice of the mass (from its twenty-third session of 1562) and, even more, in the writings of Martin Luther and John Calvin. Such Catholic preachers as J. B. Bossuet (d. 1704) and L. Bourdaloue (d. 1704) also spoke of God's vengeance and anger being appeased at the expense of his crucified Son. As a victim of divine justice, Christ was even held to suffer the pains of the damned. Themes from this penal substitutionary view linger on in the works of Hans Urs von Balthasar, Wolfhart Pannenberg, and some other twentieth-century theologians[11]

Many Christian thinkers reject this language as entailing an unacceptable vision of God, supported by misinterpretations of the

---

[9] See G. O'Collins, *Christology* (Oxford: Oxford University Press, 1995), 200–1.

[10] See P. Gilbert, H. Kohlenberger, and E. Salmann (eds.), *Cur Deus Homo* (Studia Anselmiana, 128; Rome: S. Anselmo, 1999); Sesboüé, *Jésus-Christ l'unique médiateur*, 328–45.

[11] See Sesboüé, *Jésus-Christ l'unique médiateur*, 67–79; 360–5.

scapegoat ceremony on the Jewish Day of Expiation, of the fourth suffering servant song (Isa. 52: 13–53: 12), of Jesus' cry of abandonment on the cross, and of some dramatic passages from Paul's letters (e.g. 2 Cor. 5: 21; Gal. 3: 13).[12] Victimized by human violence and not by a vindictive God, the non-violent Christ, through his self-sacrificing death as our representative (not penal substitute), removed the defilement of sin and restored a disturbed moral order. In developing his ideas on cultures and Christ as the non-violent victim of collective violence, René Girard has rightly drawn attention to some processes involved in human sin and violence.[13] Nevertheless, one must insist that the NT never speaks of redemption altering God's attitudes towards human beings and reconciling God to the world. The sending or coming of God's Son and the Spirit presupposes God's loving forgiveness. Through Christ and the Spirit, God brings about redemptive reconciliation by renewing us; it is our resistance to God that needs to be changed. Both John (e.g. John 3: 16; 1 John 4: 10) and Paul (e.g. Rom. 8: 6–11; 2 Cor. 5: 18–21) bear eloquent witness to the loving initiative of God the Father in the whole story of the redemptive reconciliation of human beings and their world. Years before Paul and John wrote, Jesus summed up his vision of God in the parable of the prodigal son, better called the parable of the merciful father (Luke 15: 11–32). Any penal substitution seems incompatible with the central message of that parable. But to argue this in detail would require examination of a full range of NT texts.

Some writers (as we saw above) and communities still maintain the language of God's 'anger' being propitiated and 'appeased' by Christ our 'penal substitute'.[14] Thus the New International Version, after translating *hilasterion* in Romans 3: 25 as 'a sacrifice of atonement', adds in a note an alternate translation: 'as the one

---

[12] In his chapter, J.-N. Aletti warns against using 2 Cor. 5: 21 to support the idea of a real transfer of sin and curse to Christ. By itself that verse does not represent fully Paul's soteriology, and its paradoxical nature defies straightforward exegesis. Tom Wright, however, argues on the basis of Rom. 2: 17–3: 9 and Gal. 3: 10–13 that Paul held that Jesus took 'Israel's curse on himself'. With reference to Rom. 8: 3, Wright understands Paul to say that God punished sin and did so in the flesh of Jesus.

[13] For a bibliography on Girard, see R. Schwager, *Must there Be Scapegoats? Violence and Redemption in the Bible* (Leominster: Gracewing, 2nd edn., 2000); J. G. Williams (ed.), *The Girard Reader* (New York: Continuum, 1997), 295–302.

[14] In his chapter, Gordon Fee marshals the difficulties against the view that 'God's wrath against sin' is propitiated, and places the language of 'wrath' correctly. Those who transgress the law become guilty, are therefore 'destined for wrath', but are forgiven by God.

who would turn aside his wrath, taking away sin'. The NIV seems guided by doctrinal convictions when thus using twelve words (in what looks like a commentary) to translate a single Greek term, which is normally rendered 'means of expiation'. Not surprisingly the NIV study edition takes 'the fuller meaning' of the Greek *hilasmos* in 1 John 2: 2 to be 'the one who turns aside God's wrath' and adds: 'God's holiness demands punishment for man's sin. God, therefore, out of love (1 John 4: 10; John 3: 16), sent his Son to make substitutionary atonement for the believer's sin. In this way the Father's wrath is propitiated (satisfied, appeased); his wrath against the Christian's sin has been turned away and directed toward Christ.' Undoubtedly the NIV and the Christian traditions it represents are right in taking seriously the terrible evil of human sin. But attributing to the NT the notion of God's anger being 'propitiated' or 'appeased' by that anger being directed against his Son does not express what Paul and John write. In Romans 3, it is *God* who lovingly provides the *hilasterion* or means of expiating the corruption of sin and destroying its power. In *The Theology of Paul the Apostle* James Dunn distances himself from talk of appeasement and propitiation of divine anger, but rightly shows how that does not involve dropping the language of 'sacrifice',[15] as Ernst Käsemann asserted.[16] Sacrificial language may be open to abuse, but it should not therefore be abandoned.[17]

The language of sacrifice expresses the costly self-giving of Christ who let himself be victimized by the powers of this world. Over and over again, the Synoptic Gospels show us how he valued every individual, and not simply the socially advantaged (e.g. Mark 10: 21), as unique and irreplaceable. Through love Christ made himself vulnerable, and his loving self-sacrifice produced life and growth; this sacrifice brought a renewed communion between human beings and the tripersonal God.[18] Through a sacrifice which comprises Christ's death and resurrection, along with the coming of the Holy Spirit, human beings were made fit to enter a new and loving fellowship

---

[15] (Grand Rapids, Mich.: Eerdmans, 1998), 212–33.

[16] In *Jesus Means Freedom* Käsemann wrote: 'If we have any concern for the clarity of the Gospel and its intelligibility to the present generation, theological responsibility compels us to abandon the ecclesiastical and biblical tradition which interprets Jesus' death as sacrificial' (Philadelphia: Fortress, 1970), 114.

[17] See the Doctrine Commission, *Mystery of Salvation*, 114–17.

[18] In expounding Christ's passion as a 'meritorious sacrifice', Thomas Aquinas stresses how, from beginning to end, it was inspired by love (*ST* 3. 48. 3 *resp.*).

with the all-holy God. Here the root of a term proves illuminating: by Christ's *sacri-ficium* or 'holy making', men and women have been made holy. His 'sacri-fice' enables them to join him in entering the very sanctuary of God (Heb. 9: 11–12, 24) and enjoy the heavenly 'banquet' (e.g. Matt. 8: 11). With this support for (loving self-)sacrifice, we move from the language of redemption to the Redeemer.

The Redeemer

While never giving Christ the title 'Redeemer', the NT calls him 'our redemption (*apolutrosis*)' (1 Cor. 1: 30) and sixteen times names him 'Saviour' (e.g. Luke 2: 11). Redemptive activity, to be summarized as deliverance from evil, expiating or cleansing from sin, and changing and reconciling through love, marks the whole story of Jesus from his incarnation through to his resurrection from the dead and coming of the Spirit. Christian writers, in particular the Greek Fathers, have associated Christ's redemptive work with the incarnation, the 'becoming flesh' of the Son of God, from whose fullness we receive 'grace upon grace' (John 1: 14, 16). In an *admirabile commercium* or 'wonderful exchange', first formulated by St Irenaeus (d. *c*.200), 'God (or the Son of God or the Word) became human, in order that we humans might become God (or be divinized).' Later Western devotional practices and writers, from Anselm of Canterbury, the Protestant Reformers, and beyond, have in various ways linked deliverance from the power of sin and death with Christ's crucifixion. Eastern Christians normally go beyond the crucifixion to insist as well on the redemptive impact of Christ's descent to the dead, his resurrection, and the coming of the Holy Spirit.

Whenever the treatment of Christ's redemptive work skips straight from the incarnation to his death and resurrection, we miss the historical mindset of the Redeemer himself—something which can be gleaned from a discerning and critical use of the Gospels. First of all, during his ministry Jesus presented his activity in the service of the present and coming divine kingdom as the victorious conflict with satanic powers (e.g. Mark 3: 27). He taught his followers to pray for deliverance 'from the evil one' (Matt. 6: 13; Mark 14: 38; Luke 11: 4). Jesus knew his redemptive work to involve liberation from sin and evil. Second, at the Last Supper he initiated the way of interpreting his death and resurrection as expiating sin which defiles human beings and damages their relationship with God. His words, 'this is my body for you' and 'this is the blood of the covenant poured out for many' (1 Cor. 11: 24; Mark 14: 24), and his prophetic gestures in breaking the bread and sharing the cup signalled, among other things, a cleansing from the defilement of evil and a new communion of life with God (1 Cor. 10: 14–17). Paul's words about Christ 'expiating sins in his blood' (Rom. 3: 25) rightly express what Jesus had already intended and done at the Last Supper.

Third, many of the actions and words of Jesus during his ministry remain almost unintelligible unless we acknowledge his redemptive love. Thus the longest and most beautiful parable, which shows a father dealing so compassionately with the painful difficulties created by the sinfulness of his two sons, never mentions love explicitly, but points transparently to the divine love at work through Jesus (Luke 15: 11–32). He presents himself as the teacher who wants to found a new family by turning his disciples into his brothers and sisters (Mark 3: 35). Such a project expresses the divine love effectively revealed in Christ. Through his loving solidarity with those to whom he ministers, he shows himself to be the merciful 'doctor' who sits at table with the sinful 'sick' (Mark 2: 15–17). He repeatedly pictures the goal of redemption as a joyful banquet which will never end, a feast of love when all will rejoice together in the kingdom of God. In short, what we know from the ministry of Jesus clearly reveals his redemptive mindset, and underpins the teaching about redemption developed by Paul and his successors. The Christian theology of redemption originated with the earthly Jesus and was not simply a post-resurrection development.[19] Two further items need to be added.

First, Tom Wright has convincingly expounded what Jesus' coming to the Jerusalem Temple implied: the 'cleansing' of the Temple and the words about the 'new Temple' to come let us glimpse Jesus' redeeming intentions. He was dramatically enacting God's promised coming to save his people.[20]

Second, apropos of the redeeming intentions of Jesus, one should recall the interesting discussion that featured such exegetes and

---

[19] For further details on the redemptive intentions of the earthly Jesus, see O'Collins, *Christology*, 54–62, 67–80.

[20] See N. T. Wright, 'Jesus' Self-Understanding', in S. T. Davis, D. Kendall, and G. O'Collins (eds.), *The Incarnation* (Oxford: Oxford University Press, 2002), 47–61.

theologians as H. U. von Balthasar, M. Hengel, J. Jeremias, W. Kasper, H. Küng, X. Léon-Dufour, R. Pesch, E. Schillebeeckx, H. Schürmann, A. Vögtle, and others. The maximalist views of Pesch and the minimalist views of Vögtle marked the two extremes.[21] But all agreed that Jesus not only anticipated his violent death but also, to some extent, interpreted in advance its redemptive value. What I missed in that protracted and interesting debate was the recognition that the value of actions can and frequently does go beyond the conscious intentions of the agent in question. Other agents, the circumstances, and the subsequent course of events often enhance the valuable effects of the agent's deed beyond, even far beyond, the good results he or she intended. The saving outcome of Jesus' death could and, I would argue, did go beyond what he intended and clearly imagined in his human mind. This brings us to the significance for redemption of his being human and divine.

Ever since Paul stressed the obedience of 'the man' Jesus in effecting justification, grace, and life (Rom. 5: 12–21), Christian teachers have acknowledged that redemption came through an agent who was not only divine but also truly one with us human beings. After Irenaeus insisted that deliverance from the forces of evil called for the union of divinity and humanity in Christ, Tertullian (d. *c*.220), Origen (d. *c*.254), St Gregory of Nazianzus (d. 389), and others endorsed the same conviction. St Basil of Caesarea (d. 379) wrote of Christ needing to take on true humanity if he were to destroy the power of sin and death (*Epistola* 261. 2). In the next century St Leo the Great (d. 461) emphasized that, unless Christ had truly assumed our humanity, the redemptive 'battle' would have 'been fought outside our nature' and we would not have experienced what we have experienced, deliverance from the power of evil (*Epistola* 31. 2). The Third Council of Constantinople (680–1), by insisting on the distinction between Christ's human and divine wills and operations, provided the doctrinal basis for acknowledging that redemption has come 'from the inside' or from one who is truly human, as well as 'from the outside' or from one who is truly divine. The mediator of redemption belonged and belongs both on God's side and on our side.[22]

---

[21] See O'Collins, *Christology*, 67–81.

[22] The chapter by Brian Daley demonstrates how, for both the Eastern and the Western Fathers of the church, our redemption depends on the identity of Jesus as divine as well as human.

But how is the relationship between the Redeemer and the redeemed to be understood?[23] Christ acted 'for us' in the sense of acting not only for our benefit and to our advantage but also 'in our place'. By acting for our sake and in our place, was he our substitute or our representative? Without always being mutually exclusive, these two ways of envisaging the relationship reveal major differences. For instance, a substitute may be passively or even violently put in the place of another person or of other persons. One thinks of hostages executed in the place of escaped prisoners of war. The escapees do not wish for this substitution to take place, and in the event they may never even learn about it. Yet such wartime episodes yield examples of those who actively chose to be substitutes and in a self-sacrificing way took the place of someone condemned to death—as St Maximilian Kolbe did at Auschwitz in 1941. Kolbe volunteered to be his fellow-prisoner's substitute, but could not be described as his representative.[24]

Representation is willed by both those represented and the representative, is normally restricted to specific matters, and may well last for only a relatively brief period. Christ freely represented human beings to God and before God; on their side they are invited to agree to this redemptive representation. Christ's activity brings deliverance but does not constitute an 'unrestricted' representation: human beings may not, for example, simply hand over to him their duty to praise and thank God. At the same time, this redemptive representation is no relatively brief affair but lasts forever. The representative role of the Redeemer leads naturally to the further question about the scope of this representation: is Christ the one Redeemer of all people?

UNIQUE AND UNIVERSAL REDEEMER?

From the time of the NT (Rom. 6: 1–11; Col. 2: 12–13), believers understood themselves to re-enact sacramentally the historical

---

[23] As Caroline Walker Bynum indicates in her chapter, Christian theology might be better served by abandoning debates over representation versus substitution and retrieving medieval notions of communion with or incorporation in Christ's suffering and death.

[24] These examples qualify Wright's example below: a Member of Parliament represents a constituency and votes in its place. The substitution created by such representation is limited in scope and lasts for only a specified term—unlike the case of Kolbe, where substitution meant the end of his entire life.

redemption effected by Christ's life, death, and resurrection. Baptism meant their symbolic dying and being buried with Christ, so as to be freed from sin and rise to a new life. But is this redemption available not only for Christian believers but also for everyone? Does the saving 'work' of Jesus reach beyond the ranks of the baptized? Who is covered by the 'for us and for our salvation' of the ancient creeds? Paul insists that Christ died 'for all' (2 Cor. 5: 14–15), without introducing any exception. Hence he can say that 'God was in Christ reconciling the world to himself' (2 Cor. 5: 19). In sharp contrast with the collective figure of Adam who brought sin and death to all human beings, the obedient Christ leads all to justification and life. The NT and the credal claim about Christ's unique and universal redemptive role may well seem arrogant and even outrageous to those who do not share this faith. Yet this common faith of Christians, even if never spelt out by a general council of the church, formed part of the basis for the formation of the World Council of Churches in 1948. The redemption of all comes only through the mediation of Jesus Christ (1 Tim. 2: 5); there is no plurality of redeemers. In the first centuries of Christianity and then in modern times, theologians have struggled to interpret and explain how and why Christ functions as the one Redeemer for all men and women of all times and places. How can he be 'the expiation for the sins of the whole world' (1 John 2: 2) and the only 'name under heaven' by which human beings can be saved (Acts 4: 12), even for those who may consciously reject his representative role on their behalf?[25]

The issue may be phrased in terms of the tension between Christ as the one way to the Father (John 14: 6), on the one hand, and the fact of the divine will to save all people (1 Tim. 2: 4), on the other. God offers to all the possibility of sharing in the saving grace brought by Christ's dying and rising, as the Second Vatican Council put it in its 1965 pastoral constitution on the church in the modern world (*Gaudium et Spes*, 22). Some contemporary writers such as John Hick (b. 1922) destroy this tension by abandoning claims to Jesus' unique status. They accept a multiplicity of saviours or mediators of redemption, who differ in degree but not in kind.[26] Others such as John Paul II and Jacques Dupuis maintain that Jesus is the unique

---

[25] See O'Collins, *Christology*, 296–305.

[26] See e.g. J. Hick, *A Christian Theology of Religions: The Rainbow of Faiths* (Louisville, Ky.: Westminster/John Knox, 1995).

(i.e. only one of his kind) and universal Redeemer, while acknowledging the 'spiritual riches' to be found in non-Christian religions
and the positive role of those religions in the salvation of their
adherents.[27]

CREATION AND REDEMPTION

Any adequate reflection on Christ's redemptive role inevitably examines the relationship between the order of redemption and that of
creation. While not saying much on the creation of human beings
and the world, the NT did add one highly significant item to the OT
teaching. Creation, and not merely redemption, occurred through
the mediation of the Son of God, who is personally identical with
Jesus Christ (e.g. John 1: 3, 10; 1 Cor. 8: 6; Col. 1: 16; Heb. 1: 1–2). In
the late second century, with his theology of Christ as the new or
final Adam 'recapitulating' all human history, Irenaeus offered a
synthesis. He saw redemption as one great drama reaching from
creation, through the incarnation and the Easter story, and on to
the final coming at the end of time. He developed in fuller detail the
Pauline view of what Christ has already effected (Rom. 4: 25–5: 11)
and of our being saved 'in hope' (Rom. 8: 24) for the full and final
redemption that has not yet come. The biblical vision of Irenaeus
held together the entire order of creation with that of redemption as
two distinguishable but interconnected moments in God's one,
saving plan for all humanity and the whole cosmos. Maximus the
Confessor (d. 622),[28] John Duns Scotus (d. 1308), Pierre Teilhard de
Chardin (d. 1955), and others maintained this unity between God's
creative and redemptive work—a unity challenged by the view of
Thomas Aquinas and others—according to which, if human beings
had not sinned, the second person of the Trinity would not have
become incarnate in our world. At least implicitly, the view of
Irenaeus enjoys the backing of the Second Vatican Council, which

---

[27] See John Paul II's 1990 encyclical, *Redemptoris Missio*, 55; J. Dupuis, *Toward a
Christian Theology of Religious Pluralism* (Maryknoll, NY: Orbis, 1997); id., *Christianity
and the Religions: From Confrontation to Dialogue* (Maryknoll, NY: Orbis, 2002).

[28] Apropos of the incarnation, Maximus wrote: 'This is the great and hidden
mystery; this is the blessed end on account of which all things were created.
This is the divine purpose foreknown prior to the beginning of created things' (*To
Thalassius* 60).

linked creation and redemption by interpreting redemption as God's renewal of creation, and presenting Christ as being actively present in the whole, universal work of salvation—from creation to the end (*Gaudium et Spes*, 9, 45).

A striking advantage in Irenaeus' vision of the link between creation and redemption, one which he never imagined, comes from its obvious power to inculcate our stewardship for the environment. Since God's redemptive plan includes the whole created world and ordains it to share in the final consummation of all things,[29] the gift of Christ's saving grace entails our moral responsibility for the rest of creation. This entailment presupposes a response to the question: how is that saving grace mediated and appropriated?

THE GRACE OF JUSTIFICATION

For those who agree that Christ brought deliverance from evil, expiation for sins, and loving reconciliation with God, the question remains: how is all that redemptive grace mediated to people now? How are sinners justified (and sanctified)? Here we reach the question posed by Martin Luther which formed the heart of the sixteenth-century religious debate: where do I find a gracious God? Or, as the Council of Trent (1545–63) put the question: how does justification through Christ's grace save and change human beings?

Both the Catholics and the Reformers agreed that all saving grace comes only through the mediation of Christ. But does God merely 'impute' the justice or saving work of Christ and judge repentant sinners to be righteous? Or does that grace make people righteous, as Catholics (and Orthodox) held and hold? From the late twentieth century, dialogues between Catholics, Lutherans, and other Protestants have studied intensely the question: how is the past redemption effected by Christ appropriated now? Even though many secondary difficulties remain to be resolved, the 'imputation of righteousness' and 'making righteous' are now widely seen as in many aspects complementary rather than mutually exclusive teachings.[30] Hence

[29] In her chapter Marguerite Shuster examines the success and failure of four classic and forty-six contemporary sermons which take up Rom. 8: 18–25 and expound the redemption God intends for the whole created order.

[30] In an unpublished work, Thomas Torrance, a leading Protestant theologian of the 20th century, recognized that justification is to be understood 'not just in terms of

the 1997 'Joint Declaration on the Doctrine of Justification', prepared by the international Catholic–Lutheran Dialogue, was officially accepted by the Catholic Church and the Lutheran World Federation.[31]

In the sixteenth century, the Catholics and the Reformers presupposed that on the visible level the church's preaching and sacraments, especially baptism and the eucharist, mediated Christ's saving grace. But the 1492 discovery of the New World, where millions of people had lived for many centuries without the slightest chance of responding in faith to Christ's message, put severe pressure on the traditional conviction, *extra ecclesiam nulla salus* (outside the church no salvation). What was and is the role of the visible church in mediating (in subordination to Christ) redemption? How does Christ's saving activity extend to those who have not professed faith in him or even heard of him?

This question has fuelled recent writing by Jacques Dupuis, Frank Sullivan,[32] and many other theologians. It clearly troubled Pope John Paul II, who at times suggested replacing the problematic 'extra' and speaking of 'sine ecclesia' (apart from the church) no salvation.[33] Is it enough to hold that all salvation implies some 'ordering' towards the church, even if such an ordering is never actuated in the case of innumerable people who live and die as honest adherents of other faiths? Then there are questions to be faced about the role of Christian believers in the salvation of others. Is it enough to recognize the 'moral' causality exercised by their public and private prayers for the salvation of all humankind? Or should theologians try to indicate how believers, in subordination to Christ, exercise some 'efficient' causality for the salvation of others?

imputed righteousness but in terms of a participation in the righteousness of Christ which is transferred to us through union with him' ('The Distinctive Character of the Reformed Tradition', 6). Precise Pauline scholarship, exemplified by the chapters of Aletti, Fee, and Wright (below), has contributed to theological restatements of the doctrine of justification.

[31] In his chapter below, Stephen Evans explores the significance of disagreements and common ground over the doctrine of justification. On the issues involved in the Joint Declaration, see A. N. S. Lane, *Justification by Faith in Catholic–Protestant Dialogue: An Evangelical Assessment* (London: T. & T. Clark, 2002); T. Schneider and G. Wenz (eds.), *Gerecht und Sünder zugleich? Ökumenische Klärungen* (Freiburg: Herder, 2001), and J. Wicks, 'Justification in a Broader Horizon', *Pro Ecclesia* 12 (2003), 473–91.

[32] See F. A. Sullivan, *Salvation Outside the Church?* (London: Geoffrey Chapman, 1992).

[33] For details see Dupuis, *Christianity and the Religions*, 205–6, 209.

Much depends here on one's view of the 'power' of prayer and refusal to play down this power by talk of 'merely moral' causality. However one evaluates the contribution of the September 2000 document from the Congregation for the Doctrine of the Faith, *Dominus Jesus*, it took seriously not only the universal, unique work of Christ as Redeemer but also the subordinate role of the church in mediating salvation.

CONCLUDING REMARKS

Such then are seven crucial issues for any theology of the redemption: (1) the universal need for redemption; (2) the nature of redemption as deliverance, expiation, and saving love; (3) the proper language for redemption and some dubious expressions; (4) the role of Christ as divine–human Redeemer in his incarnation, ministry, death, and resurrection (with the coming of the Holy Spirit); (5) Christ the unique and universal Redeemer; (6) the link between redemption and creation; (7) the appropriation of redemption through justification, along with the church's subordinate role in mediating redemption.

This list raises two questions: its order and its completeness. There could be a case for treating in second place creation and its link with redemption, before moving to the nature of redemption and the other issues just listed. Furthermore, many other significant questions can be raised. There is, to begin with, the question of relating Christ's redemptive and revealing roles. How far might we interpret his saving work as that of revealing the truth of God and human beings? Does he, to some or even a great extent, perform his redemptive role by delivering us from ignorance and showing us the truth of ultimate reality (see Daley's chapter below)? Second, there is the issue highlighted by liberation theology: what political implications does Christ's redemptive activity entail? Apropos of his own 'fresh perspective' on Paul, Wright remarks that 'the coming together of soteriology and "political theology" may indeed be the most important proposal' of his chapter (see details below). Third, the gender question: how can women acknowledge a male saviour? Undoubtedly the Christian tradition has often tied the saving significance of Christ too closely to the masculinity of Jesus and forgotten that we are redeemed through the full humanity assumed by the Word at the incarnation. How can this misleading view which still persists be remedied?[34] Fourth, the chapters to follow by David Brown and Robert Kiely could trigger a broad enquiry: do we find the richest witness to redemption in liturgy, art, music, literature, and the best films? What educational 'tools' could we discover and develop in the creative arts to heal the collective memories of atrocious crimes that encourage seemingly endless hatred, violence, and injustice? Fifth, how does a Christian view of redemption or salvation resemble and how does it differ from versions of redemption or salvation to be found elsewhere? All the great religions of the world offer their answer to the human quest for meaning and salvation. Where does the Christian answer converge and where does it diverge from those other answers? Sixth, does the chapter below by Peter Ochs establish the peremptory need to approach our central issue through prayer? Will prayer to and with the Redeemer enlighten us best about the nature and tasks of redemption? Seventh, the chapter to follow by Eleonore Stump raises the further question: what might redeem the suffering of those who have perpetrated horrendous evil?

The sheer complexity of these seven further questions and even other questions which may be put testifies to the inexhaustible richness of the deep truth of redemption. In the proper sense of a religious mystery, the redemption effected by Christ remains at the heart of Christian faith as the truth which can never be adequately explored, let alone comprehended.[35]

---

[34] See A. Carr, *Transforming Grace: Christian Tradition and Women's Experience* (New York: HarperCollins, 1988); S. Coakley, *Powers and Submissions: Spirituality, Philosophy, and Gender* (Oxford: Blackwell, 2002); J. M. Soskice, 'Blood and Defilement: Reflections on Jesus and the Symbolics of Sex', in D. Kendall and S. T. Davis (eds.), *The Convergence of Theology* (Mahwah, NJ: Paulist Press, 2001), 285–303.

[35] For some valuable criticisms and comments on this chapter, I want to thank David Brown, Caroline Walker Bynum, Sarah Coakley, Stephen Davis, Peter Ochs, and Alan Padgett.

Biblical Questions

2

Reconciliation and the Plain Sense Witness of Scripture

CHRISTOPHER SEITZ

When Clement wishes to say something theological about the crucifixion he seems singularly unable to do so in his own words. He does not even use statements from Romans or 1 Corinthians which he certainly knew. What he does is to quote the whole of Isaiah liii. This was no doubt what he was accustomed to do *as a teacher*.[1]

PREFACE

I confess that what follows is prolegomena to an account of reconciliation. It belongs to our period of historical-critical readings of the Bible that considerable confusion exists over how one approaches this or any other central theological locus. If one seeks an exegetical basis for Christian doctrine, immediately one must face the variety of the witness, and it is variety that historical contextualization has brought into such sharp relief and general prominence.

But there is another specifically Christian facet of the problem. The Christian scriptures come in the form of two testaments. Reconciliation is an especially prominent theme in the first testament. Yet how does the church hear this witness? Does the OT sound its notes directly, even as the overtones of the cross are allowed their explicit place in the chorus?[2]

---

[1] H. J. Carpenter, 'Popular Christianity and the Theologians in the Early Church', *JTS* 14 (1963), 298–9; the reference is to Clement of Rome (1 Clement 16). Before this quotation, Carpenter says (298): 'We may infer . . . that normal catechetical instruction proceeded on the basis of the threefold Name with such positive statements as we have in the Old Roman creed. Elaboration, illustration, and proof were obtained not by discussion of problems arising out of affirmations, but by acquainting the catechumen with the scriptures, especially those of the Old Testament.' Clement is used as an example of this practice.

[2] See the elegant account of this, using John Donne's 'Devotions upon Emergent Occasions', in B. S. Childs, *Biblical Theology of the Old and New Testaments* (Minneapolis: Fortress, 1992), 382–3.

Against the backdrop of quests of the historical Jesus, another specifically Christian interpretative issue must be faced. It has long been noted, quite rightly, that a possible influence on Jesus and his understanding of his mission, is to be found in Isaiah's suffering servant (Isa. 52: 13–53: 12, for which shorthand 'Isaiah 53'). Here might be a place where the per se witness of the scriptures of Israel would sound its own notes, and find correlation with the NT's own apprehension of them.[3] Moreover, there would be a movement both forward and backward, the effect of which in a two testament witness would be a larger, specifically Christian, understanding of reconciliation. The work of the servant within and on behalf of Israel would be seen, in the light of the cross, to comprehend the widest possible circle of reconciliation. Something promised, or adumbrated, or figured would both find its typological resting point, and then press forward to a larger figural significance as the full chorus of OT notes on reconciliation would begin to be heard in the light of the cross.[4]

Yet this traditional way of doing theology from the Christian scriptures has been disturbed on a number of fronts (and this is true even when it is allowed that a 'traditional' way of doing things never amounted, for example, to a single theory of the atonement). This chapter looks at one of these fronts: a prominent and quite promising account of reconciliation, undertaken within the context of a sustained effort to provide us with a maximal account of the aims, intentions, and motivations of what is referred to as the 'historical Jesus'. This is the account associated with the work of N. T. Wright (for specific citations, see below). In his portrayal, perhaps surprisingly given its interest in the effect of the OT on Jesus, the role of Isaiah's servant is diminished significantly. The consequence of this is a clear, and I believe, intentional recalibration of how the OT sounds its notes for Christian theology. This chapter will examine such an approach and point out its possible limitations for constructive theology undertaken on the basis of 'the prophets and apostles'.

---

[3] For a fine discussion of several recent treatments of atonement and biblical theology (especially those by O. Hofius and B. Janowski), see D. Bailey, 'Concepts of *Stellvertretung* in the Interpretation of Isaiah 53', in W. H. Bellinger and W. R. Farmer (eds.), *Jesus and the Suffering Servant. Isaiah 53 and Christian Origins* (Harrisburg, Pa.: Trinity Press International, 1998), 223–50.

[4] For an older account of the atonement, where such a perspective is still largely operative, see e.g. A. Lyttelton, 'The Atonement', in C. Gore (ed.), *Lux Mundi* (London: John Murray, 1889) 275–312.

I Introduction

I take redemption to be not a narrow but a large concept in respect of biblical theology. So I will not be interested in a word-study approach, helpful though that could well be, where terms related to redemption might be considered (ransom, atone, buy back, propitiate, satisfy, etc.). Also, because it strikes me as a more comprehensive category, I will in fact use the term 'reconciliation' instead of redemption in this brief essay. I mean by reconciliation the coming to rest, the settling of accounts, the making of peace between God and humanity, including creation itself. This can occur by an act of God, so we speak of 'his redeeming work' in bringing Israel from the dead or Christ in like manner.[5] It can occur as a consequence of actions in the cult, whereby God is satisfied and peace is brought where forfeit had reigned. Hartmut Gese's classic study of atonement examines how blood and sacrifice and ransoming are handled in discrete levels of OT tradition.[6] God redeems and reconciles to himself a people.

Just in the way I have formulated this opening paragraph, the assumption is that certain key categories of reconciliation arc across the two testaments. How that happens (tradition-historically, religio-historically, developmentally, figurally) is not self-evident and for the purposes of biblical theology would be necessary to establish. Because the work of Christ in reconciling pursues promises made to Israel, and through her, to the Gentiles, and because that work has been inaugurated but awaits its full-fruit settlement, when God is all in all (1 Cor. 15: 28), it is necessary that our understanding of reconciliation be properly calibrated with the twofold witness of OT and NT. Because the second witness takes its bearings from and achieves its authority as scripture on analogy with the first witness, an account of redemption or reconciliation, if it is to be successful, must be a work of biblical theology, and not one of OT or NT reflection alone.[7] That is, for the Christian it is not possible to think

---

[5] For a nice treatment of this, see R. Jenson, *Systematic Theology*, i. *The Triune God* (Oxford: Oxford University Press, 1997), 43–4.

[6] H. Gese, 'The Atonement', in *Essays on Biblical Theology*, trans. K. Crim (Minneapolis: Augsburg, 1981), 93–116.

[7] On the formation of the NT canon derived from the logic of, and on analogy with, the scriptures of Israel, see the classic formulation of Adolf von Harnack in *Bible Reading in the Early Church* trans. J. R. Wilkinson (London: Williams & Norgate,

of reconciliation in the NT independently of the OT. No better witness to this is the Song of Zechariah. That is, it is the NT which insists throughout that Christ's redeeming work picked up something that had been begun, fulfilled promises already delivered, inaugurated something whose final end is also promised in the first witness.[8]

This insistence can, however, be understood in very different ways. One way that has recently been put forward also underscores the link between the testaments at the key point of reconciliation. It believes it can give an exhaustive account of the aims and intentions of Jesus as these arise out of the narrative world to which he has ineluctable reference.

II RECONCILIATION AND 'HISTORICAL JESUS'

A recent study on the importance of Isaiah for a proper understanding of Jesus[9] reminded me of Hezekiah's tunnel. OT scholars were brought in to discuss serious issues in Isaiah interpretation, involving the suffering servant, reconciliation in Isaiah 52–3, collective personality, and so forth. The labour went on within the climate of modern Isaiah study, whereby chapters 40–55 are isolated and discussed using the nomenclature, 'Deutero-Isaiah', even as one could also see great rigour and range in assessing how much of the classic Duhmian 'second Isaiah' still made sense.[10]

As this tapping went on, in the ensuing chapters we witnessed NT scholars tapping from the other side, as it were, making their way back to Isaiah from the serious sets of questions posed by technical NT scholarship. Here too, one sensed creativity and a willingness to push beyond certain accepted models of research and inquiry.

1912). On p. 145: '[Lessing] perceived that the New Testament as a book and as the recognized fundamental document of the Christian religion originated in the Church. But Lessing did not recognize that the Book from the moment of its origin freed itself from all conditions of its birth, and at once claimed to be an *entirely independent and unconditioned authority*. This was indeed only possible because the book at once took its place beside the Old Testament, which occupied a position of absolute and unquestionable independence because it was more ancient than the Church.'

[8] For a fuller account of this, see C. Seitz, *Word Without End: The Old Testament as Abiding Theological Witness* (Grand Rapids, Mich.: Eerdmans, 1998).

[9] Bellinger and Farmer, *Jesus and the Suffering Servant*.

[10] The (now popular) conception of 'Three Isaiahs' was worked out in detail by B. Duhm, *Jesaja*, HKAT (Göttingen: Vandenhoeck & Ruprecht, 4th edn., 1922).

At the close of the book, the historian N. T. Wright was asked to offer his reflections on this important dual activity. Extending my tunnel image for a moment to his remarks, I found Wright wondering whether the two activities were properly suited, and if any success in joining the two labours could be expected.[11] In their place, Wright presented the ambitious proposal now associated with his name, whereby it is the mind of Jesus which helps us join the witness of the testaments and comprehend in the most basic sense who Jesus was and what he thought he was doing. That this latter activity ought to be central to our concerns is, for Wright, self-evident. That this is some form of biblical theology I suspect is also meant to be true.

Now this first sort of clearly historiographic concern is also manifest in the work of the other NT scholars in the volume, but it is Wright's own particular understanding of how one properly goes about historical reconstruction of the mindset of Jesus that sets his own concerns off, and here we can see how his tunnel gets built.[12] This in turn touches on how it is that, in respect of the second project, we are rightly to understand reconciliation as a category of biblical theology, in its most broadly conceived form. In order to illustrate these two points and their significance for reconciliation as a locus of biblical theology, we can do no better than consider his objections to the dual labour projects. Whatever else he may say of their positive contribution we can leave to the side.

---

[11] 'The Servant and Jesus: The Relevance of the Colloquy for the Current Quest for Jesus', in Bellinger and Farmer (eds.), *Jesus and the Suffering Servant*: 'The original meaning of Isaiah, and its re-use in subsequent Old Testament writing such as Zechariah, does tell us something about the range of available options for subsequent readers; though it is clear to me that if there is a lacuna in this conference it is at the point of discussing how Isaiah might have been read by Jesus' own contemporaries' (p. 282).

[12] By 'mindset' is meant what Wright sees as the intentions and aims of Jesus. Describing *Jesus and the Victory of God*, he says, 'the book was basically about the mindset of Jesus as he went to the cross' (C. Newman (ed.), *Jesus and the Restoration of Israel* (Downers Grove, Ill.: InterVarsity Press, 1999), 268). For a trenchant analysis of this type of appeal to 'Jesus' self-understanding' see the chapter by C. Stephen Evans ('Methodological Naturalism in Historical Biblical Scholarship') in *Jesus and the Restoration of Israel* (194–5). I agree with the statement: 'It seems remarkable that Wright can know not only what Jesus believed about himself but the manner in which the knowledge was obtained and the degree of certainty he possessed' (p. 195). There are serious christological concerns, of a traditional theological sort, crying out for attention here (see also the remarks by Gerald O'Collins in Ch. 1 above).

OT scholars tend, as Wright sees it, to view the OT with historical questions. Though valuable in themselves, these questions can become detached from how the NT witness read the OT, and especially (for Wright) from how one reconstructs Jesus' own reading of the scriptures of Israel, wherein he comprehends his mission and identity on terms Wright is concerned to make precise. One can sense immediately that Wright's concern is not anti-historical; far from it. He wants to freeze the frame of history at a later moment, in the OT's effective history.[13] He does not take up the vexed question of how OT scholarship might defend itself theologically at those points where he takes historiographic issue. That is, it might be possible to maintain a concern with the OT's effective history, as he does, which in turn is constrained by the way its per se theological voice is heard, firmly rooted in Israel's historical witness. But more on that in the course of my own remarks.

The NT scholars at work in the volume, for their part, fail to see the effective history of the OT in the same way as Wright does, and this at one crucial point, having to do with reconciliation.[14] They work backwards to the testimony of the OT, seeking to understand how Jesus or the NT read Isaiah, but their eye falls on the wrong place (so Wright sees it). It is reconciliation where the lens goes fuzziest, and this for one chief reason, according to Wright. One can see here how a conference on 'Jesus and the Suffering Servant' set its bearings from the very beginning on a course which would deviate quite strongly from Wright's own stated project.[15]

Reconciliation in connection with a theme like the suffering servant of Isaiah will naturally enough focus on the work of the servant

---

[13] See n. 11 above where this concern is expressed.

[14] For a full treatment, see *Jesus and the Victory of God* (London: SPCK, 1996), 268–74.

[15] 'I think, in fact, we have been too shortsighted in focusing on the fourth Servant Song and on the precise meaning of various phrases within it. We have reminded ourselves tirelessly that first-century readers were ignorant of Duhm's analysis and all that has followed it, and yet we have failed to take seriously, I believe, the very passage that sums up the whole of Jesus' public ministry, Isaiah 52: 7–12. "How lovely on the mountains are the feet of the *mebasser*, the herald of good tidings, the one who publishes salvation, who says to Zion, Your God reigns!"' ('The Servant and Jesus', 290). What needs clarification is whether substituting a single text from Isaiah for a focus on the servant is either (*a*) an improvement on certain of Duhm's core insights, and not simply a substitution demanded by the thesis being pursued, or (*b*) a fair reading of the plain sense of Isaiah as this might be heard by '1st-century readers' receiving this witness and unaware of a 'second Isaiah' or of 'servant songs' (i.e. differently from the analysis of Duhm and 'all that has followed it' assumed).

in atoning for sins (if the term 'atonement' is a proper way to characterize such work). It will want to know matters of exegetical consequence, as these have traditionally been handled in biblical scholarship. So, are there such things as 'servant songs'? Are these related to each other? What about context in interpretation, given the claims of form-criticism? Is the servant an individual? How is the servant working for Israel, and for the nations? Who is the servant, or is such a question answerable? Is the servant substituting for Israel, or representing Israel? Is the suffering innocent, or the consequence of sin? Is the reconciling work of the servant *sui generis*, or does it have forebears, or bear analogy with Moses, Jeremiah, Zion, and a whole range of psalm-typed righteous suffering?[16]

OT tapping has been labour-intensive and productive when it comes to these sorts of questions. It is not hard, in turn, to see how this labour might be of use to NT scholars asking about Jesus and the NT witness, in spite of Wright's very important caution: namely, that a certain kind of historical inquiry might actually become detached from the question of how, in its own day and given later exegetical parameters, Isaiah was being heard at the period of the NT's formation.

But here Wright's critique of NT scholarship takes a different, sharper turn. A focus on the suffering servant, even if it were to proceed along the lines of Wright's cautionary note, would still go astray according to him. That is the first critical suggestion I will make here. For Wright wants the eye of NT scholarship to fall on a place which he feels can and must bear the entire weight of critical reconstructions of the mind and mission of Jesus.[17] But just here it is not clear whether he is talking about the per se witness of the OT heard in its proper effective historical moment, as he insists. For the chief weight-bearing joist in his structure is in fact derived, neither from the obvious plain sense of Isaiah (to choose the OT example at hand), nor from the sorts of readings of Isaiah available at the time of the NT's formation, strictly speaking. In fact, it exists chiefly in Wright's own reconstruction and must be assessed within his reconstructed universe of meaning, which he at places calls the 'narrative

---

[16] These issues are discussed in some detail by H. Reventlow ('Basic Issues in the Interpretation of Isaiah 53') and R. Clements ('Isaiah 53 and the Restoration of Israel') in *Jesus and the Suffering Servant.*

[17] See the quotation in n. 15 above.

world' out of which the NT witness emerged. It seems to me that to insist on 'return from exile' as the chief index of the OT as heard by Jesus, or as the generating engine of the NT's plain sense witness, even as an historian like Wright might approach it, fails on the very set of constraints Wright has himself been at pains, and at times quite rightly, to put in place.[18]

It will be the argument of the next section that Wright's reifying of the 'exile' is only conceivable in the climate of higher critical work on Isaiah, as this has taken place over the past century. That in itself is not a disqualifier, yet it might explain why a disproportional focus on one historical fact in Israel's life has emerged.

What will be of greater concern is the emergence of a model for reading the NT, and indeed for reading Christian scripture as a whole, in which reconciliation no longer has chiefly to do with sacrifice, suffering, atonement, and personal, individual redemption—matters which Wright has been at pains to denounce—but instead has to do with return from exile. It will be the argument of this chapter that, in so far as this view seeks as its warrant the per se witness of the OT, it is an exaggerated and selective reading. It will follow from this that Wright's focus on 'return from exile' is an example of how certain historical questions in respect of the NT witness have been badly mishandled, especially as these have sought warrant in an historical retrieval of the mind of Jesus more exhaustive than the actual apostolic witness, and quite different in form and presentation from that self-same witness.

---

[18] Wright makes this point insistently: 'forgiveness of sins is another way of saying "end of exile"' ('The Servant and Jesus', 290); '*Forgiveness of sins is another way of saying, "return from exile"*' (*Jesus and the Victory of God*, 268). This understanding offers a contrast and corrective for those 'who live in the shadow of the medieval church, of Martin Luther, of soul-searching pietism, and now of navel-gazing self-help spiritualities' ('The Servant and Jesus', 290). Later he continues in this vein: 'I suggest, then, that the categories of sixth or fifth or fourth centuries BCE, and those of the sixteenth or subsequent centuries CE, are not necessarily good guides for our understanding of Jesus' ('The Servant and Jesus', 295). What is at stake here is the insistence that the historian can describe Jesus in such a way as to make this description normative over the biblical texts said to be influencing him (from centuries BCE), or over the subsequent history of interpretation. As we shall see, this is not an appeal to the plain sense of the NT, where the mind of Jesus is indeed set forth (though in a far more minimal way than in Wright's historical portrait). It is an appeal to Wright's historical reconstruction of Jesus' mind and the narrative world which he claims gave it content.

III ISAIAH AND RECONCILIATION

Previous sections have pointed to the difficulties any treatment of reconciliation must face, once the decision is made to work with both testaments of Christian scripture. For a project like Wright's, it is necessary to insist that the OT is guiding Jesus' sense of identity and mission, as an historical datum; and in the realm of reconciliation, certain texts of the OT have a primacy because they arise within a narrative world Jesus inhabited, imprinted by the OT's effective history. This world is not imprinted by a history-of-religions milieu only, or by traditions in motion, but by texts as we have them in the OT and can read them right now (as Wright does). To be avoided are kinds of readings which would have been alien to the NT period.

What is difficult is knowing when the plain sense of the OT is guiding, indeed constraining, Jesus' sense of his identity and mission, and where he is dramatically selecting from it. To choose the example Wright most frequently deploys: is Isaiah 52: 7–12 crucial to the presentation of Isaiah in a non-Duhmian reception?[19] Or is it crucial to Wright's reconstruction wherein return from exile is the prominent theme and displacer of other views of reconciliation?

As has been noted, Isaiah has been a place of change and fresh approaches. Old theories are falling away. The sort of cleavage one could have described, as we see above, between a strong, historically referential reading, and one more likely to have been operative at the time of Jesus, is receding. Canonical and final-form readings are arguably closer to the ways in which the NT heard the OT, not least because they have not insisted on being tied to a specific theory of historical reference, such as would have been unavailable to Jesus and his contemporaries. This is not a simple matter, but I think the point is sound.

So, for example, the conceptual world which gave us a 'second Isaiah' is clearly irrelevant from the side of NT reading. What did this conceptuality give us? First, it gave us a relatively clear biographical set of bearings from which to approach sixteen chapters of the book. A prophet, working in Babylonian exile, preached an imminent return from exile, and a glorious homecoming. Second, based upon the assured results of form-criticism, we know how this conceptual

---

[19] See Wright, 'The Servant and Jesus', 290.

framework sought to highlight individual units of text, as over against an understanding of rhetorical or dramatic coherence—within the chapters not only associated with the prophet in exile, but also and especially within the larger book as a whole. Third, the critical method isolated these chapters from the rest of the book, and at a whole range of points, but at one point at least that isolation gave rise to a quandary which sat on the mind of the interpreter, and it would not go away. If return from exile was the chief preaching theme of second Isaiah, why did the book then generate such a disappointing finale, or at least one in which return from exile had got reworked or otherwise accommodated? This quandary made its force felt all the more if the geographical conceptuality of second and third Isaiahs (Babylon and Jerusalem, respectively) was in place. Those who listened to one prophet in Babylonian exile, in chapters 40–55, were replaced by another group listening to another message (or messages) in chapters 56–66, now back in the land. What had happened to make the content and horizon of the last chapters change?

This is not to deny that, on any reading of Isaiah, the return of the dispersed—indeed from north, south, east, and west, not just from Babylon but from wherever and whenever—is a major theme of all parts of the book. What is far less clear is whether Wright's particular emphasis on 'return from exile' equals forgiveness of sins does not in fact work best with a rather dated understanding of the book of Isaiah as a whole? Ironically, it is an understanding of the book which retains far more of the odour of Duhm and the sorts of 6th–4th century BC. readings which Wright cautions against than one which might have been more operative for Jesus and his contemporaries.

I say this not to make an academic point about the recent history of Isaiah interpretation. When I read Wright, I confess to feeling surprised that, for no apparent reason I can see from the Isaiah side of the tunnel, suddenly Isaiah 52: 7–12 takes on a prominence which is argued to overshadow the work of the servant. I understand that Wright believes this is key to the narrative world within which Jesus worked, though he has failed to persuade me of this. What I do not understand is how one could read Isaiah and *comprehend from its plain sense that return from exile was a more prominent theme than the suffering and atoning work of the servant.* Indeed, I believe it quite possible to show, as I have tried in a recent NIB commentary, how the suffering servant's work is the genuine resolution of what God had spoken of through the servant and brought about in his own self-offering—the longed-for reconciliation, not just of Israel, but of the nations in a proleptic depiction.[20] Putting the cart before the horse would mean making this reconciliation somehow secondary to return from exile, as Wright has insisted.

It is a simple point, but one nonetheless compelling, that in the present literal unfolding of Isaiah, Isaiah 52: 7–12 opens on to the dramatic text of 52: 13–53: 12. Many in the history of interpretation failed to see in 52: 7–12 clear reference to a return from exile, and neither Brevard Childs nor myself interpret the text that way within the dramatic flow of Isaiah.[21] Less controversially and more importantly, a return from exile remains devoid of meaning in Isaiah without the work of the servant, whose work takes place under the conditions of suffering and death, for a people who are nowhere depicted on the other side of anything, exile or whatever.

This fact helps explain why the book of Isaiah does not end with return from exile, but presses ahead to discuss any number of new, as well as continuing, themes in chapters 56–66. Of course, Isaiah does not end there, in part for reasons all interpreters and not just Wright have long known: exile is nowhere seen as completed in the OT in general nor in Isaiah itself. But the point remains that chapters 56–66 of Isaiah are the proper conclusion of the book, and in these chapters the chief interest is in (*a*) righteousness and separation within Israel[22] and (*b*) the coming of the nations—a theme which uses exile in a quite ironic sense, unrelated to Wright's 'exile is not over' or 'exile's end equals forgiveness' themes.[23] These several themes devolve from the work of the servants, who continue the work of the servant as dramatically constituted in the final suffering servant poem. The movement from chapters 40–55 to 56–66 (or, as I argue in NIB, from 40–53 to 54–66) is chiefly a movement from the servant's work to the work of the servants, and return from exile is

[20] C. Seitz, 'The Book of Isaiah 40–66', in L. Keck (ed.), *The New Interpreter's Bible*, vi (Nashville, Tenn.: Abingdon, 2001).

[21] B. S. Childs, *Isaiah* (OT Library; Louisville, Ky.: Westminster John Knox, 2001), 406–7.

[22] See, among others, W. Beuken, 'The Main Theme of Third Isaiah: "The Servants of Yahweh"', *JSOT* 47 (1990), 67–87.

[23] So in the last chapters, the nations come into contact with Israel in exile, and are shown as bringing Zion's children back home, building the temple, and even worshipping and serving God, as priests or levites elsewhere exercise this role.

subsidiary to it (not to mention, difficult to square with it; see above).
The work of the servant is, conclusively, his suffering and atonement
for Israel (53: 4–9), which work has as a consequence, paradoxically,
the confession of the nations (52: 13–15). In the final chapters, this
reconciliation for Israel, accruing as well for the nations, brings
about strife within the household of God, with the consequence
that, by the final chapters, Israel is herself pruned (Isa. 65: 13–16),
and 'unnatural branches' are brought in (to use the image of Rom.
11: 17–24) to fulfil the work of the servant, who was to be 'light to
the nations' (42: 6). The point is that all this activity takes place
with only loose reference to 'return from exile' and certainly not in
dependence upon its having been completed. Reconciliation and
forgiveness of sins are decidedly not the same things as return from
exile.

There are many other places where this point can be made. Two
examples will have to suffice, however. The first is Lamentations 4:
22, which is cited by Wright as 'stating the matter about as clearly
and as baldly as one could wish':

> The punishment of your iniquity, O daughter Zion, is accomplished;
> He will keep you in exile no longer.

Zion is of course not in Babylonian exile nor has she been deported to
any other place of dispersion, like a Jeremiah in Egypt (Jer. 43–6).
'Exile' here is used by extension, consistent with the root meaning of
Hebrew GLH, 'to strip'. Zion has been stripped and reduced to the
lowest state. The same tableau can be seen in Isaiah, where Zion
complains she has been cast off (Isa. 49: 14; 50: 1–3). Incidentally,
the Zion–Jerusalem orientation of Isaiah 40–55 has thrown major
doubt on the notion of a 'second Isaiah in Babylonian exile' model for
reading these chapters (a position even Duhm knew was difficult to
maintain).[24] But the point remains the same. Forgiveness of sins may
well be related to Zion's reversal of fortunes, but this is unrelated to
physical deportation. No one has ever read Lamentations as
depicting Zion in physical exile in the manner implied by Wright's

---

[24] On this sticking point for older Deutero-Isaiah notions, see H. Barstad, 'Lebte
Deuterojesaja in Judäa?', *NorTT* 83 (1982), 77–87; C. C. Torrey, *The Second Isaiah:
A New Interpretation* (New York: Charles Scribner's Sons, 1928); J. Smart, *History and
Theology in Second Isaiah* (Philadelphia: Westminster, 1965); C. Seitz, *Zion's Final
Destiny* (Minneapolis: Fortress, 1991); and most recently in the Hermeneia Commen-
tary by Klaus Baltzer, *Deutero-Isaiah* (Minneapolis: Fortress, 2001).

larger argument. Perhaps it would have been better if he had evoked a theory of 'spiritual exile' from the very beginning, but I am not confident that the force of his larger conceptuality could thereby have been sustained.

A second example makes something of the same point, though from a different direction. In Deuteronomy, where physical deportation can indeed be a sign of curse and the consequence of sin and divine judgement, the narrator takes us into that place of forsakenness and guilt (Deut. 30: 1–5). This is part of the genius and subtlety of the theological portrayal of Deuteronomy: it can see a law being broken even as it is delivering it to a new generation on the banks of the Jordan.[25]

> And when all these things come upon you, the blessing and the curse, which I have set before you, and you call them to mind among all the nations where the Lord your God has driven you, and return to the Lord your God, and obey his voice in all that I command you this day, with all your heart and all your soul; then the Lord your God will restore your fortunes, and have compassion on you, and he will gather you again from all the peoples where the Lord has scattered you. (Deut. 30: 1–3)

Here we do indeed see a link between forgiveness and the gathering of God's people from the nations. But the point of significance here is that the language used to describe forgiveness is 'restoring of fortunes' and 'having compassion'. The Hebrew phrase *sub subuth* occurs throughout the Psalms and elsewhere in the OT; it does not require attachment to a concept of exile and return. Forgiveness of sins is a fully independent and sovereign act of God. The larger point is that exile and return are not, without considerable elongation, the equivalent of forgiveness of sins. Reconciliation with God entails matters of the heart, and there are too many examples in the OT to bring forward at this juncture to support what seems to me, at least, an obvious point.

IV JESUS' MINDSET

Why this discussion is important can be seen most clearly when it comes to how one believes theology is generated from the NT

---

[25] On this, see Dennis Olson's *Deuteronomy and the Death of Moses* (Overtures to Biblical Theology Series; Minneapolis: Fortress, 1994).

witness. Reconciliation for many NT scholars does indeed turn on gaining precision about matters like representation, substitution, and atonement, not least because these English terms seek to get at the thought world of Romans and the OT language of cult and sacrifice as it appears in the NT.[26] That they are happy to do so without reference to Israel's return from exile appears to approach self-evidence.

The effort to turn this way of discussing reconciliation to the side, in favour of retrieving a narrative world said to operate with return from exile as its key ingredient, is no small matter. What is at stake is an insistence that the 'mindset' of Jesus can be got at with historical tools, and that these tools can prise free an accurate picture of who Jesus thought he was, and what he was doing. This mindset, it is then argued, has at its centre certain specific views of Israel's restoration, and since this is so, no adequate understanding of reconciliation can function without recourse to such a redescription.

At this point it is necessary to remind ourselves that the NT does not need to be put through a process of historical redescription for access to the mind of Jesus (its importance for the moment being conceded) to be possible. Jesus can report his thinking about who he is and what he is doing in the apostolic witness, as indeed he does. It is a very important theological question as to how much Jesus' own specific and detailed sense of his mission truly matters for the purpose God has in mind for him, but that can be set to the side for the moment. In other words, if this were a truly critical category for the apostolic witness, it is surprising how minimal a portrait it is that we receive.

Here the issue comes to a head. After Peter's confession (Matt. 16: 13–20; Mark 8: 27–30; Luke 9: 18–20), the NT witness reports that Jesus taught his disciples that he must suffer and be killed and after this be raised from the dead (Matt. 16: 21–3; Mark 8: 31–3; Luke 9: 21–7). In explaining this further to a distraught Peter, Jesus says that the disciples too must take up the cross and follow him. Then in explaining discipleship along similar lines later, he says that the Son of Man came to serve and to give his life as a ransom for many (Matt. 20: 28; Mark 10: 45).

---

[26] Wright takes issue with this way of talking about reconciliation, as n. 18 above makes clear; (although he does not name names, it is likely Dan Bailey's brokering of the Janowski–Hofius discussion of *Stellvertretung* that Wright objects to).

It is obvious that NT scholars have wrestled with Jesus' relationship to the suffering servant in Isaiah because of the plain sense reference to 'ransom for many'.[27] It is equally obvious that many of the mechanisms of NT historical questing have decided it is important to sift the apostolic witness to Jesus, in the fourfold Gospel record, and determine which texts they can with confidence retain for a historical redescription. *What is odd is that an effort to retrieve the narrative world said to be crucial to determining Jesus's identity and mission would seek to reproportionalize the centrality of texts like Mark 10: 45 so as to give greater attention to a locus like 'return from exile', which can only by a great act of (critical) inference be given any centrality to begin with.* It in turn requires even greater effort to suggest that the witness of Isaiah points away from the servant and his atoning work (for Israel and for the nations) and toward a focus on exile as primary.

To stay with the historiographic issue a bit longer. I wonder if a category like 'witness' has been properly integrated into certain historiographic inquiries undertaken by NT scholars.[28] That the NT witness does not contain any statements from Jesus where he describes his mission as 'taking away sins by returning to Zion' must surely be significant. How can one appeal to the 'mindset' or 'intentions' of Jesus as critical to any account of his work,[29] and then in an area where such a view is provided in the witness, prefer another of one's own making? That such a move disturbs the natural affiliations

---

[27] For a serious study of the issues handled by NT scholars looking at Mark 10: 45, in debate with M. Hooker and C. K. Barrett, see R. E. Watts, 'Jesus' Death, Isaiah 53, and Mark 10: 45', in *Jesus and the Suffering Servant*, 125–51.

[28] See the recent discussion of Samuel Byrskog, *Story as History: History as Story* (WUNT 123; Tübingen: Mohr Siebeck, 2000).

[29] That there is confusion over what may be meant by 'plain sense' as I am using it is suggested by the exchange between Wright, Evans, and L. T. Johnson in C. Newman (ed.), *Jesus and the Restoration of Israel* (Downers Grove, Ill.: InterVarsity Press, 1999). Evans and Johnson contend that Wright's reproduction of the 'self-understanding of Jesus' confuses our grasp of the apostolic witness, or worse. Wright on his part simply does not register this critical contention. 'Plain sense' reading is a commitment to the final form of the witness, in its given form and arrangement. It seeks to understand the theological significance of the account by paying attention to the way in which the witness has been constituted. So, in the case of the gospel witness, the fact that a fourfold account has been provided stands as a formal warning against the production of a single narrative 'substructure' said to comprehend the 'real' or 'historical' Jesus. Plain sense reading understands the theological significance as conveyed by the canonical form of the witness. On John and the fourfold Gospel record, see Christopher Seitz, 'Booked Up: Ending John and Ending Jesus', in Seitz, *Figured Out* (Louisville, Ky.: Westminster John Knox, 2001), 91–101.

between Isaiah, Mark/Matthew, and Romans, to mention just three witnesses, cannot, it seems to me, be judged a gain.

Here may well be a case where a certain form of historiographic quest—one seeking to give us the mindset of Jesus—may actually distance us from the plain sense witness in an area so critical for Christian theology as reconciliation. The 'mindset of Jesus' begins actually to encroach on and reproportionalize the plain sense of OT and NT. Ransom language is crucial to any account of reconciliation, within Israel and within the church. Getting us to pay attention to the place of Israel in our thinking about Jesus has been a salutary thing, in the writing of Wright and elsewhere in NT studies. Yet ironically, the scriptures of Israel in their vast sweep begin to recede in favour of a certain take on them, said to be accurately provided by one on a quest to get at the aims, intentions, and motivations of Jesus through historical redescription of a certain sort. No one would dispute that exile and return are key issues in the OT. But it would be an exaggeration if we were to conclude that the OT says primarily what it says about reconciliation through this lens. Saying that this is the way Jesus saw it deflects our attention away from the plain sense of scripture, both in the OT and the NT, and especially as we seek to hear them together as twofold Christian scripture

V Conclusion

The OT is an enormously rich resource for Christian reflection on reconciliation. It is remarkably easy for a gentile Christian church to forget how fundamental were the scriptures of Israel in the early church, long before anyone contemplated anything like a second testament.[30] Indeed, even to insist they were fundamental is to suggest there might have been some serious alternative, which there was not (Marcion notwithstanding).[31] To talk about reconciliation was, then, to talk about what Jesus had done for the church and world, using what language had been provided for this in Israel's

---

[30] See W. Horbury, 'The Interpretation of the Old Testament in the Church Fathers', in M. J. Moulder (ed.), *Mikra* (Philadelphia: Fortress, 1988); Harnack, *Bible Reading in the Early Church*; Carpenter, 'Popular Christianity'.

[31] See the learned account by H. von Campenhausen, *The Formation of the Christian Bible* (Philadelphia: Fortress, 1972).

prefigured life with God in the old covenant (where Israel, servant, and nations are the operative terms) and letting that language do its fullest plain sense work.[32] The opening quotation in this chapter from Carpenter on Clement shows the instinct of the early church, which turned to Isaiah 53 for an account of the cross, without further ado.

The OT has reconciliation at the heart of its Torah. There we see the elaborate and carefully worked out system for bringing the people of Israel into right relationship with God. The life is in the blood, and God has given it for atoning for sin (Lev. 17: 11). With this simple insight, all else spills out into the gracious giving of the Torah whereby Israel can be brought back after she falls. It is a never-ending process, as Hebrews sees it, but it is a process whereby Israel sustained her walk with God all the same. Without this life-sustaining cult, Israel's walk with YHWH would have been marked by failed moralisms, darkness, and idolatry/magic.

I am not convinced that a historian working on matters of NT redescription fully understands what the impact of his or her findings about the intentions of Jesus have on the OT as first-order scripture. It could urge us to the view that the OT speaks primarily, when theories about what Jesus intends or aims in respect of it are able to carry our conviction.[33]

---

[32] On this, see C. Seitz, 'Of Mortal Appearance: Earthly Jesus and Isaiah as a Type of Christian Scripture', *Figured Out* (Louisville, Ky.: Westminster John Knox, 2001), 103–16.

[33] Consider Wright's confident claims of historiography at this point and then try to relate these to a doctrinal or constructive theological appropriation of the two-testament Christian scripture: 'Within historiography in general, and the study of Jesus as one example of it, it is also important to insist that we can in principle study human intentionality . . . serious historians have never confined themselves to asking "what happened"; they also regularly ask "why did so-and-so, or such-and-such a community, behave in the way they did?" Human motivation, including that vital but elusive category, human awareness of vocation, is a proper subject of historical study. This is not a matter of psychology' ('The Servant and Jesus', 286). Wright then proceeds to elaborate in detail, using language like 'I regard it, in fact, as historically certain that Jesus regarded himself as . . .', or it is 'overwhelmingly historically probable that Jesus regarded himself as, intended to act as, and was perceived to be acting as . . .' (ibid. 288). These near certainties find their continuation in, 'Jesus did not consider his death in terms of an abstract or ahistorical atonement theology' (ibid. 292). Here one could respond in kindred terms, 'no, that is right, his death was not abstract nor ahistorical in the least; it was even more than a piece of "critical realism"—indeed, it was a real, historical, flesh and blood certainty, and even among disbelievers and the most disinterested of historians, this is nowhere in dispute.

If this is correct, one can sense almost immediately the problem from one historical point among many: the early church did not operate with this type of conceptuality (and here we confront again the problem of discontinuity in effective history). The earliest Christian interpreters did not take a second testament, wrestle with Jesus's aims and intentions as derived from it, and then hear the OT in so far as it lined up with this redescription. One can, of course, contest their take on things. But I would prefer to seek to hear the OT as scripture guided by the sorts of concerns and constraints these early interpreters strove to be responsive to (here we may touch upon an incipient 'rule of faith'). On a matter like reconciliation, the OT as scripture has far more to say than that forgiveness of sins is chiefly about Israel's physical return from exile, however painfully she may have desired that to become a reality.

The theological point in all this is: reconciliation is what God does in Christ and has done in Israel figurally. A full figural reading of the OT will not allow the focus to move to 'exile and return', because to do so would be to historicize one aspect of forgiveness to the exclusion of others, and then give it a historical Jesus 'stamp of approval'—a stamp absent in the *plain sense presentation* of the NT witness said to be generating it.

We have come to the end of the tunnel project. The OT's per se voice has much to bring to our understanding of reconciliation. Heard in concert with the NT, we can see how, independently of 'exile and return', Paul can talk about the way Christ has laid hold of him and reconciled him to God. He can do that, not just because the Holy Spirit brought him face to face with the living Lord, but because the OT had already laid upon him, in as rich a way as possible, the figures of reconciliation Christ had come to 'fill full'. Any account of reconciliation for the Christian church will gladly attend to this same richness, with the fervent hope that the tunnel might reach into the heart of those brought near in Christ Jesus, the 'desire of the nations'. That is what is meant by reconciliation for the church, even a church in exile.[34]

Jesus died a death on a cross.' We do not even need to know what Jesus thought about that death, even though the Gospels provide us with some measure of his self-understanding in the plain sense witness, to know that it happened and that it happened as an execution.

[34] E. Radner, *The End of the Church: A Pneumatology of Christian Division in the West* (Grand Rapids, Mich.: Eerdmans, 1998).

3

Paul and the Metaphors for Salvation: Some Reflections on Pauline Soteriology

GORDON D. FEE

At our last 'summit' I noted in passing that Paul's central concern theologically is 'salvation in Christ'.[1] But this is a phrase that needs unpacking. First, the *supposition* of 'salvation in Christ' is the triadic nature of God, since it is predicated on the love of God the Father, is effected through the death and resurrection of Christ the Son, and is made effective through the Spirit of God who is also the Spirit of the Son. Second, the *goal* of salvation is not simply the saving of individuals and fitting them for heaven, as it were, but the creation of a people for God's name, reconstituted by a new covenant. Third, the *framework* of God's 'salvation in Christ' is thoroughly eschatological, meaning that Christ's death and resurrection and the gift of the Spirit mark the turning of the ages, whereby God has set in motion the new creation, in which all things eventually will be made new. Fourth, the *means* of 'salvation in Christ' is Christ's death on the cross and his subsequent resurrection in which death itself has been defeated.

In the two preceding summits, my papers dealt with the first of these propositions: (1) the Trinitarian presuppositions of Pauline theology, focusing especially on the person and role of the Spirit; and (2) Paul's incarnational understanding of the person of Christ the Son. In this chapter I wish to examine (in overview fashion) the other three of these propositions, focusing first on the goal of salvation in Christ, and second on the 'new creation' nature of such salvation, and then finally looking at the nature/means of salvation through the lens of some of the Pauline metaphors.

---

[1] See 'St. Paul and the Incarnation: A Reassessment of the Data', in S. T. Davis, D. Kendall, and G. O'Collins (eds.), *The Incarnation: An Interdisciplinary Symposium on the Incarnation of the Son of God* (Oxford: Oxford University Press, 2002), 63.

I THE GOAL OF SALVATION IN CHRIST

From my perspective, one of the weaknesses of much Protestant theology is its proclivity for a soteriology devoid of ecclesiology. That is, the tendency is to focus on salvation in an individualistic way that loses the 'people of God' dimension of Paul's soteriology. This is due in large part to a presuppositional emphasis on discontinuity between the two covenants, with very little appreciation for the significant dimension of continuity. To be sure, discontinuity resides in the not insignificant reality that entrance into the people of God under the New Covenant happens one by one through faith in Christ Jesus and the gift of the Spirit.[2] But to embrace that point of emphasis to the neglect of the equally important 'people of God' dimension to Christ's saving work is to miss Paul by too much.

Paul simply cannot help himself, since both his own history as a Jew and his calling as apostle to the Gentiles presuppose that the goal of God's saving work in Christ is to create an end-time people for God's name out of both Jew and Gentile together. This passion finds expression especially in Galatians and Romans,[3] where the issue is not primarily justification by faith, but Jew and Gentile together as one people of God predicated on the work of Christ and the Spirit and realized by faith. After all, the whole argument of Romans climaxes in 15: 5–13, 'so that with one mind and one voice you [Jew and Gentile together] may glorify the God and Father of our Lord Jesus Christ' (v. 6), which is followed by a catena of four OT passages which focus on the inclusion of Gentiles. Similarly Galatians concludes with a repetition of Paul's aphorism, 'Neither circumcision nor uncircumsion means anything; what counts is a new creation'[4] (6: 15), followed by a benediction on all who follow this 'rule', who are then described as 'God's Israel'.

---

[2] This presupposes the reality that Paul's letters were all written to first-generation adult converts, who became so through faith in Christ and the gift of the Spirit. How second-generation believers become members of the household of God is an area of huge debate and division among later Christians—in part because Paul simply does not speak specifically to this question.

[3] It is a primary driving concern in Ephesians as well, where the emphasis is more clearly on ecclesiology rather than soteriology as such.

[4] This aphorism occurs first in 1 Cor. 7: 19: 'Neither circumcision nor uncircumsion means anything; what counts is keeping God's commands' (!). It also occurs earlier in Gal. 5: 6, where it is followed by 'what counts is faith expressing itself through love'.

Paul's own calling is thus expressed in keeping with this concern: 'But when God, who... called me by his grace, was pleased to reveal his Son in me so that I might preach him among the Gentiles' (Gal. 1: 15–16; cf. Rom. 15: 15b–19). Luke's version goes: 'I am sending you to the [Gentiles] to open their eyes and turn them from darkness to light, and from the power of Satan to God, so that they *may receive forgiveness of sins and a place among those* who are sanctified by faith in me' (Acts 26: 17–18). Although the language is Luke's, the content is certainly Paul's. Thus Paul expresses his self-understanding by echoing the language of Isaiah, who had envisioned the inclusion of Gentiles in the eschatological people of God. This inclusion, which stands at the very beginning of Isaiah (2: 1–5), finds expression several times thereafter.[5] Both Paul's and Luke's versions of Paul's call echo the second of Isaiah's servant songs (47: 1–7).[6]

This vision, in turn, takes us back to Genesis 12: 2–3, where God establishes a covenant with Abraham that 'I will make you into a great nation', whose final goal is 'and all peoples on earth will be blessed through you'. Israel's failure in this regard is what is picked up eschatologically in the prophetic tradition. And it is this tradition to which Paul is indebted.

It is not surprising, therefore, that Paul's language for the people of God, which now includes Gentiles, is simply an extension of the language of the former covenant. The most common is 'saints', which is a direct borrowing from the language of Daniel 7: 18 and 22, which in turn is itself an echo of Exodus 19: 5–6. Crucial for Paul's use of this term is that fact that 'the saints' included 'all nations and peoples of every language' (Dan. 7: 14). The same sense of continuity is found in his usage of *ekklesia*, which of course also has the advantage of being a term well known in the Greek world. But Paul's usage is determined by its appearance in the Septuagint as a translation of *qahal*, when referring to the 'congregation' of Israel. The same is true

---

[5] See 11: 10 (LXX, cited as the fourth and final passage in the catena of Rom. 15: 9–12); 42: 6; 49: 6. Since these latter two appear in the servant songs, it is not surprising that Paul sees Isa. 54: 1 (at the conclusion of the final servant song) as fulfilled by Gentile inclusion (Gal. 4: 27); see his use of Isa. 65: 1 in Rom. 10: 20, and of Hos. 2: 20 and 1: 10 in Rom. 9: 25–6. Gentile inclusion is found elsewhere in the prophetic tradition in Mic. 4: 1–2; Zeph. 3: 9; Zech 8: 20–2; 14: 16–19.

[6] Paul echoes both vv. 1 and 6: 'Before I was born the Lord called me; from my birth he made mention of my name' (cf. v. 5, 'he who formed me in the womb to be his servant'), and 'I will make you a light for the Gentiles' (cf. 42: 6). The latter is echoed in the Lucan version.

of his use of 'election' and 'new covenant' language as well.[7] Equally telling is Paul's use of 'temple' imagery for the people of God in a given location (1 Cor. 3: 16–17; 2 Cor. 6: 16; Eph. 2: 20), which picks up the crucial 'presence of God' motif from the Old Testament, and which in Ephesians 2: 20–2 is explicitly applied to the reality of Jew and Gentile as one people of God.

This concern with the people of God is found in other ways in Paul as well. It is of more than passing interest that most of his letters to churches are addressed to whole congregations, not to a leader or leaders. Indeed, even when leaders (plural) are included in the salutation in Philippians 1: 1, they are so as an addendum ('along with the *episkopoi* and *diakonoi*'). Moreover, even when a problem in the church is the direct result of individuals' wrongdoings, Paul never addresses the wrongdoers directly, but calls on the whole church to deal with the issue as a community matter. See, for example, the arguments in 1 Corinthians 5: 1–13 and 6: 1–12. At issue in each case is clearly the community as God's people in Corinth[8]— although the individual sinner(s) are not overlooked. But they are to be dealt with by the community.

All of this to point out, then, that for Paul 'salvation in Christ' still has the creation of a people for God's name as its goal, and that this concern is to be seen in continuity with the people of God as constituted by the former covenant.

II SALVATION IN CHRIST AS THE NEW CREATION

One further facet of this concern needs to be highlighted, namely Paul's use of 'new creation' terminology to speak of the *result* of God's saving event in Christ. Related to this is his use of 'image of God' language. Even though 'new creation' language as such occurs only

---

[7] For 'election' see 1 Thess. 1: 4; 2 Thess. 2: 12; Col. 3: 12; Eph. 1: 4, 11; for 'new covenant' see 1 Cor. 11: 25; 2 Cor. 3: 6–17; cf. Gal 4: 24 and Rom. 2: 29 (echoing Deut. 30: 6).

[8] e.g. 'when you are assembled and I am with you in Spirit, and the power of the Lord Jesus is present, hand this man over to Satan' (1 Cor. 5: 4–5); 'Get rid of the old yeast so that you may be a new unleavened batch of dough' (v. 7); 'Expel the wicked person from among you' (v. 13, citing Leviticus). Cf. 6: 1–6, which focuses on the church's own failure to act on a deed that has been taken 'before the ungodly'. In this case, Paul finally speaks to the two litigants (in vv. 7–8 and 9–10), but his focus is primarily on what this has meant as a failure for the whole community.

twice in Paul (2 Cor. 5: 17; Gal. 6: 15; but cf. Rom. 8: 18–25), it nonetheless is a significant theme in his theology. Two facets of this usage in Paul are important here: his use of new creation language in its own right, but especially in light of his usage of 'image of God' and 'Second Adam' language with regard to Christ.

New creation theology is articulated in two ways by Paul. First, in the key passage (2 Cor. 5: 14–17) Paul is arguing again (cf. 1 Cor. 1: 18–4: 21) for both his gospel of a crucified Messiah and his own cruciform apostleship. He asserts that the new creation brought about by Christ's death and resurrection nullifies viewing anyone/anything from the 'old age' perspective (*kata sarka*, 'according to the flesh'). Why? Because Christ's death has brought the whole human race under the sentence of death (v. 14), so that those who live in God's new order do so for the one who died for them and was raised again (v. 15). Thus being 'in Christ' means belonging to the new creation: the old has gone, the new has come (v. 17). This radical, new-order point of view—resurrection life marked by the cross—lies at the heart of everything Paul thinks and does (cf. Phil. 3: 4–14).

This leads, second, to a series of texts in Paul which picks up 'second exodus' imagery from Isaiah 40–66: God is about to do a 'new thing' (Isa. 43: 18–19), and in the end will establish 'new heavens and a new earth' (Isa. 65: 17; 66: 22–3). In Paul this theme is applied to believers, who through association with Christ's death and resurrection have themselves experienced death and being raised to newness of life (Rom. 6: 1–14; 7: 4–6; Col. 3: 1–11; Eph. 4: 20–4). Common to these texts, either explicitly (Rom. 6: 1–14) or implicitly (e.g. Col. 3: 1–11 with 2: 9–12), is an association with Christian baptism. Colossians 3: 1–11 is especially noteworthy, since it concludes: 'Here there is no Greek and Jew, circumcised and uncircumcised, barbarian, Scythian, slave and free, but Christ is all, and is in all.' That is, in the new order already set in motion through Christ's death and resurrection the value-based distinctions between people—ethnicity and status—no longer obtain.

Crucial to this view of things is Paul's use of 'image of God' language, which clearly echoes Genesis 1: 26–7. Since God's 'image-bearers' are to be his vice-regents in 'charge' of the creation, there is every reason to believe that behind this usage is a common feature of suzerainty in the ancient Near East. One way for people to be reminded of a suzerain's sovereignty was by placing 'images' of himself throughout the land(s) as visual reminders of that sovereignty. Thus God is expressing his own sovereignty over creation by placing it under his 'image-bearers', man and woman. What was distorted in the Fall was 'the image of God' in humanity; and this is precisely where, in Paul's theology, Christ enters history as the one who is bringing about the new creation, restoring the image. He is himself the 'new Adam', the one who *in his humanity is the perfect image-bearer* of the eternal God (2 Cor. 4: 4; Col. 1: 15).

Thus the two places where Christ is seen as the 'second Adam' are at the beginning point of Adam's fall (his sin) and its end result (death). First, in contrast to Adam's ushering sin—and with it, death—into the world, Christ ushered in the time of grace and righteousness (Rom. 5: 12–21); second, in contrast to Adam's sin that brought (eternal) death, Christ as the last Adam brought life and resurrection through his own resurrection (1 Cor. 15: 21–2, 45–59). But even more significantly for our present purposes is the fact that in saving a people for God's name, Christ is described as the 'firstborn among many brothers and sisters', who have been predestined themselves to be 'conformed into the image of [God's] Son' (Rom. 8: 29; cf. Col. 2: 10–11). It is as though God's people by the Spirit were looking into a mirror and beholding not their own, but Christ's, image, and thus are being transformed into that same image, from one degree of glory to another (2 Cor. 3: 17–18). In the Spirit, Christ thus effects the new creation by restoring humanity back into the divine image.

In Pauline theology, therefore, Christ's saving work is not only (re)creating a people for God's name, but at the same time this people is to be part of the new creation, who in their own lives and in their life together are God's image-bearers on this planet. And this is why Paul's energies are given almost totally to exhorting and encouraging his congregations to live out this calling as God's people wherever they are.

I start this overview of 'redemption in Paul' with these realities, because I turn now to survey the primary metaphors[9] Paul uses to speak about entry into this newly constituted people of God. And this is where the major point of discontinuity emerges—because entry

---

[9] By 'primary' I mean those that occur most often in contexts where 'salvation in Christ' is the subject matter. 'Metaphor' throughout this chapter carries its standard sense of an implied comparison, in which the figure enhances the literal reality through evocative imagery.

into this people happens at the individual level as by faith they appropriate Christ's saving work in their behalf.

III SALVATION IN CHRIST: SOME PRELIMINARY MATTERS

My reason for choosing to examine the various Pauline metaphors for salvation is twofold: first, because one of the missing elements in the Pauline letters is any explanation as to *how* the death of Christ effected salvation for us, and the closest we can get to that question, it seems to me, is by way of Paul's metaphors; second, because as a NT scholar I have been dissatisfied for many years with historic Protestantism's settling on one metaphor ('justification') as Paul's primary way of speaking about salvation—so much so that it is sometimes not recognized for the metaphor that it actually is. Thus another reason for examining Paul's soteriology by way of his metaphors is to be reminded that, although metaphors do indeed give expression to *one dimension of a reality*, no one of them is adequate to embrace *the whole of that reality*. Before examining several of the key metaphors, some very important preliminary words about Pauline soteriology are in order. As noted at the outset, 'salvation in Christ' is the cooperative work of the three persons of the Trinity. Although this is the language of a later time, it faithfully captures a significant reality in Paul's letters; for in some twenty creedal moments in his letters where he reminds believers of their salvation—and no two of them are alike—almost all of them are framed in a triadic way.[10] The point to make here is threefold.

First, for Paul salvation is an especially *theological* reality, in the sense that it is both a *reflection* of God's *character* and the *result* of God's *initiative*. Whatever else, and at this point Paul is at one with his OT heritage, salvation is God's thing—from beginning to end. God in love initiated it; God effected it through Christ's death on the cross; God brings it to bear in our lives by the Spirit. If our understanding of God's character has been distorted by our own fallenness and thus hidden from view (2 Cor. 4: 4), then salvation in Christ is

---

[10] On this point see my 'Paul and the Trinity: The Experience of Christ and the Spirit for Paul's Understanding of God', in S. T. Davis, D. Kendall, and G. O'Collins (eds), *The Trinity* (Oxford: Oxford University Press, 1999), 52–7.

both a reflection and result of God's character being manifested in the world.

What is revealed is in full continuity with the OT: that God is full of mercy and loves his fallen creatures who by their own sinfulness are destined for 'wrath'.[11] In the death of God's Son on the cross, we come full face with God's active love: 'God demonstrated his own love for us in this: While we were still sinners, Christ died for us' (Rom. 5: 8, TNIV). Thus, contrary to many popular Christian 'theologies', Christ did not die in order to make it possible for God to love us, who were otherwise unlovable. Rather, he died precisely because God loved us even while we were still sinners and enemies.

Second, Christ's *death* on the *cross* is the place where God effected his remedy for the human condition. From beginning to end, the focus is here. Earlier than all his letters Paul had already embraced the commonly held creed: 'Christ died for our sins, according to the Scriptures' (1 Cor. 15: 3). In his earliest letter he declares that 'God did not appoint us to suffer wrath, but to receive salvation through our Lord Jesus Christ, who *died for us*, so that . . . we may live together with him' (1 Thess. 5: 9–10). And in one of his last letters it is still the same: 'Jesus Christ . . . *gave himself for us* to redeem us from all wickedness' (Tit. 2: 13–14). And such language can be found everywhere in between.[12] In these texts we find recurring language, seldom explained, but full of theological grist—death, the cross, blood. All of these speak of the same reality: that God effected salvation through Christ's *death*, a death that took place on the *cross*, in which Christ poured out his *blood*.

This extravagant expression of divine love is at the same time the 'divine scandal' (1 Cor. 1: 18–25), whereby God chose to redeem our fallen race through a *crucified Messiah*—the ultimate oxymoron.[13]

---

[11] This troublesome word in most instances in Paul refers not to an 'emotion' of anger or indignation, but to God's future punitive judgement of those who have rejected him. See BAGD 720–1, and the discussion below (s. v).

[12] See 1 Cor. 1: 18–25; 2: 1–2; 2 Cor. 5: 14–15; Gal. 1: 4; 2: 15–25; 6: 14–15; Rom. 3: 21–6; 5: 6–11; 6: 10; 8: 34; 14: 9; Col. 1: 19–22; 2: 14–15; Eph. 1: 7; 2: 16; Phil. 2: 8.

[13] Made so by the fact that 'Messiah' had come to represent power and glory, God's way of triumphing over hated foes, while 'crucifixion' was the most horrifying and humiliating death known in antiquity, reserved by the Romans for insurrectionists (which is how Jesus died) and for runaway, or otherwise incorrigible, slaves. Paul clearly recognizes the inherent difficulty with the Christian message for both Jews (God himself 'cursed' Jesus by having him hanged on a tree) and Gentiles (whose world-view simply could not contain such folly in a God); see 1 Cor. 1: 18–25.

And so the early Christians were faced with the double difficulty: that their Messiah conquered not through military might but as God's suffering servant, who had been crucified as an insurrectionist; and that this message was God's good news for Jew and Gentile alike. It is little wonder that the earliest visual symbol of the Christian faith was not the cross, but the fish (to visually represent the acrostic *ἰχθύς*), whose fifth letter served to embrace the reality of the cross (Christ as Saviour).

Third, it is important to repeat here that no one metaphor embraces the whole of Pauline soteriology. There are at least two reasons for this. First, here we are dealing with another divine mystery, which is simply too large to be captured in a single metaphor. Second, and for me this is the important point, in almost every case Paul's choice of metaphor is determined by the aspect of human sinfulness that is in immediate purview. Slaves to sin (and law) are 'redeemed'; those in enmity to God are 'reconciled'; those who are guilty of transgressing the law are 'justified'.

Evidence of this reality can be seen in two 'freestanding'[14] passages in 1 Corinthians, where Paul wants to remind them of their former life as pagans and their present life in Christ. In both cases, one metaphor simply will not do. So in 1: 30, as God's own expression of 'wisdom' in saving the Corinthian 'nobodies' (1: 26–8), he set forth Christ to be their 'righteousness (justification), sanctification, and redemption'. Two of these metaphors are picked up again in 6: 11, where Paul reminds them of the past sinful way of life (vv. 9–10) from which God has saved them: 'But you were washed, you were sanctified, you were justified in the name of our Lord Jesus Christ and by the Spirit of our God'. With these one might also compare Romans 3: 24–5, where in two clauses of a single sentence Paul changes metaphors three times: 'all [Jew and Gentile alike] are *justified* freely by [God's] grace through the *redemption* that is in Christ Jesus, whom God presented as a *hilasterion* (atoning sacrifice)'. The point is that no one of these is itself the whole thing, and the 'whole thing' must be recognized as embracing each one and all of them.

With these crucial 'preliminaries' before us, let us turn then to examine four out of the many Pauline metaphors to see how they 'work' as describing one aspect of the saving work of Christ.

---

[14] By this I mean that they do not occur in a passage that is dealing with soteriology as such, which means further that there is no mention of sin.

IV REDEMPTION

I begin with 'redemption' both because that is the theme of this book and because it is one of the two Pauline metaphors that has deep roots in the OT story. It is also one of the more abused metaphors in the history of the church, when metaphors are turned into exact equivalents of reality. The metaphor itself has two OT settings. The first is the ultimate defining moment in Israel's history—God's deliverance of his people from the bondage of Egyptian slavery. Not surprisingly this is the setting that predominates in Paul's usage. The other setting is slavery in general, where a 'purchase' is involved, bringing freedom or change of ownership by payment of a ransom.

In Pauline usage only the first setting is in view when Paul images Christ's death as freeing believers from sin's bondage. The second is used when the emphasis is on being 'purchased' so as to *belong to* Christ (1 Cor. 6: 20; 7: 23). It is precisely the confusion of these metaphorical settings and emphases that has led to the primary abuse of the metaphor: to see people as 'purchased' from, or by payment to, Satan. Not only is this *not* a Pauline view of things, but in both cases when he uses the metaphor in this way his emphasis is on being purchased *for* God—not *from* anything—thus coming under Christ's ownership. The first of these (6: 20) is a clear play on the fact that when a slave is 'purchased', they are thought of in terms of their 'bodies'. Since Christ has 'purchased' their bodies, Paul argues with some Corinthian men who are insisting on the 'freedom' to go to the prostitutes, their bodies now belong to God and are destined for resurrection (v. 14); and believers must therefore glorify in their bodies the God who so 'purchased' them for his own purposes.

But Paul's primary use of the metaphor of redemption presupposes the exodus narrative, so that the unbeliever is imaged as enslaved to/ by sin[15] (and sometimes the law) as Israel was enslaved in Egypt. It should be noted that the imagery of sin as enslavement and bondage occurs more often than the actual language of 'redemption', in

---

[15] This imagery, it should be noted, is never used by Paul in reference to enslavement to Satan, although in Gal. 4: 3 and 9 he uses the imagery of enslavement to the *stoicheia*, which in the latter case now includes the law.

which cases other verbs (especially 'set free') serve the same metaphorical function. This is especially so in the long argument in
Romans 6 that believers need no longer live under sin's mastery.
The whole passage is predicated on the 'freedom' from sin and death
that has been effected by Christ's death on the cross (6: 1–10). The
rest of the argument in Romans 6 spells out the consequences in
terms of living for God in freedom, no longer enslaved by sin to do its
bidding. The same imagery is picked up again in 7: 6, 14 and 8: 2,
where the one 'sold as a slave to sin' (7: 14) has been set free from the
'law' of sin and death by a third 'law', that of the Spirit who gives life
through Christ Jesus.

For the purposes of this study Paul's use of redemption imagery in
Galatians 3: 13–14, which is picked up again in 4: 5–6, is especially
important, since along with 2 Corinthians 5: 21 this is the closest one
comes in the Pauline corpus to an *explicitly* substitutionary understanding of Christ's death. But in this case, in contrast with 2
Corinthians 5: 21, the redemption is related to 'enslavement' to the
law, not to sin. Thus in a paragraph (Gal. 3: 10–14) contrasting those
who are ἐξ ἔργων νόμου (predicated on doing law) with those who
are ἐκ πίστεως Χριστοῦ (predicated on trusting Christ, vv. 6–9), Paul
chooses two OT texts to describe the 'curse' of such people. They are
under the 'curse' of Deuteronomy 27: 26, if they 'do not *continue to do
everything* written in the Book of the Law' (TNIV); and therefore they
cannot be 'by faith' (by which the righteous *live*), since commitment
to 'doing the law' means that 'the one who does these things [= lives
by the law] will live *by them*' (Lev. 18: 5).

Paul's point is that these two ways of 'living' stand in diametric
opposition to each other. One lives 'by faith' or 'by doing law'; and
the one who lives by 'doing law' is under that very curse—of having
to live by the law and thus not by faith, and by implication outside
God's 'blessing'. That this is what the paragraph is all about is
made clear by the concluding twin purpose clauses in verse 14:
that the blessing of Abraham might be for the Gentiles through
Christ, who have received the promised Spirit by faith. But to get
there—to the promised 'blessing' that includes the Gentiles—Paul
reminds them of how 'the curse of the Law' (so understood) was
removed: 'Christ *redeemed* us from the curse of the Law by becoming
a curse for us, for it is written, "Cursed is everyone who is hung on a
tree" '. Paul thus clearly sees Christ's death as substitutionary; but in
this case it is hardly 'penal substitution' for our sins. Rather, as Paul

will elaborate in 4: 4–7, Christ was 'born under the law' precisely so that he might 'redeem those under the law'.

It should be noted further that in both Romans and Galatians, Paul's use of this OT imagery of God's deliverance of his people from bondage (to the law (Galatians) as well as to sin (Romans)) is joined to the contemporary Graeco-Roman image of 'adoption as sons'. The word used in both cases ($vio\theta\epsilon\sigma\acute{\iota}a$) is a technical term for the adoption of a male heir in a culture where many families had no son(s) to inherit the estate. The conjunction of these terms (redemption, adoption) in Romans 8: 23 suggests by proximity and implication that it underlies the use of the same metaphor earlier in 8: 15.

The passage in Galatians 4 is the paradigm for Paul's use of these now-combined metaphors. Speaking to Gentiles who are being 'compelled' by some (6: 12) to come under the law, Paul picks up from 3: 23–5 the metaphor of the law as a pedagogue (as imagery for the useful function of the law). But the pedagogue (usually a slave) in fact had a degree of mastery over the 'heir' who has not yet reached his majority (vv. 1–2). That leads then to an application (v. 3) that envisages 'us' (= Paul and the Gentile Galatians) as enslaved to the *stoicheia* of the world. Thus in a stroke of inspired genius Paul images 'slavery' to the law, and thus to sin (v. 9), as the equivalent of the Gentiles' life-long enslavement in fear to the 'powers'. And such multi-dimensional bondage is what Christ has come to free 'us' from. Thus in twin purpose clauses (v. 5), he concludes his sentence that began in verse 4 by pointing to Christ's redemption from the enslavement of the law, which at the same time included 'adoption as sons'. The evidence for such 'adoption' with its concomitant deliverance from slavery is the gift of the Spirit of the Son, who from within the heart of the believer cries out to God in the language of the Son, 'Abba'. And so the argument that began in 3: 1 concludes with 'not a slave, but a son', then an 'heir'—and all of this 'through God', meaning by God's design and doing (Gal. 4: 7).

In the end, therefore, this metaphor functions to press home one reality of post-conversion life with regard to sin. The believer is neither helplessly under sin's bondage nor, because of sin, positioned as a slave outside the family of God. On the other side, the believer has been 'purchased at great cost' to be God's 'slave', meaning free to do his bidding through the power of the Spirit. It should be noted finally that Paul's interest in the metaphor is primarily with the *what* ('redemption') and the *how* ('the cross'); the closest he comes to the 'how it works' question is in Galatians 3: 13, that Christ 'became a curse for us' (= came under God's 'curse' to 'redeem' us from the curse of living by law) so that Gentiles might receive the 'blessing' of life in the Spirit. To press it in ways that Paul himself does not take would seem to be a dubious way of treating metaphors.

V Hilasterion (Means of Atonement)

This is the second metaphor that derives from the OT story, in this case from the sacrificial system. Given the rich possibilities of sacrificial imagery (consider Hebrews, for example), it appears surprisingly infrequently in Paul. Most likely he does not make full use of it because he was a Pharisee of the Diaspora, for whom the sacrificial system would long have been a past reality as far as his understanding of being Jewish was concerned. Moreover, his call as apostle to the Gentiles probably should be factored in as well.

Nonetheless, 'sacrificial' language occurs just often enough,[16] and in such off-handed ways, that one would neglect it among the Pauline metaphors at one's own loss. I begin by noting Paul's *language* in this regard, since both its place in context and the 'logic' of its usage in Paul are not immediately apparent. There are four passages in which such language appears that speak of Christ's saving work. In their chronological order of appearance they are:

Christ our Passover was sacrificed for us   (1 Cor. 5: 7)
God presented Christ as a *hilasterion* by his blood   (Rom. 3: 25)
What the Law could not do, God did by sending his own Son in the likeness of sinful humanity to be a sin offering (καὶ περὶ ἁμαρτίας)[17]   (Rom. 8: 3)
just as Christ loved us and gave himself up for us as a fragrant offering and sacrifice to God   (Eph. 5: 2)

Another set of texts also needs to be noted in this regard, namely Paul's use of the imagery of 'blood' as a way of speaking about

---

[16] Indeed, Paul is not adverse to sacerdotal language as such. He uses it most frequently, however, to refer to ministry of some kind, sometimes where he or others assume the role of the priest in making an 'offering' to God (e.g. Rom. 15: 16; 2 Cor. 9: 12; Phil. 2: 17; 4: 18).

[17] This is a debatable one. For the likelihood that the TNIV has it right in this instance see N. T. Wright, *The Climax of the Covenant* (Minneapolis: Fortress, 1991), 220–5, who comes to this conclusion by noting that the LXX uses the phrase περὶ ἁμαρτίας to translate 'sin offering'.

Christ's death in our behalf. There are eight of these, one of which appears in conjunction with *hilasterion* in Romans 3: 25 (see below). Three others appear in connection with the eucharist in 1 Corinthians ('the new covenant in my blood', 11: 25; picked up again in v. 27; cf 10: 16). The other four are what give us reason to pause, since they serve as a reference to Christ's death in sentences where metaphors other than the sacrificial system are at work. Thus:

Since we have been *justified* by his blood   (Rom. 5: 9)
... through [Christ] to reconcile to himself all things ... by making peace through his blood, shed on the cross   (Col. 1: 20)
In him [Christ] we have redemption through his blood, the forgiveness of sins   (Eph. 1: 7)
But now in Christ Jesus you who once were far away have been brought near by the blood of Christ.   (Eph. 2: 13)

Several summarizing observations may be made regarding these data, before looking specifically at the probable meaning of *hilasterion* in Romans 3: 25. First, in terms of actual usage, the sacerdotal system does not provide the primary metaphor for salvation in Paul. Nonetheless, sacrificial language is *presuppositional* to Paul's understanding of Christ's death on the cross. The fact that 'blood' language is used in conjunction with the other three metaphors under consideration in this chapter, which themselves have no immediate referent to the sacrificial system, suggests that for Paul Christ's death on the cross was always understood as 'sacrificial' in some way. Finally, we should note that in contrast to the other metaphors under purview, this one has no specific contextual referent as such, nor is any specific understanding of sin in view when it is used. These observations, I would think, should lead us to use a degree of caution when coming to the usage in Romans 3, to which we now turn.

I begin by making the observation that Romans 3: 24–5 is not an example of 'mixing' metaphors; rather it is a primary example of the fact that no single metaphor will suffice for Paul. As already noted, what is at stake for Paul in Romans is whether Gentiles must bear the marks of the former covenant in order to be full members of the people of God as constituted under the new covenant. The metaphor of 'justification' therefore predominates because in this kind of argumentation 'sin' is understood as a 'transgression' of *the law*. Such transgression puts one under potential condemnation, which in turn leads to fear and sometimes guilt. But this *use* of the metaphor has no specific OT referent in terms of salvific relationship to God. Thus, even though the 'law-court' imagery presupposed is probably that of civil justice being handled at the city gates—which in the Jewish world would indeed have to do with the law—Paul's Gentile believers would find an easy 'transfer' to the Roman legal system.

The point to be made here, then, is that the most likely reason for Paul's adding the metaphors of 'redemption' and *hilasterion* to that of 'justification' is that, even though a verdict of 'condemnation' could lead to death, the metaphor itself lacks any inherent referent to a 'substitute' death for the convicted. I propose that it was in order to overcome this deficiency in 'justification' itself that Paul felt compelled to add the second and third metaphors, so as to put this metaphor as well in the context of Christ's death. This is then expressed in 'shorthand' in 5: 9, 'since we have now been justified by his blood'. But even here, the use of 'by his blood', which picks up 'Christ died for [us]' in verses 6 and 8, causes Paul once more to abandon the metaphor of justification (for reconciliation in this case).

So why does Paul use the word *hilasterion*, a Pauline *hapax*, to pick up the imagery of the sacrificial system in this argument about *justification*, and what is his intended referent by the use of such a metaphor?[18] There are four things to note in order to establish a frame of reference. First, the word group of which this is a part has in general the idea of the 'appeasement' of a deity who has been alienated by human wrongdoing. However, second, the complication posed by this particular word is that, apart from an idiosyncratic use by the Greek translator of Ezekiel,[19] the only referent it has in biblical Greek (LXX and NT) is to the *covering* (traditionally, 'mercy-seat') of the 'ark of the covenant' in the most holy place. The first point of confusion comes, third, from its use in the Graeco-Roman world, where it was used for 'that which served as an instrument for regaining the goodwill of a deity' (BAGD). And, fourth, its present usage is made the more complex by the modifier 'in/with his blood',

---

[18] There is, of course, an enormous bibliography with reference to this question. I do not mean to be glib by not engaging that literature in this discussion. What I have tried to do rather, for both this metaphor and the next two ('reconciliation', 'justification'), is to offer a fresh look at the data, with the metaphorical nature of the language as the first concern.

[19] In three instances in 43: 14–20, where it is used to translate צזרה (ledge).

which does not seem at first blush to function well as a modifier of 'mercy-seat'.

At issue finally in this passage is whether Paul is using it in the Septuagintal way (to refer to the covering itself, probably as a metonymy for the place of atonement or the atonement itself), or whether he is using it in the Graeco-Roman way to refer to Christ as the means either of propitiation or expiation. There are several good reasons for believing it was the former that Paul had in mind by using this word as a deliberately pregnant metaphor.

First, it should be noted that, whenever Paul elsewhere uses sacerdotal language, it can be demonstrated rather conclusively that he is echoing the language of the OT sacrificial system.[20] One would seem to need compelling reasons to think otherwise here. Second, that this word is a metonymy for the *place of atonement* (only on the Day of Atonement) is strengthened by the two qualifying prepositional phrases that follow.[21] The *hilasterion* is the 'place' of atonement, made so by the 'blood' of the atonement, which happens only on the Day of Atonement. And the reason for it was to have an annual sacrifice 'for the people of Israel once in the year for *all* their sins' (Lev. 16: 34), including inadvertent sins. It is this latter feature that calls forth the next prepositional phrase. For this is how God in his justice has now handled the past sins of the Gentiles. By use of the pregnant metaphor *hilasterion* accompanied by the phrase 'with his blood', Paul thus offers Christ as the replacement of the 'mercy-seat' with its sprinkled blood on the Day of Atonement; at the same time as a pregnant metaphor it functions to accommodate the 'inadvertent'

---

[20] See e.g. my Philippians commentary on Phil. 2: 17 and 4: 18 (*Paul's Letter to the Philippians* (Grand Rapids, Mich.: Eerdmans, 1996), 251–5, 451).

[21] This sentence (which extends from v. 22b to v. 26) is a famous crux; but it can in fact be shown to hold together quite well. At issue from the appearance of ἱλαστήριον on, is what to do with the several prepositional phrases that follow. Some things seem certain: (1) that, despite the word order, the phrase 'in his blood' is not the object of 'through faith' (as NIV, but now corrected in the TNIV), since nowhere in Paul does the Greek preposition ἐν follow the word 'faith' as its object (= 'trust *in* someone'); rather the phrase 'through faith' stands up front to make sure that this crucial idea does not get lost in the process of changing metaphors; (2) that even though the following compounding of prepositional phrases (*en/eis/dia/en/pros/en/eis*) is especially complex, a degree of sense can nonetheless be made; the first *en* phrase is either instrumental ('by') or accompaniment ('with'); the *eis* and *pros* can only be purpose, held together in temporal tension by the language of 'in former times' and 'in the present time'.

sins of the Gentiles who now realize forgiveness together with Jews through Christ's poured-out blood on the cross.[22]

Those who reject this view are divided as to whether what is realized in Christ's death as *hilasterion* (in the Greek sense) is 'propitiation' (appeasing God's wrath) or 'expiation' (provision for removing an impediment between people and God). Those who historically have favoured 'propitiation' do so in part because this argument begins in 1: 18 with the language of 'God's wrath', which is expressed in the present tense. Thus what is being propitiated is God's wrath against human sin.

But the difficulty with this view is threefold. First, it leans towards the Graeco-Roman meaning of the word; but in so doing, Paul would have given the word a new twist—that God has 'propitiated' himself. This is not difficult in itself (after all, one can do wonderful things with metaphors!). The questions are: *why* would Paul do this double twist with a well-known biblical word, and *would* his readers have caught on?

Second, the greater issue is how 'the wrath of God' fits into the argument at this point. In most of Paul's use of this language, it refers to God's future punitive judgement on those who have rejected him. Moreover, not one of the occurrences of this word in the Pauline corpus is associated with sacrificial language. For example, Jesus '*rescues* us from the coming wrath' (1 Thess. 1: 10); 'God did not appoint us to suffer wrath but to receive *salvation* through our Lord Jesus Christ' (5: 9). Thus, even in Romans (5: 9) Paul states, 'Since we have *now* been *justified* by his blood, how much more *shall* we be *saved* from [God's] wrath.'

Third, and of equal import, the OT does not speak of the sacrificial system as a way of removing God's wrath from his people. Not only is that not said anywhere explicitly in the texts, but for the most part a quite different picture emerges. For example, in the great penitential psalms (32, 51) the appeal is to God's mercy and his willingness to forgive sin. Indeed, in Psalm 51 the psalmist explicitly rejects sacrifices as a means of forgiveness. What God delights in are the sacrifices of a broken, repentant heart (vv. 16–17), and that in turn will lead to proper sacrifices (v. 19).

---

[22] For a brief presentation of this point of view, see also J. Roloff, '*ἱλαστήριον*', in *Exegetical Dictionary of the New Testament*, ii (Grand Rapids, Mich.: Eerdmans, 1991), 85–6.

All of this to say, then, that what we learn theologically from Paul's use of sacrificial metaphors, especially his metonymous use of 'blood' and *hilasterion*, is that Christ's death has been 'for us'[23] in some way, and, whatever else, it has been effective. How much we theologize by our own extrapolation of the metaphor, in ways Paul himself does not do, would seem to be moot.

VI RECONCILIATION

Of the 'metaphors' of salvation looked at in this chapter, reconciliation is probably the least metaphorical as such. Here we move into the sphere of personal relationships, and human sin in this case is seen as 'hostility' or 'enmity', and perhaps 'estrangement'.

The language of reconciliation occurs four times in Paul's letters (2 Cor. 5: 18–20; Rom. 5: 9–10; Col. 1: 19–22; Eph. 2: 16), and in each case he is addressing Gentiles, sometimes Gentiles and Jews together (Romans, Ephesians). Although the settings in each of these uses differ considerably, two things are constant. First, God initiates the reconciliation and brings it about through the death of Christ. Thus, 'God was, in Christ,[24] reconciling the world to himself' (2 Cor. 5: 19), or 'God was pleased . . . through him to reconcile to himself all things' (Col. 1: 19–20). Second, God does so to overcome the Gentiles' former alienation and enmity against himself. Thus, 'Once you were alienated from God and were enemies . . . because of your evil behaviour. But now God has reconciled you by Christ's physical body through death' (Col. 1: 21–2), or 'while we were God's enemies, we were reconciled to him through the death of his Son' (Rom. 5: 10).

Finally, in two cases the estrangement is first of all between human beings, which God overcomes by reconciling both to himself through Christ. In 2 Corinthians 5, Paul is wrestling (again) with the Corinthians' attitude towards himself (as 5: 13 makes plain).[25] Thus

---

[23] I have chosen in this study not to deal with the preposition ὑπέρ, except to point out that some kind of 'substitution' seems to be demanded in many of its occurrences. On this issue see BAGD A1a*e*, and D. B. Wallace, *Greek Grammar Beyond the Basics* (Grand Rapids, Mich.: Zondervan, 1996), 383–9.

[24] I am among those who think Paul's word order here is deliberate: θεὸς ἦν ἐν Χριστῷ can mean either (or both) that God was in Christ doing the reconciling, or that God, in Christ, was reconciling. Perhaps the double meaning can be captured by translating 'God in Christ was reconciling? . . .'.

[25] The TNIV has wonderfully captured the sense: 'If we are "out of our mind," as some say, it is for God; if we are in our right mind, it is for you.'

the argument that follows is intended to force them into a world-view based on the new creation, that death and resurrection with Christ radically changes one's perspective. 'All this is from God', he urges in verse 18, and with that he uses the metaphor of reconciliation, the ministry of which God has given to Paul (basically the reconciliation of the world to God). Then at the end he turns to the Corinthians themselves and urges, 'Be reconciled to God', meaning by implication that their present enmity towards God's ambassador is equally enmity towards God.

But, typically for Paul, since such an imperative might appear to put the emphasis on their action, he concludes by making clear that 'reconciliation' with God is something God himself has effected through the death of Christ. Returning momentarily to where he began in verses 14 and 15 (that Christ's having died for all means that all are under the sentence of death, and only those raised by Christ now live in the new aeon), he spells out what that means, but does so now in terms of 'sin' and 'righteousness'. God made him who did not know sin by experience to become sin (perhaps a 'sin offering') for us, so that in him we might take on the righteousness of God. How Paul understands Christ's 'being made sin for us' and our 'becoming the righteousness of God in him' are areas of huge debate;[26] at this point I simply note that for Paul the way God effected reconciliation was by his own putting forth Christ in death for us (probably sacrificial, not judicial, language).

In Ephesians 2, the context is (once more) Jew and Gentile as one people of God. Addressing Gentiles primarily (the 'you' in vv. 11–13 and 19 are clearly Gentiles), he argues that Christ is our peace, who by his death has created one new people (actually, a 'new humanity'), doing so in order to 'reconcile both of them to God through the cross'. The point, of course, is that by their common reconciliation to God through Christ they should be similarly reconciled to one another as well.

And so, even though it moves much closer to reality than metaphor, as metaphor reconciliation is language used by Paul when human hostility towards God and one another has been overcome by the death of Christ. Again, there is no theologizing on Paul's part,

---

[26] See e.g. N. T. Wright, 'On Becoming the Righteousness of God: 2 Corinthians 5: 21', in D. M. Hay (ed.), *Pauline Theology*, ii. *1 and 2 Corinthians* (Minneapolis: Fortress, 1993), 200–8; and J.-N. Aletti's chapter below.

nor is it at all clear *how* Christ's death brings about this reconciliation. Thus, it functions as yet another metaphor pointing to the
effective nature of the cross in dealing with human sin, but without
explanation or elaboration.

VII JUSTIFICATION

Some of what needs to be said about Paul's use of the metaphor of
'justification' has already been said above in section V. There I noted
that: (1) the language of justification emerges in Paul primarily
where the issue is over whether Gentile believers must also come
under the Mosaic law; (2) while the primary referent for the metaphor itself has to do with 'breaking the law' in the OT, it is seldom
used as language for redemption or salvation as such; and (3) 'justification' is to be taken seriously as a metaphor, and precisely for this
reason it is inadequate to carry the full weight of Paul's understanding of what God did through the death of Christ.

My concern here is twofold: (1) to elaborate on the limited use of
this metaphor in Paul, even in the two major letters where it occurs
(Galatians and Romans), which is what forces us (2) to try to ferret
out Paul's own understanding of its implications.

The problem that many Protestants face when coming to this
metaphor is that they have an innate resistance to seeing it as a
metaphor at all. My guess is that this stems from two factors. First,
the heart of Pauline theology is that God saves by his grace alone, to
which the human response is faith—in Pauline language (often
forgotten) a 'faith that works itself out in love' (Gal. 5: 6). It is the
attachment of 'by faith' to the metaphor of 'justification' that is most
likely the crucial point. Yet this is an ungrounded anxiety. The fact
that the emphasis on 'by faith alone' occurs most often with the
language of justification does not mean that it is *dependent* on this
metaphor for its meaning. We have already noted that 'by faith' is
also attached to the sacrificial metaphor in Romans 3: 25. Moreover,
before Galatians and Romans were written, Paul speaks of the 'faith'
of both the Thessalonians and Corinthians quite apart from forensic
language;[27] and in the one instance in 1 Corinthians where he does

---

[27] See 1 Thess. 1: 7–8; 3: 2–10; 2 Thess. 2: 12–13; 1 Cor. 2: 5; 3: 5; 15: 2, 11; 2 Cor. 1:
24; 4: 13; 5: 7.

use forensic language (6: 11, as one of three metaphors), he does so quite apart from the mention of faith. Furthermore, when for the final time in his extant letters (Ephesians) Paul deals with the similar issue of Jew and Gentile as one people of God, based on faith in the work of Christ (ch. 2; see esp. 2: 8), he manages to do so without using the forensic metaphor once in the entire letter! So while it is true that Paul tends to emphasize 'by faith' when using this metaphor, he does so precisely because he is arguing against those who would emphasize 'doing law'.

Second, making 'justification' the *primary* way of speaking about 'salvation in Christ' stood in some obvious tension with the actual data. Hence its advocates (albeit probably unconsciously) learnt— and taught others—to read all of scripture by means of a 'canon within the canon'. This view was asserted in a most straightforward way by E. J. Carnell in *The Case for Orthodox Theology*,[28] as though it should be plain to any who read the texts for themselves. In a five-step programme of hermeneutics, he argued that the NT interprets the OT, that the Epistles interpret the Gospels, and that 'systematic passages interpret the incidental', which for him meant that the whole canon was finally interpreted on the basis of Romans and Galatians!

To get here, however, one must read Romans as though it were not *ad hoc* in the same way as Galatians, and that it thus represents a compendium of Pauline theology. Not only does this seem to be a skewed reading of this letter, it founders on the evidence within both Romans and Galatians. Here are the hard data. (1) Apart from 1 Corinthians 6: 11 noted above (where the forensic metaphor occurs as one of three metaphors and without connection to 'faith'), this metaphor occurs in only three of Paul's letters (Galatians, Romans, Philippians). (2) In each case it occurs in a context of controversy as to whether Gentiles who have trusted Christ must also adhere to aspects of the Mosaic Law. (3) The metaphor does not appear all the way through these documents,[29] but only when the issue of 'doing

---

[28] Philadelphia: Westminster Press, 1959. I am here contending with the content of ch. 4, 'Hermeneutics', pp. 51–65.

[29] Indeed, in Philippians it is incidental at best, occurring in 3: 9 as a response to 3: 6 (Paul's being 'blameless' as to the 'righteousness found in the law'), which in turn responds to the 'boasting' of the 'mutilators of the flesh' in vv. 2–4. In reality, Paul says, true righteousness means to 'be found in Christ, not having a righteousness of my own based on law, but the righteousness from God based on faith'.

law' as well as having faith emerges. (4) Perhaps most surprising of all, Paul rarely connects 'justification' directly to the death of Christ, although that is clearly presupposed in most cases.

Thus in Galatians the metaphor appears in the early argumentation of 2: 16–3: 24; it is picked up again only in the final applicational moment in 5: 4–5. Paul's point otherwise is that 'having begun by the Spirit (received through faith), one comes to completion by the same Spirit' (3: 3), which is what the last part of the letter is all about (5: 13–6: 10). The Spirit is God's sufficiency for Gentiles to do what the law could not do, and thus to make the law irrelevant (5: 18, 22–3). When Paul actually speaks of the work of Christ itself, he consistently focuses on the cross, but only indirectly (in 2: 21) as the place of 'justification'. Otherwise the emphasis is on Christ's giving himself 'for me/us'. In 1: 4 he celebrates Christ as the one 'who gave himself for our sins to rescue us from the present evil age' (cf. 6: 14), and in 2: 20 the focus is on death to the law accompanied by life through 'the Son of God who loved me and gave himself for me'. Otherwise the work of Christ is expressed by the metaphor of 're-demption' (3: 13; 4: 4–6; cf. 1: 4).

Similarly in Romans, what makes it possible for Jew and Gentile to be the one people of God is the fact that in Christ God has brought the time of the law to an end (7: 1–6; 8: 2, 4; 10: 4), and has ushered in the time of the Spirit (2: 29; 7: 6; 8: 2–17). Thus, both Jew and Gentile, equally guilty of sin (by transgressing the law), may equally be justified through faith in Christ (3: 21–4). But precisely at that point, as noted above, when Paul speaks of the actual work of Christ on our behalf, he shifts to metaphors of redemption and sacrifice. From that point on, the metaphor of justification reappears only in the crucial argument of chapter 4, with its 'conclusion' in 5: 1–11, and in 9: 30–10: 21, where he picks up the issue of Jewish failure and Gentile inclusion. Moreover, the tie of this metaphor to the cross itself, though implied at several points (3: 24; 4: 25; 8: 3–4), is made explicit in this letter only in 5: 9: 'Since we have been justified by his blood'. And whatever else, nowhere is it suggested that Christ's is a 'substitute death' in the sense that one *who is not guilty dies for the guilty* to release them from the penalty of their transgressions. Rather it is the guilty who are pictured as dying and rising with Christ (6: 1–11; 7: 4–6), whose death and resurrection make possible our own.

This is not to downplay 'justification by faith' in Paul; rather, it is to see it for what it is—a pregnant metaphor used when sin is understood as transgression of the law, which brings guilt/condemnation and leads to experiencing God's wrath (2: 5, 9; 4: 15; 5: 9; and esp. 7: 13–25). Thus it is not an insignificant metaphor, but neither is it the whole. What is important for our purposes is that seeing it for what it is—one metaphor among many and used only when transgression of the law is in view—should lighten the debate over certain aspects of the metaphor, a debate that occurs primarily because so much is at stake once it is made the whole thing.

That leads me finally to offer an opinion about the 'meaning' of the metaphor. The debate swirls around two matters: (1) whether in justifying the ungodly (Rom. 4: 5), God merely 'declares' the guilty to be justified or actually makes the justified person righteous in some way; (2) what actually transpires with regard to the believer when she or he is thus 'justified'. Are they 'acquitted' or 'pardoned/forgiven'? I conclude with a few brief words about each matter.

It seems to me that the first issue is the unfortunate outcome of pressing metaphors by making them 'walk on all fours', which happens precisely because all other metaphors are collapsed into this one. Why, one wonders, should Christ's work on our behalf with regard to our transgressions be a matter of either/or rather than both/and? Since one can line up texts on both sides of this debate, should it not finally occur to us that it depends on what emphasis one finds in Paul as to which of these realities is in view? Thus, it seems to me that there can be little question that the 'ungodly' are 'declared' justified. But for Paul that would never be an adequate understanding of Christian conversion, precisely because it leaves out the most important ingredient—the coming of the Spirit to dwell in the believer.

Evidence for this is writ large in the corpus, but nowhere more boldly than in Galatians 3: 1–5. Paul here begins his argument that the Galatian Gentiles do not need to come under the law because of their own experience of the Spirit—at the beginning (vv. 2–3), from that point on (v. 4), and including currently (v. 5). This, then, becomes the predicate for the argument from scripture that follows (3: 6–4: 7); and it is picked up again in the concluding argument, where Paul deals with the question of 'what happens to righteousness (in terms of ethical life) if one does away with the law?' The answer, as always, is the cross of Christ (5: 24) and the gift of the Spirit. Paul simply would not understand 'justification' as a declaration without the accompanying activity of the Spirit. After all, his concern is about 'salvation', which is Trinitarian at its core, so that (Gal. 4: 5–6) God sent his Son to redeem and to secure adoption, and he sent the Spirit of his Son to effect the adoption (not to mention 'justification') in the life of the believer.[30]

On the matter of what the metaphor 'means', I find the language of 'acquittal' especially difficult when dealing with Paul. Acquittal by definition means to be found 'not guilty'. But that is surely to miss Paul's use of the metaphor. Whatever else is true of the one who has transgressed the law, that person is guilty before God and destined for wrath. Christ's death, therefore, does not bring about acquittal. If we are to keep the metaphor alive, then the 'meaning' must be something close to 'pardon' or 'forgiveness', which imply that the transgressor has been found guilty but forgiven. This, after all, is at the heart of Paul's own Jewish heritage, as is made plain in the penitential psalms, one of which is cited by Paul at the heart of his argument about 'justification through Christ' (Rom. 4: 7–8, citing Ps. 32: 1–2): 'Blessed is the one whose iniquities are *forgiven*, whose sin is *covered*; blessed is the one against whom the Lord *will not reckon sin*' (cf. Pss. 51 and 130).

Such a debate, it seems to me, is the result of pressing a metaphor on the basis of its original setting, rather than on the basis of Paul's own usage. While the metaphor assumes the setting of the court of law, it finds its meaning in God's saving action in Christ that is already presaged in the story of the former covenant. So as with the other metaphors, 'justification' is to be understood in connection with the understanding of sin under purview. Sin as 'trangression of the law' is the similar experience of Jew and Gentile alike (Rom. 2: 1–3: 20); and since the law only exposes sin—indeed gives it life so that it overpowers the transgressor and leads to death—God has brought the time of the law to an end through the 'justifying' work of Christ and the empowering of the Spirit.

Thus in sum: 'salvation in Christ', which stands at the heart of Pauline theology, is the outworking of the Trinity and has 'a people for God's name' as its goal. The means of salvation is the death of Christ on the cross, an event of such monumental proportions that it

---

[30] It should be noted in passing that the division of Rom. 1–8 into 'justification' and 'sanctification' is arbitrary and unrelated to what Paul is doing. Both of these words function together as metaphors for conversion in 1 Cor. 1: 30 and 6: 11. Salvation is a 'package deal' in Paul, a many-splendoured reality that cannot be so neatly divided up.

cannot be embraced by a single metaphor. Its simplest expression is that 'Christ died for our sins'. What that means to the one who is joined to the people of God through faith in Christ is expressed by Paul with a variety of metaphors, no one of which is the whole, but each of which is part of the whole. Which metaphor gets special attention at any given moment is dependent on the perspective on human fallenness in view. *How* the cross works is never carefully spelt out in Paul, but *the fact* that it works is evidenced by our *redemption* from enslavement to sin and the law and our *adoption* as God's own children and heirs, by Christ's being set forth as a *hilasterion* (place/means of atonement) in our behalf, by God's *reconciliation* of his enemies to himself, and by God's *justifying* the ungodly, not reckoning their trespasses against them but instead offering forgiveness and pardon. In the end, all of this is made effective by the Spirit.

4

Redemption from the New Perspective?
Towards a Multi-Layered Pauline
Theology of the Cross

N. T. WRIGHT

I INTRODUCTION

Calling something 'new' is always risky, and the 'new perspective' on Paul, now a quarter of a century old since it was introduced by Ed Sanders in 1977, is starting to look rather frayed around the edges. Others have written its history; some are now trying to write its epitaph.[1] I come neither to bury Sanders nor to praise him, but to do two things simultaneously: to look at Paul's doctrine of 'redemption' from (one version of) the perspective Sanders proposed, and in so doing to see what if anything can be redeemed from his proposal. I am conscious that the current wave of gravediggers are making room for more than one coffin, and that some of them at least want to bury N. T. W. along with E. P. S. (and indeed J. D. G. D.). But I am inclined to believe that the rumours of my theological demise have been exaggerated, and that the modified and developed version of the

---

[1] Representative works of the New Perspective include E. P. Sanders, *Paul and Palestinian Judaism: A Comparison of Patterns of Religion* (Minneapolis: Fortress, 1977), James D. G. Dunn, *Jesus, Paul, and the Law: Studies in Mark and Galatians* (Louisville, Ky.: Westminster/John Knox Press, 1990); N. T. Wright, *What St Paul Really Said: Was Paul of Tarsus the Real Founder of Christianity?* (Grand Rapids, Mich.: Eerdmans, 1997). Among recent, critical responses, see Seyoon Kim, *Paul and the New Perspective: Second Thoughts on the Origin of Paul's Gospel* (Grand Rapids, Mich.: Eerdmans, 2001); Andrew A. Das, *Paul, the Law, and the Covenant* (Peabody, Mass.: Hendrickson, 2001); Simon J. Gathercole, *Where is Boasting? Early Jewish Soteriology and Paul's Response in Romans 1–5* (Grand Rapids, Mich.: Eerdmans, 2002).

'new perspective' (hereafter NP) which I adopt possesses not only life but considerable explanatory and exegetical power.

A few brief introductory notes on the various topics thus introduced. First, as to the NP: Sanders's proposed reading of Paul had at its heart a massively argued proposal about first-century Judaism, in which Sanders substantially followed the protest of H.-J. Schoeps a generation before and G. F. Moore a generation before that. Judaism was not, basically, a religion of self-help moralism, a kind of early Semitic Pelagianism, but was a religion in which the keeping of the law mattered not because people were trying to earn their membership in God's people but because they were eager to demonstrate it. Law-keeping was not part of 'getting in' but of 'staying in'—two categories which become thematic for Sanders. Keeping the law within the 'staying in' mode is what he calls 'covenantal nomism', another thematic technical term.

This proposal cuts most deeply against the Lutheran readings of Paul which have been common coin in New Testament scholarship for a long time, and also in many non-Lutheran parts of the church which have assumed that its account of Judaism (enshrined in such monumental works as Strack-Billerbeck and the Kittel *Wörterbuch*) was historically accurate. Sanders is clearly motivated by the desire to do justice to first-century Judaism rather than caricature it in the interest of Christian apologetic. Painting the 'background' dark in order to make the jewel of the gospel shine more brightly—the very word 'background' has become taboo, carrying as it does the implication that one might be studying Judaism not for itself but in order to contrast it with Christianity to the advantage of the latter—must be abjured in the interests of objective study of the different 'patterns of religion'. As in all his work, Sanders belongs within the post-Holocaust movement of scholarship, trying to get away from a polarization between Judaism and Christianity and to show their many convergences. Indeed, though Sanders does acknowledge that Paul held a critique of Judaism (in this he does better than his teacher, W. D. Davies, who in other respects paved the way for him), this critique is minimal and simply a reflex of Paul's new experience: Paul has found salvation in Christ, and so deduces that there must have been a problem with Judaism. He begins with the solution and then postulates a plight, rather than the old theory in which Paul began with a problem (variously described) to which he found the answer in Christ. The implicit conclusion from a good deal of

Sanders's work, as in many other contemporary writers, is that these two religions at least are more or less equally valid paths to salvation. Sanders is clear that Paul does not say that himself, but he constantly hints that it will not take a large step beyond Paul for us to do so.

As the subtitle of his book indicates, Sanders's proposal is about religion, not theology. Indeed, when it comes to theology both his initial book and his subsequent ones are unsystematic, and do not address in any sustained way the major topics of Pauline theology (christology, justification, the cross, etc.). If anything, Sanders simply assumes that the big words like justification, atonement, salvation, redemption and so on all converge in meaning. His major proposal about interpreting Paul himself does not need to explore that territory too far, because the emphasis lies elsewhere: he divides Paul's thought, in a traditional fashion, between 'juristic' categories and 'participationist' categories, and, following Schweitzer and Davies, declares that the latter are primary and central, and that the former are ancillary and more situational or polemical. Thus he regards 'being in Christ' as central, and 'justification' as more peripheral. This has obvious exegetical spin-offs (e.g. reading Rom. 5–8 as more central to Paul's thought than Rom. 1–4), though as Sanders has published no commentaries we cannot see exactly how it might all play out. It is noticeable, however, that he has difficulty in fitting Romans 2: 1–16 into the mind of Paul, and that he is forced to dismiss the complex Romans 7 as tortured rambling.

Second, the relation of my own reading of Paul to the NP. Perhaps the most important point is this: had the dominant view of Paul prior to Sanders been Reformed rather than Lutheran, the NP might never have been necessary. I began my graduate work on Paul with just such a Reformed standpoint, and in many respects found Sanders an ally rather than an adversary. Since this will be counter-intuitive to some, an explanation is needed.

From (at least) Calvin onwards, reaching something of a climax in the Romans commentary of Charles Cranfield, exegetes in the Reformed tradition found in Paul a view of the Jewish law which was far more positive than Lutheran exegesis had assumed. I am not sure that this tradition ever did full justice to second Temple Judaism, but at least it did not start from the assumption that the law itself was basically a bad thing ripe for abolition. (Notice how this works out in exegesis of the notorious crux at Rom. 10: 4: is Christ the abolition, end, completion, goal, or fulfilment of the law? Or what?) After all, in

Reformed theology the Torah was given in the first place within a historical scheme, not to enable the Israelites to keep it and so earn their membership in God's people, but to enable them, *as a people already redeemed through the Exodus*, to demonstrate and work out the implications of their membership and vocation. The (at least partial) convergence of Sanders's reading of Judaism with a Reformed view of the law makes it all the more ironic that the anti-NP movement is today centred not least in Reformed circles such as the Presbyterian Church of America and Westminster Theological Seminary; but this sort of thing is frequent in the history of ideas. What I am concerned with at the moment is to stress that there were various readings of Paul and Judaism already on offer and that Sanders's protest was directed against one (albeit the mainstream one) among them, one which was already under attack (not that most Lutherans noticed) from the Reformed side.

I arrived at my own understanding after some years of struggling to make Cranfield's reading of Romans fit with what Paul actually says in Galatians—something Cranfield, I think, never achieved. I was not satisfied with the shallow developmental analyses offered by various scholars, according to which Paul was opposed to the law in Galatians and in favour of it in Romans, and so on.[2] I found the clue in Romans 10: 3: Paul's fellow Jews, he says, 'were ignorant of God's righteousness, and were seeking to establish their own, and so did not submit to God's righteousness'. *Their own*: not a 'righteousness', a status of membership in God's people, which might be obtained by assiduous and moralistic self-help Torah-keeping, but *a covenant status which would be for Jews and Jews only*. It would be what I called a 'national righteousness'. Dunn followed this with his proposal, which I fully endorse, that the 'works of the Law', against which Paul warned in both Galatians and Romans, were not any and every legal 'work' done out of a desire to earn good marks in some heavenly ledger account, but were the 'works of Torah' which marked out Jews over against their pagan neighbours: sabbath, circumcision, and food laws. I have shown in considerable detail that this proposal works exegetically, verse by verse and line by line, through Romans, and I have sketched out the way it works in Galatians.

[2] John W. Drane, *Paul, Libertine or Legalist? A Study in the Theology of the Major Epistles* (London: SPCK, 1975); Hans Hübner, *Law in Paul's Thought* (ET; Edinburgh: T. & T. Clark, 1984).

In particular, it makes sense of first-century Judaism. A recent attempt to prove that there was a 'variegated nomism' in the second Temple period has indeed succeeded in bringing out various nuances which go beyond what Sanders had said.[3] But, despite the attempt in the book's final summary to suggest otherwise,[4] it has not basically undercut the overall emphasis of his work or mine. Nobody has succeeded in proving that Judaism was after all the kind of proto-Pelagianism which it would need to have been for the normal Lutheran (and, in some circles, 'evangelical') understanding to be correct. In particular, remarkably, nobody in the entire project noticed that the one second Temple passage in which 'works of Torah' were thematic (4QMMT section C) referred not to 'works of the law' as something to be done in order to *earn* membership in the community, or salvation, or justification, but as things to be done in order to *mark out in the present* the community that would be vindicated in the future. The question being addressed is not: 'how do you *become* a true Jew?', but 'how are you *marked out in the present as* a true Jew?' The parameters of the discussion are eschatological, looking ahead to the last day; the assumption is that at the last day some Jews but not all will be vindicated by God; the question is, how can you tell here and now who it is that will be vindicated in the future. This has exactly the same *shape* and *form* as Paul's doctrine of justification, but as we shall see different *content*, appropriate for his Jesus-shaped construal of both problem and solution.

But this is to run ahead of myself. Two more remarks, one on a major weakness of Sanders's proposal, and one on a strength.

First, the weakness. Sanders declares that prior to his conversion Paul had no problem—no unquiet conscience, no difficulty keeping the law, no existential angst of the kind normally imagined within the ruling paradigm. Here Sanders, like Stendahl before him, rightly emphasized Philippians 3: 2–6.[5] As a result, he says, Paul moved not 'from plight to solution', first being aware of a problem and then finding Christ as the answer to it, but 'from solution to plight', first finding 'salvation' in Christ (what this word would mean if there was no sense of plight is not clear) and then deducing that there must

---

[3] D. A. Carson, Peter T. O'Brien, and Mark A. Seifrid (eds.), *The Complexities of Second Temple Judaism*, i. *Justification and Variegated Nomism* (WUNT 2. 140; Tübingen: Mohr-Siebeck; Grand Rapids, Mich.: Baker, 2001).

[4] Ibid. 543–8.

[5] *Paul Among Jews and Gentiles and Other Essays* (Philadelphia: Fortress, 1976).

have been some kind of 'plight' to which this 'salvation' was the answer. This explains, according to Sanders, the seemingly muddled nature of Paul's critique of Israel: he is flailing around, accusing Judaism and the Torah of various inconsistent things because this was not the real centre of his thought.

But this ignores the enormous problem, like the elephant in the living room, of which every first-century Jew—and particularly a Pharisee—would be aware. Israel was not free. The Torah was not being observed. The wrong people were running the Temple. The promises had not yet come true. YHWH had not yet returned to Zion. The Messiah had not appeared. The Gentiles were not coming to Jerusalem to learn wisdom from the true God, but were coming there instead to impose their will, their 'justice', their way of life. All of this is what I, drawing on many strands in second Temple Judaism, have characterized in terms of 'continuing exile': despite the geographical 'return' several centuries earlier, Israel found herself living in a story whose last major marker was destruction at the hands of Babylon, a destruction only superficially reversed in the geographical return. The main exception to this reading of the second Temple period must be Ben-Sirach, and I suspect that Saul of Tarsus would have had little time for that work, with its near-idolization of the pre-Hasmonean high priest. Thus I believe we must say that Saul of Tarsus had a 'problem' all right: not so much the 'problem' often imagined within pious Protestantism, but the problem that Israel was still unredeemed, still in exile.

This enables us to locate Sanders's proposal about Paul moving from solution to plight as the second half of a two-stage movement of thought. I agree that Paul offers an analysis of 'the problem' (Israel's problem, and the world's problem, the problem of all humankind) which bears all the marks of retrospective understanding. He has rethought the problem in terms of the gospel, in terms of the God-given solution. (He is, to that extent, a good Barthian, learning to look at everything, including the world and sin, in the light of Jesus Christ.) But he has precisely *re*thought the problem. He has not invented it from scratch. *Paul's analysis of the problem of Israel, the world, and humankind is his revision, in the light of the gospel, of the problem of which he was already thoroughly well aware.* He already knows that Israel was 'still in exile': as a Christian, he understands that in a still deeper sense, witnessed in Romans 2: 17–24 and 7: 7–25. He already knows that the Gentiles were idolaters and that idolatry was destructive of genuine image-bearing human-ness; as a Christian, he understands that in a still deeper sense, witnessed in Romans 1: 18–2: 16. What is more—and this lies close to the heart of his freshly worked theology of the cross, the main subject of this paper—he may already have glimpsed, as Jesus and the prophets before him had done, the dangerous truth that Israel's problem was related to the world's problem, in the sense not just that Israel was the innocent victim and the world was the guilty aggres-sor, but that Israel herself was composed of human beings who, despite being given Torah and Temple, were themselves still sinners. Whether he has already thought of it like that or not, this is the point he now offers as the most profound analysis: *Israel too is in Adam*. This is one of the driving insights that carries him forward from Romans 2: 17–24 to 7: 7–25 and on, crucially, to 9: 30–10: 21. Thus, over against Sanders's proposal that Paul moved simply 'from solution to plight', I suggest that we can watch Paul as he moves from his earlier understanding of 'plight', to the 'solution' offered in Christ, and thence to a deeper, but not a totally new, understanding of the 'plight' of Israel and the world. And, since it is to this 'plight' that the cross and resurrection of the Messiah are the answer, this points us clearly on to our main theme.

Second, the strength of Sanders's proposal. The NP enables us, at a stroke, to make sense of one area which has long been controverted in Paul. Why does Paul insist, in 1 Corinthians 8–10 and Romans 14, that one must not divide the community over issues of what you eat and which holy days you keep, while also insisting, in several places, including 1 Corinthians 5 and 6, that there are certain types of behaviour for which there must be zero tolerance? This has been a problem for those who think that the key issue in his theology is 'keeping rules' over against 'trusting God'. But when we line up the matter in a post-NP way, the answer is: because food and holy days are things which threaten to divide the community along ethnic lines, whereas sexual ethics (or their non-observance) would divide the community in terms of what it means to be a renewed-in-Christ human being. Personal holiness matters even more for the Christian than it did for the Jew, because in Christ we have died to sin and come alive into God's new world; but personal holiness has nothing to do with the 'works of the law' by which ethnic Israel was demarcated.

I thus agree with several aspects of Sanders's proposal while differing from it in some ways and going beyond it in others. I am

not surprised that some conservative Christians have found Sanders's proposal not to their taste. It contains a strong streak of
relativism, and that was bound to be unwelcome. He shows little
appreciation of Paul's view of either God, Jesus, or the Spirit. But I am
saddened that many have imagined they have nothing to learn from
Sanders's massive scholarship and have run howling back into the
arms of Luther. In some cases—these are, I think, the saddest of all—
they have been reduced to appealing over the head of the New
Testament to the tradition of the sixteenth century, which is all the
more ironic when we reflect that Luther, Melanchthon, Calvin, and
the rest would certainly have advised us to read the New Testament
even better than they did, not to set up their own work as a new
authoritative tradition, a fixed lens through which the Bible would
have to be viewed for ever afterwards. And what has been on offer in
post-Sanders scholarship, including my own, has not been a slavish
following of Sanders, but an insistence on rereading Paul with our
eyes and ears open to the many-sided nature of second Temple
Judaism, and a recognition that none of our traditions may yet
have learnt all that the apostle has to teach us.

Our present summit need not concern itself, I guess, with the detail
of these debates. But it has been important to sketch them out,
because the theme of redemption is clearly central to some of them
at least. I hope it will be clear that a (not uncritical) post-Sanders
reading will enable us to take huge strides forward in our understanding of redemption, which has itself of course been contentious
in various areas, not least ecumenical discussion. (I think of the
perennial squabbles about justification, and also of the echoes of
the Jansenist controversy in some Roman rejection of anything
approaching penal substitution.) Sanders did not himself attempt to
locate and explicate Paul's theology of redemption within his overall
argument. Can we do so, and what will happen to the NP if we do?

Before I move to positive statements, though, a word about two
other movements which I regard as vital for a proper, historically
and theologically sensitive, reading of Paul. First, there is the *narrative* reading of Paul which, pioneered by Richard Hays twenty years
ago, has been found increasingly fruitful, and goes with Hays's
equally important stress on Paul's fresh reading of scripture. Basically, Paul grounds his theology again and again not in isolated
prooftexts (one of Sanders's many weaknesses was to suggest this)
but in a reading of scripture which, like many second Temple Jewish

readings, picked up its fundamental quality as the story of the creator and covenant God with the world and with Israel. It is central to Paul's world-view that this long story has now come to its climax in Jesus, the Jewish Messiah (another failing of Sanders is that he does not explore the significance of *Christos* in Paul), and that the church, not least his own apostolic ministry, is called to implement that achievement in a continuation of the same story in a new mode. This, I suspect, is one of the main things that recent anti-NP writers have objected to, which is the more ironic in that it was not part of Sanders's platform: that when Paul is talking of salvation, he, like his Jewish contemporaries, was thinking in terms of the eschatological scheme in which 'the present evil age' would give way to 'the age to come', seen as a dramatic turn-around within a continuing history, rather than a snatching of God's people out of the space–time world altogether. (Notice how, within the traditional paradigm, Rom. 8: 18–28, which is structurally one of Paul's most emphatic passages, becomes marginalized in favour of a supposed message of individual salvation away from the world.) When Paul draws on scripture, whether it be Genesis, Deuteronomy, Isaiah, or Habakkuk, he is more often than not aware of, and intending to resonate with, the place of the scripture in question within a longer narrative. This is where the motif of 'return from exile' is so important, though still so controverted. The best example is the use of Deuteronomy 30 in Romans 10: 5–8, exactly parallel to the use of the same passage in 4QMMT. Paul believes himself to be living in a story, the real story of the real world, which stretches back to creation, and comes forward, through Abraham, the exodus, the monarchy, the prophets, to the exile, which in the political and theological sense has continued to his own day. He believes that the real return from exile, which is also the new 'exodus', has taken place in Jesus the Messiah, and that this has brought to birth the 'new age', the 'age to come', by freeing God's people from 'the present evil age'.

Within this new age, there are new tasks, of which Paul's Gentile mission, in all its many facets of evangelism, church planting, and maintaining, is a central one. The story will continue until God is finally 'all in all', when the cosmos itself has been set free from its bondage to decay and God's people are finally given the new, resurrection bodies that correspond to that of Jesus himself. As I said, the real objection to the NP within certain conservative circles seems actually to be an objection to this reading of Paul as the theologian of

a salvation which is not *away from* the world but *for* the world.
Narrative readings of Paul are thus not simply a new fad, a postmodern trick played on an ancient text, an attempt to award Paul an
honorary Doctor of Letters from Yale. They reflect, at a very deep
level, the fact that he is as much a theologian of creation as of
redemption, and of alerting us to the fact that his theology of redemption is precisely a theology of renewed, redeemed creation. They
reflect, also at a deep level, the fact that (though he seldom mentions
the word) he is a theologian of *covenant*, expounding Genesis 15 and
wrestling with the apparent tension between the foundational covenant promises to Abraham and the subsequent covenant with
Moses (Rom. 4; Gal. 3). The two are intimately related: God's covenant promises to Abraham always were the road towards the redemption of humankind and creation as a whole (e.g. new covenant in 2
Cor. 3 leading to new creation in chapter 5; and the argument from
Abraham back to Adam in Rom. 4–5). I use 'covenant' in this sense
as a shorthand way of drawing attention to the fact that, though of
course Paul believes that God's purpose has been achieved through
the dramatic, apocalyptic event of the cross, cutting across all
human pride and immanent process, this is nevertheless the fulfilment precisely *of* that larger, longer purpose. What God did in the
cross and resurrection of the Messiah, and the gift of the Spirit, was
what he had promised Abraham he would do: that is what I meant
by referring to those events as 'the climax of the covenant'. Paul does
not think in detached aphorisms or theological slogans, but in large
stories, including the story within which he believes himself to be
playing a vital role. That is the framework for the various narratives
that we find embedded, and fruit-bearing, within his letters.

The second movement which must be factored in to any fully
fledged reading of Paul is the new awareness of the *political* dimension of all his thought.[6] Though there are many flaws in the work of
Richard Horsley on this subject, he has pioneered the way for us
to see what I have called 'the fresh perspective on Paul', according to
which the gospel of Jesus the Messiah impinges directly on the other
'gospel' which was making great inroads into the same world,
namely, that of Caesar. As I have argued elsewhere, for Paul it was
central that if Jesus was 'Lord' then Caesar was not. This, too, has an

---

[6] See N. T. Wright, 'A Fresh Perspective on Paul?', *Bulletin of the John Rylands
Library*, 83 (2002), 21–39, with full references.

inescapable narrative dimension, and indeed a recognition of the narrative and historical nature of Paul's thought, as above, precipitates us into the political arena: the story of Rome, with its vivid eschatology of empire (a thousand years of preparation, and now—Caesar!), was to be subverted by the story of Israel, climaxing in Jesus. Paul fell heir to the long tradition of Jewish critique of pagan empire, stretching back to Isaiah, Jeremiah, and Daniel. This was never a dualist rejection of every aspect of empire (think of Cyrus, of Jeremiah telling the exiles to settle down in Babylon, of Daniel confounding the pagans and then resuming his senior position in the civil service). Paul is equally emphatic on God's desire for good government and policing (Rom. 13); this has nothing to do with a right-wing or *laissez-faire* political attitude, but in the Jewish tradition sits perfectly well alongside a statement of God's sovereignty over all human kingdoms.

In particular, if we are to have any historical sensitivity to the meaning of the cross in Paul's thinking, we must place at the very centre the awareness of the cross that every first-century person, Jew and pagan alike, would share. This is where the political meaning of Paul's gospel bites most deeply, where the 'fresh perspective' in its turn offers insights on a Pauline view of redemption. Granted that crucifixion was widespread as a punishment for all sorts of people, particularly at the lowest end of the social scale, it was particularly used—and had been used in Palestine in Jesus' lifetime—as a way both of punishing revolutionaries and of warning those who might imitate them. The cross already said, with all its violent symbolic power, that Caesar ruled the world, and that those who stood in his way would be both shamed and obliterated. To get at this today we might draw on a variety of images: the world-famous photo of a small, naked Vietnamese girl, terrified and tearful; the demolition of a Palestinian home; the burning of a synagogue in 1930s Berlin, or of a church in today's Sudan; imperial tanks sweeping into a resistant city (Russian ones, in Prague; Chinese, in Tiananmen Square?). Brute force, dehumanizing humiliation, shameful death: that was the symbolic message of the cross, and that was the symbol that came, from Paul onwards, to speak of the love of the true God, the love which had somehow conquered the principalities and powers.

I propose, then, that the true insights of the NP should be blended with a narratival and political reading of Paul, and that when we do this we find the possibility of a multi-faceted theology of redemption emerging from his writings. There are several ways of approaching this topic: for present purposes I shall do so by considering the place of the cross within seven implicit narratives in Paul's writings.

II REDEMPTION IN PAUL

(i) Overview

What do we mean by 'redemption'? I take it that for the purposes of the Redemption Summit we are using the word in a broad sense, to denote the action(s) whereby God rescues human beings, and (if we are being biblical) the whole cosmos, from the state of sin, decay, and death to which they have become subject. This broad sense includes, but goes beyond, the meaning of Jesus' crucifixion on the one hand and the 'application' of redemption ('call', faith, justification, glorification, to use some of Paul's terms) on the other. It is thus very nearly coextensive with 'salvation', seen also in a broad sense.

These big, somewhat floppy terms can get in the way, not least because Paul uses them in a much more precise sense, so that most of them fit together snugly in his mind like adjacent, but not identical, pieces of a jigsaw. Thus, with regard to 'redemption', Paul seems clearly to have in mind not just the often-noted slave-market metaphor in which someone buys the slave his or her freedom but the more specifically Jewish meaning in which God rescues Israel from the historical slave-market of Egypt. As I have argued elsewhere (that phrase applies to most of what will now follow), the context of Romans 3: 24 and 8: 23, two of Paul's key uses of *apolytrosis*, strongly suggests an Exodus-interpretation: human beings in the present, and the whole creation in the future, are rescued from slavery to sin and death as Israel was rescued from slavery in Egypt. Paul uses the word again in 1 Corinthians 1: 30, in a string alongside *sophia*, *dikaiosyne*, and *hagiasmos*, which tells us little about the precise meaning he attaches to the word, though later in the letter he does speak of 'Christ our Passover' being sacrificed for us (5: 7). Two of the uses in Ephesians (1: 7 and 4: 30) reflect the same present/future balance as the two in Romans; the third (1: 14) seems to be a more restricted metaphor, part of the picture of a 'down-payment' guaranteeing 'full possession'. The one remaining Pauline use of the word, Colossians 1: 14, belongs with Romans 3: 24 and Ephesians 1: 7.

But of course our topic is wider than simply the occurrences of the word normally translated 'redemption'. Part of the difficulty now emerges: God's action to rescue humans and the world is such a constant topic in Paul's letters, and he says so many different things about it in so many different contexts, that without launching into a full exegesis of most of the letters I cannot really do justice to the multi-faceted nature of his thought. Nevertheless, I may attempt a proposal, at least for the sake of discussion. My proposal is that Paul's thought about Jesus as Israel's Messiah, the one in whom God's promises to Israel and, through Israel, to the world are fulfilled, functions as the vital turning point in no fewer than seven interlocking narratives which form the backbone of all his thought. Understanding how the cross in particular functions in each of these will take us close to a presentation of the heart of his theology.

(ii) Biblical Narratives in the Background

Standing over all the stories that make up the narrative substructure of Paul's thought, we find frequent reference to the Exodus. Romans 8 uses Exodus-language of the whole creation, and of the people of God travelling through the wilderness towards their 'inheritance'. Similarly, Galatians 4: 1–11 speaks of God's people as being enslaved, and then, at the right time (the time for the Abrahamic promises to be fulfilled, as in Genesis 15 which Paul has been expounding in the previous chapter), God sending forth his Son and his Spirit to rescue those who are 'under the law'. This is of course heavily ironic in that, in the original Exodus-story, the law is God's good gift to the newly redeemed people, whereas here it is a force or power from whose enslavement people need to be freed. Perhaps the most obvious point (at least, thus it seems to me) is Romans 6, where those in Christ come through the waters of baptism, symbolizing the dying and rising of and with Christ, and so pass from the slavery of sin to the new life of sanctification.

The story of the Exodus is re-used in various ways both in the OT and NT, and in the latter, as in some other second Temple contexts, it gives shape in particular to stories and prophecies about the 'return from exile'. As indicated above, I use this as a shorthand way of referring to the widespread second Temple belief (as in Daniel 9) that the true 'exile' continued long after the geographical return, leading to speculation about when the real 'redemption', in other words, the New Exodus, would take place. Israel was once again enslaved to the pagans, as in Egypt, and God would act decisively on her behalf. This is, to choose a couple of examples at random, the message of the last chapters of the Wisdom of Solomon, or of the final segments of Tobit. Just as in 4QMMT and Baruch, Paul draws on the passage in Deuteronomy 30 which prophesies this 'real return from exile' (Rom. 10: 5–9), and I have argued that the same theme is also present in his use of Leviticus in Galatians 3: 12.[7] The 'curse' of the Torah is not an abstract threat hanging over all who break some abstract moral law, an early version of Kant's Categorical Imperative; according to Deuteronomy, it is the historical and physical punishment which consists of disaster within the land and finally expulsion from it. Israel's continuing shameful exile (see Rom. 2: 17–24, quoting Isa. 52: 5 and Exod. 36: 20) needs a new act of God's covenant faithfulness, as in Daniel 9: 16, to bring Israel and hence the world through to the long-promised and long-awaited state of renewal, restoration, and redemption.

If exile is the problem, the servant is the answer—at least according to Isaiah 40–55. Though this remains controversial, I now regard it as a fixed point that Paul made extensive though subtle use of the servant songs at several places in his writings, and, we may infer from his almost casual references, at considerably more places in the thinking that lay behind the writings we have. An obvious example is Romans 4: 24–5, where the entire train of thought of 3: 21 – 4: 25, is summed up in a formulaic sentence which clearly evokes Isaiah 53 and to which Paul refers in his statements about the 'obedience of the one man' in 5: 12–21. Not that Paul has removed the servant from his wider Isaian context: chapters 40–55 are all about the righteousness of God through which the powers of the world are defeated and God's people in consequence rescued—the New Exodus, in other words. And, within the servant story itself, but obviously going much wider in Jewish thought as a whole, we cannot ignore Paul's regular use of sacrificial terminology. Our difficulty here is not so much in recognizing that Paul sees Jesus' death as a sacrifice as in working out what he might

---

[7] See N. T. Wright, *The Climax of the Covenant: Christ and the Law in Pauline Theology* (Edinburgh: T. T. Clark, 1991), ch. 7.

have meant by this, since our knowledge of how second Temple Jews understood the theology of sacrifice is remarkably thin.[8] This is bound to remain a question mark within this chapter as a whole: how precisely did Paul understand Jesus' death as a sacrifice, and how does this integrate with all the other things he says? If we could answer this more satisfactorily we would take another large step, I think, to integrating several other aspects of his thought.

These are the narratives—the exodus, the return from exile, the offering of sacrifices—which help to frame and shape the seven key stories which Paul is telling, in each of which the redeeming death of Jesus the Messiah is the central point. I must now set them out one by one before attempting integration.

(iii) The Seven Key Stories, and the Cross within Them

The *first story* Paul tells, by implication throughout, is that of *creation and new creation*. A consistently Jewish thinker, Paul never imagines that creation is evil; it is the good creation of the good God, and to be enjoyed as such. But, in line with much apocalyptic thought, Paul believes that God is planning to renew creation, to bring it out of its present state of decay and death and into the new world where it would find its true fulfilment. The classic passage for this is of course Rom. 8: 18–27, which as we saw offers one of the rare occurrences of the word 'redemption' itself. Paul does not mention the cross in that passage itself, but the sufferings of Christians, which are, for him, the sharing of Christ's sufferings, hold the key to the current state of affairs through which the world must pass to attain its final deliverance from decay.

This explains why, at the end of Galatians (6: 14–15), Paul can suddenly broaden the horizon of what has been up till then a sharply focused discussion. I suspect that many at the Redemption Summit sang a few days earlier Charles Wesley's version of redemption:

> Forbid it, Lord, that I should boast,
> Save in the cross of Christ my God;
> All the vain things that charm me most,
> I sacrifice them to his blood.

---

[8] On the clear reference to the 'sin-offering' in Rom. 8: 3 see my commentary and the other works there cited: *Romans*, in the *New Interpreter's Bible*, (Nashville, Tenn.: Abingdon, 2002). See also Jean-Noël Aletti's remarks below about the difficulty of knowing how Paul and contemporary Judaeans understood the Day of Atonement.

> Were the whole realm of nature mine
> That were an offering far too small;
> Love so amazing, so divine,
> Demands my soul, my life, my all.

A wonderful statement of Christian devotion; yet, as with other hymns from the same period, we may question whether it does full justice to the scope of what Paul actually says: 'through whom the world has been crucified to me, and I to the world; for neither circumcision is anything, nor uncircumcision, but new creation'. The 'to me' is clearly important, and the 'new creation' is focused on the new creation that consists in the Spirit-called people defined by faith as opposed to membership in ethnic Israel; but what Paul is saying about himself, and about all God's people in Christ, is not just that *they* have changed, but that they live in a landscape which has decisively changed. The world as a whole has been crucified in the crucifixion of the Messiah, and a new world has been brought to birth. This is presumably why he can say in Colossians 1: 23 that the gospel has already been proclaimed to every creature under heaven: when Jesus died and rose again, the cosmos as a whole became a different place. This is also closely linked to the famous 2 Corinthians 5: 17: 'anyone in Christ is new creation—the old things have gone, and look, new things have come into being'. That passage, too, belongs closely with a massive statement both of the cross of Jesus and of the way the cross has worked its way through Paul's apostolic ministry, as we shall see later. What seems to be happening is that Paul understands the death of Jesus, and the continuing resonances of that death in the suffering of the church, as the hinge upon which the door of world history turns. From that moment, the forces of decay and death have suffered their major defeat, and from now on new creation is under way, with its first signs being the new life of those who believe the gospel. 'New creation' thus refers to the actual people concerned, not over against the rest of the world but as the sign of the new life that will one day flood the entire creation.

The *second* great *narrative* which Paul has in mind throughout his writing is the story of Israel. This is more complicated, because Israel is the people called to bear God's solution to the problem of the world and yet now ensnared, themselves, within the same problem. Paul shows dozens of signs that he is following through the Israel-story in the same way as many other second Temple writers: the Abrahamic promises as God's solution to the problem of the world, the Exodus as the first great fulfilment of those promises, the Torah as God's good gift to his redeemed people, designed to stop them going to the bad until the final fulfilment . . . and then the catastrophe of exile, with Torah itself turning against Israel and condemning it. What can God do now about the promises? What will happen to the divine plan to bless the whole world through Israel?

This is exactly the way Paul sets up the problem in two classic passages, Romans 2: 17–3: 9 and Galatians 3: 6–12. The answer, in both cases, is the death of Jesus, bursting through the blockage in the historical fulfilment of the divine purposes. In Romans, Jesus appears as the Messiah, the faithful Israelite, whose redeeming death (3: 24–6) is the means of God's now declaring that all who share this faith are 'righteous', that is, members of the sin-forgiven family (3: 27–31), and that this is how God has fulfilled the Abrahamic promises (4: 1–25). In Galatians, more specifically, the curse of exile which had bottled up the promises and prevented them getting through to the Gentiles, leaving Israel itself under condemnation, is dealt with by the death of Jesus: he takes Israel's curse on himself (and thus, at one remove, the world's curse, though this is not what is in view in this passage, despite efforts to employ it as a generalized statement of 'atonement theology'), making it possible at last for 'the blessing of Abraham to come on the Gentiles' and also that 'we' (in other words, Jews who had been under the very specific 'curse' of Deuteronomy) might receive the promise of the Spirit through faith. In other words, the covenant has been renewed at last—through the death of Jesus as Israel's representative Messiah.

In other words, I do not think that Paul's train of thought ran, as so many have suggested: (*a*) Jesus was crucified, therefore he was under God's curse, therefore he cannot have been the Messiah; and then (*b*) God raised him from the dead, therefore he cannot have been cursed, therefore his death must have been redemptive. Paul is quite clear that Jesus *did* bear the curse, not that he didn't.

This explains, among many other things, why Paul says at the start of Galatians (the point in the letter when we might expect a thematic statement) that 'our Lord Jesus the Messiah gave himself for our sins, to deliver us from the present evil age according to the will of God our Father' (1: 3–4). And this in turn brings into view the central statement of the common early creed quoted by Paul in 1 Corinthians 15: 3: the Messiah 'died for our sins according to the scriptures'. Galatians 1: 4 shows very clearly what this means,

offering once more a historical understanding rather than a dehis-
toricized atonement-theory. For a second Temple Jew, soaked in
passages like Daniel 9, the present parlous state of Israel, which
(following Daniel and many other writers) I have characterized as
'continuing exile', was the result of Israel's sins. The ancient Israelites had sinned, and had gone into exile; now their successors, even
those living back in the land, had continued to sin, and as a result the
final redemption, the real 'return from exile', was delayed. (Think, for
instance, of Malachi.) The problem of sin is thus not simply that it
separates the individual from God in his or her existential spirituality
(true though that is as well). The problem is that Israel's sins are
keeping Israel in exile. Conversely, if somehow Israel's sins were to be
dealt with, finished with, and blotted out, then exile could be undone
and the people could go free—and with them the whole world,
waiting for Israel to be redeemed (as in e.g. Isa. 55, not by coinci-
dence as we shall see). Thus, for the moment, Israel languishes in
'the present evil age', waiting for 'the age to come' to arrive, the time
of redemption and forgiveness. And this forgiveness will not mean
simply that individuals can now enter into a happy and intimate
relationship with their heavenly Father, true again though that is.
The point is that, if sins are forgiven, exile will be over, the rule of the
evil powers will be broken, and Israel—and the rest of the world—
will be summoned to enjoy, and take part in, God's renewed world.
This is what Paul believes has happened with the death of Jesus. In
neither passage does he *explain* how it is that the death of Jesus
delivers us from the evil age; the equation depends on two other
things, which he supplies plentifully elsewhere, not least in 1 Corinthians 15 itself: (*a*) Jesus was and is Israel's representative Messiah;
(*b*) God raised him from the dead (note 1 Cor. 15: 17: if the Messiah
isn't raised, your faith is futile, *and you are still in your sins*, in other
words, the new age has not begun).

The story of the crucified Messiah is thus at the heart of Paul's way
of telling the story of how Israel has been brought to the very depth of
exile and has now been rescued to live as God's new creation. The
sharpest statement of this comes at the end of Galatians 2:

I through the Torah died to Torah, that I might live to God. I have been
crucified with the Messiah; however, I am alive, yet it is not me, but the
Messiah lives in me. And the life I now live in the flesh, I live by faith in
the Son of God, who loved me and gave himself for me. I do not nullify God's

grace; for if covenant membership came by Torah, then the Messiah died for no reason. (Gal. 2: 19–21)

This spills over into the next story (and all these stories are in any case interlocked); yet I cannot resist putting it here. The point of all that Paul is saying, to Peter at Antioch and, through the telling of that incident, to the Galatians as they 'overhear' the Paul/Peter debate, or at least Paul's side of it, is not that he, Paul, has had a particular spiritual experience or that he now enjoys a particular kind of spiritual life. The point of it all is that Paul is here standing, as in one or two other places, as the typical Israelite. He has stated the general principle in Galatians 2: 15–16: though we are by birth Jews, not 'Gentile sinners', we know that God declares 'righteous' not those who rely on 'works of Torah', but those whose status depends on the faithfulness of the Messiah. Paul's point, in other words, is that through the faithful death of the Messiah God has acted *to transform the category of 'the righteous'*, so that it now denotes not those who are defined by Torah but those who are defined by the Messiah. And 'those who are defined by the Messiah' means those who have died and come to life in and with him; those, in other words, who have been co-crucified with him (v. 19). Here the cross determines the death of the old identity: the Messiah, Israel's representative, dies, therefore Israel dies according to the flesh. And, by implication, the resurrection determines the new life of the new identity: the Messiah, Israel's representative, 'lives to God' (Gal. 2: 19, cf. Rom. 6: 10), and those who are 'in him' possess this same new life. That which was said in the plural in Gal. 1: 3–4 is now brought into the sharp singular, not (once again) because Paul is special but because he is paradigmatic: 'the Son of God loved me and gave himself for me' (Gal. 2: 20). The final verse sums up the effect of the cross on the story of Israel: if Torah could have defined covenant membership, the Messiah would not have needed to die, but (so Paul clearly implies) the fact that the Messiah *did* need to die indicates that Israel, as defined by Torah, needed to die and to come through to a new sort of life, a life in which the promises would at last be fulfilled.

The *third* great *narrative* which Paul offers is embedded within the second, as the second is in the first: it is the story of Torah. Torah is almost personified in some Pauline passages, and its multiple ambiguities have precipitated a huge secondary literature. The crucial passages are again in Galatians and Romans. In Galatians 4: 1–7,

Paul tells the story of Israel being redeemed from Torah as though Torah were a new sort of Pharaoh, an enslaving power. Torah has become, in fact, identified as one of the *stoicheia tou kosmou*, the 'elements of the world', which I take to mean the shabby line-up of the tutelary deities of the nations, the subdivine beings to whom the world has been entrusted until the time of fulfilment. This explains how Paul can say that in their former state the ex-Gentile Galatians had been enslaved to beings that by nature were not divine, but had now been set free by God's 'knowing' of them (4: 8–9). Paul can then chide them with turning *back* to the 'elements' once more (4: 9b), when what they were seeking to do was to embrace Torah, presumably in the hope of getting 'further in' within the people of the true God than they had been able to do by believing in Jesus and being baptized. The only way we can make sense of this is to remind ourselves, from 3: 21–5, that the God-given Torah had a *deliberately negative purpose*, to shut up Israel under a new kind of slavery until the ultimate redemption, which has now been accomplished through 'the son of God', his sending, his birth, and his 'being under Torah' (4: 4). Though Paul does not mention Jesus' death at this point we should surely infer it.

We should do so not least in the light of the parallel in Romans 7: 1–8: 11. Once again I refer to my commentary for fuller treatment. The main point to be drawn out here is found in two seminal statements, Romans 7: 4 and 8: 3–4.

Paul's advance summary in 7: 4 is very close to Galatians 2: 16–21: 'you died to the law through the body of the Messiah, so that you could belong to another, to the one who was raised from the dead, so that you could bear fruit for God'. Briefly, the point is this: Torah had bound Israel, not to God as had been thought, but to Adam (see Rom. 5: 20; 6: 14; 7: 1–3). The death of the Messiah is then to be counted as the death of his people; so those who, formerly under Torah, die with the Messiah to the Torah are set free from the bond that binds them to Adam (the 'former husband' of 7: 1–3, like the 'old man' of 6: 6). As a result, they are free for a new life, a life in the risen Christ, a life of 'being fruitful' as Adam had originally been commanded. This points the way forwards into the exposition of chapter 7, where Torah demonstrates that Israel is indeed in Adam (7: 7–12), and that Israel, even though possessing Torah as God's gift and rejoicing in it as such, finds that all Torah can do is condemn and kill, not because there is anything wrong with Torah but because there is something right about Torah—it must point out sin and condemn it. That's what it's there for. Israel's ultimate problem is not the fact of possessing Torah, but the fact of possessing it *while being a sinful people, a people in Adam.*

Torah, however, has throughout this process had an important and God-given negative purpose: to draw sin onto one place, luring it forwards to concentrate all its efforts at one spot. That is the meaning of the otherwise puzzling 5: 20. And when this has been done, then the trap can be sprung: sin, the real culprit (does Paul, in personifying 'sin', take a step towards identifying it with the serpent in the garden, and hence with 'the satan'?), must be condemned. This is the closest Paul comes to saying in so many words what so many of his interpreters have attributed to him: that the death of Jesus was the ultimate moment of judicial condemnation, of God's punishment: 'God, sending his own son in the likeness of sinful flesh and as a sin-offering, condemned sin in the flesh.' This is strongly penal language. However, Paul does not say either that God punished Jesus or that God punished Jesus for 'my sins'; much of the previous chapter has been devoted to demonstrating that, for the pious Jew under Torah, 'it is not I that do it, but sin dwelling in me'. What Paul says is that God punished *sin*—in the flesh, that is, the flesh of Jesus. Of course, this amounts to the same thing in practice; Jesus' crucifixion was not one whit less horrible, shameful, disgusting, and agonizing for the fact that God was punishing sin rather than punishing Jesus, since of course the point was that he had come 'in the likeness of sinful flesh'. But this theological analysis of the event indicates well enough, I think, how close the traditional penal theories of the atonement come to his meaning while yet not allowing for its subtlety. The point within this third story is that Torah, God's agent in the necessarily negative period between Moses and Jesus, was used to draw sin onto one place—Israel, and thence to Israel's representative, the Messiah—so that, in his crucifixion, it could be punished at last as it deserved. And in that punishment—here the penal substitutionary theory makes its perfectly valid point—'there is now no condemnation for those who are in Christ Jesus' (8: 1). No condemnation for Christ's people because God has condemned sin in the flesh of Christ: that is the perfectly Pauline point underneath the substitutionary language that has proved so powerful for some and so problematic for others.

This leads us to the *fourth story*, which is that of the human race. This is central to the whole presentation and, though this treatment is still very brief, it will be somewhat longer than that of the other stories. 'All sinned, and came short of the glory of God; and they are justified by his grace as a gift through the redemption which is in Messiah Jesus' (Rom. 3: 23–4). Redemption is the means of justification. How can we understand this? 'Justification' has, since Augustine at least, often been understood as more or less coterminous with 'conversion'. Traditional Reformed theology has spelt things out in more detail in terms of an 'ordo salutis' which comes close, in my view, to the substance of what Paul is saying without always reflecting his use of key terms. My contention here—and this explains the anger directed against my view in some circles—is that Paul does not use the verb like this. This is where I not only agree with Sanders in seeing that Paul is talking about the coming together of Jew and Gentile in Christ, but go beyond him into a far more precise definition of 'justification'.

When Paul speaks of the initial hearing-the-gospel-and-coming-to-faith he speaks of the 'call' of God (see 1 Cor. 1: 26; Gal. 1: 15; spelt out in 1 Thess. 1: 4; 2: 13). In the decisive, crystal-clear summary at the end of Romans 8 he distinguishes 'call' from 'justify' within the sequence of God's actions. Thus, despite generations who have read it this way, I conclude that Romans 3: 21–6 *does not describe how someone becomes a Christian*, but describes rather the grounds on which God declares that certain persons, despite their all alike being sinful, are declared to be members of his covenant family. This declaration is not what brings people into the family; it is what certifies— against the expectation of those who might still assume that the Jew/Gentile distinction operates in perpetuity— that all who are 'of the faith of Jesus' are full members, circumcised and uncircumcised alike. That this is Paul's meaning ought to have been clear long ago from verses 29 and 30, which explain the nature of the 'boasting' in 3: 27–8; but the Lutheran reading of the passage, according to which 'boasting' meant 'self-righteous legalism, trying to earn God's favour', has been so strong that even good exegetes have been content to see verse 29 as a transition to a different theme. God 'justifies' all alike on the basis of faith; that is, exactly as in Galatians 2: 15–21, God regards all the faithful alike as fully members of the same single family, and as belonging side by side at the same table.

Thus, despite generations of zealous evangelistic use of Romans 3: 21–6 as describing and facilitating 'conversion', I do not think this is what the passage is basically about. 'Justification' is not about 'entry', about 'getting in'; this is where Sanders, I think, failed to draw the appropriate conclusion from his own thesis. Nor is it exactly about 'staying in'. It is about God declaring that someone *is* in. It defines the community.

In the light of this, what can we say about the cross in verses 24–6? How does Paul explain more precisely the meaning of 'the redemption which is in Messiah Jesus'?

The main thing to say is that it is *cultic*. God 'put him forth'—the word is used in the LXX of the shewbread—as a *hilasterion*, through his faithfulness (i.e. his obedience-to-death, as in 5: 12–21), by means of his blood. Much debate has poured forth on the precise meaning of *hilasterion*, and much has been invested in making this the vital turning point in atonement theology. By itself the word probably cannot bear that weight. Strong indications point to a propitiatory significance, but this is not enough to force the whole passage into the normal straitjacket of 'we sinned; God punished Jesus instead; we go free'. The main point is that, as with the sacrifices of the OT, the death of Jesus is the means whereby the God of infinite justice can nevertheless declare that certain people truly are his people, are *dikaioi*: that is, they are covenant members, and their sins are forgiven. That was what the covenant was always designed to do, and in Jesus the Messiah the object has been attained. I have argued in my commentary that Paul is here drawing on ideas connected to the sacrificial death of the martyrs, which in turn point back to second Temple readings of Isaiah 53; and the fact that Paul refers to that passage when summing up the place of Jesus' death in the argument of this section (4: 24–5) gives this strong support. The servant dies 'for our trespasses/iniquities', in order to put into effect God's righteousness and salvation.

There can be no question but that Isaiah 53 has in mind some kind of substitution: the servant is innocent, yet bears the fate of the guilty. (See too Rom. 8. 3, discussed briefly above.) Paul has made it very clear in his initial statement of human guilt that the characteristic human position is to know God's decree that certain types of behaviour deserve death, and yet to practise and approve them. Now he describes the Messiah dying 'on behalf of' the weak, the sinful, as the outworking of God's love (Rom. 5: 8), resulting in people being 'justified', that is, declared to be in the right, in the present, and being assured of final salvation (Rom. 5: 9). (Paul here draws on the same seam of thought as we saw in Gal. 1: 3–4 and 1 Cor. 15: 3.) And, as the paragraph reaches its climax in Romans 5: 10, Paul speaks of enemies being reconciled, and of those now reconciled then being saved the more easily. The fact that he has just spoken of God's wrath (Rom. 5: 9) ought to warn us against too readily assuming that 'enemies' describes only the subjective state of rebellious human beings; the mystery is that God simultaneously was turned against the human race in wrath (Rom. 1: 18) and turned towards it in love (Rom. 5: 8). The day we fathom that mystery will be the day we understand Paul's atonement theology.

Where has this taken us in following the fourth story? The whole human race, sinful and unable to defend itself (Rom. 3: 19–20), finds itself addressed by a love which declares that Jesus, the Jewish Messiah, has died for it and risen again. When this message is preached, and the Spirit works powerfully through this gospel, this constitutes the 'call' (Rom. 1: 16–17; 1 Cor. 12: 3; Gal.1: 15; 1 Thess. 2: 13), resulting in the faith that Jesus is indeed Lord and that God raised him from the dead (Rom. 4: 24–5; 10: 9). This 'call' is itself possible because of what Jesus has already done, because of the new world that has come into being through his dying and rising (see story 1 above); but as it is applied, through the word and the Spirit, to the individual heart it invites the surprised, newly believing person to reflect on the status he or she now has. This is the status of 'righteous', and it is grounded in what has been achieved on the cross. By only a small expansion of Romans 5: 6–10 we can see the point. Those who were weak are now strong; those who were unaware of God's love are now grasped by it; those who were sinners are now accounted such no longer; those who were unrighteous are now righteous, those facing wrath are now rescued from it; those who were enemies are now reconciled and, once more, rescued. All this has taken place because of the death of Jesus, and the new life which flows from it. All of this constitutes 'the redemption which is in Messiah Jesus'. And all of this points on, in the argument of Romans 5–8 and the theology of Paul as a whole, to the climax in Romans 8: those who share Christ's sufferings will share his glory, his dominion over the redeemed cosmos.

At the heart of this we find the strange combination of two apparently opposite ideas: the Messiah dies, therefore his people die with him; the Messiah dies, therefore his people do not die. Though these are often played off against one another ('representation' versus 'substitution'), I have already said enough to show that they belong closely with one another. Substitution (he dies, we do not) makes sense within the context of representation (the Member of Parliament *represents* the constituents, and therefore is qualified to act, particularly to speak and vote, *in their place*). Representation is important not least because it creates the context for substitution.

Within the story of the human race as a whole we find the Pauline story of the individual human being, summarized in Romans 8: 29–30. When someone becomes a Christian, this is rooted in God's inscrutable will, not in their own initiative; Paul has little to say about this, but (here and in e.g. 1 Thess. 1: 4–5) it is clear that when the gospel works powerfully to change hearts and lives, Paul traces this not to the worthiness of the hearer but to the grace of God (he may well, of course, have in mind passages like Deut. 7: 6–8). For our purposes the key events are the three final ones in Romans 8: 29–30: those God called, he also justified; those he justified, he also glorified.

This should make it clear that when Paul wants to refer to the initial event of someone's becoming a Christian he does not use the term 'justify' and its cognates. He uses 'call', and he glosses this, as we saw, with a theology of the preaching of the gospel, the 'word', in the power of the Spirit. 'Call' denotes the event that people often refer to as 'conversion', though of course whereas 'conversion' draws attention to the change of heart and mind in the person concerned, the word 'call' draws attention to God's action and hence places that change of heart and mind already in the category of 'obedience' as well as 'faith' (see e.g. Rom. 1: 5). The 'call' thus does indeed evoke faith, faith that Jesus is Lord and that God raised him from the dead.

The verb 'justify' does not, then, denote the initial moment of coming-to-faith, but (when used in the present—see below) the declaration which God makes on the basis of that faith. Justification in the present is God's declaration, based on that faith alone rather than anything in the ethnic, gendered, moral, or social background of the person concerned, that this person is indeed a member of the covenant family, one whose sins are forgiven and for whom there is 'no condemnation'. Justification thus points forwards to 'glorifica-tion', Paul's larger term for the eventual goal. I note that this is a larger category than 'sanctification', though it includes it en route (not least by means of baptism; there is, unfortunately, no space for

Romans 6 in this chapter). I also note that the concrete referent is the final resurrection (Rom. 8: 11), not simply a post-mortem life of bliss in 'heaven' or wherever, something about which Paul has almost nothing to say.

What then does Paul mean by 'justification'? Once we clear our minds of the referent the word has had in much of the last 1600 years, and listen carefully to what he says, we discover three things. When we listen to its OT echoes, the word is *covenantal*: it refers to the declaration that these people are members of God's true people. But because this declaration is always made in the face of the accusation of sin, and in the light of God's determination to put the world to rights precisely through the Abrahamic covenant, the word is also *forensic*: the 'law-court' categories are not simply snatched from a different and perhaps conflicting metaphorical home base, but rather explain how it is that the covenantal purpose is worked out. And the word is also, especially, *eschatological*. It can be used in both past and future as well as present, and indeed the past justification and the future justification determine the meaning of the present. This will become clear if we lay these senses out.

In Romans 2: 1–16 Paul speaks of 'justification' in the future: those who by patience in well-doing seek for glory, honour, and immortality will be given the life of the age to come, and this is to be seen as 'justification', that is, God's final declaration that they are his people. This future 'declaration' will consist in God's raising these people from the dead; this same event can thus properly be described, also, as 'salvation', since it will be the means of rescuing people from the state of death; and, as we saw, as 'glorification', stressing the new role for God's redeemed humanity within God's new world.

In Romans 4: 25 Paul declares that Jesus was 'put to death for our trespasses, and raised for our justification'. The connection implied by 'for' in this double statement is highly contested, but for present purposes the point is that Paul is looking back to a past event which somehow grounds the justification that we enjoy in the present. It is the event which he can sum up as the 'act of obedience' of Jesus Christ, or as his 'faithfulness'.

Thus Romans 3: 21–31, and indeed Romans 4 which roots it in God's covenant promises, speaks of a *present* justification which is based on the action of the faithful Messiah in the past and which *anticipates* the verdict of the future. When someone believes the gospel—when, in other words, the 'call' takes place, as above—then the verdict of the future is brought forward into the present. As in 4QMMT, this is how that which will be revealed on the last day— namely, who God's true people really are—is known in advance. But whereas in 4QMMT the evidence was to be the performance of certain specified 'works of Torah', namely the regulations which marked out the Essenes from other Jews, and whereas for the Pharisees (or their Christian analogues whom we can assume to have been Paul's partners in controversy) the evidence was to be the performance of the 'works of Torah' which marked out Jews from their pagan neighbours, that is, sabbath, food-laws, and circumcision, for Paul the evidence is simply Christ-faith: belief that Jesus is Lord and that God raised him from the dead. This faith, the obedient response to God's call, is the appropriate evidence for this declaration, both because it is the sign of the Christ-life (note how the faith of the believer mirrors the faithfulness of Jesus the Messiah in Rom. 3: 22) and because, since it is the work of the Spirit through the gospel, it is the sign of that upon which final assurance is based. 'The one who began a good work in you will bring it to completion at the day of the Messiah' (Phil. 1. 6). This is where Paul's whole theme of the Spirit as *arrabon*, 'down-payment', makes its contribution to a fully blown theology of justification.

I thus note that, despite the loose language (and theology) we often find in this area, Paul does not speak of 'salvation by faith' (except for Eph. 2: 8, which raises other questions). Once we free 'justification' from meaning 'conversion' or anything like it, we cut loose from the sterile and often tortuous debates about 'faith and works' that have taken place in an environment many miles removed from second Temple Judaism, namely the European controversies of the sixteenth and some subsequent centuries. Paul would, of course, have scoffed at Pelagian-style self-help moralism, but this is not what Romans and Galatians are about. He believed, like most Jews of his day, in a final judgement which would be 'according to works', and did not in any way see that as compromising his position on justification, God's declaration in the present that all believers belong to his true people. 'Justification' is a technically precise way of saying something Paul was eager to say and many of his readers have completely missed: that all those who believe in Jesus as the risen Lord belong in the same family, no matter what their social or moral status or background.

So much for the fourth story Paul is telling. I turn *fifthly*, much more briefly, to a very specific outworking of the same narrative, namely the story of Paul's apostolic vocation. Two passages are particularly significant: Philippians 3: 4–11 and 2 Corinthians as a whole. In Philippians Paul applies the pattern he has set out in 2: 6–11 to his own life. Whatever gain he had, he counted as loss because of the Messiah. His goal is 'to know him and the power of his resurrection and the fellowship of his sufferings, becoming conformed to his death, if somehow I may attain to the resurrection from the dead'. I have argued elsewhere that this is not said for the sake of autobiography, but in order to highlight the pattern of Jesus' dying and rising as being etched into Paul's apostolic work so that it may serve as a pattern. He wants the Philippians to imitate him; they cannot do this directly, since none of them had been zealous Pharisaic Jews as he describes himself to have been. The solution is found at the end of the chapter, where Paul's description of Jesus seems deliberately to echo Roman imperial rhetoric about Caesar. Paul is hinting, I suggest, that the Philippians, some of whom at least will have been Roman citizens, and all of whom may have found benefit in the city's status as a Roman colony, must sit as loose to their privileges as he has to his.[9]

Paul's second letter to Corinth reveals the cross not so much etched into Paul's apostolic work as burnt deep into it with a branding-iron. Passage after passage makes it clear that the cross is not only the means whereby the Christian obtains initial forgiveness, the new start of the gospel, but also the way and pattern of life, especially for those to whom the gospel is entrusted. It is at the heart of this exposition of Paul's apostolic ministry that we find one of the most famous statements of his *theologia crucis*, in 2 Corinthians 5: 20–1: 'We act as ambassadors for the Messiah, as though God were making his appeal through us. On behalf of the Messiah we entreat people: be reconciled to God! God made the one who knew no sin to be sin on our behalf, so that in him we might become God's righteousness.'

Again, I have argued elsewhere for a different interpretation to the normal one.[10] I start from two fixed points. First, it is highly probable

[9] See N. T. Wright, 'Paul's Gospel and Caesar's Empire', in Richard A. Horsley (ed.), *Paul and Politics: Ekklesia, Israel, Imperium, Interpretation. Essays in Honor of Krister Stendahl* (Harrisburg, Pa.: Trinity Press International, 2000), 160–83.

[10] 'On Becoming the Righteousness of God: 2 Corinthians 5: 21', in D. M. Hay (ed.), *Pauline Theology*, ii (Minneapolis: Augsburg Fortress, 1993), 200–8.

that when Paul writes *dikaiosyne theou*, as here and in several passages in Romans, he is not referring to the status which he and all Christians have, the status of 'righteous' which is God's gift. That he describes as the righteous status which comes *from* God (*he ek theou dikaiosune*, Phil. 3: 9). Rather, he refers to God's own covenant faithfulness. (This is strengthened further by the oddity of saying 'become', had he meant that this righteous status was 'reckoned' to them, as in Rom. 4 or Gal. 3.) Second, reading the verse the normal way, as a statement of abstract atonement theology in which our sins are credited to Jesus and his righteousness is credited to us (something Paul says nowhere else), destroys the force of the passage, in which Paul is building up to a crescendo not about soteriology but about the inner logic of his apostolic ministry. In fact, the normal reading of the passage often results in v. 21 falling off the end of the discussion; or, sometimes, in the treating of v. 20 as if it were a direct appeal to the Corinthians themselves (by the unwarranted addition of 'you'), rather than a broad statement of Paul's apostolic activity. These two fixed points suggest the following reading: that the cross of Jesus the Messiah is (among many other things) the means by which the failings and limitations of the apostle and his work, and particularly his personal sins, are dealt with, setting him free to *become*, to embody, to encapsulate, and show forth in his own work, that covenant faithfulness of God whose initial unveiling in the faithful death of Jesus (Rom. 3: 21–6) stands behind everything Paul believes, writes, and attempts. I therefore read v. 21, not as a statement of God's righteousness, still less Christ's righteousness, being imputed, imparted or otherwise transferred to the believer, but as a statement of God's own covenant faithfulness being embodied in the apostolic work which is causing Paul so much grief throughout the letter.

This still leaves, however, the first half of the verse: 'For our sake [God] made [the Messiah], who knew no sin, to be sin for us.' Though Paul does not mention the death of Jesus specifically, the wider context has been full of it (especially e.g. 4: 7–15), and the mention of God's reconciling work in the Messiah (5: 18–19) fits closely with his cross-shaped reconciliation theology in Romans 5: 9–10 and Colossians 1: 20, 22. Once again there may be cultic overtones: to make something to be 'sin' could be a way of referring to the sin-offering. But this should not take away from the central statement: God's making the sinless one to be sin on our behalf. Once again the closest OT passage seems to be Isaiah 53, where the innocent one is wounded for our transgressions and bruised for our iniquities. It may be, though, that Paul is not simply explaining that in his death Jesus has borne 'our' sin, that is, including that of the apostles themselves, in order that they might be fit embodiments of God's covenant faithfulness. He may also, or even primarily, be referring to Jesus' sin-bearing death as the model for, and the locus of, the suffering which the apostle must now undergo as he brings the message of reconciliation. It is 'in him', after all, that the apostles 'become' God's covenant faithfulness. Once again the parallel with Colossians 1 suggests itself: Paul fills up in his own flesh what was lacking in the Messiah's afflictions for the sake of his body, the church (1: 24).

Colossians 1 points us to the *sixth story* which Paul is aware of telling throughout his work: that of the powers of the world. Briefly, and confusingly, the powers—every single one of them, in heaven and earth—are created in, through, and for the Messiah, God's beloved son (1: 16), and then are reconciled through him (1: 20). The reader of Paul's great poem is puzzled: why, if they were created by him, did they need to be reconciled? The poem clearly presupposes some sort of 'fall', or rebellion of the powers. This is confirmed in Colossians 2: 15. The cross of Jesus, instead of being as one might suppose the place where the powers celebrated a triumph over him, stripping him naked and holding him up to public contempt, is to be seen as the place where Jesus celebrated *his* triumph over *them*.

This victory over the powers, and their consequent reconciliation, sets the stage for Paul's reworking of the ancient Jewish theme of the one sovereign God and the powers of the world, spiritual and political (a modern distinction to which, notoriously, neither Jewish nor Pauline thought corresponds). Alongside Colossians 1 we must place 1 Corinthians 2: 8: 'None of the rulers of this age knew [the hidden wisdom of God]; if they had, they wouldn't have crucified the Lord of Glory.' Three things are going on here, points at which Paul is picking up Jewish political theology where the Wisdom of Solomon left off and taking it forward. First, he implies that the wisdom of Israel's God is what the world's rulers really need, if they are to do their job properly and avoid judgement from the world's true Sovereign. Second, he implies that had they recognized Jesus himself as wisdom incarnate, they would have done him homage rather than executing him. Third, he implies that their killing of Jesus was in fact their acquiescence in their own demise, since his death was (as in

Col. 2) the means whereby their stranglehold over the human race was broken at last.

This is where, I suggest, Paul's theology of the cross confronts, in principle, the power of Rome. As I have argued in various places, both in structure and in detail Paul ranges the gospel of Jesus against the gospel of Caesar, and the place of the cross within the Jesus-message offers a wonderful subversion of the place of the cross within Caesar's empire. I cannot go further into this here, but unless this is taken seriously one whole aspect of Paul's understanding of Jesus' death is in danger of being ignored.

The *seventh and last story* we note is that of God himself. It may seem a step too far towards process theology to imagine God himself having a 'story'; yet when Paul tells the story of Israel this is really the obverse of the other story looming up behind, the story of the creator and covenant God. This is, surely, what Romans 9–11 is all about; were there more space, I would try to demonstrate that that entire section of the book is radically shaped around the cross of Israel's Messiah. Israel follows the Messiah into judgement, and is now free, if it wants, to abandon unbelief and find new life. But Romans 9–11 is itself based on the earlier sections of the letter, and in 5–8 we find God as the subject of the story all through, implicitly or explicitly, particularly as the one whose love is embodied and exemplified in Jesus' death (5: 6–10; 8: 31–9). We must not miss the importance of this: over against all kenotic christologies that flirt with the idea of the Son of God somehow 'stopping being God' for a while in order to become incarnate and die, Paul insists that when Jesus dies what we are seeing is the love of God in action. If the one who died on the cross was not somehow identified with the one true God, then his death would reveal, not how much God loved, but how much God managed to escape the consequences of genuine love.

In fact, the passage traditionally quoted in favour of a 'kenotic' christology makes this point very well. Philippians 2: 6–11 turns on the little word *dio* at the start of v. 9: *therefore* God has given him the name above every name, that every tongue should confess that Jesus, Messiah, is *kyrios*. The LXX references, especially to Isaiah 45: 23, indicate what is in mind: the One God, who will not share his glory with another, has shared it with Jesus—precisely because he has been 'obedient to death, yes, the death of the cross'. For Paul in Philippians, the crucifixion of Jesus is not something which happened *despite* the fact that he was God incarnate, but *because* of it. He has done what only God can do.

(iv) Conclusion: The Cross within Paul's Storied World

I have tried to show, in all too incomplete a fashion, the role that the cross played in seven of the key interlocking stories which contribute to the rich texture of Paul's theological and practical writing. Ideally, I should now work through the material from one or two more angles, establishing some cross-sectioned references and so homing in the more accurately on the way Paul's mind and arguments worked. But I have said enough to show, I think, both that the New Perspective, by highlighting key aspects of second Temple Judaism and by loosening the grip of a wooden Lutheran-style analysis, has opened up all kinds of new possibilities, even though within the NP itself these were not followed up in the way I have now done. I have also tried to indicate how the fresh perspective plays out, though there again there is much more to be said. Certainly Paul believed that through his costly apostolic work (story 5) and through the creation, by the gospel, of a renewed non-ethno-specific human family (story 4), Caesar's grandiose claim to bring justice, freedom, and peace to the world (story 6) was being challenged by God's counter-claim, which, like Caesar's, hinged decisively on the cross. This coming together of soteriology and 'political theology' may indeed be the most important proposal of this chapter.

But I have tried to show, in particular, how narrative readings of Paul can shed fresh light on well-known and contentious areas. I do not think I have made these areas less contentious, but I hope I have conveyed something of the excitement and drama that they had for Paul himself and can, I believe, still have today. 'Redemption' is one of those heavy, stodgy words that sit amongst Christian vocabulary the way suet puddings sit amongst the other food on the plate. I hope I have indicated that for Paul this was a word which spoke of promise fulfilled, of freedom attained, of the faithful love of God and the journey home to the 'inheritance'—in other words, of exodus. In a world ringing once more with the familiar imperial rhetoric of freedom, it is good to be reminded that there is another way of telling the story.

5

God made Christ to be Sin (2 Corinthians 5: 21): Reflections on a Pauline Paradox

JEAN-NOËL ALETTI, SJ

2 Corinthians 5: 21 is known as one of the most difficult Pauline statements because of its paradoxical style and the issue at stake. Even recently the verse has been interpreted as if Christ had really become a sinner: 'Paul teaches that Christ became the receptacle of the power of sin and its curse... Though innocent and sinless, Christ become a transgressor through an act of substitution... A real transfer of sin and curse to Christ was essential. Christ must truly become polluted.'[1] Such an exegesis has a long history, in both Protestant and Roman Catholic traditions, as two representative texts make clear:

No doubt the prophets all foresaw that Christ would become the greatest transgressor, murderer, adulterer, thief, rebel, and blasphemer that ever was or could be in the world. Being made a sacrifice for the sins of the whole world, he is not now an innocent person without sins, not now the Son of God born of the Virgin Mary, but a sinner who carries the sin of Paul, who was a blasphemer, an oppressor and a persecutor; of Peter, who denied Christ; of David, who was an adulterer and a murderer and caused the Gentiles to blaspheme the name of the Lord. In short, Christ bears all sins, but he received the sins that we had committed; they are laid on his own body, that he might make satisfaction for them with his own blood.[2]

The divinity has found the means to merge harmoniously the very strong union of God and humankind with the extreme desolation that the

---

[1] B. H. McLean, *The Cursed Christ. Mediterranean Expulsion Rituals and Pauline Soteriology* (JSNT Supplement Series, 126; Sheffield: Sheffield Academic Press, 1996), 144.

[2] M. Luther, *Galatians* (The Crossway Classic Commentaries; Wheaton, Ill.: Crossway Books, 1998), 151.

man Jesus Christ endured when he was persistently assailed by the divine retaliation.[3]

In the last decades these views have been seriously challenged for theological reasons.[4] But what does current exegesis of the verse say about it? It seems useful to delve a little more into the issues raised by the Pauline paradoxes.

I THE BORDERS AND THE OUTLINE OF 2 CORINTHIANS 5: 18–21

It is not so easy to divide the flow of Paul's argumentation into small units.[5] But, if we pay attention to the repetitions in the passage, we can identify a series of *reversiones* (see table).[6] If the rhetorical function of the verses is taken into consideration, it turns out that v. 18 is an introductory statement (*a* = God's reconciling work in/through Christ; *b* = the apostolic ministry of reconciliation) and vv. 19–21 the unfolding of the themes (in a chiastic order, *ABB'A'*). As S. E. Porter said, '[t]he outline makes clear that Paul uses the repeated lines to aid in defining what antecedent lines mean.'[7] This outline is typical of the way Paul develops his arguments, by making clearer and clearer his initial statements (here *a* and *b*). As a consequence of the *reversio*: (1) the prepositional phrases of *a* and *A*, 'through Christ' and 'in Christ' seem to form a *polyptoton*;[8] (2) v. 21 takes up v. 19ab

---

[3] J.-B. Bossuet, 'Carême des Minimes, 26 mars 1660', *Œuvres*, iii (Paris: Lebarq–DDB, 1916), 388. For other samples of this interpretation, see B. Sesboüé, *Jésus Christ l'unique médiateur. Essai sur la rédemption et le salut*, i (Paris: Desclée, 1988), where he reports some upsetting interpretations of 2 Cor. 5: 21 (often taken in connection with Gal. 3: 13): e.g. 58, 67, 69, 76, 82, 91, 117–18, 211, 308–9, 314–15, 359, 369, 386.

[4] See Sesboüé, *Jésus Christ l'unique médiateur*, who shows at length why the views which follow that line of interpretation are gruesome.

[5] Several commentators consider the unit to extend from 5: 11 to 6: 10. But since a discussion regarding the scope of the unit would take me too far, I will consider here only the verses immediately preceding 2 Corinthians 5: 21.

[6] The phenomenon has partially been described by S. E. Porter, Καταλλάσσω *in Ancient Greek Literature, with Reference to the Pauline Writings* (Estudios de Filologia Neotestamentaria, 5; Córdoba: Ediciónes El Almendro, 1994), 128–9. In English the *reversio* is often called *chiasma*, even though a *chiasma* is only a species of *reversio*. Here the *chiasma* covers only vv. 19–21.

[7] Ibid. 129.

[8] In our languages a *polyptoton* consists in a repetition of words derived from the same root but with a different ending. In Greek it is a repetition of the same word (noun, pronoun, or adjective) in different cases (*poly* = multiple; *ptoton* comes from *ptôsis*, which means *case*).

a = 18a	All these things are from God who reconciled us to himself, through Christ,		
b = 18b	and gave us the ministry of reconciliation.		
A = 19ab	That is, God was in Christ reconciling the world to himself,	God's action	⎫
B = 19c	not reckoning their trespasses against them, and entrusting to us the message of reconciliation.	Ministry assigned	⎬ God's action
B′ = 20	So we are ambassadors on behalf of Christ, since God is making his appeal through us. We entreat [you] on behalf of Christ, be reconciled to God	Ministry performed	⎫ Paul's exhortation
A′ = 21	The one who did not know sin he made [to be] sin on our behalf, so that in him we might become the righteousness of God.	God's action	⎬

and must be seen as an explanation of it; (3) vv. 19–21 can be divided in two: (i) the mention of God's action of reconciliation in *AB*, and (ii) Paul's exhortation in *B′A′*. (4) The subunits BB′ wherein Paul mentions his apostolic ministry of reconciliation, are surrounded by those referring to the divine action of reconciliation (*A* and *A′*). Hence, the apostolic exhortation to reconciliation is the effect of God's action of reconciliation and must be related to it. Moreover, the contiguity of *AA′* (God's initiative and action in Christ) and *BB′* (the apostolic exhortation to response to God's initiative) means that both elements are essential for a correct understanding of Paul's reflection on our salvation. (5) The variation of the tense of the verbs can be interpreted as follows: the reconciliation has already been accomplished by God (past tense in *AA′*) and is actualized through Paul's ministry in the present time (present tense in *B′*). (6) V. 21 not only repeats v. 19ab, but also develops and specifies it; in doing so, Paul indicates that his ministry consists in making explicit God's plan of reconciliation. Thus, v. 21 requires all our attention, since it is an expansion of the Pauline doctrine of reconciliation. Unfortunately, this verse is much more elliptic than the preceding ones (vv. 18a and 19ab) which it is supposed to explain and illustrate.

II The Verse within its Context (vv. 18–21)

Even if no monograph on our passage[9] has yet appeared,[10] nevertheless several studies have paid attention to the theme of reconciliation
in the Pauline letters and are relevant for our purpose.[11]

(i) The Origin of the Vocabulary of Reconciliation

Breytenbach established that the idea of reconciliation does not come
from the Hebrew Bible nor from the Judaism of Paul's age but from
the diplomatic vocabulary of the Hellenistic world:[12] καταλλάσσω
('reconcile') and its cognates are essentially secular (and not religious) terms. They must be sharply distinguished from words for
atonement, especially [ἐξ]ιλάσκεσθαι ('appease') which derives from
the cultic tradition of the Bible. The LXX does not translate *kpr* with
the καταλλασσω root. There is consequently no semantic or historical
reason to link the origins of the Pauline notion of reconciliation with

---

[9] Since I cannot provide here a thorough exegesis of the passage, let me simply
mention that the τὰ πάντα of v. 18 probably refers to the work of God detailed in the
preceding verses (vv. 14, 16–17). See how R. P. Martin understands the logic of the
reasoning and paraphrases it: 'The old order has gone, to be replaced by the new ...
And this new order in all respects is God's doing' (2 *Corinthians* (Word Biblical
Commentary; Waco, Tex.: Word Books, 1986), 135). As for the aorist active participle
καταλλάξοαντος which occurs in the same v. 18 (see also v. 19), Porter says it is
apparently the earliest instance to be found in ancient Greek literature of God being
said to effect reconciliation by giving up his own anger against humankind. Compare
this usage with 2 Macc. 1: 5; 7: 33; 8: 29, where God is asked to accept to be reconciled
(passive voice) with his people, who asked for forgiveness.

[10] The collective volume edited by J. P. Lewis, *Interpreting 2 Corinthians 5: 14–21: An
Exercise in Hermeneutics* (Studies in the Bible and Early Christianity, 17; Lewiston, NY:
Mellen Press, 1989), cannot be called a monograph.

[11] C. Breytenbach, *Versöhnung. Eine Studie zur paulinischen Soteriologie* (WUNT 60;
Neukirchen-Vluyn: Neukirchener Verlag, 1989); id., 'Versöhnung, Stellvertretung und
Sühne: Semantische und Traditionsgeschichtliche Bemerkungen am Beispiel der paulinischen Briefe', *NTS* 39 (1993), 59–79; Porter, Καταλλάσσω (the entire ch. 6 deals
with 2 Cor. 5: 18–21; see 125–44); id., 'Reconciliation and 2 Corinthians 5, 18–21', in
R. Bieringer (ed.), *The Corinthian Correspondence* (BETL 125; Leuven: Peeters, 1996),
693–705; John T. Fitzgerald, 'Paul and Paradigm Shifts: Reconciliation and its Linkage
Group', in T. Engberg-Pedersen (ed.), *Paul Beyond the Judaism/Hellenism Divide* (Louisville, Ky: Westminster John Knox Press, 2001), 241–62.

[12] See e.g. the verb πρεσβεύομεν in 2 Cor. 5: 20. The application of this vocabulary
seems to be peculiar to Paul and to Hellenistic Judaism; see 2 Macc. 1: 5; 8: 29; Philo,
Vita Moses 2. 166–7 about Moses' mediation; Josephus, *Bellum* 5. 415; *Antiquitates* 7.
153; and 3. 315, again about Moses' mediation.

the OT theology of atonement. According to Breytenbach, it is Paul who first merged these two different semantic fields,[13] when he said that reconciliation was made possible through the representative atoning death of Christ.[14]

If the origin of the vocabulary of reconciliation is diplomatic, nonetheless its usage was not restricted to the diplomatic realm,[15] because it was also used for private relationships in the household and between friends, and merged with other semantic fields like that of atonement, as it is attested in Plato[16] and in Dionysius of Halicarnassus (first century BCE): 'For the gods themselves are disposed to forgive the offences of men and are easily *reconciled*; and there have been many here now who, though greatly sinning against them, *have appeased* their anger by *prayers* and *sacrifices*.'[17]

(ii) The Shift of the Paradigm

Thus Paul took up an old Greek and Hellenistic semantic field. But he did so with two major changes.[18] (1) He 'shift[ed] the paradigm by making God, the offended party, the one who takes the initiative in reconciliation'.[19] Habitually, envoys were sent by those who were in difficult and desperate circumstances, and who therefore were anxious to end the conflict and resume friendly relations;[20] instead, Paul appears as an ambassador for Christ (the envoy of God).[21] (2) If the ancient texts talked about the good will of the offended or stronger party, in Paul's letters it is God (and not humankind) who pays damages to reconcile human beings with himself (2 Cor. 5: 21 deals with this point).[22]

---

[13] Breytenbach, *Versöhnung*, 119–20.

[14] Ibid. 221. So Paul would have mixed two different backgrounds, Greek and Jewish.

[15] Fitzgerald stresses the fact that reparations of various kinds were necessary in order to appease the estranged party: 'The necessity of making reparations was a standard precondition in the reconciliation of warring nations' ('Paul and Paradigm Shifts', 251). See e.g. Polybius, *Historia* 4. 52. 6–9; 21. 16. 9; and 21. 17. 1–8.

[16] See Plato, *Menexenus* 241a (reconciliation through prayers and sacrifices).

[17] *Ant. Rom.* 8. 50. 4. 1–6 (mentioned by Fitzgerald; for other examples, see the same article).

[18] On Paul's shift of the paradigm, see Fitzgerald, 'Paul and Paradigm Shifts', 252–7.

[19] Ibid. 253.

[20] The note of urgency is common to Paul (see 2 Cor. 5: 21) and his predecessors.

[21] Fitzgerald, 'Paul and Paradigm Shifts', 254.

[22] Let us note that Paul does not say that God reconciled himself with us but that he reconciled us with himself.

(iii) The Reconciliation Vocabulary and Paul's Experience

The reconciliation vocabulary occurs in the NT only in the Pauline letters, where it describes a change of relationship between God and humankind (Rom. 5: 10, 11; 11: 15; 2 Cor. 5: 18, 19, 20),[23] and, as just said above, 'the Pauline usage of the terminology represents a real innovation in *Religionsgeschichte*'.[24] But why did Paul use the metaphor of reconciliation? Is it the conflict between the Corinthian church and himself that led the apostle to use the reconciliation category for the interpretation of Christ's death? But in this passage there is no mention of a conflict between Paul and the Corinthian church;[25] and if there had been a conflict, it would have been between them and God, as 2 Corinthians 5: 20 makes clear ('be reconciled *to God*'). According to Kim, the best explanation for the usage of the metaphor is that it comes from Paul's experience on the Damascus Road where Christ reconciled the persecutor of the churches with himself.[26] Even though this point is not decisive for the exegesis of 2 Corinthians 5, 18–21, let us admit Kim's plausible assumption.

(iv) Reconciliation Already Effected or Not?

Whether or not the reconciliation vocabulary is anchored in Paul's experience, the major problem comes from its paradoxical usage. On one hand, it seems that we have already been reconciled through Christ's death (see vv. 18a and 19a) and, on the other, it seems that we are not yet reconciled, as Paul says in v. 20: 'we entreat you on behalf of Christ, *be reconciled* to God'.[27] But what is the exact meaning of the aorist imperative 'be reconciled'? Is 2 Corinthians 5: 21 the first time Paul announces reconciliation to the Corinthian communities? Or does he ask them to actively and dynamically adhere to the process of reconciliation operated by God?

---

[23] See also in the prison letters Col. 1: 22 and Eph. 2: 16. Col. 1: 20 stands alone in mentioning a reconciliation between creatures.

[24] S. Kim, *Paul and the New Perspective: Second Thoughts on the Origin of Paul's Gospel* (Grand Rapids, Mich.: Eerdmans, 2002), 218. (Ch. 6, '2 Corinthians 5: 11–21 and the Origin of Paul's Concept of Reconciliation', 214–38, was published in *NovT* 39 (1997), 360–84.)

[25] Observation made by Kim, *Paul*, 219.

[26] Ibid. 214.   [27] NRSV trans.

Let me first analyse the syntactic structure. According to R. Bell,[28] the construction 'was ... reconciling' is not periphrastic but has to be interpreted as two different phrases, the second being juxtaposed with the first: 'God was in Christ, [and then][29] reconciling the world to himself.' Bell reproaches the exegetes with saying that the formulation is periphrastic, but he does not justify his own position. As a matter of fact, his translation would be correct only if the participle καταλλάσσων were circumstantial; and here the only possible modality would be temporal, so that one should read: 'God was in Christ when he reconciled the world to himself'. But the *reversio* singled out above (the parallel between *a* and *A*, then between *A* and *A'*) shows that this is not the point stressed by Paul. What then does the statement 'God was in Christ' mean? According to Bell, it states the divinity of Christ. But it must be recalled that the passage does not aim at underlining Christ's divine rank. Moreover, the syntactic arrangement of v. 19a is best explained in terms of the chiasm,[30] through which Paul shows the encompassing presence of God.

According to Porter,[31] the phrase 'was ... reconciling' is the most complex issue of the passage. It is a periphrastic construction, with two possible translations: 'God was in/through Christ reconciling the world to himself.' Porter goes on: 'the periphrastic is a marked form; in other words, its use when a simple form is available draws attention to the verbal action it represents. In this context it was apparently used by Paul to draw attention to his statements regarding God's work of reconciliation',[32] namely its modalities described by the two subsequent participles. How should we interpret the present participle 'reconciling'? Does it describe a continuing action? The same action of reconciliation may also be described in two different ways or aspects: as a fulfilled action, with the aorist participle ('reconciled', v. 18), and as a continuing action, with the present participle as in v. 19.[33] Let us observe only that the same

---

[28] R. H. Bell, 'Sacrifice and Christology in Paul', *JTS* 53 (2002), 1–27 (esp. 11).

[29] Or 'therefore'. Bell reminds us that this interpretation had been suggested centuries ago by Calvin, in his commentary on 2 Corinthians (*ad locum*), according to whom Paul states 'first, that God was in Christ and then that by this intervention He was reconciling the world to himself'.

[30] God at the fringes ($a + a'$), then his action ($b + b'$), and, in the middle, the means (*c*) and the beneficiaries (*c'*). Bell thinks that his translation makes God present at Calvary (p. 12), but the text does not need that translation to draw such a conclusion, since God is the subject of the verb *katallassō*.   [31] Porter, Καταλλάσσω, 132–9.

[32] Ibid. 137.   [33] Porter, Καταλλάσσω, 137.

chain—imperfect of 'to be' + present active participle—occurs elsewhere: in Galatians 1: 22, 23, and Philippians 2: 26, and already
more than 200 times in the LXX, where it indicates repetition or
duration. Thus, the phrase 'was . . . reconciling' would be a semitism
and hint at the process of reconciliation. In M. Lang's opinion,
however, the participle 'reconciling' would rather function as a
predicate noun; hence, the temporal aspect would play no role in
this construction.[34] Of these two diverging opinions, Porter's one fits
better with the chiastic *dispositio* of the passage, wherein v. 19 (= *A*)
prepares v. 21 (= *A'*) which in turn appears to be an expansion of v.
19. So, vv. 19 and 21 refer to the past, namely to Christ's death
through which God reconciled humankind with himself.

As to the aorist imperative 'be reconciled', it means 'be reconciled
now, in the present time'. But why does Paul use a passive form? 'With
the passive form, God is appropriately the goal of the action of the
verb, since he is the one to whom, through the work of Christ, one is
to be reconciled.'[35] But this explanation does not really account for
the form; actually, its use is paradoxical and aims at stressing the
reversal of situation: let us not forget that in the OT texts, as in 2
Maccabees 1: 5; 7: 33; 8: 29, mentioned above in n. 9, it is God who
was asked to be reconciled (passive voice) with his people who were
looking for forgiveness. Hence, in imploring the Corinthians to be
reconciled with God, Paul addresses the Corinthian community as
if they were the offended partner, and he implores them to accept
(v. 20) the compensation already provided by God (vv. 19ab and 21):
the roles are reversed! It goes without saying that Paul's expression is
deliberately paradoxical. But to what purpose?

(v) The Logic of the Passage

Before I reflect on the function of the Pauline paradoxes, let me try to
rephrase the logic of the passage. Paul's statements suppose that (i)
the relationship between God and humankind should have been
friendly, (ii) the situation of enmity was caused by human transgressions or faults (v. 19b),[36] (iii) reparation had to be made (by the

---

[34] M. Lang, 'Erwägungen zu 2 Kor 5, 19a', *BibNotiz* 84 (1996), 46–50.

[35] Porter, Καταλλάσσω, 141.

[36] But Paul does not say anything about the nature of the offence. With regard to
the wording of v. 19b, let me remark that, as in Rom. 4: 8, Paul probably hints at Ps 31:
2 (LXX).

human offenders or delinquents), and (iv) there is reconciliation only after reparation. The paradox here is that it was the offended partner (and not the offender) who made reparation and in a totally unexpected way—not only by declaring that he forgives or does not count the offences, but by making Christ to be sin for our sake (v. 21). This last declaration is the most challenging and requires accurate exegesis.

III   AN EXEGESIS OF 2 CORINTHIANS 5: 21

Most commentators note the absence of a syntactic link (called *parataxis*) between vv. 20 and 21.[37] But it should be added that since the subject of the verb (God) is not mentioned, the verse cannot be separated from the last word, (*God*), of the preceding verse (v. 20); moreover, the *reversio* singled out above shows that A (v. 19) and A' (v. 21) are related and actually that A' is supposed to make A more explicit. Consequently, it is impossible to separate v. 21 from what comes before. And since the verse has been read in so many ways,[38] I prefer, before proposing my own translation, to list the major interpretations of the verse.

(i) The Syntactic and Semantic Structure of the Verse

A perfect chiastic outline of the whole statement must be abandoned,[39] even though several commentators underline a chiastic sequence of the characters.[40] But if we pay attention to the order of the phrases, a *reversio* may be singled out in the first part of the verse: 'knew'—'sin'— 'us'—'sin'—'he made'.[41] With regard to

---

[37] For a thorough analysis of v. 21, see R. Bieringer, 'Sünde und Gerechtigkeit in 2 Korinther 5, 21', in R. Bieringer and J. Lambrecht, *Studies in 2 Corinthians* (BETL 112; Leuven: Peeters, 1994), 461–514. I will not repeat Bieringer's detailed survey of all the preceding exegetical positions: the reader should read the verse with the help of Bieringer's study or of a recent commentary.

[38] But with regard to the first part of the verse (τὸν μὴ γνόντα ἁμαρτίαν ὑπὲρ ἡμῶν ἁμαρτίαν ἐποίησεν), all commentators consider that the first accusative ('him') is the direct object, and the second ('sin') attributed to that object; the phrase has been rightly translated by all English Bibles 'he made him *to be* sin'.

[39] See the discussion by Bieringer, 'Sünde und Gerechtigkeit', 464–6.

[40] In the following order: (*a*) Christ (who did not know sin), (*b*) (for) us, (*b'*) (we), (*a'*) in/through him, (Christ).

[41] The rationale of this *reversio* is syntactic (*a* = verb—*b* = noun—*c* = pronoun—*b* = noun—*a* = verb) and semantic (the repetition of the *b*-element, namely the noun ἁμαρτία).

the syntactic order, it must be said that, when the normal order is reversed, the emphasis lies on the first phrase—'the one who knew no sin'. The meaning of this syntactic phenomenon will be dealt with in the next paragraphs.

With regard to the semantic features, let me note two major oppositions, (i) within the first part of the verse ('the one who did not know sin'/'he made him to be sin') and (ii) between the first and the second part of the verse, namely between 'sin' and 'righteousness'. Both oppositions are dynamic, since they describe a change of state, a move from one extreme to another.

(ii) *The First Two Phrases of the Verse*

In the opinion of most commentators, the first phrase ('the one who did not know sin') does not mean that Christ ignored what sin is or that he had no contact with the reality of sin (because Christ met sinners and demons during his life), but that he never sinned.

With regard to the meaning of the phrase 'for us' ($\dot{v}\pi\grave{\epsilon}\rho$ $\dot{\eta}\mu\hat{\omega}\nu$) Bieringer thinks that there are two major readings: (i) substitution ('instead of us', 'in our place', 'on our behalf') and (ii) benevolence ('for our benefit', 'for our sake').[42] Both translations may be supported by the context and other Pauline passages. The first finds its confirmation in the preceding verses, when Paul says 'one has died for all' ($\dot{v}\pi\grave{\epsilon}\rho$ $\pi\acute{a}\nu\tau\omega\nu$, v. 14), and 'We entreat you *on behalf of* Christ ($\dot{v}\pi\grave{\epsilon}\rho$ $X\rho\iota\sigma\tauo\hat{v}$, v. 20)'. Why would the meaning of the preposition $\dot{v}\pi\acute{\epsilon}\rho$ change from one verse to another? But, as has been noted by many commentators, the second translation can be supported by the second part of the verse, since the benefit we obtained through God's act of reconciliation in Christ was our total transformation. Moreover, it is very well attested in other soteriological Pauline statements.[43] Since the translation of the phrase depends on our overall understanding of the verse, I will study it with the subsequent phrase.

(iii) *'He made him to be Sin'*

With regard to this phrase most recent commentaries draw heavily on Bieringer's article. Readers may see for themselves how this

---

[42] Bieringer, 'Sünde und Gerechtigkeit', 473–94.
[43] See Rom. 5: 8; 8: 31, 32, 34; 15: 30; I Cor. I: 13; 11: 24; 2 Cor. I: 11; Gal. 2: 20; 3: 13; I Thess. 5: 10.

author describes and examines the different readings. I will not take up the entire discussion but only refer in passing to the positions in order to focus on their theological consequences.

1. *The incarnation designated?* Some commentators think that Christ's becoming sin alludes to his incarnation and they read the verse in light of Romans 8: 3. Of course, if Jesus suffered because of the effects of sin, it is because he assumed flesh and became a human being. But the preceding verses (vv. 14–15) clearly focus on Christ's reconciliatory death; since vv. 18–21 take up the same idea by means of another semantic field, the hypothesis is improbable.

2. *Sin offering or apotropaeic rite?* This was Augustine's initial translation: 'Deus fecit Christum "peccatum", id est sacrificium pro peccato (vel pro peccatis)',[44] which has been taken up by many other commentators down the centuries.[45]

With this reading the verse becomes very clear: God wanted Christ to become a sin offering, an innocent victim whose death would reconcile us to himself. The clause can be paraphrased this way: 'The one who did not sin, God made him to be a sin offering'. If this is the meaning of the second 'sin' ($\dot{\alpha}\mu\alpha\rho\tau\acute{\iota}\alpha$), then there is no opposition between the beginning and the end of the clause. Since the victim of a sin offering must be blameless and sinless,[46] Jesus could not have been made a sin offering if he had sinned. But, since the phrase 'the one who knew no sin' comes first, it is stressed.[47] That is to say, what is stressed is more the uniqueness of the one who did not sin than his innocence. The use of the definite article indicates an operation of designation: 'the one who' could be paraphrased 'the *only* one who', and, to be sure, Christ was the only one to satisfy that condition. It is

[44] See e.g. *Epist.* n. 140; *Quaestionum in heptateuchum libri septem* 4; *Quaest. numerorum*, quaest. 12; *Sermones* 134; *De gratia e de peccato originali* 2. 32. 37.

[45] On the history of this interpretation see L. Sabourin, *Rédemption sacrificielle; Une enquête exégétique* (Brussels: Desclée de Brouwer, 1961); he rewrote his essay in collaboration with S. Lyonnet, *Sin, Redemption and Sacrifice* (AnBib 48; Rome: Pontifical Biblical Institute, 1970), 185–296. See also N. T. Wright, 'On Becoming the Righteousness of God: 2 Corinthians 5: 21', in D. M. Hay (ed.), *Pauline Theology*, ii. 1 and 2 *Corinthians* (Minneapolis, Minn.: Fortress, 1991), 200–8, at 206 and 207; Martin, 2 *Corinthians*: 'The text is leaning on an Old Testament testimony, namely Isa. 53: 10 where "offering for sin" חטאת is what is implied in $\dot{\alpha}\mu\alpha\rho\tau\acute{\iota}\alpha$.'

[46] Objection raised by Bell, 'Sacrifice', 13.

[47] As said above, in Greek, when the complement precedes the verb and the subject, it is emphasized.

also worth adding that the Hellenistic background, where the ideas of reconciliation and expiation were already combined,[48] could confirm such an interpretation.

Although it is theologically sound and in agreement with other Pauline texts,[49] this solution raises problems as Bieringer and others have shown.[50] Without repeating their arguments, all that I need to do here is to emphasize that, when it designates a sin offering, 'sin' is usually preceded by the preposition 'about' (περί), and if Paul had wanted to hint unambiguously at the sacrificial field, he would have used the stereotyped phrase περὶ ἁμαρτίας, as for example in Romans 8: 3. It could be objected that there are some exceptions in the OT,[51] but, with the verb 'to make' (ποιέω), the sequence is 'make a sin offering' (ποιέω τὸ περὶ τῆς ἁμαρτίας) or the like,[52] but never ποιέω ἁμαρτίαν, which means 'to sin'.[53] So, if it pointed to a sin offering but lacked the preposition περί, the sequence ποιέω + ἁμαρτίαν would lead the reader astray. It would be the only such NT usage. Could Paul's readers grasp this unique usage of the word without any formal indication, especially since the preceding occurrence of ἁμαρτία in v. 21 clearly designates the reality of sin? To that observation it has been responded that the verse is not typically Pauline, and thus that 'there is no need to be embarrassed by the absence of Pauline parallels'.[54] But such a response is irrelevant, because the rhetorical techniques are wholly Pauline, as a comparison with other paradoxical affirmations confirms. Against the sacrificial meaning of the word, the parallelism between Galatians 3: 13–14 and 2 Corinthians 5: 21 has been

---

[48] See Dionysius of Halicarnassus' passage mentioned above in II(i).

[49] See e.g. my essay on Rom. 8: 3: J.-N. Aletti, 'Romans 8: The Incarnation and its Redemptive Impact', in S. T. Davis, D. Kendall, and G. O'Collins (eds.), *The Incarnation* (Oxford: Oxford University Press, 2002), 93–115.

[50] Bieringer, 'Sünde und Gerechtigkeit', 480–4, where Sabourin's arguments are examined at length. If ἁμαρτία designates a sin offering, since the sacrificial victim must be without sin to be accepted by God, then the opposition between sin and righteousness disappears.

[51] See Lev. 4: 21, 24; 5: 12; 6: 18, where the noun ἁμαρτία designates a sin offering—this is a metonymy.

[52] Lev. 9: 7, 22; 14: 19; Num. 6: 16; ποιέω τὰ ὑπὲρ ἁμαρτίας in Ezek. 43: 25; 45: 17; see also Lev. 4: 20; 15: 15, 30; 23: 19; Num. 6: 11. The wording of Lev. 15: 15, 30 shows that if Paul had intended sin offering, he would have written: τὸν μὴ γνόντα ἁμαρτίαν ὑπὲρ ἡμῶν περσὶ ἁμαρτίας ἐποίησεν.

[53] Tob. (S) 12: 10; 14: 7.

[54] Martin, *2 Corinthians*, 157.

v. 21a = Christ		v. 21b = We	
did not know sin	was made to be sin	[did not know God's righteousness]	became God's righteousness

invoked, because in both passages the oppositions and the unfolding of the ideas are the same (Christ → curse/sin, so that we may become blessed/righteous). Actually, in both parts of v. 21 there is a transfer from one state to another,[55] and, as the chart makes clear, the logic of the verse is that Christ's transfer from one state to another is the condition for our own transfer. But if the meaning of the phrase 'he made sin' (ἁμαρτίαν ἐποίησεν) is that Christ was made a sin offering, then there has been no transfer (from one state to another), since a sin offering must be kept away from any kind of sin and impurity. For that reason, as many commentators agree, the sin offering interpretation must be abandoned.

Because blood—and, therefore, sacrifice—has no function and is not even mentioned in Galatians 3: 13 and 2 Corinthians 5: 21, McLean thinks that neither Greek nor Jewish sacrifice can provide an adequate analogy for interpreting Paul's theory of atonement.[56] But if 2 Corinthians 5: 21 does not allude to sacrificial rites and especially not to sin offering, might we read the verse as if God had made Christ to be a scapegoat? In other words, does 2 Corinthians 5: 21 allude to an apotropaeic rite? Since the apotropaeic paradigm was deeply rooted in ancient Mediterranean culture and religion—and not only in Israel[57]—the hypothesis cannot a priori be rejected, and Galatians 3: 13, where the word κατάρα (curse) explicitly occurs, could support it.[58] Given that a scapegoat was a sin bearer,[59] the identification of Christ with sin in 2 Corinthians 5: 21 could also allude to that rite. Nonetheless, according to Leviticus 16, on the Day of Atonement, there were two goats, one to be offered to God as a sin offering and the other as a scapegoat to be sent into

---

[55] Let us keep in mind that the second accusative ἁμαρτίαν is attributed to the direct object.

[56] McLean, *The Cursed Christ*, 64.   [57] Ibid. 65–104.

[58] This conclusion supposes that the scapegoat was a curse bearer.

[59] See Lev. 16: 21–2.

the wilderness: the rites were inseparable, and atonement was not obtained through one alone; on that day, all the rites had to be performed. Moreover, with regard to atonement, it is difficult to know what importance Paul and Judaism of that period gave to the scapegoat.[60] If we now attend to the semantics of 2 Corinthians 5: 21, we must acknowledge that in identifying Christ with sin, the verse uses a metonymy, and it is necessary to identify the function of this rhetorical device before searching for the religious background(s)[61] of the verse.

3. Christ as sinner?[62] If the second occurrence of 'sin' does not mean 'sin offering' but designates the reality of sin, is it an abstract for a concrete?[63] The phrase 'he made [him] sin' can be considered as the opposite of v. 19b, which mentions the 'trespasses' of humankind: Christ who did not sin was made to be sin, which means, in the opinion of many ancient and contemporary critics, that he was punished in our place and that our transgressions have been counted against him.[64] Moreover, many interpreters argue: if, on one hand, we attend to the strict parallelism between *sin* (v. 21a) and *righteousness* (v. 21b), and if, on the other hand, we admit that believers really became righteous, is it not necessary to conclude that Christ became a sinner and a transgressor,

---

[60] In that respect, Rom. 3: 25, the only text wherein the atonement vocabulary occurs, discloses a sacrificial (and not an apotropaeic) background.

[61] As usually happens in the Pauline letters, in the same verse or pericope the background may be multiple. I proved this for Rom. 7: 7–25 (J. N. Aletti, 'Rm 7. 7–25 encore une fois: Enjeux et propositions', *NTS* 48 (2002), 358–76); and one of my doctoral students did the same for the entire Letter to the Galatians (M. Rastoin, *Tarse et Jérusalem: La Double Culture paulinienne à l'œuvre en Gal 3, 6–4, 7*, to appear in AnBib). This could be confirmed in all the other letters. For that reason, as regards the background, it is better not to make a hasty decision.

[62] In the opinion of many commentators this interpretation is incompatible with the preceding one. But some of them think that both are compatible. See e.g. P. Ellingworth, 'For our sake God Made him Share our Sin? (2 Corinthians 5. 21, GNB)', *BibTrans* 38 (1987), 237–41, according to whom the best choice for translating 2 Cor. 5: 21 seems to be between the language of identification ('for our sake God made him one with human sinfulness') and the language of sin offering ('for our sake God made the sinless one a victim for sin'). Ellingworth adds that the first interpretation could be expressed in the text, and the second in a note.

[63] See e.g. BAGD (entry ἁμαρτία): 'As abstract for concrete τὸν μὴ γνόντα ἁ. ὑπὲρ ἡμῶν ἁμαρτίαν ἐποίησεν (God) *made him, who never sinned, to be sin* (i.e. the guilty one) *for our sakes* 2Co 5, 21'.

[64] So, among many others, Porter, *Καταλλάσσω*, 142.

otherwise the opposition between the two substantives (sin/right-eousness) would fail?[65]

This reading of v. 21 raises some difficult questions: since Christ is entirely passive, he is not responsible for his and our changes of state; only God is responsible, as the only active protagonist. But how could God, who hates sin, transform good into evil and an innocent person into a sinner? One might object that God did not transform Christ into a sinner, but associated him with all sinners and charged him with their sins. Thus, even though he did not sin, Christ would be taken to be guilty. To this objection I respond that Paul does not use a judicial vocabulary here.[66] God is not said to accuse, charge, judge, or punish.

4. Toward a right interpretation of the metonymy   To interpret correctly the rhetorical thrust of our passage, it is necessary to keep in mind that metonymy expresses effect for cause (sin for the sinner) or cause for effect (sin for the effects of sin). In the latter case, it would mean that, although he was not a sinner, Christ was encompassed and struck by sin, and that what sin is and does has been fully manifested in him—namely, in his rejection, suffering, and death. Since metonymy does not describe inclusive (as the synecdoche does: *pars pro toto* and vice versa, etc.) but contiguous relationships (the cause for the result and vice versa, etc.), Paul would thus say that without having sinned Christ suffered so much from sin that he was identified with it.[67] By rephrasing McLean's assertion cited at the beginning of this study, it could be said that if there had been a real transfer of sin to Christ, that does not necessarily mean that he became a transgressor.[68]

This interpretation must be preferred to the preceding one (Christ becoming a sinner) for two reasons at least. (i) In this verse, nothing is said about human responsibility (and/or guilt), because everything underlines God's paradoxical initiative and action; (ii) if the reader

---

[65] In addition to all those mentioned by Bieringer, see Bell on these verses, 'Sacrifice', 13–14 (p. 13: 'Christ was made to be "sin" which by *metonymy* means made to be a "sinner" '; my emphasis).

[66] In such a case, Paul would have used adjectives like ἔνοχος (+ gen.) or ὑπόδικος. See 1 Cor. 11: 27; Rom. 3: 19.

[67] If I am not mistaken, this is Bieringer's position, 'Sünde und Gerechtigkeit', 491–2: Christ became one thing with the reality of sin and its consequences.

[68] McLean, *The Cursed Christ*, 144.

had to understand that Christ was made a sinner, it would have been much easier and *ad rem* to use the substantive 'sinner'. But in the Pauline letters all the occurrences of this word designate those who reject God and are his enemies; and, to be sure, Christ was never separated from God.[69] Metonymy is a subtle device, which prevents us from saying that Christ sinned and (worse) was an enemy of God, and which nonetheless stresses that in Jesus Christ, the crucified,[70] we can see the deadly results and nature of sin.

I have just said that metonymy depicts contiguous relationships. Thus, all the circumstances which stress how Christ has been struck by sin so as to die can be included in the connotations of the metonymy of v. 21: Jesus' contemporaries unjustly charged him (with blasphemy) and condemned him; he was vilified as a sinner by those standing around the cross, because they were convinced that he was a curse bearer—the supreme perversion of sin is when innocents are condemned and die as if they were sinners.[71] For the same reason, the metonymy of v. 21 may also apply to the NT passages wherein Christ is said to have borne our diseases and sins.[72]

The upshot of this discussion is that, even though I take account of the linguistic and rhetorical phenomena of the passage, I have not eliminated all its difficulties. Paul does not say *why* and *how* the fact that Christ was identified with sin made all sinners become God's righteousness: the connection between the becoming sin of Christ and our becoming righteousness of God is neither unfolded nor explained. For that reason, I have to reflect on the function of the paradoxical statements in v. 21a.

(iv) 'So that in him we might become the righteousness of God'[73]

This final clause provides the reason for Christ's change of condition. In a word, the radical nature of God's action had a *salvific* motivation: the identification of Christ with sin was not a goal in itself!

---

[69] Paul says in another letter: 'The death he [Christ] died, he died to sin' (Rom. 6: 10, NRSV). Thus, exegetes must confront apparently contradictory Pauline statements. See below, 'Theological Reflections', s. IV.

[70] As has been said above, the preceding context (v. 14–15) invites us to acknowledge that the statements about reconciliation (v. 18–21) are centred on the death of Christ.

[71] As Naboth in 1 Kgs. 21: 13.   [72] See Matt. 8: 17 (citing Isa. 53: 4–5).

[73] NRSV translation. On that clause, see Wright, 'On Becoming the Righteousness of God'; R. K. Moore, '2 Cor. 5, 21: The Interpretative Key to Paul's Use of *ΔΙΚΑΙΟΣΥΝΗ ΘΕΟΥ*?', in Bieringer (ed.), *The Corinthian Correspondence*, 707–15.

This shows that God wanted to operate our transformation at all costs.

Paul could have expressed the restoration of the relationship between the partners with the covenant vocabulary. One commentator even suggests that the final clause be rather translated 'so that in him we might become God's covenant-faithfulness'.[74] It must nevertheless be recalled that in his soteriological statements the Apostle does not use the covenant vocabulary but expresses the change of state of believers with other categories—righteousness, sonship, and the like.[75] Besides, the opposition between sin and righteousness is biblical in general and Pauline in particular.[76]

What kind of genitive is 'of God'? Is it objective (righteousness which counts before God), of origin (righteousness coming from God), subjective (righteousness operated by God),[77] or possessive (God's own attribute)? Is 'the righteousness of God' here a human status bestowed by God or a human status which counts before God or, rather, an inner transformation operated by God without any human cooperation and implying deeds that conform to God's will? In other words, does the clause describe a human quality, an internal and moral transformation, or a divine attribute? The 'we might become' signals that we have been transformed: our righteousness is not a pure forensic declaration, but a real new human feature. As a result, the word 'righteousness' is an 'abstractum pro concreto': we became *righteous*![78] But if Paul uses such a rhetorical device, is it (i) to draw a perfect parallelism between the words 'righteousness' of v. 21b and 'sin' of v. 21a, and (ii) to signal that our righteousness is entirely due to God's salvific action? The genitive 'of God' is primarily subjective, since the change has been operated in us by God. But the clear-cut opposition between sin and righteousness does not eliminate the difference between Christ and us: if we were sinners and became righteous, Christ did not become a sinner, even though he

---

[74] Wright, 'On Becoming the Righteousness of God', 206.

[75] See J.-N. Aletti, 'Le Statut de l'Église dans les lettres pauliniennes: Réflexions sur quelques paradoxes', *Bib.* 83 (2002), 153–74.

[76] See e.g. Prov. 14: 34; Sir. 26: 28–9; Rom. 6: 7, 16, 18, 20; 8: 10; Gal. 2: 17.

[77] Bieringer, 'Sünde und Gerechtigkeit', 509; if so, the genitive means: 'von (und vor) Gott gerechtfertigte Menschen'.

[78] That kind of metonymy appears several times in the OT. See e.g. Isa. 42: 6 and 49: 8 ('I have given you as a *covenant* to the people').

was identified with sin. So the use of the metonymy permitted Paul to bring together asymmetrical situations.

With regard to the last phrase of the verse ἐν αὐτῷ, the commentators translate it in two different ways: 'in him' or 'through him'. The major options so far taken have been examined by Moore, who himself concludes that the ἐν αὐτῷ is instrumental.[79] But, if we keep in mind the chiastic structure of the passage, especially the parallelism between A and A', it seems preferable to conclude that the ἐν αὐτῷ of v. 21b cannot be read apart from the 'in Christ' of v. 19a, which in turn cannot be separated from the 'through Christ' of v. 18a. As has been suggested above, Christ's mediation is expressed in different ways, by means of a *polyptoton*, and the two formulations are complementary. If Paul finishes the passage with ἐν αὐτῷ, it is to say that the righteousness we have obtained is inseparable from (that of) Christ. In other words, all what we are and have, is *christologically* coloured.

(v) Summary

Let me distill the results of my exegesis into some short statements. Of the two main readings of v. 21a, the sacrificial one (God made Christ to be a sin offering) and the one seeing Christ identified with the mortal effects of sin, I preferred the latter for reasons I do not need to repeat. But, as I have acknowledged, even that reading cannot account for the paradoxical formulation of the verse; since Paul does not justify his declarations, the exegesis is to some extent conjectural. But the clearest effect of the paradox is to stress the (apparently) foolish way through which God operated reconciliation. And such a formulation must be examined.

IV THEOLOGICAL REFLECTIONS

(i) The Silences of v. 21 and Paul's Soteriology

I have so far analysed what Paul says. But the main feature of the verse is its laconic or elliptical makeup. The Apostle does not say that God made Christ to be sin because of our transgressions, that Christ is no longer sin because God raised him from the dead and made him to

---

[79] Moore, '2 Cor 5, 21', 714–15.

be righteousness, or that in sharing his own righteousness we become righteous. Above all, unlike such other passages as Romans 5: 8 and Galatians 2: 20, nothing is said about the will and love of God and Christ (who is totally passive in 2 Cor. 5: 21). Clearly, this text does not represent all the Apostle's soteriology. It could even be added that it seems in clear opposition to other passages, like Romans 6: 10, where it is explicitly stated that 'the death [Christ] died, he died to sin' (NRSV). Is Paul capable of espousing mutually contradictory positions? And if the salvific motivation is clearly expressed in v. 21b, the connection between the becoming sin of Christ and our becoming 'righteousness of God' receives no explanation. Why did God go to that extreme? If Paul neither justifies his statements nor provides further explanations, this gives full strength to the paradox he unfolds in v. 21a. The question is then: why does he employ such a paradox?

(ii) The Pauline Paradoxes

I cannot expatiate here upon the theme. Let me only say that, in addition to 2 Corinthians 5: 21, the Apostle has formulated other paradoxes, all as strong as can be. There have been so far very few studies of his paradoxes.[80] But they are worthy of study, because all of them raise problems. The most difficult paradoxes deal with Christ's death: God made the wisdom of the world foolish through the foolishness of the cross (1 Cor. 1: 21–2); 'He gave his Son up' (Rom. 8: 32)—formulations that associate paradox and exaggeration.[81] Certainly Paul knows a rhetorical technique called *correctio* that can tone down his statements and does not hesitate to use it every now and then.[82] Unfortunately, the *correctio* never accompanies his paradoxes, especially those expressing the mystery of the crucified one (see Gal. 3: 13–14; 2 Cor. 5: 21; 8: 9). How can the one who dispossessed himself

---

[80] To my knowledge, there is only one monograph available, that of G. Hotze, *Paradoxien bei Paulus: Untersuchungen zu einer elementaren Denkform in seiner Theologie* (Münster: Aschendorff, 1997).

[81] In addition to the paradoxes describing God's ways in Christ (Rom. 11: 32; Gal. 3: 13–14; 2 Cor. 5: 21; 8: 9), there are paradoxes regarding the situation of the believers (1 Cor. 1: 26–31; 9: 19; 2 Cor. 11: 30; 12: 10; Gal. 5: 13; Phil. 3: 2–11). Paradoxes are a typical feature of Paul's style and theology.

[82] This rhetorical device consists in a semantic clarification by addition of a phrase ('not *x*, but *y*', and also '*x* or, better, *y*'). See Rom. 4: 4; 7: 15b, 17, 19, 20; 11: 11; 2 Cor. 5: 7. On the topic, see N. Schneider, *Die rhetorische Eigenart der paulinischen Antithese* (Tübingen: Mohr Siebeck, 1970).

of everything enrich others and the one who became a curse be a blessing? Paul does not give any response!

Why does he not tone down his paradoxes? Most likely he wants to stress that God's ways cannot be mentally digested and that Christ's death cannot be announced except through the rhetoric of exaggeration. What can we say when the offended partner himself provides the means to reconciliation and permits his only Son to be mortally struck by sin? For sure, it is up to us, exegetes, to show the profound coherence and the foundation of Paul's paradoxical affirmations, but this task cannot be thoroughly fulfilled: Paul's paradoxes espouse and describe God's mysterious will and ways.

V CONCLUSION

We have seen that, according to J. T. Fitzgerald, Paul operated a shift of paradigm when he reversed the roles in the reconciliation process between God and humankind.[83] I now raise the same question with regard to a possible shift of paradigm in the interpretation of 2 Corinthians 5: 21. Augustine initiated the sin offering reading of the verse and Luther decisively supported that of Christ's sinfulness. But what is the trend at the present time? If one of the readings cannot eclipse the other, there is nonetheless a clear shift in exegetical procedures. Our conclusions are not drawn any longer from theological presuppositions, but rather from a painstaking exegesis of the verse. For that reason I have myself paid attention to the exegetical reasons provided by current studies and I have tried to go a little further.

After having presented 2 Corinthians 5: 21 within its literary context, this chapter deals with the two main readings of v. 21a, the sacrificial one (God made Christ to be a sin offering) and the one seeing Christ identified with the mortal effects of sin. The second is preferred here, but even that reading cannot account for the paradoxical formulations of the verse. Since Paul does not justify his declarations, every exegesis is to some extent conjectural. If Paul uses a paradox, it is because he wants to make sure that God's way cannot be mentally digested and that Christ's death cannot be announced except through the rhetoric of exaggeration.

---

[83] Fitzgerald, 'Paul and Paradigm Shifts'.

6

Israel's Redeemer is the One to Whom and with Whom She Prays

PETER OCHS

PREFACE

The most important book of Jewish theology is the prayer book, or *siddur*. And, within the *siddur*, the most important Jewish theology of redemption is displayed in the daily morning prayer service, or *shacharit*. Before offering a careful reading of the structure of this service, I would like to share a few thoughts on why I believe both Christian and Jewish theologians would have much to gain from studying the *siddur* as a source for contemporary Jewish theology.

The context out of which I offer these remarks is not 'Judaism in general', but a particular movement of what I will label 'postliberal Jewish theology', which also works in dialogue with a current movement of 'postliberal Christian theology'. For postliberal theologians, both Jewish and Christian, theology is performed prayerfully. This means both that it is performed in relation to the revealed word of the eternal God *and* that this relation, and therefore this theology, is always specific to some time. The time of postliberal Jewish theology is after the Shoah and after modernity. This means the time when the Jewish people is still struggling to give new voice to a covenant that, in some senses, died (God forbid) in the Shoah. And it seeks to find this voice at a time when the great 'isms' of modern civilization have lost their hegemony. The question for Jewish theology at such a time is this: is Israel's covenant with God still alive after the Shoah? Or, God forbid, has the covenant died? Or, as the Jewish people has found after every horrible destruction in its history, will one epoch of the covenant—one articulation of Judaism—indeed die, but then another one come to life? That is, does Israel's covenant suffer a death, as it were, and then resurrection? These may be strange questions to ask, but a careful reading of Judaism's salvation history suggests that they reflect the strangeness of Israel's intimate relation with God. In our corporate finitude and temporality, Israel is wedded to the infinite and eternal God! We do what we can to serve this God in each particular epoch and civilization of our history, but then it seems that a given time of service has passed, the season has come and gone, and we die—I mean we really do, or how else can we describe the time of enslavement in ancient Egypt, the destruction of the First Temple and the exile that followed it, the destruction of the Second Temple and the diaspora that followed it, the destruction of Spanish Jewish civilization and the expulsion and exile that followed it, and so many other such caesuras in our history, and then the Shoah? We would be foolish not to see the pattern. But we would also be wrong not to read in it signs of the sober hope that characterizes Jewish eschatology and to feel this hope right now, at this time in the story when our generation should be preparing for the resurrection that follows the death of our grandparents and their form of Judaism. We cannot be sure, of course (and I note these things with a characteristically Jewish mix of sad memory, fallibilism, and eschatological industry), but we should leave open the possibility that we belong to the generation that begins to experience the next Judaism.

Postliberal Jewish theology is a theology of Jews who believe this time of change is upon us. They believe that the purpose of theology at such a time is not to describe some eternal features of the people Israel's relation to God, nor to construct some new edifice of Jewish belief. Its purpose is, instead, to serve the process of rebirth and reformation that may characterize this moment in salvation history. If this is the time they believe it may be, then postliberal Jewish theology should be an activity of Israel's prayerful relation to the God who would now appear as her Redeemer. For this generation's grandparents, He did not appear this way, and they who live today fall silent in the face of this memory. But they do not live at the time of their grandparents. They do not know why God appears to them now as Redeemer, but they do not believe this appearing is of their choosing, nor that they have reason to greet it with either silence or guilt or fear or scepticism. They greet this Redeemer God, instead, as they greet the God to whom they pray the daily morning prayer service. This means that they greet the Redeemer God prayerfully, as one who hears their cries and responds to them. It also means that they greet the God of the morning prayer service as Redeemer, and this, as we shall see, is a God who responds to their cries by instructing them and enlisting them in His redeeming work. Morning prayer is the service of light after darkness, rebirth after a sleep that is like death: a time for this generation of Israel to see past its past.

Postliberal Jewish theologians can imagine other periods in salvation history: times when theologians become philosophers (exploring the limits of rational reflection on the signs of God's presence in the world) or when they become systematizers (constructing possible models for enacting divine law in a particular social context). But they recognize that their current task finds its model in prayer. This is theology in the service of petition (giving voice to their community's yearnings at a time of profound transformation), of praise (giving voice to their community's discovery that God can once again be named Redeemer), and of service itself (articulating this lesson of morning prayer: that the God who redeems Israel enlists Israel, now, as new agent of redemption).

> tzur yisrael, kuma b'eztrat yisrael . . . goalenu . . . baruch ata adoshem, ga'al yisrael . . .
> Rock of Israel, rise up to Israel's aid . . . , redeem us. Blessed are you, Hashem, who redeemed Israel.

The most important book of Jewish theology is the prayerbook, or *siddur*. And, within the *siddur*, the most important Jewish theology of redemption is displayed in the daily morning prayer service, or *shacharit*. It is traditional (but not doctrinal) to speak of four, sequential sections in *shacharit*: the Morning Blessings (*birchot hashachar*), the Verses of Praise (*pesuke d'zimra*), the Sh'ma and its blessings, and the Amidah (the standing prayer, or *tefillah*, 'reflective prayer').[1] The

---

[1] I will not offer scholarly documentation for each of my claims and suggestions about the morning service, but will note here the various sources and commentaries I draw on. I offer my own translations from the traditional *nusach* of the Ashkenazi *shacharit*, aided by the following Hebrew editions with English translations: *Ha-Siddur Ha-shalem, Daily Prayerbook*, trans. Philip Birnbaum (New York: Hebrew Publishing Co., 1949); *Siddur Sim Shalom: A Prayerbook for Shabbat, Festivals, and Weekdays*, ed. and trans. Jules Harlow (New York: The Rabbinical Assembly and The United Synagogue of America, 1985); *The Complete Art Scroll Siddur; Weekday/Sabbath/Festival*, trans. Nasson Scherman (Brooklyn: Mesorah Publications, 1988); *My People's Prayer Book: Traditional Prayers, Modern Commentaries*, ed. Lawrence A. Hoffman, i. *The Sh'ma and Its Blessings*; ii. (Woodstock, Vt.: Jewish Lights Pub., 1997, 1998). For historical background and rabbinic as well as modern commentary, I draw on: *My People's Prayer Book*; A. Z. Idelsohn, *Jewish Liturgy and its Development* (New York: Schocken,

final blessing of the Sh'ma section is the 'Blessing of Redemption' (*birchat ha-geulah*), which extols the God of Israel, by whose own hand ancient Israel was delivered from bondage in Egypt. After recounting *that* work of 'salvation' (*yeshuah*), 'liberation' (*pidayon*), 'rescue' (*hatsalah*), and 'redemption' (*geulah*), the blessing concludes with a plea for yet another redemption: 'Rock of Israel, rise up to Israel's aid; deliver Judah and Israel, as You promised. Our Redeemer (*goalenu*): . . . Blessed are You, Hashem, who redeemed Israel (*ga'al yisrael*)'. Israel's Redeemer is the One who heard her prayers in the past and rescued her; her Redeemer is the One from whom Israel waits for a future deliverance; and her Redeemer is the One to whom she prays now. For the *shacharit* service, redemption is therefore not merely an eschatological activity: provided we take 'eschatology' to refer, not only to a 'final end', but also to the hoped-for end of any prayer of petition—'meantime ends', we might say, in which God hears and responds to the prayers that mark this immediate world as a world also of suffering. To be Redeemer is to bring each world of suffering to an end, and we live through many such worlds.

In this chapter, I will focus on this third identity of Israel's Redeemer, as the One who hears her prayers now, and responds. My attention is therefore drawn, in particular, to a transition in the *shacharit* service, from the 'Blessing of Redemption' that I just introduced to the Amidah that immediately follows it. In the Blessing of Redemption, the worshipper is led to identify with Israel, sharing her experience of redemption in the past and then offering a petition on behalf of her redemption in the future. After its initial 'Blessings of Praise', the Amidah *appears* to continue and extend this genre of petition: leading the worshipper to share in Israel's requests, to the Holy One, for a return to Jerusalem, in a realm of justice, health, and peace. As I will suggest, however, the Amidah could also be read, blessing by blessing, as leading the worshipper to share so intimately in the depth and mystery of God's holiness that, with Israel, the worshipper comes to share in God's work of *tikkun olam*, repairing and redeeming this world. My attention is drawn, in other words, to the possibility that the *shacharit* service offers the worshipper an opportunity to exchange petition for redemptive work.

1932); Joseph Heinemann, *Prayer in the Talmud: Forms and Patterns* (Berlin and New York: de Gruyter, 1977); Lawrence Hoffman, *The Canonization of the Synagogue Service* (Notre Dame, Ind.: University of Notre Dame Press, 1979); Max Kadushin, *Worship and Ethics* (Binghamton, NY: Global Pub., 2001).

As noted, my reading follows the traditional division of *shacharit* into four sequential sections. My interpretations are prompted by two postulates. The first is that a theology of Jewish worship arises from attention not only to the language and semantics of the prayers, but also to a reasonable depiction of the worshipper's experience of praying these prayers, in their assigned sequence, day in and day out. '*The* worshipper' refers here to an ideal type, constructed out of a variety of individually partial evidences: Mishnaic and Talmudic discussions of the prayers, the ocean of suggestions (varied and conflictual) that are displayed in post-Talmudic commentaries from the Gaonic period to today, and the interpreter's immediate sense of what matters most to us today. However informed by the sources, such a depiction is inevitably marked by context and subjective choice. The second postulate is that the four sections of the morning service draw the worshipper through four stages of preparation for the day to come. Depending on the reader's preferred mode of discourse, the stages may be characterized as 'levels of redemptive activity' and as 'levels of consciousness',[2] or 'levels of ensoulment'. (I have a personal preference for the latter two, as ways of correlating phenomenological categories with traditional rabbinic references to three levels of soul: *nefesh*, *neshamah*, and *ruach*. Outside of specific kabbalistic traditions, I read rabbinic discussions of these terms as merely suggestive, rather than doctrinal.[3]) The levels of ensoulment (or consciousness) are accumulative, so that a fourth stage includes and presupposes the previous three. In order to discuss a fourth stage (in the Amidah), I must therefore also introduce the first three. The merit of these two postulates is strictly practical: they offer a way for contemporary readers to draw on the *siddur* as a resource for theological instruction. I believe that the second postulate is particularly useful for theologies of redemption that consider redemption as an activity in this world, as well as at its end, and as an activity that

---

[2] I am wary of this discourse, lest it psychologize the movement of prayer; but 'consciousness' is often a useful rubric for contemporary readers, particularly those who study religious experience phenomenologically.

[3] As far as I know, there is no rabbinic source, or later commentary, that correlates the sections of prayer to specific levels of consciousness or ensoulment I identify here. There are ample references, in more general terms, however, to the spiritual depths achieved in prayer and to different depths that can be achieved in the different sections. The references extend from allusions in the rabbinic literature to more detailed analyses in Chasidic and other spiritualist and pietistic literature.

engages the worshipper (or seeker) in direct relation to the God to whom one prays.

VOCABULARY

The Four Sections of Shacharit

(1) The Morning Blessings (*birchot hashachar*) begin with the very first act of the worshipper's day: opening the eyes and reciting, *modeh ani*, 'Grateful am I to You, O ever-living Ruler, for graciously restoring my soul...' There follow various preliminary blessings of the day, often recited at home even by those who then attend a public prayer service. (2) 'Verses of Praise/Song' (*pesuke d'zimrah*): for the most part, these are biblical psalms of praise for God's work of creation, among them Psalms 145–50. (3) 'The Sh'ma and its Blessings': this section is Israel's call to worship, named after its central and defining prayer: 'Hear, O Israel, Hashem (YHVH) is our God, Hashem alone' (Deut. 6: 4–9). (4) 'The Amidah' ('Standing Prayer'). This climactic section of nineteen blessings is named, alternately, *shmoneh esre* ('The Eighteen', referring to the eighteen blessings that originally comprised it), *tefillah* ('The Prayer', *per se*, which I prefer to gloss as 'Reflexive Prayer', from the root meanings of *l'hitpallel*).

Four Terms of Ensoulment

(1) *nefesh*, which I will gloss as 'animated soul' (as in *nefesh kal chai*, 'the soul of all living beings', or *pikuach nefesh*, 'to save a life', or *nafshi yatsah b'dabru*, 'my soul failed me when he spoke', Song of Songs 5: 6). I prefer the term 'animated', rather than 'animal', so as not to suggest that this soul is somehow subordinated to the 'higher' souls of language and relation. (2) *neshamah*, usually translated 'breathing soul' (as in *kol od n'Sh'mato bo*, 'as long as there is breath in one's body'). I will also gloss it, somewhat tendentiously, as the 'relational soul' (as in *niSh'mat kol chai*, 'the soul of every living being'). (3) *yisrael*. Naming 'Israel' one level of ensoulment is strictly my own neologism. (4) *ruach*, usually translated 'spirit', etymologically 'wind', or also 'divine spirit' (as in *ruach elohim m'rachefet 'al p'nei hamayim*, 'The spirit of God hovered over the face of the waters'). I also gloss it, tendentiously, 'divine-image', simply to distinguish the divine-spirit of God from the divine-spirit that enters us.

A THEOLOGY OF REDEMPTION IN PRAYER (1)

Making use of this vocabulary, I find it helpful to envision the Morning Blessings as awakening 'attention to' (*kavvanah 1*) the worshipper's 'animated soul', or *nefesh*. To 'awaken attention to something' means to turn the worshipper's attention to, or more precisely (since 'worshipper' is an everyday term), to awaken a 'reflexive relation to'. Of the many terms for 'praying', such reflexivity has its prototype in what is sometimes characterized as 'prayer per se', or *tefillah*, of which the prototypical ritual is the Amidah (or, in other words, the Amidah enacts the worshipper's reflexivity per se). Each section of prayer contributes to this accumulated reflexivity, through its own defining type of prayer (although each section includes elements of all the other forms of prayer as well). In these terms, I envision the Verses of Praise as awakening the 'relational/linguistic soul', or *neshamah*, and the Sh'ma, as awakening *yisrael*, as the petitioning and redeeming soul. In this portrayal, each soul builds on and presupposes the previous one, so that *yisrael* is also animated (bodily and active) and relational/linguistic.

I will say that, by awakening attention to the animated soul, the Morning Blessings enable the worshipper to rediscover the animated soul, at once, as sign of the creator's handiwork (*maaseh b'reshit*) and as instrument of Hashem's activity on earth. Thus, for example, the Blessings begin with gratitude for God's 'mercifully restoring my soul (*nefesh*)'—plain enough! Then, after washing the hands, the worshipper recites a blessing formula for being commanded to wash the hands. Then, donning the prayer-shawl (*tallit*), the worshipper declares 'Bless Hashem, O my soul (*nefesh*)'. Later, come blessings for 'God's forming the human being with a system of ducts and tubes', for 'commanding us to study Torah', and for 'giving the cock intelligence to distinguish between day and night [and wake us up!]'. In other words, as waking life rushes back into the body, the worshipper awakens to the animated soul as ground of the day's activities. While the animated soul may first show itself most conspicuously in the body's inner movements, from blood flow to the stream of outer consciousness, it soon shows itself to be the ground of movement in all subsequent levels of soul as well. That is why a theology of redemption cannot bypass attention to the Morning Blessings: prayers for redemption must emerge out of disruptions in the animated soul (which means out of actual, worldly suffering, rather than merely imagined distress), and, as we will see in the Amidah, redemptive responses to prayer must be re-embodied in the animated soul as well.

In different terms, we may say that the Morning Blessings awaken a first practice of reflexivity, reflecting on the inner movements of the created being who awakens every morning from sleep ('Blessed are You . . . Who removes sleep from my eyes and slumber from my eyelids'). For the rabbinic sages, sleep is also a kind of death—a separation of various souls from the animated body—and a time of dreaming. In this sense, sleep brings two forms of nearness to God: to be separated from the individuated body and to be visited by dream states. Waking means leaving both these states of dream and of separation and thus leaving these particular forms of closeness to God. It is significant that blessing, *berachah*, is the signal prayer form of this section, since *berachah* is the form that most clearly marks *both* the radical separation between God and this world, in its stark corporeality, *and* the miracle of God's indwelling that corporeality (where 'to indwell' glosses *l'shachen*, and 'indwelling' glosses *shechinah*). Through this indwelling, God becomes 'nigh unto' his creatures ('This Teaching . . . is not beyond reach . . . ; it is very close to you' (*karov elecha*: Deut. 30: 11, 14)). Although not a prayer of the morning service, the simplest *berachah* to teach as illustration of this phenomenon is the blessing over bread (which also serves as the all-inclusive blessing over a regular meal). 'Blessed are You, Hashem our God, Ruler of the Universe, who brings forth bread from the earth'. The blessing is recited as the bread is broken, and then, while the worshipper/eater's attention (*kavvanah*) remains fully on the details of the blessing, the bread is consumed. In this way, the words and significance of the blessing is directly embodied in the literal taste of the bread, just as the blessing identifies Hashem as the immediate source of bringing the bread out of the ground into our mouths. In a semiotic vocabulary, we may refer to the bread as Sign of God the creator *with respect to* (or as interpreted by) the words of blessing. In phenomenological terms, we may say that the blessing transforms bread as a part of the natural world into a sign of God's presence in the created world—where 'sign' refers not to a distant symbol or metaphor, but to an indexical sign of the embodied presence of God. In the same way, the Morning Blessings as a whole transform the worshipper's body, otherwise perceived only as part of the natural world of the morning, into an indexical sign of the creator's presence. As movement and life stream back into the worshipper's body, the blessings awaken attention to that streaming as an aspect of God's presence in this world. This, as we will see, is the presence of our Redeemer.

To awaken attention to the animated soul is also to awaken attention to that soul's aporias, burdens, and crises. This burdened attention, as we shall see, is in fact the condition for petitionary prayer. For now, however, such burdens remain muted, merely suggested, for example, in the burdened memory of the initial verses of Psalm 30, which serves as the transitional prayer between Morning Blessings and Verses of Praise. *aromimecha hashem ki dilitani v'lo simakhta oyvaay li*: 'I will raise You up (awaken my attention to you), O my God, because you have saved me and not allowed my enemies to rejoice over me...'

A THEOLOGY OF REDEMPTION IN PRAYER (2)

Psalm 30 introduces the second part of the service and its 'Verses of Praise'. For the most part, these are biblical psalms of praise for God's work of creation. In most cases, the collection omits those psalms of inner transformation that trace the individual's (typically David's) having been redeemed from the terrible assault of his enemies which, he discovered, was also a mark of his own inner sin. While the latter psalms end in praise, the Verses of Psalm tend to be all praise: wonder, gratitude and thanksgiving for what God has done in enabling all creatures to celebrate animated life here on this earth. Only the introductory Psalm 30 offers a token reminder of burdens that have already been experienced (last night when we fell into the death of sleep, or some other past time when we have been brought low), of relief for the redemption that has already been experienced, and of the gratitude we feel now for having received such relief and for anticipating that we may receive it again. The psalm foreshadows a subsequent stage of prayer: the God whom we now praise as Creator is the same One whom we will soon petition, as our Redeemer. We will soon complain about the sufferings of the animated soul in this world, and this complaint will be a critical mark of what we might label the pragmatic dimension of Jewish soteriology: which is never to abstract away from and thus override or forget the material/

animate dimension of all prayers of petition. As we will see in the Amidah: prayers for redemption always arise out of prayers for the relief of earthly suffering.

For now, however, it is all praise, and the praise awakens attention to something more than the animated soul. In many of the psalms of this section, the subject is a symphony of such souls—many animated souls, on many levels, as if the object of praise were the entire symphony, or at least various series of relations among souls. 'Shout praise to Hashem, all the earth' (Ps. 100); 'Praise Him all angels... Praise Him sun and moon...Praise Hashem from the earth, sea monsters and ocean depths' (Ps. 148). In this sense, the Verses of Praise awaken attention to *neshamah* as relational soul, or not merely individuated souls. In various ways, however, the subjects of praise are not only animated souls in their relatedness, but also the languages through which such souls come to relationship. These include divine languages of creation ('Blessed be the One who spoke and, behold, the world was, blessed is He') and of instruction ('He declares His word to Jacob'); angelic languages of praise ('Praise Him all His hosts'); and earthly languages of song ('with songs of Your servant David we will praise You'), thanksgiving ('Give thanks to Hashem'), and praise ('praised be your Name'). Through these verses, the worshipper attends to a soul that joins animated souls (*nefashot*) together into such varieties of collection as 'world' (*olam*), 'peoples' (*amim*, but in their plurality not individuality), 'earth' (*arets*), 'heaven' (*shamayim*), 'His hosts' (*ts'va'av*), and the 'broken hearted' (*sh'vore lev*).

These collections of souls are worthy of praise the way every *nefesh* is worthy, but many times over: they display the wonder of divine creativity, but many times over. As hinted in Psalm 30, however, the collections appear to merit praise for another reason as well. Animated souls suffer as well as flourish, and the multiplicity of souls has something, as yet undisclosed, to do with the redemption of suffering souls. This something is anticipated in a series of prayers that concludes the second section of *shacharit* and prepare the way for the third section, the Sh'ma. The series links 1 Chronicles 29: 10–13 to Nehemiah 9: 6–11 to Exodus 14: 30–1 to Exodus 15: 1–18.

David said, Blessed are You, Hashem, God of Israel our Father...
You, alone, are Hashem, who made heaven...You are Hashem God who chose Avram and brought him out of Ur...You made a covenant with

him ... You saw the affliction of our ancestors in Egypt ... and [You] heard
their cry ...
On that day Hashem saved Israel from the hand of the Egyptians ...
Then Moses and the Children of Israel sang this song to Hashem ...

All of a sudden, out of the symphony of souls from Psalms 145–50,
the Verses of Praise turn to the history of a particular, named collection of animated souls, *yisrael*, and the praise is not merely for the
One who formed Israel, but also for the One who redeemed it from its
trials.

So far, we have only hints (in Ps. 30) about the suffering of
animated souls and only hints (in the Verses) about the role that
relational souls may play in repairing this suffering. Now, however,
in this history of Israel, the Verses tell us not only that relational
souls may also suffer, but also how they have previously been
rescued from their suffering. We learn that the collection of souls
that suffers also has a proper name (*yisrael*), that it suffers from the
actions of another named collection (*mitsrayim*), and that Hashem
may act as the suffering collection's Redeemer, to this end enlisting
the aid of individual, named members of the collection (Moses, or
later David). We are, therefore, already in the subject matter of the
third section of *shacharit*, but not yet within its distinctive mode of
practice and presentation.

A THEOLOGY OF REDEMPTION IN PRAYER (3)

The third section is named after its central and defining prayer:
the Sh'ma (Deut. 6: 4–9). This is Israel's call to worship, which
also serves as a call to the soul that joins God in the work of
earthly redemption. The section is introduced, fittingly, by a call
for one specific community of worshippers to come together to
worship.

Barchu et hashem hamevorach. Baruch hashem hamevorach l'olam va-ed.
[The prayer leader's call:] Bless Hashem who is to be blessed.
[The congregation's response:] Bless Hashem who is to be blessed forever and
ever.

The call is a *command*, and, for the first time in the morning service,
the section is marked by imperatives. This is also the first prayer that
is formally led by a prayer-leader, and the first to be prayed only

before a quorum (*minyan*) of at least ten worshippers.[4] The call marks the beginning, in other words, of a cohortative as well as imperative level of prayer and of soulful activity. As consequence and condition of the call, the worshippers constitute a formal body, a congregation (*kahal*). It is as if the *kahal* constituted the people Israel, and the leader were led by Moses. And that, in fact, is the explicit model for the Sh'ma itself:

Sh'ma yisrael hashem elohenu hashem echad. Baruch shem c'vod malkhuto l'olam va'ed.
[Moses' call, recited by all congregants:] Hear, O Israel, Hashem is our God, Hashem alone.
[Israel's response, recited silently by all congregants:] Blessed is the name of His glorious sovereignty, for ever and ever.

The leader calls a specific community of Israel into being as a particular set of relations among a particular collection of animated beings. These beings are called, moreover, to attend to their shared relation to the God who created them, who has made a covenant with them by way of their ancestors, and who instructs them in their conduct as a covenanted people. They are called, furthermore, to respond antiphonically to the call. Following the postulates that guide this chapter, I infer that, as an entire section of prayer, the Sh'ma awakens the worshipper to attend to a dimension of soul for which I can find no better name than *yisrael* itself. In short, this dimension includes both animated soul and relational soul as its ground but includes as well the following characteristics of *yisrael* (as soul) which are essential to any soul that engages in a redemptive relation with the God of Israel:[5]

(1) *yisrael* is a 'people' (*'am*), defined as a collection of relational souls each and every one of which also shares in a single collection-identity *yisrael* (comparable, in set-theory, to a 'class character'),[6] so that:

---

[4] I am overlooking the *kaddish*, chanted at the close of each section only in the presence of a *minyan*.

[5] Christian readers may, at this point, want to ask about the redemptive relation of Israel both to other peoples and to the church. In the Appendix to this chapter, I respond to this question by offering comments on George Lindbeck's theology of the church as Israel.

[6] This description is derived from Charles Peirce's model of a continuous whole. See P. Ochs, 'Continuity as Vagueness: The Mathematical Antecedents of Peirce's semiotics', *Semiotica*, 963–4 (1993), 244; and Charles Sanders Peirce, *Collected Papers*, vi (Cambridge, Mass.: Harvard Press, 1931, 1932, 1958), 174–6; 4.561 n., 4.642, 7.535 n.

(2) all relations among every member of the people *also* shares in the identity *yisrael*, and so that:

(3) each member of *yisrael* may be redescribed as a human being (adam), defined as a collection of its own attributes, each and every attribute of which *also* shares in the individual-identity *yisrael*. Furthermore,

(4) *yisrael* as a people may also be redescribed as a collection of its own attributes, with the features characterized in (3), so that:

(5) these attributes are also collected into subgroups, defined by such dimensions as 'historical identity' (relation to itself in different periods of time), 'political identity' (relation to other such peoples), and 'covenantal identity' (relation to God).

As member of *yisrael*, an individual human being displays both animated soul, relational soul, and *yisrael* itself, as what we may also call a redemptive soul. As we have seen, the animated soul may suffer but cannot, by itself, enter into relations with a redeemer; it cannot be rescued by another. The relational soul brings the animated soul into relations that may potentially serve as instruments of rescue or redemption, but mere collections of relational souls cannot actualize this potential. *Yisrael* brings to a collection of relational souls the capacity to actualize this potential. The Call to Worship and the Sh'ma awaken the worshipper's attention to the source of this capacity: Hashem alone. Hashem is 'to be blessed', because Hashem, alone (*echad*), is the source of Israel's blessings: the source of the character that transforms a collection of human beings into an actual instrument of redemption. In the biblical narratives, covenant ceremonies represent the transformational events through which, at once, a collection of relational souls becomes *yisrael* and *yisrael* enters into covenantal bond with Hashem. The voice of the Sh'ma section is imperative, cohortative, and antiphonic, because this section is no mere narrative of Israel's life, but an activity through which the worshipper actually rejoins or reawakens his or her own membership in Israel's covenant. In this sense, worshipping the Sh'ma section awakens the worshipper's capacity to enter into redemptive relations.

In-between the Call to Worship and the call of the Sh'ma, there is one subsection that remains in the voice of praise and not yet that of covenantal directives. This is a reflection on the order of creation (*maasaeh b'reshit*). Each of the first two sections of *shacharit* offered related reflections on creation, but with the following differences. In Morning Blessings, creation appeared only as the animation of a single creature. In Verses of Praise, creation appeared as a symphony of such creatures, brought in relations through various kinds of language. In the present section, however, creation appears as a *seder*, a specific ordering that, as we will see, provides a setting for the ordering of relational souls into peoplehood and, thus, into instruments of redemptive activity.

Blessed are You...who forms light and creates darkness...
Who mercifully gives light to the earth and to those who dwell on it. And who, in his goodness, daily renews (*m'chadesh*) the order of creation (*maaseh b'reshit*).

This time, reflective attention to creation is not merely hortatory, but also analytic. The worshipper is brought not only to praise creation but also to understand how it works: how God does it, and, that, we will see, also suggests how we might participate in the process ourselves!

Blessed God, great in knowledge, designed and activated the sun's rays...He placed lights around His throne...He fashions ministering angels...

These accounts bring us inside an aspect of God's creative process: disclosing details that are wondrous to behold, but even more wondrous to study, should we, in any sense, come to imitate or share in God's actions. We should not overlook the fact that, consonant with its pragmatism, rabbinic Judaism also makes room for what we call scientific activity. The prime example in medieval Judaism was medicine: along with prayers for healing, rabbinic Judaism urged the pursuit of all legitimate means of knowledge that enable us to assist God in the task of healing. But by what means could we engage actively in the Redeemer's work, rather than limit our responsibilities to those of patients, who wait?

With a great love have You loved us, Hashem our God.... For the sake of our ancestors who trusted in You and You taught them the laws of life, be gracious to us as well and teach us.

Our prayer, it appears, is not merely for rescue, but also for instruction, that we, too, may learn the laws of life:

Our father, merciful father..., have compassion on us and strengthen our hearts to understand and to discern, to listen, to learn, and to teach, to observe, to enact and gladly fulfil all the teachings of your Torah.

To engage actively in your work, we seek to understand and enact your teaching. This is neither piety alone, nor science alone, but piety and science: knowledge and imitation of what God does as creator of the world and of what God commands as revealer of Torah. For this task, 'Blessed are You, Hashem, who chooses His people Israel with love.' *Yisrael* is covenanted so that it will understand, discern, listen, learn, teach, observe, enact, and gladly fulfil the example of God the Creator and the instructions of God the Revealer.

And what of the promises of God the Redeemer? The verses that follow the Sh'ma awaken the worshipper to share in the lessons of God the Creator ('If you . . . love Hashem your God . . . , I will give rain for your land at the right season'), to follow the teachings of God the Revealer ('tell Israel . . . to make fringes on the corners of their garments . . . , so that when you look upon [them] you will remember to do all the commands of Hashem'), and to trust in the faithfulness of God the Redeemer (who 'was always our ancestors' help' and 'redeemed us . . . from the house of bondage'). It is not yet clear, however, to what extent Israel may or may not draw on the lessons of creation and the teachings of revelation to share in God's work of redemption. The Sh'ma section ends with the most vivid portrayal of Israel as one who merited and received God's saving work and who waits for such salvation, again, in the future. Were the morning service to end with this portrayal, then the telos of *shacharit* as a whole would be to unite the animated—and relational—soul in Israel as one who merits, prays for, and awaits yet another redemption.

You were always the help of our ancestors, a shield for them and for their children, our deliverer in every generation . . . You are the first and You are the last. We have no Ruler, Redeemer, or Saviour but You. You rescued us (*gealtanu*) from Egypt; You redeemed us (*p'ditanu*) from the house of bondage. The firstborn of the Egyptians were slain; Your firstborn were saved. You split the waters of the sea. The faithful you rescued; the wicked drowned. . . . Then Your beloved sang hymns of acclamation, extolling You with psalms of adoration . . .

Who is like You, Lord, among all that is worshipped? . . .

The redeemed (*geulim*) sang a new song for You. . . . 'The Lord shall reign throughout all time.' Rock of Israel, rise to Israel's defence. Fulfil Your promise to deliver (*fede*) Judah and Israel. Our Redeemer (*goalenu*) is the Holy One of Israel, *hashem tseva'ot* is His Name. Blessed are You, Hashem, Redeemer (*ga'al*) of Israel.

A THEOLOGY OF REDEMPTION IN PRAYER (4)

Of the sections of morning prayer, the Amidah is at once the most clearly petitionary—the most personal and embodied (as the most animate, the most relational)—and yet, at the same time, the most removed from the concrete particularity and selfhood of the petitioner. In the latter sense, the Amidah is the place of holiness (*kedushah*) in the Morning Service: the place of most intimate relation to God as holy other. In the former sense, the Amidah is the place of concrete yearning. This paradox marks the Amidah, within the service, as the most likely context for possible union with the divine: not a union that obliterates the worshipper's identities (as animated and relational soul, and as Israel), but one that marries them to *ruach* as the indwelling presence of the divine. The conditions for such 'marriage' are set through the Amidah's sequence of nineteen (originally eighteen) blessings, traditionally subordered into three groups: (A) blessings of praise (1–3), (B) blessings of petition (4–16), and (C) blessings of thanksgiving (17–19). Within the space of this chapter, I will focus on the three blessings of (A) and brief overviews of the sequence of blessings in (B).

BLESSINGS OF PRAISE

Just after extolling the 'Rock of Israel' for redeeming Israel from bondage, the worshipper faces the direction of Jerusalem, takes three steps backwards (receding before the presence of the 'holy King') and three steps forward (addressing the King), bows, and requests, 'My Lord, open my lips, and let my mouth declare Your praise'. Then, the first blessing begins:

Blessed are You, Hashem our God and God of our ancestors, God of Abraham, God of Isaac, and God of Jacob,[7] great, mighty, awesome, exalted God, who bestows loving kindness, O Creator of all, who remembers the kind deeds of our ancestors and, lovingly, brings a Redeemer to their children's children for the sake of His Name.... Blessed are You, Hashem, Protector of Abraham.

---

[7] Today, many non-Orthodox congregations add 'God of Sarah, God of Rebecca, God of Rachel, and God of Leah'.

Traditionally labelled *avot*, 'Ancestors' (or 'Patriarchs'), the first blessing invokes the rabbinic doctrine of *zekhut 'avot*, 'Merits of the Ancestors': appealing to God to care for us (the worshipper's people Israel) in memory of the 'patriarchs' (or also, in liberal versions, 'matriarchs') fidelity to Him. Jewish theologians debate the degree to which the blessing appeals to Abraham's covenant for its own sake, renewed in each generation, or to Israel's variable achievements (meriting divine mercy, measure for measure). Either way, one context is clear: one cannot petition God by oneself, but only as member of a trans-generational people who has known God and been known by God for generations. In this sense, the *avot* blessing completes the awakening of souls that began in the second section of the morning service. The foundation of petition is the individual, animated soul, but the soul that hears prayers answered—and thus shares in redemption—shares in the relationality that was praised in psalms and commanded in the Sh'ma. In the Sh'ma, this is the relationality that draws all the individuals of Israel into the people Israel and the people Israel into covenant with the God who redeems them from bondage in Egypt. As the Amidah continues, we may witness the awakening of attention to that covenant itself as another dimension of soul.

The second Blessing of Praise is traditionally labelled *g'vurot*, 'God's Power':

You are forever mighty, Hashem; giving life to the dead, You are a mighty saviour (*rav l'hoshiah*). You sustain life with loving kindness, give life to the dead with abundant mercy, support the fallen, heal the sick, free the captives, and keep faith with those who sleep in the dust.... Who is like You?... Blessed are you, Hashem, who gives life to the dead.

The God who would redeem the worshipping community is mighty beyond all comparison, not only creating life, but also mighty enough to restore life to those who have lost it. There is thus nothing worthy of life for which we may not pray. This, I fear, is not merely a hopeful thought, but also a terrifying one: to think that we have intimate, covenantal relation with a power that can undo the very order He has put into this creation, that creatures live and die! While the Amidah completes the prayers of Israel, it also draws the worshipper into the precincts of a *mysterium tremendum* that appears to open levels of relationality and of ensoulment that exceed those we have encountered thus far. I cannot imagine, therefore, that the worshipper belongs only to Israel at this moment. The worshipper's participation in Israel is by no means superseded—the Amidah's Blessings of Petition speak within the terms of Israel's earthly life—but the third Blessing of Praise appears to draw the life of Israel into relation with something still greater. Following my postulate—that subsequent levels of ensoulment are cumulative—any subsequent awakening must also be animated, relational, and communally corporate (or of the 'form of Israel'). We cannot, therefore, be speaking of some 'universal soul', meaning what late modernists dub a 'species consciousness' that lacks any corporate communality and, thus, any encompassing animated life. It may be helpful at this point to reintroduce the term 'person' to refer to the kind of animation that also includes within itself the relationality I attributed to *neshamah* and the communality I attribute to *yisrael*. If so, any ensoulment that is awakened beyond the consciousness of Israel (if I can still use the term 'soul' at this level) should retain a personhood that is wanting in any of the modern notions of either species consciousness or universal humanity. It should refer to a person or personhood that is also present, or embodied, in Israel, but that could be embodied in other corporate souls as well: if, that is, we use the term 'Israel' as token of the type *Israel*. If, however, we use the term 'Israel' to refer to the form, then there is reason to apply the name 'Israel' to this person as well. If only for the sake of terminological clarity, we might want to avoid the latter option.

There are at least two sources in Judaism for alternative names for this person/personhood. Philo provides the name 'Logos', as both the divine self-image and the embodiment of that image as what we might relabel 'Divine Intelligence in the world'. Early Jewish mysticism—influenced at once by Zoroastrian sources, second Temple period commentaries on Ezekiel, and, later, by Neoplatonic sources—applies to God's self-imaging such names as *adam ha-kadmon* (The Primordial Adam), *metatron*, and *michael* (as Archangel). There is no space here to delve with any depth into the details of the early kabbalah. For our purposes, it will suffice to note that the Jewish tradition already offers precedents for personifying a dimension of ensoulment that is neither limited to, nor supersedes, the name Israel. This suggests that the logic we use to discuss these matters cannot be one that is limited to the law of excluded middle. In medieval discourse, we are in the realm of the *analogia fidei*. The philosopher John Deely argues that the medieval logic of analogic reasoning is best articulated in the semiotic of John Poinsot (John of St Thomas).[8] I argue elsewhere that the semiotic of Charles Peirce provides both Poinsot's and Augustine's semiotic a non-propositional logic appropriate to contemporary discourse.[9] I call this 'the logic of redemption' (appropriate to our theme, indeed, but too detailed to spell out in this chapter). However defined, this logic enables us to describe the activities of a dimension of soul (still using that word for now, despite its limitations) that presents itself in different ways in different tokens and on what we might call different dimensions of awakening. Depending on one's domain of inquiry, these dimensions can be depicted as dimensions of ensoulment, of consciousness, or of prayer. Returning to the discourse of morning prayer, we may depict each dimension of ensoulment as a dimension of the subsequent level: referring to *nefesh*, *neshamah*, and Israel as dimensions of a fourth soul that, to avoid the need for explanatory detail, I will simply label, 'Divine-image', imagining that on each of its dimensions, the Divine-image appears in many different tokens.

For the worshipper who, having recited the Sh'ma, now takes three steps back, three forward, bows, and begins to pray the Amidah, the One he or she called Redeemer (*goel*), may now also be called Divine-image. The third Blessing of Praise in the Amidah is traditionally called *kedushah*, or Holiness. When recited communally, this blessing re-enacts, antiphonically, Isaiah's vision of the celestial doxology:

We sanctify your name in this world as it is sanctified in the heavens above, as it is written by your prophet:
And [each angel] will call to the other, saying:
Holy, Holy, Holy is Hashem of hosts, the whole world is filled with his glory
. . . Blessed is the glory of Hashem from His place
. . . Hashem shall rule forever, your God, oh Zion, from generation to generation, Hallelujah!

The worshipper enters the *mysterium tremendum*, the holy of holies. Holiness, *kedushah*, is a 'place' of utter alterity and separateness that should defy the kinds of categorizations I am attempting in this

---

[8] See John Deely, *New Beginnings, Early Modern Philosophy and Postmodern Thought* (Toronto: University of Toronto Press, 1994), *passim*.

[9] P. Ochs, *Peirce, Pragmatism and the Logic of Scripture* (Cambridge: Cambridge University Press, 1998), 233–5, 311–13; and a forthcoming essay.

chapter. This should be one lesson of Moses' encounter in Exodus 3. 'What shall I say Your Name is?' Moses asks the Holy One. The Holy One, we might say, should not answer, but He does. In this sense, honouring the tradition of Nachmanides (the medieval commentator Moses ben Nachman), our approach leads us to suggest that the names God offers, from *eyeh* to *yhvh*, are neither clearly disclosed names (essential identities) nor efforts to refrain from naming. To think, after all, in the terms God can/God cannot be named is to invoke the very law of the excluded middle whose logic is confounded by this dimension of encounter with the Divine-image. Our approach, therefore, keeps us from both sides of Maimonidean essentialism (which illustrates the consequences of interpreting Exodus 3 within the terms of a propositional logic). On one side, Maimonides identifies the name, *eyeh asher eyeh*, with the self-disclosure of the One whose existence is implied by his essence (substance). On the other side, Maimonides also argues for apophasis. Nachmanides' alternative, disregarding the law of excluded middle, is to suggest that the divine names disclose particular relations between *Hashem* and the One who prays to *Hashem* in this time in this context: 'Am I not named according to My acts? . . . I say to you, Israel, who cries in bondage, I am the one who will be with you where I will be with you; I will be with you in your suffering.' Similarly, the worshipper who utters the *kedushah* stands within the precinct of the One who redeemed Israel, repairs all wounds, and restores even the dead to life. The worshipper stands now within the Divine-image itself, which has no image, yet this is its image: this moment in which the angels declare, 'Holy, Holy, Holy is *Hashem*'. To stand in the presence of the Redeemer, and thus to stand in that present-absence we call the Holy One, is to stand in the Divine-image as *kevod Hashem*, the glory of the One who cannot be named but is named in Exodus 3. This, we may say, is the height and depth of the Rabbinic Morning Prayer Service. There is reason to say that this is the worshipper's moment of redemption, and it is available every morning, in fact, three times a day, in the thrice daily repetition of the Amidah. In this sense, it is not that there is final redemption here, in this world, before the endtime, but that this is the endtime, or what we may call a 'meantime endtime'. To stand in presence of the Holy One is to stand in the Redeemer's endtime, which is our participation, now, in the world to come (*olam haba*), in the Divine Presence (*shekhinah*), the eternal Shabbat, the Garden of Eden.

There is, however, also reason to say that the one who worships the *kedushah* is not in the endtime, but is here, in this world (*olam hazeh*). This is the world in which our prayers are ultimately tears, like the tears of Israel in bondage, in which we are surrounded, even while standing in the Divine Presence, by a world of suffering, yearning for the Redeemer. These prayers occupy a space that is both of this world and of the world to come; there is no contradiction here, simply a logic that is irreducible to the law of excluded middle. Were that not the case, either we would have no reason to pray, or no capacity nor hope to do so. There are therefore prayers to offer after the *kedushah* and after the Blessings of Praise. For the worshipper, it is on one level like stepping out of the Garden of Eden, except that this time the Divine Presence embraces one's shoulders, like the *tallit* or white prayer shawl. It is life in the veil of tears but in the immediate company of the Redeemer. The step between the third blessing and the fourth, the first of the Blessings of Petition, does not come as a Fall, or a moment of defeat. Like the end of the Sabbath, Saturday night, the beginning of the first day of the week, the first Blessing of Petition comes as the beginning of divine service in this world.

We call the second section of the Amidah the 'Blessings of Petition', but, having passed into the presence of the Divine-image, the worshipper is now an agent of redemption, rather than a subject of petition. In Platonic terms, the worshipper has gone back into the cave, but surrounded with light. In the terms of Exodus, we are no longer on the way to the Mountain, but on the way from it: burdened not with a sense of our own suffering, but with the weight of Torah, or the Word (*hadibbur*, the divine 'spoken-word'). This Word may be seen, furthermore, as a person. The Divine-image that Israel encountered as the face of its Redeemer is now the hand on Israel's shoulder, and Israel is now agent of *tikkun olam*, or repair of the world in service to the Divine Name who is the Divine Word.

The first Blessing of Petition displays Israel's new agency. 'You graciously endow humanity with knowledge ... blessed are You, *Hashem*, gracious giver of knowledge.' Knowledge, *da'at*, is intimate knowledge, as in intercourse: not knowledge as possession or identification, but as intimate relation with, as when we say, 'I know you well'. As agent of the work of redemption, the worshipper reasons with the Divine Word. This surprising implication of the order of blessings offers us a glimpse into tropes that dominate the kabbalistic literature: worship is not merely Israel's petition to God, but also her being dressed, within worship, with the divine presence. The morning service, from its first blessings through the *kedushah*, is a channel to the worshipper's participation in the work of redemption. The thirteen Blessings of Petition may be read, from outside the experiential context of worship, as an ordered series of requests to grant Israel answers to all her petitions (from blessing 4–16):

(4) seeking intimate knowledge of God: holy knowledge (*da'at*) as being-with the Redeemer;

(5) seeking repentance, to be drawn back to Torah and divine service (*avodah*);

(6) seeking forgiveness (*s'lichah*);

(7) seeking redemption from affliction (*geulah*);

(8) seeking healing from all wounds (*refuah*);

(9) seeking blessings for the land ('of the year or season', *shanim*): conditions for agricultural productivity;

(10) seeking the ingathering of Israel from exile (*kibbutz galuyot*): the restoration of community;

(11) seeking justice (*mishpat*), through the restoration of a system of justice;

(12) seeking relief from enemies (*malshinim*, slanderers or informants) inside and outside the community;

(13) seeking righteousness and piety, through the restoration of pious and righteous leaders (*chasidim, tsadikim*);

(14) seeking the restoration of divine presence to Jerusalem (*yerushalayim*);

(15) seeking the messiah and the coming of salvation (*yeshuah*);

(16) asking God to hear this prayer (*tefillah*).

The blessings may also be read, however, from within the practice of worship, as that unfolding of holiness through which Israel will work in the world as agent of such answers. From this perspective, the worshipper with the divine presence (identifying the worshipper here with worshipping Israel) is to be agent of Torah and divine service, of forgiveness, of redemption from affliction, of healing, of care for the land, of the community's (Israel's) ingathering, of justice, of protection from enemies, of righteousness and piety, of the restoration of Jerusalem as place of God, of bringing the messiah.

Among contemporary practitioners of the kabbalah, the Chasidic communities bear the strongest tradition of turning to prayer and acts of charity and loving kindness as means of sharing, directly, in the Redeemer's work in this world. In Abraham Heschel's words, God is also in search of us, and that also means in search of our assistance. Modern Jews, including modern Orthodox Jews, are often wary of such tropes, claims, and beliefs. In a previous time after Destruction (the *chorban, or* Destruction of the Second Temple), the sages of the Mishnah declared a time to 'do for God' (*et la-asot lashem*). This was a time, given the exigencies of the moment, to take on responsibilities, or pursue levels of knowledge, previously open only to others. Living in another time after destruction, religious Jews may need, once again, to do for the redeeming God, indeed to be with the redeeming God, in ways they may not previously have envisioned.

APPENDIX: THE CHURCH AS ISRAEL?

According to the approach of this chapter, the third section of *shacharit*, the Sh'ma, awakens the worshipper to *yisrael* as what I have termed a redemptive soul. In these terms, Israel illustrates the form through which the animated—and relational—souls enter into redemptive relations with the God of Israel. I have not yet asked what this reading would imply about the relation of Israel to other redemptive souls, or what I have named 'peoples'. Within a collection devoted primarily to Christian theologies of redemption, this question should lead us to ask, as well, what relation *yisrael* would have to the church as redemptive soul.

In rabbinic tradition, the Tower of Babel story is read as evidence that there are a plurality, in fact precisely seventy, natural languages in the world, so that whenever God speaks one word, it is heard in seventy ways, one way for each linguistic/relational order, which means one way for each people, and each way articulates a way of redemption. This cannot be emphasized more; for a dominant strain in Rabbinic Judaism, the Tower of Babel story indicates the fact that, after Adam left the Garden, and in the face of the reality of human violence, there must be a plurality of languages to receive the divine word. Since, after Noah, that divine word becomes the exclusive source of humanity's redemption, *this plurality of languages and thus peoples is the irreducible instrument of redemption*. In this world, before the final endtime, it is an act of idolatry for humans to seek to reduce these seventy languages to one: such efforts are what we would now call totalitarian. Does this mean, however, that the people Israel are the sole instrument of worldly redemption?

There are two ways to respond to this question. From one perspective, the earthly Israel is none other than the earthly Israel, what later acquired the name 'The Jewish People', and it is only one of seventy instruments of worldly redemption. The people Israel know themselves only by way of a divine word addressed to them. This word indicates that they should serve as a 'light to the nations', which means that way they behave should be instructive to others, as a light or teaching of a relationship between God and humanity. But, as the prophets made clear, from Amos on, each nation must concretize the path of redemption in a way that is specific to its relation to God's revealing and redeeming speech. From this perspective, the people Israel must be ignorant of the particular paths of redemption to be fulfilled by sixty-nine other peoples.

From another perspective, God's relation to Israel represents a figure or type or form of worldly redemption, and the term 'light' in 'light to the nations' refers to form, figure, or type. The critical point—in many ways the defining point for Western religious history—is to understand appropriately what it means for Israel to represent this form, figure, or type. Of many options, I will take time here to comment on two that should be appropriate and one that is not.

George Lindbeck's current project of reinstating the Christian trope of 'The Church as Israel', represents one appropriate path.[10] In his terms the two inappropriate paths for the church are either to deny that the church is Israel or to affirm it in a supersessionist way. I will comment here only on the latter. For the church to claim that it, alone, realizes the form Israel—it and not the Jewish people—is in most cases a simple category error. A form is a form, so that the form 'Israel' must be general with respect to any concrete instance or token of it. If the 'Church as Israel' means the earthly institutions of the church fulfil the form 'Israel', then the form 'Israel' remains a form that could still, at the same time, be fulfilled by other tokens as well, and it is a category error to speak of one token as excluding others. Of course, this would be a category error according to the rabbinic reading of the Tower of Babel. If, however, 'the Church as Israel' means that the church as form is synonymous with 'Israel as form' then the supersessionist reading represents either an effort to disregard one of the attributes of form or simply a contestation of the biblical record of Israel. In the former case, it is the effort to retain both the generality of form (the distribution of any form or type over an indefinite class of tokens) but at the same time the determinacy of a single token. In these terms, the supersessionist claim is logically confusing. If,

---

[10] See George A. Lindbeck, *The Church in a Postliberal Age*, ed. J. Buckley (London: SCM Press, 2002); George Lindbeck, 'Postmodern Hermeneutics and Jewish–Christian Dialogue: A Case Study', and 'What of the Future? A Christian Response', in T. Frymer-Kensky, D. Novak, P. Ochs, D. F. Sandmel, and M. A. Signer (eds.), *Christianity in Jewish Terms* (Boulder, Colo.: Westview Press, 2000), 106–13, 357–66.

however, the supersessionist claim simply contests the record of Israel, then we end up with either one of two conundrums. On the one hand, a super-sessionist church may both affirm and deny the meaning of Israel as form: as if to say, 'yes, we are Israel but no, the form Israel is not what the form Israel appears to be'. In this case, the rabbinic thinker is simply puzzled about why the church would need to claim Israel rather than simply abandon it. On the other hand, a supersessionist church may represent something about which rabbinic Judaism will have much less to say: a claim that the creator/revealer/redeemer God has himself refined the form 'Israel'. On this reading, the generality of form has in fact been married to the singularity of a single token, and this marriage is the incarnation. In Christ, therefore, historical time has been fulfilled, and the form 'Israel' has assumed a token that is itself the final token of the redemptive form of all seventy peoples through whom God redeems the world. This is, indeed, a conundrum since the claim entails no logical error but only the claim that God has altered the rules of logic in this case. Since this case would represent the end of time, there is no logical error in claiming that the end of time would display the means through which the form of divine redemption is realized in its tokens.

The force of Lindbeck's argument against supersessionism would have to be consequentialist or pragmatic rather than 'logical', in the way I have used logic in the previous paragraph. The objection to supersessionism must be any or all of the following. One objection is that the history of Jewish/Christian relations culminating in the Shoah demonstrates that superses-sionism kills and, thus, that its consequence in this life of the world of tokens subverts the form of the life of Israel (both Israel as Israel per se and as Christ). In this way, supersessionism represents a material if not a merely 'logical' contradiction. Another objection is that supersessionism cannot provide an adequate account of this time between the times, or the historical space between Christ's first and second coming. If the church fulfils and thus refines the form of Israel in the incarnation, then this refined form must still be distinguished from its tokens (the behaviour of all seventy nations) in the period between the first and second comings. If so, the form Israel/church or Israel/Christ re-enacts the logic of Israel as a form separable from its tokens. A supersessionist church would both replay and subvert the same logic.

I cannot say more on this issue, since it is a matter for intra-Christian theological reflection on the meaning of 'Israel' as instrument of redemption. Within the frame of rabbinic Judaism, I need only reiterate the obvious: that the Jewish people in this day must regard a supersessionist church as an obstacle to redemption. As for the church that simply separates itself from Israel, removing its identification with the form Israel, then this move may or may not represent an obstacle to redemption. If it simply means that the church is 'another religion', then the move is simply puzzling. Shall we suggest that the church is a religion of the Septuagint, for example, with no soteriological relation to the church as reader of Tanakh? The difference would be innocuous, unless the church were to make claims, nonetheless, about Israel. In this case, such an 'other' religion would become an obstacle again to redemption. The obverse is then most interesting theologically. If the alternatives to identifying the church as Israel are either explicitly or potentially troubling, we are left with the surprising conclusion that, for rabbinic Judaism after the Shoah, non-supersessionist identifications of the church with Israel may serve the redemption history of the Jewish people. (Or at the very least, may serve that history better than any other option for the church.)

Patristic and Medieval Periods

7

'He Himself is Our Peace' (Ephesians 2: 14): Early Christian Views of Redemption in Christ

BRIAN DALEY, SJ

A year or so ago, I had the opportunity to deliver a series of lectures in Oxford on the christology of the Fathers. While I was there, I had a number of conversations on the subject with an old friend who is also a theologian and a Patristic scholar, and at one point he raised a question that he said he had long been unable to answer in a satisfactory way for himself: granted that God desires to save humanity from its own self-destructive course of sin and alienation, granted that God wishes to intervene in history and to reconcile his creatures with himself through some kind of revelation and atonement, why must we think that he did this through an incarnate Son? Why does it not make just as much sense to think of God redeeming the world through a delegate, an appointed mediator or broker of reconciliation, who is himself a creature? Why, in other words, does Christian soteriology—as has often been argued—require a Nicene or even an Athanasian, rather than an Arian understanding of the saviour?

Put in such a direct form, the question left me, too, struggling for a satisfactory answer. The classic position of the Christian West, of course—which Anselm's brilliantly conceived explanation in *Cur Deus Homo?* develops—is that the work of atonement had to be a human work, if it was to satisfy for human debt, yet a work of such infinite value that only God could be its agent. Anselm's conversation partner, the monk Boso, summarizes the archbishop's position neatly towards the end of book 2:

You...have shown that it was not right that the restoration of human nature should be left undone, and that it could not have been brought about unless man repaid what he owed to God. This debt was so large that, although no one but man owed it, only God was capable of repaying it, assuming that there should be a man identical with God. Hence it was a necessity that God should take man into the unity of his person, so that one who ought, by virtue of his nature, to make the repayment and was not capable of doing so, should be one who, by virtue of his person, was capable of it.[1]

So the incarnation, in Anselm's view, is reasonable—indeed, logically necessary, if God is to reclaim his lost human creatures—as the condition of possibility for an effective act of redemption, conceived as the settling of humanity's ancient and inconceivably enormous debt to its offended creator. As an act of sheer freedom and grace on God's part, it is also the ultimate revelation of God's love for humanity, so that 'a greater and juster mercy cannot be imagined'.[2]

Ingenious and well-crafted as Anselm's argument for the incarnation as the necessary basis for human redemption is, it continues to raise questions for critically minded Christians. One might ask, for instance, whether the repayment of debt is the only or even the best way of conceiving humanity's situation of need and alienation before God, or whether Anselm's understanding of sin as a violation of God's infinite honour gets to the real root of human wickedness for the thinking of a more egalitarian culture such as ours. More importantly, perhaps, Anselm's argument seems to beg the question my Oxford friend raised. Granting that the final intellectual explanation (if there can be such!) of Christianity's understanding of Christ must be soteriological—that what we say of his person must be rooted in what we understand to be his role in the whole history of God's healing and life-giving involvement in human history, God's unceasing effort to form and reform for himself a holy people—why should it be impossible that the agent of this divine work of redemption should be a created delegate, rather than God assuming 'the form of a servant' and becoming human? Why must the Saviour 'pay the debt', carry out the work, simply 'from his own resources' as a human being, or be himself the offended divine Master to whom the debt is due? In a soteriology resting on the conception of redemption as a restorative transaction between God and humanity, provided the initiative for the transaction comes from God and God is its

---

[1] Anselm of Canterbury, *Why God Became Man*, 2. 18 (trans. Janet Fairweather), in *Anselm of Canterbury: The Major Works*, ed. Brian Davies and G. R. Evans (Oxford and New York: Oxford University Press, 1998), 348.

[2] Ibid. 2. 20 (354).

recipient, why does the agent of the transaction need to be God's incarnate Son?

My task here is not to reflect on Anselm's understanding of redemption and its implications for the person of Christ, or on the later tradition of Western soteriology, which has remained largely dominated by Anselm's focus on what Christ did to set things right between humanity and God. My task is instead to reflect, in broad and synthetic strokes, on the understanding or understandings of redemption that characterized the early centuries of Christian theology: how was soteriology first articulated by Christian writers, and how were the questions about God's intervention to restore us to friendship with himself first framed by those whom we call the Fathers of the church? But I hope not simply to fulfil a task; my thesis here is that an answer to my friend's question can really best be found not in a post-Anselmian soteriology, whatever its form, that is essentially focused on the *work* of Christ to save us, but rather in the most widespread Patristic approach to soteriology, which seems to me essentially focused on the *person* of Christ, as being in itself the realization of salvation. The soteriology of the early church, I want to argue, most commonly understands redemption or salvation as being *achieved in Jesus' identity* rather than *accomplished as his work*; whereas Western soteriology since Anselm typically takes redemption as something Jesus has done for us by his *actions*, above all by his death in innocence on the cross, and usually goes on to argue that this saving action requires he be both divine and human at once. Patristic soteriology, both Eastern and Western, tends to see redemption as already achieved in that personal *union* of God and a man—a union beginning in Jesus, uniquely rooted in him, but ultimately involving every human being willing to accept this new identity of human divinity or divinized humanity as their own future. Let me attempt to sketch out this soteriology of union a bit more fully.

I IMAGES OF SALVATION

(i) Biblical Images

Perhaps the central message of Christian preaching is that the life, death, and resurrection of Jesus of Nazareth is the key to our own ultimate welfare, if we are ready to accept the church's proclamation about him in faith and to let it change our lives. Just how Jesus' being and actions do affect us in this decisively beneficial way, however, defies simple expression, let alone adequate explanation. Christians are forced to speak of it in images, most of them drawn either from everyday life in the ancient world or from the cultic and legal language of ancient Israel.[3] Perhaps the most general of these, in the writings of the NT, is the word 'salvation' (*sōtēria*) itself, which carries meanings of 'welfare' and 'safety' as well as bodily health. In the NT, it is used to refer to the eschatological fulfilment of Israel's hope (e.g. Rom. 13: 11; John 4: 22), to a cure (e.g. Luke 6: 9; 8: 48, 50) or an exorcism (e.g. Luke 8: 36)—particularly in the vocabulary of Luke—and to Paul's release from imprisonment and prosecution (Phil. 1: 19), as well as to the present stamina and confidence in the midst of trouble of those who believe in Christ (2 Cor. 6: 2; 1 Pet. 1: 9). Another familiar term is that of 'redemption' (*apolytrōsis*), which rests on the image of 'buying back' a slave or a prisoner from servitude (see Lev. 25: 48–9); in the NT, this image is used in a number of passages for the liberating effect on us—liberating, presumably, from the domination of sin—of Christ's offering of himself on the cross (Rom. 3. 24; 1 Cor. 1: 30; Eph. 1: 7; Col. 1: 14; Heb. 9: 12). Paul occasionally speaks of the transformation worked by faith and baptism in his readers as God's 'liberating' them (*eleutheroun*) from slavery to the power of sin (Rom. 6: 18, 8: 2) or to the observance of all the details of the Law (Gal. 5: 1; cf. 4: 21–6), while John presents Jesus as promising that 'the Truth' revealed by Jesus will set believers free from servitude to sin (John 8: 32–6). Closely connected with 'redemption' in some of these passages is 'the forgiveness of sins' (*aphesis tōn hamartiōn*) (Eph. 1: 7; Col. 1: 14; cf. Rom. 3: 25), which the Gospels present as a central aspect of the Kingdom of God proclaimed by Jesus (e.g. Mark 2: 5, 10) and Acts identifies as the first effect of the gift of the Holy Spirit to those who believe in the risen Lord (Acts 2: 38). 'Redemption' is also associated in some passages (Rom. 3: 24–5; Eph. 1: 7; Col. 1: 14; cf. 1 Cor. 6: 20) with the 'price' of the blood of

---

[3] For comprehensive surveys of the language of soteriology in the NT, see Hastings Rashdall, *The Idea of Atonement in Christian Theology* (London: Macmillan, 1919), 3–189; C. Ryder Smith, *The Bible Doctrine of Salvation* (London: Epworth Press, 1941); Brian E. Daley, 'Soteriologie in der Bibel', in L. Scheffczyk, A. Grillmeier, and M. Seybold (eds.), *Handbuch der Dogmengeschichte*, iii/2a (Freiburg: Herder, 1978), 1–54; E. Schillebeeckx, *Christ: The Experience of Jesus as Lord* (New York: Seabury, 1980), 468–511.

Christ, shed as part of an expiatory or cleansing sacrifice modelled on those of Jewish worship (see Lev. 6: 17–23; Lev. 16); in Rom. 3: 25, Jesus the redeemer is spoken of as one 'whom God put forward as an expiation (*hilastērion*) by his blood', suggesting the view of Jesus' death as cleansing sacrifice which is developed at greater length in Hebrews (e.g. 9: 11–14; see 1 John 2: 2: *hilasmos*). Closely connected with the expiatory shedding of Jesus' blood is also the notion of 'sanctification' (*hagiasmos*), which in the Hebrew Bible signifies the identification of something or someone with God through an act of ritual purification (e.g. Lev. 21: 8; Jos. 3: 5); in a number of NT passages, Jesus' offering of himself in sacrifice is seen as 'sanctifying' the community of believers (John 17: 17; Eph. 5: 26; Heb. 10: 10; cf. 1 Thess. 4: 3). Other NT texts speak of the effect of Jesus' life and death on the believer in more social or legal categories: as working the 'reconciliation' (*katallagē*) of an alienated humanity, even of all creation, with God (e.g. Rom. 5: 10–11; 11: 15; 2 Cor. 5: 18–19; Col. 1:20, 22), or as 'acquitting' or 'justifying' (*dikaioun*, etc.)—that is, declaring 'just' or innocent—those previously convicted of sin by God's tribunal (Rom. 3: 24–6; 5: 6–9, 16, 18–21).[4] All these images, and others one might possibly name, are attempts to express the conviction of the earliest Christians that Jesus' work of healing and exorcism, which accompanied his proclamation of the coming Kingdom of God, continued to be felt powerfully in the transformed lives of those who accepted the news of his resurrection from the dead and received the gift of the Holy Spirit, and that in the light of that gospel and the power of that Spirit even his death could be seen as the unsurpassable source of freedom and life, and as the basis of a new relationship with God for all humanity.

(ii) Patristic Images

The Church Fathers drew constantly, of course, on this wealth of NT images for their own attempts to describe the effect of Jesus' life and death on what they regarded as the transformed life of the Christian community. No single image or category seems to have

---

[4] To 'justify' the guilty was seen as 'an abomination to the Lord' by Proverbs 17: 15. Much of the shock-value of Paul's presentation, in Romans, of the effect of Jesus' 'act of righteousness' and obedience, as shown on the cross, rests on the fact that it leads to the acquittal or 'justification' of the guilty.

been dominant in their thought; rather, the same abundance of soteriological metaphor can be found, even within single works and single passages, that is found in the NT—sometimes in rather bewildering juxtaposition. Without attempting to be exhaustive, and without suggesting that there are any discernible historical trends in the use or predominance of these categories, let me briefly describe some of the ways in which the Fathers use and subtly transform these biblical themes, in speaking of the saving action of Christ.[5]

1. Communication imagery: revelation and the image of God   For many Patristic authors, the most basic way in which Jesus gives new life and freedom to the human race is by revealing in human terms the transcendent reality of God, who is the undying source of life. This approach to understanding salvation is clear, for instance, in Irenaeus' great treatise *Against the Heresies*, composed at the end of the second century. Unlike the Valentinian teachers he is criticizing, who promised release from enslavement to the oppressive forces of human materiality and human institutions through esoteric revisionist narratives of the origin of things, Irenaeus insists that God's 'express will' is that humans should know him, even though this requires God's own intervention in the form of self-revelation in creation.[6] Although God's Word reveals the Father to us in creation,[7] it is above all in the Word's incarnation that the Father is revealed: 'for the Father is the invisible of the Son, but the Son is the visible of the Father. And for that reason everyone called him "the Christ" while he was present [on earth], and named him "God".'[8] The saving importance of this revelation, for Irenaeus, is that the ultimate

---

[5] For other synthetic treatments of the images and categories Patristic soteriology, see Rashdall, *Idea of Atonement*, 189–350; Gustaf Aulén, *Christus Victor* (London: SPCK, 1965), 16–60; H. E. W. Turner, *The Patristic Doctrine of Redemption* (London: Mowbray, 1952); Basil Studer, 'Die Soteriologie der Väter', *Handbuch der Dogmengeschichte*, iii/2a, 55–225; Basil Studer, *Trinity and Incarnation: The Faith of the Early Church* (Edinburgh: T. & T. Clark, 1993); and the thoughtful, if more generic, survey by Michael Slusser, 'Primitive Christian Soteriological Themes', *Theological Studies*, 44 (1983), 555–69. One Patristic passage in which at least an attempt is made to distinguish more clearly between two important soteriological terms is Ps.-Dionysius, *De Divinis Nominibus* 8. 9. There the author identifies 'salvation' (*sōtēria*) as the divine activity of preserving the health and well-being of creation by keeping all things in proper order, while 'redemption' (*apolutrōsis*) carries the further suggestion of a healing of disorder and a restoration of lost health.

[6] *Adv. Haer.* 4. 6. 3–5.   [7] Ibid.

[8] Ibid. 4. 6. 6 (trans. based on Greek fragment).

source of enduring life, for creatures, is nothing less than to see the glory, the dazzlingly beautiful reality, of God. So he writes, in a celebrated passage in book 4 of *Against the Heresies*:

For as those who see the light are within the light, and partake of its brilliance, so those who see God are in God, and receive of his splendour. But his splendour vivifies them; those, therefore, who see God receive life. And for this reason, he, although beyond comprehension and boundless and invisible, rendered himself visible and comprehensible and within the capacity of those who believe, that he might vivify those who receive and behold him through faith. . . . It is not possible to live apart from life, and the means of life is found in fellowship with God; but fellowship with God is to know God, and to enjoy his goodness. Human creatures therefore shall see God, that they may live, being made immortal by that sight, and attaining even unto God . . . For the glory of God is a living human being, and the life of the human being consists in beholding God.[9]

It is the Word's revelation of himself in human form that makes clear what Genesis means in saying we are made in the image of God, and that restores that image to its full 'likeness' to the creative Word on which the image is modelled: 'When the Word of God became flesh, . . . he both showed forth the true image, by himself becoming what was his image, and he re-established the likeness in a stable way, making the human being resemble the invisible Father, by means of the visible Word'.[10]

Irenaeus' conviction that experiential knowledge of the glory of God, made possible for humans only in Christ, is itself the only source of indestructible life for us, is echoed by many later Fathers. Origen, for instance, imagines the goal of Christ's revelation in history to be the union of intellectual creatures with God and with each other through contemplative knowledge, so that, in Paul's words, 'God will be all in all' (1 Cor. 15: 28):

Everything which the rational mind, purged of all the filth of vices and thoroughly cleansed from every shadow of wickedness, can feel or understand or think, all will be God; nor will it feel anything other than God from that time on, but it will think God, will see God, will hold on to God, and all its movements will be God.[11]

---

[9] Ibid. 4. 20. 5–7, trans. A. Roberts and J. Donaldson, *Ante-Nicene Fathers I* (repr. Grand Rapids, Mich.: Eerdmans, 1977), 489–90 (altered).
[10] *Adv. Haer.* 5. 16. 2.   [11] *De Principiis* 3. 6. 3.

Athanasius, too, writing a century after Origen, develops a similar theme, and connects it as Irenaeus had done with the theme of the image of God from Genesis 1: 26–7. Arguing that the first effect of human sin was the loss of the direct, intimate knowledge of God that itself communicates incorruptible life and makes us 'rational' (*logikoi*) by the presence of the Logos within us, Athanasius sees the first task of God in saving fallen humanity to be the revelation of the Word. So he writes, in *On the Incarnation*:

> God, who has the power over all things, when he was making the human race through his own Word, saw the weakness of their nature, that it was not sufficient of itself to know its maker . . . [But] taking pity on the human race, for he is good, he did not leave them destitute of the knowledge of himself, lest they should find no profit in existing at all. For what profit is it to creatures if they did not know their maker? Or how could they be rational without knowing the Word?[12]

After humanity, through disobedience, lost its ability to know God, and with it its status as God's image, its share in God's incorruptible life, and even its distinctive rationality, God was bound by his own goodness to restore these lost gifts: 'What, then, was God to do? What else was to be done, save the renewing of that which was in God's image, so that by it human beings might once more be able to know him? But how could this have come to pass, save by the presence of the very image of God, our Lord Jesus Christ?'[13] In Athanasius' view, then, as in that of Irenaeus and Origen and many other Fathers, the heart of Jesus' life-giving work was his revelation to darkened human minds of the reality of God, a revelation that in itself brought a restored relationship and a renewal of life.

2. Therapeutic imagery: cleansing and healing   For Athanasius, the state of humanity after its fall from grace is best described as 'corruption' (*phthora*), a state of moral and physical frailty natural to them as animals, but originally held at bay by God's 'second gift' of a share in his Word. Deprived of this participation, which included both knowledge of God and a likeness to the Word's role in the cosmos through the sovereignty of reason in the human microcosm, humanity has grown more and more corrupt, in Athanasius' view, subject to a kind

---

[12] *De Incarnatione* 11, trans. A. Robertson (*NPNF* 2/4; repr. Grand Rapids, Mich.: Eerdmans, 1978), 42 (altered).

[13] *De Incarn.* 13 (Robertson 43 (altered)).

of epidemic of evil.[14] So the coming of the Word in human flesh not only reveals God in new clarity, but 'gives life to the body'—his own, presumably, and the human body generally—'and cleanses it, even though it was mortal'.[15]

Augustine, too, makes this cleansing and healing effect of Christ's work of revelation clear in book 4 of *On the Trinity*, one of his most important essays in soteriology. Here Augustine argues that the ultimate state of health for the human creature is eternal life, and for the mind this means the contemplation of truth, in its eternal fullness; in this life of change, this vision of truth begins in the limited vision of faith in Christ:

> so now we accord faith to the things done in time for our sakes, and are purified by it, in order that when we come to sight, and truth succeeds to faith, eternity might likewise succeed to mortality.... To those who already believe [Christ] speaks as follows, in order that they may abide in the word of faith, and thence come to truth and thus be set free from death and be conducted through to eternity: 'If you abide in my word you are really my disciples.' Then as though they asked 'To what purpose?', he continues: 'And you will know the truth.' Again, as though they said, 'And what use is truth to mortals?', he concludes: 'And the truth will set you free' (John 8: 31). What from, if not from death, from perishability, from liability to change.[16]

Of course, Augustine uses the language of healing for God's saving action much more widely, too. In the *Confessions*, especially, he often speaks of Christ as the 'physician' who heals him from the 'tumour' of pride and the 'ulcer of self-indulgence with a cool, sure hand'.[17] But in *De Trinitate* 4, the emphasis is clearly on the healing and

---

[14] *De Incarn.* 4–6.   [15] Ibid. 17.

[16] *De Trinitate* 4. 24, trans. Edmund Hill (Brooklyn: New City, 1991), 169–70 (punctuation altered). Augustine makes a similar point in *De Civitate Dei* 11. 2, specifically connecting it with Christ's role as Mediator and Way. Our greatest human blessing, he says, is to know 'the immutable substance of God', which God reveals to the mind through the presence of Truth within it. But since the mind is so darkened by sin that it cannot know truth 'until it has been renewed from day to day, and healed, and made capable of such great felicity', it had to be 'imbued with faith, and so purified'. This healing and purifying work has been done by God in the incarnation of 'the Truth itself, God's son' (trans. R. W. Dyson (Cambridge: Cambridge University Press, 1998), 450–1). It is God's self-revelation in Christ the Mediator which heals and saves.

[17] *Conf.* 3. 1. 1; cf. 2. 7. 15 (God as physician); 6. 4. 6 (healing of the soul's eye by the medicine of faith); 7. 7. 12 (healing of 'swelling' of pride); 7. 18. 24 (healing of weakness by the 'milk' of Christ's wisdom); 9. 1. 1 (God has drawn out the poison from his heart); 10. 28. 39 (God as physician, heals wounds). Cf. *Enar. in Ps. 118* 9. 2; *In*

cleansing of the mind, in its ability to know God and so find life—a cleansing and healing made possible only by God's humble self-emptying, to become and transform what we are:

Our enlightenment is to participate in the Word, that is, in that 'life which is the light of men' (John 1: 4). Yet we were absolutely incapable of such participation and quite unfit for it, so unclean were we through sin, so we had to be cleansed. Furthermore, the only thing to cleanse the wicked and the proud is the blood of the just man and the humility of God; to contemplate God, which by nature we are not, we would have to be cleansed by him who became what by nature we are and what by sin we are not. By nature we are not God; by nature we are men; by sin we are not just. So God became a just man to intercede with God for sinful man.[18]

3. Payment imagery: sacrifice and ransom   The language of sacrifice appears in almost every context in which the Fathers speak of the effect and meaning of Christ's death, although it is rare for them to explain its use at any length; it is simply part of the NT tradition, and doubtless was reinforced by the traditional ways of celebrating the Eucharist. Ignatius of Antioch, for instance, seems to see the dividing line between sham Christianity and real Christianity to be both the ability to acknowledge the flesh-and-blood reality of Jesus, and the willingness to 'imitate the Passion of my God' in shedding one's own blood for the faith.[19] He greets the church at Philadelphia 'in the blood of Jesus Christ', and remarks on their 'deep, abiding joy in the Passion of our Lord';[20] it is unity with the rest of the faithful, as expressed in obedience to their bishop and the sharing of a single Eucharist, that shows they are not 'at variance with the Passion', but rather united by the flesh and blood of Jesus at a single 'sacrificial altar'.[21] Augustine, again, in the fourth book of *De Trinitate*, echoing the theology of Hebrews, contrasts pagan sacrifices, offered to demons in a spirit of pride, with the true sacrifice of Christ; for

---

Jo. Evang. 110. 7. See R. Arbesmann, 'The Concept of "Christus Medicus" in St. Augustine', *Traditio*, 10 (1954), 1–28; J. William Harmless, 'Christ the Pediatrician: Infant Baptism and Christological Imagery in the Pelagian Controversy', *Augustinian Studies*, 28 (1997), 7–34.

[18] *De Trin.* 4. 4 (trans. Hill, 154–5).   [19] *De Trin.* 4. 4 (trans. Hill, 154–5).
[20] *Phil.* praef.
[21] Ibid. 3. 3–4. 1. See also *Eph.* 18. 1, and *Trall.* 2. 1, 11. 1, for references to the cross as the source of eternal life and unity for believers.

true sacrifice can only be correctly offered by a holy and just priest, and only if what is offered is received from those for whom it is offered, and only if it is without fault so that it can be offered for the purification of men with many faults. This is certainly what everyone desires who wants sacrifice offered for him to God. What priest then could there be as just and holy as the only Son of God...? And what could be so suitably taken from men to be offered for them as human flesh?...And what could be so acceptably offered and received as the body of our priest, which has been made into the flesh of our sacrifice?[22]

More often, Patristic authors associate the sacrificial value of Christ's blood with Christ's intervention to repay the debt humanity has incurred by sin. Athanasius, for instance, seems to use this debt-language unreflectively, as he develops his narrative of the restoration in humanity of the damaged image of God:

By offering unto death the body he himself had taken, as an offering and a sacrifice free from any stain, straightway [Christ] put away death from all his peers by the offering of an equivalent. For, being over all, the Word of God naturally, by offering his own temple and corporeal instrument for the life of all, satisfied the debt by his death. And thus he, the incorruptible Son of God, being joined with all by a like nature, naturally clothed all with incorruption...[23]

Nestorius, too, in his celebrated sermon of 429 that unleashed the *Theotokos* controversy, elaborates a picture of humanity held bound by an unpayable debt to God—a debt of unrealized goodness and obedience—apparently based on Romans 3: 23. So 'Christ assumed the person (*prosōpon*) of the debt-ridden nature, and by its mediation paid the debt back as a son of Adam'.[24] In Nestorius' treatment, Christ pays our debt not simply by dying on the cross, but by the whole shape of his virtuous and obedient life, which comes to a climax in his death.[25] More often, however, Patristic writers tend to identify the 'debt' paid on humanity's behalf by Christ as a debt owed to the devil—a position based on a reading of Colossians 2: 14–15, but one which Anselm would later strenuously oppose.[26]

---

[22] *De Trin.* 4. 19 (trans. Hill, 166).

[23] *De Incarn.* 9 (trans. Robertson, NPNF 2/4, 41); see also *De Incarn.* 20.

[24] Nestorius, 'First Sermon against the Theotokos', in Richard A. Norris, Jr. (trans. and ed.), *The Christological Controversy* (Philadelphia: Fortress, 1980), 126–7.

[25] Ibid. 127.

[26] See *Cur Deus Homo?* 1. 7. The basis of this idea seems to have been Col. 2: 13–15, which speaks of the death and resurrection of Jesus both in terms of the cancellation of debt and of the defeat of the demons, and thus suggests a connection between the two

Nestorius' contemporary Proclus, for instance, in a sermon delivered in Constantinople promoting Mary's *Theotokos* title which may have unleashed Nestorius' sharp rejoinder, depicts the plight of humanity before the incarnation precisely in these terms:

The human race owed a great deal and was unable to pay. Through Adam, all of us signed the bill for sin. The devil held us as slaves; he produced the deed for us, using as paper our vulnerable body. The wicked forger stands there, shaking the bill at us and demanding payment ... The human being could not save himself, for he was himself the debtor. No angel was strong enough to buy him free, for none had such a ransom. A sinless one had to die for sinners: this was the only solution left for our plight.[27]

Augustine, in the same book of *De Trinitate* I have already quoted several times, adopts this interpretation of Jesus' death as the cancellation of a debt to the devil. Having summarized the narrative of the fall from Genesis, as a story of the fatal deception of humanity by the devil as 'mediator of death', Augustine interprets Jesus' 'mediation of life' in terms of both the payment of debt and the settlement of a legal claim.

For our sakes the Lord paid this one death which he did not owe in order that the death we do owe might do us no harm ... So by a death of the flesh the devil lost man, who had yielded to his seduction, and whom he had thus as it were acquired full property rights over, and being himself liable to no corruption of flesh and blood had held in thrall in his weakness and poverty and the frailness of this mortal body, like one seemingly rich and powerful ... Yet in being slain in his innocence by the wicked one, who was acting against us as it were with just rights, [Christ] won the case against him with the justest of all rights, and thus 'led captive the captivity' (Ps. 68: 19; Eph. 4. 8) that was instituted for sin, and delivers us from the captivity we justly endured for sin, and by his just blood unjustly shed 'cancelled the I.O.U.' (Col. 2: 14) of death, and justified and redeemed sinners.[28]

images: 'God made [you] alive together with him [i.e. Jesus], having forgiven us all our trespasses, having cancelled the bond which stood against us with its legal demands; this he set aside, nailing it to the cross. He disarmed the principalities and powers and made a public example of them, triumphing over them in him.'

[27] Proclus of Constantinople, *Sermon on Mary*, ed. E. Schwartz, *Acta Conciliorum Oecumenicorum* (Berlin: De Gruyter, 1927), I. I, I. 105.

[28] *De Trin.* 4. 17 (Hill, 165). Augustine develops this same understanding of the blood of Christ as 'a kind of price' paid to the devil, in a bargain which eventually destroys the devil's power over humanity, in *De Trin.* 13. 19–21. His emphasis here, like Anselm's in the 11th cent., is on the innocence and freedom of the incarnate Son of God, which gives his death—normally the punishment of sin—its unique value.

In this interpretation of the value of Jesus' death, it is not so much the cleansing power of his blood, shed in sacrifice, which frees humanity from the ancient domination of sin and death, as the fact that God the Son, who is not liable to death in his humanity because he is free of sin, chooses to die out of love for fallen creatures. It is his power and freedom as incarnate Son, not simply his human act of dying, which make his death valuable.[29]

4. *Conflict imagery: defeat of death and the devil*   Closely connected with this theme of the life and death of Jesus as discharging humanity's debt to the powers of evil is the broader soteriological image of his death and resurrection as triumph: what Gustaf Aulén, in his influential study of 1931, calls 'the classic idea of the Atonement'.[30] The most striking version of this way of conceiving the value of Jesus' death is doubtless that of Gregory of Nyssa's *Catechetical Discourse*. Wishing to avoid any notion of evil as a substance, or any suggestion of a lack of wisdom in God's original act of creation, Gregory has emphasized both the changeableness inherent to any creature and the 'envy' and deceit of previously fallen angels as the explanation for the fall of a humanity naturally made to be virtuous.[31] As a result of giving in to the devil's deceit, however, Gregory assumes that human beings have ceded to him a kind of legitimate power over their lives, exercised in the dominance of sin and the fear of death; God, in his justice, may 'buy back' those who have sold themselves into slavery, but may not simply wrest them from the devil's power by violence.[32] Gregory's narration of this buying back, this redemption, has an imaginative boldness to it that seems unmistakably playful. The devil, he argues, is always a lover of power, a seeker for glamorous

---

Augustine writes: 'The devil was holding on to our sins, and using them to keep us deservedly fixed in death. He who had none of his own discharged them, and was undeservedly led away by the other to death. Such was the value of that blood, that he who killed Christ even with a momentary death he did not owe would no longer have the right to hold anyone who had put on Christ in an eternal death he did owe.' (*De Trin.* 13. 21; trans. Hill, 360)

[29] This point is also of central importance for Anselm: see *Cur Deus Homo?* 2. 10–11.
[30] 'This type of view may be described provisionally as the "dramatic." Its central theme is the idea of the Atonement as a Divine conflict and victory; Christ—Christus Victor—fights against and triumphs over the evil powers in the world, the "tyrants" under which mankind is in bondage and suffering, and in Him God reconciles the world to Himself' (Gustaf Aulén, *Christus Victor*, trans. A. G. Hebert (London: SPCK, 1965), 4.
[31] *Or. Cat.* (GNO iii/4; Leiden, 1996), 24–6.   [32] Ibid. 57–8.

new acquisitions; the divine beauty of the incarnate Word, radiating
the glory and power of God, seemed an irresistible prize to him, one
that he was even willing to take under his power as a substitute for
the whole of humanity.

When the enemy saw such power, he recognized in Christ a bargain which
offered him more than he held. For this reason, he chose him as the ransom
for those he had shut up in death's prison. Since, however, he could not look
upon the direct vision of God, he had to see him clothed in some part of that
flesh which he already held captive through sin. Consequently the Deity was
veiled in flesh, so that the enemy, by seeing something familiar and natural
to him, might not be terrified at the approach of transcendent power...
Hence it was that God, in order to make himself easily accessible to him who
sought the ransom for us, veiled himself in our nature. In that way, as it is
with greedy fish, he might swallow the Godhead like a fishhook along with
the flesh, which was the bait. Thus, when life came to dwell with death and
light shone upon darkness, their contraries might vanish away. For it is not
in the nature of darkness to endure the presence of light, nor can death exist
where life is active.[33]

As a result of the 'deception' of the incarnation, then, Gregory
suggests that the devil, the original deceiver, himself 'swallowed'
God along with the man Jesus—swallowed God up into death, the
realm of his own power—and in so doing assimilated the cure for his
own wickedness, allowing the very realm of death to meet its end.[34]
   The portrayal of Christ's death as a triumphal defeat of death itself,
understood as a threatening power linked with sin and the personified forces of evil, is a widespread theme in early Christian writing,
even apart from Gregory of Nyssa's particular form of the narrative.
Athanasius, for instance, who points in his treatise *On the Incarnation*
to the palpable vitality of the Christian church of his own day as a
sign of the continuing force of Christ's resurrection in believers, sees
this as proof that his death was a victory: 'For if, as our argument
showed, death has been brought to naught, and because of Christ all

---

[33] *Or. Cat.* (*GNO* iii/4; Leiden, 1996), 60–2; trans. Cyril C. Richardson, ed. Edward R.
Hardy (Philadelphia: Westminster, 1954), 300–1.
[34] Gregory held a clear version of the Origenist doctrine of *apokatastasis* or universal
salvation, based on the inherently limited character of evil; see Brian E. Daley, *The Hope
of the Early Church* (Cambridge: Cambridge University Press, 1991; 2nd edn., Peabody,
Mass.: Hendrickson, 2003), 85–7. It is likely that he assumed the evil spirits will also be
included among the saved.

tread him underfoot, much more did he himself first tread him down with his own body, and bring him to naught'.[35]

A century and a half before Athanasius, in fact, Melito of Sardis had taken an equally dramatic approach to interpreting the meaning of Christ's suffering and death as the final defeat anticipated figurally in the Exodus and celebrated in the Jewish Pasch, for the misery imposed upon humanity by sin and the death that accompanied it. Sin was the 'inheritance' that an inconstant Adam left to his children,[36] and death was both its favourite instrument and its inevitable result. But Christ, who is himself free from sin and death, came from heaven and 'wrapped himself in the suffering one' by taking a body: 'Through the spirit which cannot die he slew the manslayer death . . . This is the one who clad death in shame, and, as Moses did to Pharaoh, made the devil grieve . . . This is the one who delivered us from slavery to freedom, from darkness into light, from death into life, from tyranny into an eternal Kingdom'.[37] 'Redemption' here becomes not simply a transaction to end the claims of the powers that enslave humanity, but their outright defeat in Jesus' own personal victory over death.

One might find these themes, based on NT images, and others like them, in the works of almost every Patristic author, woven into the texture of broader theological argument or made into the subject of preaching and meditation. All I have been able to do here is point to a few classic examples, and to suggest their significance for their authors as ways of conceiving the effect of the life and death of Christ on the believer and the church. To see how such images are often simply compounded and mingled, with great suggestive power but without much attempt at further interpretation or analysis, we might simply take a brief and summary look at one of the 'spiritual homilies' attributed to Macarius of Egypt—works probably written as exhortations for the charismatic 'Messalian' sect in East Syria in the

---

[35] *De Incarn.* 30 (trans. Robertson 52). It seems undeniable that this treatise of Athanasius served as a model for Gregory of Nyssa's *Catechetical Discourse*, even though Gregory takes a very different approach to many issues.

[36] Melito of Sardis, *On Pascha* 49.

[37] Ibid. 66, 68, trans. Alastair Stewart-Sykes (Crestwood, NY: St Vladimir's, 2001), 54–5. Cf. *On Pascha*, 101–2, where Christ says: 'I set free the condemned. I give life to the dead. I raise up the entombed. Who will contradict me? . . . I am he who destroys death, and triumphs over the enemy, and crushes Hades, and binds the strong man, and bears humanity off to the heavenly heights' (Stewart-Sykes, 65).

last two decades of the fourth century.[38] In Homily 11, the author—
often identified by modern scholars as a certain Symeon of Mesopo-
tamia—begins by speaking of the transforming presence of God in
the souls and bodies of the devout as 'heavenly fire' (1). As a power
that melts and reshapes what contains it, this fire 'even now forms
an image in the soul, which will be manifested exteriorly in the
resurrection'. In a typically broad range of picturesque images and
comparisons, the author goes on to reflect on the origin and dynam-
ics of this saving work of God in the believer. Through the disobedience of the first pair, the devil and death 'gained power over every
soul and completely destroyed the image of Adam' (5). But God, the
creator of body and soul, 'renews and forms a heavenly image and
recreates the soul anew, so that Adam again may be king over death
and lord over all creatures'(6). To aid in this renewal, God commands
disciples to give away their material goods and seek their treasure in
heaven (7); so the first meaning of the story of the bronze serpent in
Numbers 21 is that 'all those who were bound to Satan by earthly
cares' might turn their gaze upwards 'and attend to more transcendent things from above' (8). Yet the real meaning of the bronze serpent
is that it is 'a type of the body of the Lord. The body which he took
from Mary he raised on the cross . . . And so the dead body conquered
and slew the serpent, living and creeping in the hearts of men' (9). So
the story of the bronze serpent reveals that 'in the dead body there is
life. Here is redemption, here is light. Here the Lord comes to death
and argues with death. He orders that death release, from hell and
death, the souls and give them back to him' (10). The author then
presents a personified death, shaken, bringing forth 'the signed
documents of indentured slaves' to argue against the invasion of
the victorious Christ into his realm. Christ answers: 'I bought back
the body that was sold to you by the first Adam. I tore up the contract
that enslaved humanity to you. Indeed, I satisfied Adam's debts
when I was crucified and I descended into hell. And I command
you, O Hell, O Darkness, O Death, release the imprisoned souls of
the children of Adam' (10).

---

[38] For a discussion of the authorship and setting of these homilies, see esp.
Hermann Dörries, *Symeon von Mesopotamien. Die Überlieferung der messalianschen
Makarios-Schriften* (Texte und Untersuchungen, 55/1; Leipzig: Hinricks, 1941); idem,
Die Theologie des Makarios/Symeon (Göttingen: Vandenhoeck & Ruprecht, 1978). I quote
here, with some alterations, from the trans. of George A. Maloney, *Pseudo-Macarius:
The Fifty Spiritual Homilies and the Great Letter* (New York: Paulist Press, 1992), 90–7.

The author goes on to apply this picture of Jesus in Hades to his conquest of the individual heart: 'For your heart is a tomb and a sepulchre...But the Lord descends into the souls of those who seek him. He goes into the depths of the hellish heart and there he commands death, saying: "Release those captive souls that seek after me..."' (11). This saving entry of Christ into the heart is like a rescuer striking shackles off the hands and feet of a prisoner, or like a swimmer striking out into a raging river to rescue a drowning person (12). So Jesus 'penetrates into two places, the depths of hell and the deepest region of the human heart, where the soul with all its thoughts is held captive by death. And he leads out of the dark depths the dead Adam' (12).

In this homily, the author has combined a number of traditional images for the saving work of Christ in dizzying succession: the restoration of the original image of God in both the souls and the bodies of the descendants of Adam; the bronze serpent of Numbers 21, identified with the crucified and exalted Jesus in John 3: 14 (cf. 12: 32); Jesus' triumphant defeat of death and conquest of Hades; salvation as the cancellation of a bill of debt, the release of captives, the rescue of those in danger. As the images slip one into another, the homily's underlying exhortation is rooted in the overarching narrative of the incarnation, and in the application of its meaning both to humanity as a whole and to individual believers:

For this reason [Christ] descended, so that he might save sinners, raise up the dead, and bring new life to those wounded by death, and to enlighten those who lay in darkness. The Lord truly came and called us to be God's adopted sons, to enter into a holy city, ever at peace, to possess a living [sonship] that will endure forever, to share an incorruptible glory. Let us singly strive to come to a good end after a good beginning! (15)

II Redemption and the Person of Christ

One element noticeable in all these soteriological images used by the Fathers is that they suggest salvation is not simply something Jesus *achieved* or *earned* for the human race by acting on our behalf, as an appointed agent of mediation between humanity and God. Rather, they all presuppose that salvation—however one imagines and describes it—is first of all something Jesus brought about *in his own person*, and that our change of status or relationship to God, our restored health and well-being as creatures of God, has already begun in what has happened to Jesus. It is the very person of Jesus, for instance, which—for Irenaeus or Athanasius—achieves the full revelation of God's grace and glory in the fallen world, remaking the damaged image (in Athanasius' understanding) or bringing it (as Irenaeus suggests) from simply being an image to being God's full likeness. It is in Jesus' own humanity, as Gregory of Nyssa and Augustine insist, that the process of the transformation and liberation of human nature is revealed, which for us begins in this life as growing freedom from the passions, and will reach its climax at the end of time in bodily resurrection. It is in Jesus' death that the indebtedness of fallen humanity is nullified, and in his resurrection that the hold of death and guilt on human nature is triumphantly broken: not simply because a ransom of some kind has been paid—to God or to the devil—but because Jesus has begun in his own person a new humanity, radiant with life and free of the enslaving obligations of the old order. Let us try to reflect briefly, and again only in very broad strokes, on how this understanding of Christ as not only the *agent* but also the *locus* of human salvation is articulated in Patristic theology.

(i) Identification with Christ

In a celebrated phrase later echoed by Gerard Manley Hopkins, Irenaeus asserts that the best way to refute Gnostic heresy is to follow 'the only true and steadfast teacher, the Word of God, our Lord Jesus Christ, who did, through his immense love, become what we are, that he might bring us to be what he is himself'.[39] For virtually the whole of the Patristic tradition, Eastern and Western, the final fulfilment of the human vocation is to have the full reality of God's image, in which we were originally created, restored within us through our identification with the Word of God—our original image—who has 'become flesh and dwelt among us' (John 1: 14). In his treatise *On the Nature of the Human Person*, for instance, Nemesius of Emesa—a fourth-century Syrian bishop and philosopher who may have been

---

[39] *Adv. Haer.* 5, praef. trans. A. Roberts and J. Donaldson: ANF I, 526 (altered). See the conclusion of Hopkins' poem, 'That Nature is a Heraclitean Fire, and of the Comfort of the Resurrection', 'In a flash, at a trumpet crash, I am all at once what Christ is, since he was what I am . . .'. *The Poems of Gerard Manley Hopkins*, ed. W. H. Gardner and N. H. MacKenzie (Oxford: Oxford University Press, 1970), 106.

a correspondent of the Cappadocian Fathers[40]—exclaims lyrically, in the midst of an otherwise rather technical philosophical and medical treatise:

[Man] is the creature for whose sake God became human, so that this creature might attain incorruption and escape corruption, might reign on high, being made after the image and likeness of God, dwelling with Christ as a child of God, and might be throned above all rule and all authority. Who, then, can fully express the pre-eminence of so singular a creature?[41]

Augustine, in book 21 of *The City of God*, gives eloquent expression to the 'exchange' of qualities that has come about as a result of the incarnation of the Word: he has taken our infirmities on himself, that we might 'participate in his immortality and righteousness' and regain the original perfection of our nature.[42] And his contemporary Cyril of Alexandria, in his exegesis of John 14: 20 ('In that day you will know that I am in my Father, and you in me, and I in you'), speaks of the restoration of the divine image through Christ in terms that could serve as a summary of this central theme in ancient soteriology. After telling the story of our original creation in grace, and of our fall through misuse of the freedom that is part of the image of God in us, Cyril continues:

It was not possible for the human person to escape death in any other way, since he was of a corruptible nature, but by gaining once again that primordial grace, and sharing in the God who holds all things together in being, as he brings forth life through the Son in the Spirit. Therefore God has become a sharer in flesh and blood (cf. Heb. 2: 14); that is, he became human, though he exists by nature as life—he who is the only Word of God the Father—that he might unite himself to corrupted flesh by the structure of his own nature, ineffably and indescribably and in a way only he understands, and might bestow on it again his own life, revealing it to be a participant, through him, in God his Father. For he is 'the Mediator between God and humans' (1 Tim. 2: 5), as Scripture says...For 'the Word became flesh,' according to the words of John. He bore our nature, reshaping it to share his own life. And he

---

[40] Letters 198–201 of Gregory of Nazianzus are addressed to a certain Nemesius, who seems to have been still a pagan, and was governor of the Roman province of Cappadocia; it is possible that he is the same Nemesius who later, as a Christian, wrote this treatise. On his use of Origen's exegesis, see Eiliv Skard, 'Nemesiosstudien I. Nemesios und die Genesisexegese des Origenes', *Symbolae Osloenses*, 15–16 (1936), 23–43.

[41] *De Nat. Hom.* 10, trans. William Telfer (Library of Christian Classics, 4; Philadelphia: Westminster, 1955), 254–5.

[42] *De Civ. Dei* 21. 15.

is in us: for surely we have become participants in him, and we have him in ourselves through the Spirit. For this reason, we have come to be 'partakers in the divine nature' (2 Pet. 1: 4), and are called sons and daughters: for we have the Father himself within us through the Son.[43]

It is only by union with God, according to Cyril's classic argument, by participation in God's very being and inner relationships, that human creatures find indestructible life in place of the death we have brought upon ourselves; and this union comes to us as a gift, through the Son's prior identification of himself with our humanity, and through his own life-giving Spirit, which he has breathed upon us. Redemption, in other words, is more than simply God's acquittal of a guilty humanity; it is the restoration to humanity of a share in the life of the Trinity, specifically through the outpouring of the Holy Spirit on the church by the glorified Christ.[44]

(ii) Transformation of Human Nature

The result of this restored identification of human nature with God in Christ, for most Patristic writers, is a transformation of humanity in both its internal and external aspects: a transformation that begins during this life in the forgiveness of sin and human growth in holiness, and that will reach its fulfilment in the resurrection of the body. Gregory of Nyssa sketches out this transformation in a number of his works, in terms of the gradual acquisition by the human creature of divine characteristics—first the moral characteristics, the virtues, that reflect God's perfection, and ultimately the radiant physical qualities of Jesus' risen body: 'Incorruptibility, glory, honour and power, which are agreed to be characteristic of the divine nature, formerly belonged to the one made in God's image, and are expected to be ours again', when our passions have been purged away and our nature restored to its 'original state'.[45] Gregory's

---

[43] Cyril of Alexandria, *Commentary on the Gospel of John* 9: 1, on John 14: 20, ed. P. E. Pusey (Oxford: Oxford University Press, 1872; repr. Brussels: Culture et Civilisation, 1965), ii. 485–6 (PG 74. 280AC). For a discussion of this passage in the context of Cyril's theology of salvation, see Daniel A. Keating, 'Divinization in Cyril: The Appropriation of Divine Life', in Thomas G. Weinandy and Daniel A. Keating (eds.), *The Theology of St. Cyril of Alexandria* (London: T. & T. Clark, 2003), 149–85, esp. 151–2.

[44] See Brian E. Daley, 'The Fullness of the Saving God: Cyril of Alexandria on the Holy Spirit', in Weinandy and Keating, *Theology of St. Cyril* 113–48, esp. 136–44.

[45] Gregory of Nyssa, *De Anima et Resurrectione* (PG 46. 157A; trans. Catherine Roth (Crestwood, NY: St Vladimir's, 1993), 119). For Gregory's understanding of the foundation of this reshaping of human nature in the person of Christ, see Brian E. Daley,

contemporary, the Pseudo-Macarius, in another homily, refers to this inner and outer transformation in similar terms:

Just as the interior glory of Christ covered his body [on the Mount of Transfiguration] and shone completely, in the same way also in the saints the interior power of Christ in them, in that day [i.e. at the resurrection], will be poured out exteriorly upon their bodies. For even now, at this time, they are in their minds participators of his substance and nature.[46]

Augustine, in book 4 of *The Trinity*, speaks of the death and resurrection of Christ as being both the 'sacrament' and the 'model' (*exemplum*) of our own death and resurrection: our 'model' as an example of how we should face death and hope for a bodily resurrection, but our 'sacrament' as a sign of the 'crucifixion of the inner man' that is required for our moral conversion, as well as of our 'inner resurrection' to a spiritual understanding of the person of Christ, and the 'ascent' of our desires to seek God alone.[47] Once again, our identification with Christ makes possible in us a passage from death to life, from materiality to spirituality, from sin to holiness, that is both the outcome and the imitation of his own paschal mystery.

(iii) Transformation of the Human Community

For most Patristic writers, the redemption achieved in the risen Christ is realized not simply in individual believers, in their restoration to the divine image, but also in a restored and revivified human community. Athanasius, for instance, in his treatise *On the Incarnation*, takes the somewhat risky step of pointing to the present life of the church—to the growing number of converts, and to heroism of Christian martyrs and ascetics, as well as the heroic virtue of many ordinary believers—as a living proof of the Easter gospel:

Of the resurrection of the body to immortality accomplished by Christ, the common Saviour and true life of all, the demonstration by facts is clearer than arguments . . . For now that the Saviour works such great things among men and women, and day by day is invisibly persuading so great a multitude

'Divine Transcendence and Human Transformation: Gregory of Nyssa's Anti-Apollinarian Christology', *Studia Patristica*, 32 (1997), 87–95; repr. *Modern Theology*, 18 (2002), 497–506.

[46] Pseudo-Macarius, *Homily* 15. 38 (trans. Maloney, 122–3).
[47] *De Trin.* 4. 6.

from every side, from those who live both in Greece and in foreign lands, to come over to his faith, and all to obey his teaching, will anyone still hold his mind in doubt whether a resurrection has been accomplished by the Saviour, and whether Christ is alive—or rather, is himself life?[48]

Cyril of Alexandria, in a later passage in the *Commentary on John*, emphasizes the unity of the church, joined as the one body of Christ primarily through its sharing in his eucharistic body, as the most dramatic outcome of the shared divine life that is redemption:

[The Son] came to be at once God and a human being, so that by joining together in himself things that are widely separate in nature and have diverged from all kinship with each other, he might reveal humanity as a participant and 'sharer in the divine nature' (2 Pet. 1: 4) . . . So the Mystery of Christ has come into being as a kind of beginning, a way for us to share in the Holy Spirit and in unity with God: all of us are made holy in that Mystery, as we have already shown. That we might, then, come together into unity with God and each other, and might ourselves be mingled as one, even though we stand apart individually in our souls and bodies by the differences we recognize in each of us, the Only-begotten contrived a way, devised by the wisdom that is his own and by the will of the Father: blessing[49] those who believe in him by a single body—namely his own—through sacramental sharing, he made them into members of a single body[50] with himself and with each other.[51]

This view of the transformation of disparate individuals, people of mixed religious background and moral virtue, into a single community marked by holiness and charismatic gifts, as a result of the incarnation of the Word, becomes an increasingly frequent theme in later Greek Patristic theology, and is especially emphasized in the writings of Maximus the Confessor. Maximus frequently emphasizes that the 'Mystery hidden from the ages and now revealed to the saints' (Col. 1: 26) is simply the mystery of Christ's person: 'the ineffable, incomprehensible union of divinity and humanity'.[52] The union of divine and human realities in the single person of the Son is, in Maximus' view, 'the preconceived end, for whose sake all

---

[48] *De Incarn.* 30 (trans. Robertson, NPNF 2/4, 52 (altered)).

[49] The Greek word, *eulogōn*, means 'to-bless', but is also used in Christian texts, by Cyril's time, to refer to the consecration of the eucharistic elements.

[50] Literally, 'concorporeal' (*syssōmous*).

[51] Cyril of Alexandria, Comm. *In Joan.* 11. 11, on John 17: 20–1 (ed. Pusey, ii. 734–6; PG 74. 557D–560A).

[52] *Quaestiones ad Thalassium* 60 (CCG 22. 73, ll. 10–12; PG 90. 620C).

things exist, ... the Mystery that circumscribes the ages'.[53] It is this union, begun in Christ, that reaches out now in the church to include all believers, through an experiential understanding of God's own reality present among us, and through participation in 'the good things that are above nature' and that bring all our restless motion, as creatures in search of God, to final rest.[54] Maximus argues, in fact, in a celebrated passage in his *Ambigua*, that this unifying work of God, first accomplished in the composite person of the incarnate Word, results not simply in human community on earth, or in the eschatological City of God, but in the healing of all the ancient divisions that have polarized reality since the start of creation: divisions between created and uncreated, intelligible and sensible, heavenly and earthly, the pre-lapsarian and the post-lapsarian world, even male and female. All of them are to be overcome in the renewal and reunification of creation, within itself and with God, that has now begun in the person of Christ:

By his own initiative, he joins together the natural ruptures in all of the natural universe, and brings to fulfilment the universal meanings (*logoi*) of individual things, by which the unification of the divided is realized. He reveals and carries out the great will of God his Father, 'summing up all things in himself, things in heaven and things on earth' (Eph. 1: 10), since all were created in him. Indeed, he has initiated this universal unification of all things with himself, by beginning with our divided selves, and has become a complete human being, from our stock, for our sakes, in our way—possessing completely what is ours except for sin ... With us and through us, he embraces the extreme opposites of all creation, using all that lies between them as his own members ... He sums up all things divinely in himself and reveals that all creation is one, like any human being.[55]

This unification of creation, in itself and with its transcendent creator, begun in Christ's person, is for Maximus the goal of God's single, creative, and redemptive plan from the beginning of time: 'the ineffable Mystery by which human beings shall become divine'.[56] The theme of 'divinization', of the participation by creatures in God's own characteristics and even in his inner life—always by his grace, and always in a finite way—is of course a constant

---

[53] Ibid. (CCG 22. 75, ll. 40–3; PG 90. 621AB).
[54] Ibid. (CCG 22. 77, ll. 81–2; cf. ll. 49–76; PG 90. 624 A; cf. 621BD).
[55] *Ambigua* 41 (PG 91. 1308D–1309A; 1312A).
[56] *Quaestiones ad Thalassium* 22 (CCG 7. 137, l. 33; PG 90. 317D).

theme in Greek and Latin Patristic literature, from Irenaeus to Athanasius and the Cappadocians, to Augustine and beyond.[57] In his twenty-second *Answer to Thalassius*, Maximus sees the end of the first stage of this process as already reached in the incarnation:

For if [the Word] himself has accepted the completion of his mystical activity of becoming human,[58] being made like us in every way except sin alone, and if he has descended to the lower parts of the earth, where the tyranny of sin had driven the human race, then surely he will also allow his mystical activity of letting humanity be made divine be realized by making us like himself, except only for essential identity with him . . .

So the end of the ages has, in truth, come upon us who presently, through the grace that is ours in Christ, will lay hold of the good things that are beyond the ages and beyond our own nature, as a gift. Types and foreshadowings of these good things, which now lie at hand, are the virtuous patterns of our lives and the intelligible characteristics of the things that we can naturally know.[59] Through them, God is always willing to become human in worthy people. Blessed, then, is the person who, after making God human in himself through wisdom, and after bringing to fulfilment the beginning of such a mystery, undergoes the experience of becoming, by grace, divine. He will never find a limit to this constant process.[60]

---

[57] The best survey of this theme in Greek Patristic literature is still Jules Gross, *The Divinization of the Christian according to the Greek Fathers*, trans. Paul A. Onica (Anaheim, Calif.: A. & C. Press, 2002). For Augustine's treatment, see esp. Gerald Bonner, 'St. Augustine's Concept of Deification', *Journal of Theological Studies*, 37 (1986), 369–86.

[58] Maximus assumes here that the previous stages of salvation history have witnessed a gradual incarnation of God's Word, now brought to a completion in the person of Jesus. The phrase *mystikē energeia*, literally 'mystical activity', seems to mean the active realization of a divine plan that is both God's self-communication and the involvement of creatures in himself.

[59] Maximus here echoes the Origenist tradition that our way to God begins in the acquisition of moral virtue (*praktikē*), moves on then to the knowledge of God in creation (*theoria physikē*, 'natural contemplation'), and reaches its goal in a participatory, affective 'knowledge' of the God who is beyond knowledge (*theologia*). See also Maximus, *Cap. Gn.* 1. 14; 1. 32; 1. 37–9; 2. 16; *Myst.* 2.

[60] *Quaest. Ad Thal.* 22 (CCG 7. 139, ll. 36–46; 142–3, ll. 99–108). In the last sentences, Maximus contrasts (as he has done throughout this little essay) the 'active' and the 'passive' stages of human growth towards divinization: the active phase, responding to God's active involvement in human history, consists in the imitation of Christ and the effort to free ourselves of the 'passions' and to grow in virtue; the passive phase, which succeeds it, is an increasing focus on contemplation and love, sustained more and more by God's grace and relying less and less on human effort. It is this latter, passive phase, he believes, that will characterize eternal life.

III CONCLUSIONS

I have made a wide and scattered survey, in these pages, of some of the principal images and concepts in which the Fathers of the church attempt to speak of redemption in Christ. Clearly one might point to other themes, other images; and one might refer to countless other early Christian authors and texts to fill out the picture. My analysis makes no claim at being exhaustive. But the main point, I think, remains valid: that for most of the Fathers, redemption or salvation is to be identified not simply as the new relationship between humanity and God that has come into being as the effect of Jesus' sacrifice for us, of his death on our behalf on the cross; rather, it is identified as the union, the living interpenetration, of God and humanity that is first fully realized in his own person. It is in the incarnation of the Word, seen as an event which includes the whole life of Jesus, rather than simply in his crucifixion or his resurrection, that the 'event' of redemption is to be found; the crucifixion and resurrection of Christ are of course seen as inseparable stages in his incarnate history, revealing in fullness what the incarnation means, but they are not considered saving events in isolation from his whole life as Word made flesh.

Does this mean that Patristic writers disconnect human redemption from the cross of Jesus? Clearly not. For most of them, rather, it is the 'self-emptying' of the eternal Son and Word (to use the terminology of Phil. 2: 5–11)—his taking on the 'form of a servant' in place of 'the form of God', the whole course of divine self-humiliation that leads to his death on the cross but begins simply in his birth as a normal, vulnerable human being—that is the real story of redemption. The 'way' of Jesus, which leads to a share in God's eternal life, Augustine often emphasizes, is the 'way of humility' that leads to the cross, but includes the whole course of the Word's incarnate existence.[61] For Gregory of Nyssa, too, the scandal of Jesus, which 'blunts the faith of little minds', is not simply Jesus' death; it is 'the human

---

[61] On Augustine's view of the Son's self-humiliation as the cure for human pride, see e.g. *Conf* 7. 18. 24; *De cat. rud.* 4. 8; *Enar. in Ps.* 35. 17; 118. 9. 2; on the cross as the key to understanding this healing, see *Enar. in Ps.* 70. 2. 9. For a discussion of an implied 'hermeneutics of the cross' in the *Enarrationes in Psalmos*, see Michael C. McCarthy, 'The Revelatory Psalm: A Fundamental Theology of Augustine's Enarrationes in Psalmos' (Diss. University of Notre Dame, 2003), 155–81.

birth, the advance from infancy to manhood, the eating and drinking, the weariness, the sleep, the grief, the tears, the false accusations, the trial, the cross, the death, and the putting in the tomb'.[62] It is precisely this scandalous involvement in the present lot of fallen humanity, in Gregory's view, that works its transformation.

The importance of Jesus' death on the cross, for most of the Fathers, is that it reveals the full extent of this divine involvement, the willingness of God to take on, in all freedom, the most lurid effects of human sin.[63] So the cross itself plays, in early Christian literature, a largely symbolic or iconic role, reminding us not only of Jesus' suffering, but also of the unifying and life-giving effect of his presence in history.[64] And the meaning of Jesus' death on the cross, in most Patristic texts, is to be found in the context of God the Son's whole journey through human weakness to divine life. In the words of Irenaeus,

> Just as he was human, in order to be put to the test, so he was also the Word, in order to be glorified. For the Word remained quiet while he was being tested and crucified, and while he died, but was fully present to the human being in his victory and his endurance and his acts of beneficence and his rising from the dead and his ascending into heaven. This, therefore, was the Son of God, our Lord, existing as the Word of the Father and as the Son of Man ... so that just as the head has risen from the dead, the rest of the body—the body of every human being found among the living—should also rise, when the time of his condemnation for disobedience is fulfilled, coming together in all its members and joints, and strengthened by the growth of God ... [65]

For Irenaeus and for the Patristic tradition after him, redemption is really inclusion in the whole story of Jesus.

Three things should be kept in mind, if we are to make sense of what may seem odd to us post-medieval Christians in this approach to redemption. First, the Fathers make no clear distinction (as some Protestant theologians would later do) between the justification of

---

[62] *Or. Cat.* (GNO iii/4, 36. 21–37. 2).   [63] See e.g. Athanasius, *De Inc.* 22–5.

[64] See e.g. Justin, *Apology* 1. 55; Gregory of Nyssa, *Or. Cat.* (GNO iii/4, 78. 19–81. 8). For a reflection on the cross as the real 'tree of life', see the anonymous 4th-cent. Paschal homily attributed to Hippolytus, 51 (SC 27. 177). On Justin's conception of the symbolic significance of the cross, see also Michel Fédou, 'La Vision de la Croix dans l'œuvre de saint Justin, "philosophe et martyr" ', *Recherches Augustiniennes*, 19 (1984), 29–210.

[65] *Adv. Haer.* 3. 19. 3 (trans. mine; up to 'ascending into heaven' the trans. relies on a fragment of the original Greek text).

sinners, as a judicial act of God, and their sanctification by the presence of the Holy Spirit in them, uniting them to Christ as children of the Father. God saves us by giving us new life, a restored identity as images of his Word; that life already makes us genuinely new people, in union with Christ our head. Second, the theological distinctions we tend to make between christology and soteriology or christology and theological anthropology are really modern distinctions—based on the division of theological 'tracts' in the modern university curriculum—and not Patristic ones. For most of the Fathers, as we have seen, as for NT writings like Ephesians and Colossians, the 'Mystery of Christ' is both the reality of his person and the reality of our transformation by personal and communal involvement with him. Third, the way most of the Fathers conceive of the working out of this mystery depends to a large extent on their ability to think figurally or typologically, not only in interpreting biblical texts and events, but in imagining our relationship to God through Christ. It is less difficult for them than it probably is for us to conceive of what 'happened' to Jesus, even of what 'happened' in the Word's coming into the world in Jesus, as 'happening' also, by grace, to us and in us. Christ is not simply an agent on our behalf before God—we are included in his actions and in his life. The rise of a more transactional model for conceiving his 'work' of redemption, in the medieval West, must be seen in the context of the growth of a new approach to scripture and the gospel in the twelfth century, more driven by logic and by analytical thinking than by contemplative assimilation, more concerned with the 'literal' or 'historical' sense of the scriptural text than with the range of possible 'surplus' meanings hidden in it, which involve the church and the individual believer. When theologians no longer think typologically, they must search for other ways of explaining how Christ's person and actions can have an effect on us. Without typology, it seems almost inevitable that one will conceive of the Saviour more as an agent than as a representative or inclusive person.

It is only in the framework of this earlier, more typological approach to salvation in Jesus, however, that the question posed by my Oxford friend really seems to find a satisfactory answer. God must work our salvation by becoming one of us, rather than by acting through a creature (such as the Arian Christ) delegated to do his work in the world, simply because salvation cannot be conceived simply as a 'work', however dramatic and however providential. The reason, as the Fathers intuitively grasped, is that salvation simply *is* God's personal presence among us, as 'Emmanuel'. Only by that presence does he begin in our human nature and community the process of purification and transformation that in the end allows us to be fully present to God: as sons and daughters with the Son, in the power of the Holy Spirit; as participants in God's life and inner relationships, 'sharers in the divine nature'.

In many of his encyclicals and other writings, Pope John Paul II likes to quote a phrase from the Second Vatican Council's Pastoral Constitution on the Church in the Modern World, *Gaudium et Spes*:

The truth is that only in the mystery of the incarnate Word does the mystery of human existence take on light. For Adam, the first human being, was a figure of him who was to come, namely Christ the Lord. Christ, the final Adam, by the revelation of the mystery of the Father and his love, fully reveals humanity to the human race, and makes humanity's supreme calling clear.[66]

It is a thought with which most of the Fathers would heartily agree. What the NT has to tell us, after all, is really that our humanity, at its best—our humanity redeemed from all that has alienated and marred it through history—is to be found in Christ, and that what he promises us is only 'that we shall be like him, for we shall see him as he is' (1 John 3: 2).

---

[66] *Gaudium et Spes*, 22.

8

The Power in the Blood
Sacrifice, Satisfaction, and Substitution in
Late Medieval Soteriology[1]

CAROLINE WALKER BYNUM

'...We are reconciled to God through the death of his Son'
(Rom. 5: 10). Where is this reconciliation, this remission of
sin?...In this chalice, [Christ] says, 'of the blood of the New
Testament, which is poured out for you' (Matt. 26: 28; Luke 22:
20)....We obtain it by the interceding death of the only Begot-
ten and are justified by grace in the same blood...Why, you ask
me, by blood when he could have done it by word. I ask the
same question. It is given to me only to know that it is so, not
why it is so.

(Bernard of Clairvaux)

I REVISIONS TO THE TRADITIONAL ACCOUNT

Recent discussions of the history of soteriology argue that two distinct understandings of redemption (or atonement) emerged in the
twelfth century: Anselm of Canterbury's theory of satisfaction and
Peter Abelard's exemplarism.[2] Anselm's *Cur Deus Homo?* jettisoned,
we are told, the older idea that Christ saved humankind by tricking

---

[1] With apologies to David Sabean, whose wonderful collection of essays with almost
the same title has little to do with blood; see *Power in the Blood: Popular Culture and
Village Discourse in Early Modern Germany* (Cambridge: Cambridge University Press,
1984). My thanks to Roberta Bondi and Joel Kaye for extremely helpful readings
as, respectively, theologian and historian.

[2] See Anthony W. Bartlett, *Cross Purposes: The Violent Grammar of Christian Atone-
ment* (Harrisburg, Pa.: Trinity Press International, 2001). The classic statements are
Hastings Rashdall, *The Idea of Atonement in Christian Theology* (London: Macmillan &
Co., 1919), and Jean Rivière, *Le Dogme de la rédemption: Essai d'étude historique* (Paris:
Lecoffre, 1905). For a quick summary of the standard textbook account, see the article
'Atonement', in F. L. Cross and E. A. Livingstone (eds.), *The Oxford Dictionary of the
Christian Church* (3rd edn., Oxford: Oxford University Press, 1997), 122–4.

the devil or ransoming man from his power, and argued instead that Christ satisfies and redeems the debt man owes to God because of human disobedience. In accord with the early scholastic search for the 'necessary reasons' of things, Anselm (d. 1109) argued that payment for sin must be made, since a simple declaration of absolution would unjustly equate justice and mercy; hence salvation must come via a God-man—that is, a union of Christ (who, being God, *can* pay the debt of sin, although he does not owe it) with humanity (who cannot pay but must). In many recent interpretations of Anselm, the heart of this argument is understood to lie in the idea that Christ is a 'substitute' for us in 'satisfying' God; he is also a 'sacrifice' (Anselm uses the word repeatedly), offered in atonement for human evil and guilt.[3] Abelard (d. 1142), on the other hand, in his famous commentary on Romans, is understood to have rejected the idea that bloodshed could rectify disorder in the universe. If God wished to forgive, he would simply do so; therefore Christ's death on the cross provides not expiation but rather a pattern for Christians to imitate and a spiritual awakening of, a turn-on to, love.

Recent scholarship often tries to justify one theory or the other but usually favours Abelard. It also, however, insists that Anselmian satisfaction was increasingly understood as a theory that Christ substitutes not only for our debt but also for the punishment we must endure (something Anselm nowhere said). Moreover, it argues that substitution theory, often in the form of 'penal substitution' (substitution for punishment), dominated late medieval theology and culminated in the sixteenth century in both Protestant and Catholic formulations (however vastly different their implications) that Christ's death on the cross is both satisfaction and sacrifice.

[3] As a number of scholars have pointed out, medieval theologians assume both eucharist and crucifixion to be 'sacrifice' *pro nobis* but tend not to theorize the concept. See Jaroslav Pelikan, *The Christian Tradition: A History of the Development of Doctrine*, iii. *The Growth of Medieval Theology (600–1300)* (Chicago: University of Chicago Press, 1978), 106–57 and 184–214, and P. J. Fitzpatrick, 'On Eucharistic Sacrifice in the Middle Ages', in S. W. Sykes (ed.) *Sacrifice and Redemption: Durham Essays in Theology* (Cambridge: Cambridge University Press, 1991), 129–56. The context in which they use the word indicates, however, that sacrifice means expiation and not just—as some modern theorists would have it—liberation of life or reconciliation. See Jose Thachil, *The Vedic and the Christian Concept of Sacrifice* (Kerala: Pontifical Institute of Theology and Philosophy, 1985); M. F. C. Bourdillon, 'Sacrifice', in Paul Barry Clark and Andrew Linzey (eds.), *Dictionary of Ethics, Theology and Society* (London and New York: Routledge, 1996), 734–7; and Sykes, *Sacrifice and Redemption*. And see at nn. 34–6.

At this violent turn of the twenty-first century, historians and theologians alike are pondering anew what they see as the violent implications of this theory of satisfaction, substitution, and sacrifice. A certain number, sometimes returning to the ideas of René Girard popular in the 1980s, want to see the period from 1100 to 1600 as a culture of persecution, scapegoating, and terrorism to which such soteriology significantly contributed.[4] Hence Anselm—at least as later understood—becomes the villain; and Abelard's understanding of redemption is regretted as the great medieval missed opportunity. If medieval perceptions are useful at all to think with, they are seen, then, as object lessons, as theological inducements to violence that must be avoided at all cost. Anselmian satisfaction or sacrifice should be replaced with a concept of the crucifix as reconciliation and embrace.[5] Abelardian exemplarism should be recuperated but also refigured into what Anthony Bartlett calls an 'abyssal' response— one in which Christ's assumption of suffering allows us the possibility of fundamental psychological reorientation.[6]

There seems to be a lot wrong with this general picture, some of it trivial for the project of this book but some of it of great importance. First, Anselmian and Abelardian understandings of Christ's work of

---

[4] Bartlett, *Cross Purposes*. See also Mark I. Wallace and Theophus H. Smith (eds.), *Curing Violence* (Sonoma, Calif.: Polebridge Press, 1994) and Mitchell Merback, 'Reverberations of Guilt and Violence, Resonances of Peace: A Comment on Caroline Walker Bynum's Lecture', *Bulletin of the German Historical Institute*, 30 (2002), 37–50. For recent, negative views of the later Middle Ages, see R. I. Moore, *The Formation of a Persecuting Society: Power and Deviance in Western Europe, 950–1250* (New York: B. Blackwell, 1987), and Jean Delumeau, *Sin and Fear: The Emergence of a Western Guilt Culture, Thirteenth–Eighteenth Centuries*, trans. E. Nicholson (New York: St Martin's Press, 1990). For a dismissal of much of medieval (and modern) atonement theory as amoral or 'nothing less than terrorism', see E. L. Peterman's entry, 'Redemption, theology of', in the *New Catholic Encyclopedia* (1967), reproduced, largely unchanged, in vol. 12 of the 2003 edn., pp. 973–89. I have dealt with some of these issues in 'Violent Imagery in Late Medieval Piety', *Bulletin of the German Historical Institute*, 30 (Spring 2002), 3–36.

[5] e.g. Edward Hulmes, 'The Semantics of Sacrifice', in *Sacrifice and Redemption*, 265–81; Miroslav Volf, *Exclusion and Embrace: A Theological Exploration of Identity, Otherness and Reconciliation* (Nashville, Tenn.: Abingdon Press, 1996), and idem, 'Forgiveness, Reconciliation, and Justice: A Theological Contribution to a More Peaceful Social Environment', *Millennium: Journal of International Studies*, 29/3 (2000), 861–77.

[6] Bartlett, *Cross Purposes*. And for a similar reinterpretation, without the extravagance of Bartlett or the use of Girard, see I. U. Dalferth, 'Christ Died for us: Reflections on the Sacrificial Language of Salvation', in *Sacrifice and Redemption*, 299–325. On Girard, see Robert G. Hamerton-Kelly, 'Religion and the Thought of René Girard: An Introduction', in *Curing Violence*, 3–24, and R. Schwager, *Must there be Scapegoats? Violence and Redemption in the Bible* (2nd edn., Leominster: Gracewing, 2000).

redemption were far closer to each other than such a simplified survey suggests. Anselm and the great critic of Abelard, Bernard of Clairvaux (d. 1153), both speak at length of the impact of Christ's example on the hearts of Christians. Indeed, Abelard's position, although usually labelled exemplarism, is better understood as a theory of response, for his argument in the Romans commentary stresses less example and *imitatio* than the idea that Christ's self-sacrifice for us is a stimulus that compels the response of repentance and love. Both Anselm and Bernard in fact agree with Abelard that empathetic participation in Christ's suffering arouses humankind to a love that is the first step towards return and reconciliation.[7] Moreover, Abelard himself, who never intended his commentary on Romans to be a complete soteriology, speaks even there of Christ's love providing justification—that is, offering something objective that repairs the chasm opened in the universe by sin. Like Bernard and Anselm, Abelard sees both the cross and the mass as sacrifice and satisfaction.[8] In other words, there are subjective and objective elements in the theories of both Anselm and Abelard.[9] Indeed, to all twelfth-century thinkers, Christ's suffering on the cross both induces response and effects ontological repair; it wrenches the hearts of humans towards empathy and healing, and it provides a totally undeserved and God-given bridge across the breach torn in the cosmos by Adam's disobedience in the garden of Eden.

Hence it is quite wrong to see two redemption theories warring for precedence in the twelfth century. Moreover, what I am calling Abelardian response and what is generally labelled Anselmian satisfaction together constitute (along with vestiges of earlier positions) the redemption theory of the later Middle Ages and the sixteenth century. Peter Lombard (d. 1160), whose *Sentences* became the theological textbook for medieval universities, expresses well the standard and multi-faceted medieval theory of the atonement. The Lombard retained the early medieval idea that Christ on the cross defeats the

---

[7] See below at n. 28.

[8] Abelard, 'Exposition of the Epistle to the Romans', bk 2, cc. 1–4; in E. R. Fairweather (ed. and trans.), *A Scholastic Miscellany: Anselm to Ockham* (The Library of Christian Classics, 10; Philadelphia: Westminster Press, 1946), 276–87, and the quotation in n. 25 below.

[9] The most balanced account of the entire issue is Pelikan, *Christian Tradition*, iii. *Growth*, 106–57; and see D. E. Luscombe, 'St. Anselm and Abelard', *Anselm Studies: An Occasional Journal*, 1 (1983), 207–29.

devil. He maintained (without using the word itself) that satisfaction is due for sin and is paid by Christ, and he clearly, unlike Anselm, saw such satisfaction as substitute punishment. He also argued for redemption as the enkindling of love:

But how are we loosed from sin through his death? Because by his death, as the Apostle says (Rom. 5: 8), the love of God is committed to us, that is, a special and praiseworthy love of God towards us appears, in that he gives his Son over unto death for our sins. And a pledge of such great love having been shown to us, we are moved and kindled to the love of God who did such a great thing for us; and by this we are justified—that is, loosed from sin, we are made just. Therefore the death of Christ justifies us, since through it love is excited in our hearts.[10]

A careful reading of Thomas Aquinas—the other thinker usually discussed in textbook treatments of the atonement—shows also a complex theory where response and satisfaction interweave.[11] Modern accounts often claim that Aquinas (d. 1274) shifts the soteriological focus to an insistence that satisfaction is not necessitated by the structure of the universe (as Anselm is understood to argue) but rather willed by a God who is, in fourteenth- and fifteenth-century theology, increasingly understood as absolute will or power. But the idea that God chose blood satisfaction as his means when he might have chosen other ways is implicit in earlier theology (see the passage from Bernard of Clairvaux quoted above as epigraph); and the shift from understanding Christ's death as imperative to understanding it as 'appropriate' (Aquinas' term) is not, in my judgement, a major one for soteriology itself. What is important is that Aquinas, like later thinkers such as Wyclif (d. 1384), Gerson (d. 1429), Cusanus (d. 1464) and Gabriel Biel (d. 1495), holds that the blood of the cross is sacrifice, satisfaction, and the enkindling of love.[12] There are not then two redemption theories (Abelardian and Anselmian) in the Middle Ages but one.

---

[10] Peter Lombard, *Sententiae in IV libris distinctae*, 2 vols. (Grottaferrata: Collegium S. Bonaventurae, 1971–81), bk 3, dist. 19. 1, ii. 118. And see D. E. DeClerck, 'Questions de sotériologie médiévale', *Recherches de théologie ancienne et médiévale*, 13 (1946), 150–84, and 14 (1947), 32–64, on the later history of the Lombard's teaching.

[11] *ST* 3. 46–9 and 83.

[12] Jaroslav Pelikan, *The Christian Tradition: A History of the Development of Doctrine*, iv. *Reformation of Church and Dogma (1300–1700)* (Chicago: University of Chicago Press, 1983), 22–5. On Biel, see Heiko Oberman, *The Harvest of Medieval Theology: Gabriel Biel and Late Medieval Nominalism* (Cambridge, Mass.: Harvard University Press, 1963), 266–75.

It is true that, within this theory, one strand—which was built upon at the Council of Trent—figures redemption as a kind of exchange and expresses it in almost quantitative terms. Christ is seen as offering to God in man's stead and on man's behalf an uncoerced and sinless obedience which so far outweighs human debt that the additional merits earned suffice for whatever recompense humans will ever need to make for their sins. But even at the level of university-trained theologians, satisfaction and exchange are still part of a theology in which the cross is also the object of *compassio* and *imitatio*. And, as such, it is not just a pattern to be built into the life of the Christian (although the sudden outburst of stigmata and other paramystical phenomena in the thirteenth century warns us not to ignore literal *imitatio*) but also a suffering and self-giving presence in which the individual is enclosed and thereby lifted to heaven. In discussing the 'appropriateness' of the passion, Aquinas asked why God chose to save by violence, which is surely 'a severance or lapse' of nature. Among the many answers he gives, the first is that God chose to save by death and blood so that man might know how much God loves him and be 'stirred to love' in return.[13] Hence even in university discourse, Christ's death not only restores the balance of the universe so that sinners can draw upon it for redemption; it is also a vast well of blood in which the Christian encounters and becomes one with love.

Giving greater precision to the abstruse pronouncements of medieval professors may not matter much to the broad concerns of this book, but there are three other necessary corrections to the conventional story that matter more. The first is to point out that theology is no more to be equated with the writings of university intellectuals in the period from 1100 to 1600 than it is today. Social and cultural historians have been perhaps more sensitive to this point recently than theologians or historians of theology, who have been too inclined to jump in their accounts diachronically from Aquinas' *Summa Theologica* to the Augsburg Confession or synchronically from Anselm's *Cur Deus Homo?* to the pogrom at Mainz and the First Crusade. Bernard McGinn, Barbara Newman, and Nicolas Watson have each tried to argue that the period from 1200 to 1500 saw a vernacular theology alongside a scholastic

---

[13] *ST* 3. 46. 3.

one.[14] Their accounts differ in locating this theology in, respectively, the contemplative tradition, the emergence of women's piety, and the rise of vernacular languages (and national identities), but the point is clear. Theology in the later Middle Ages was done not only in university debates, which focused increasingly narrowly on a few disputed points, heavy in philosophical consequence, but also in the sermons, hymns, devotional manuals, prayer books, broadsides, pamphlets, and pilgrim guides provided for a partially literate laity and in the practices, both liturgical (such as devotion to the eucharistic host) and extra-liturgical (such as flagellant processions), of religious and lay folk alike.

My second point is connected to this. We cannot understand the late medieval theology of atonement and redemption or its legacy in modern theology if we isolate it from surrounding ideas. The themes of satisfaction and exchange, of sacrifice, of suffering and compassion, of substitution, representation, and participation that undergird it undergirded as well late medieval eucharistic theology and the theology of purgatory. We will not understand the centrality of the Man of Sorrows in redemption without considering his mode of presence in the mass; we will not understand suffering in atonement unless we understand its place in the theology and piety of purgatory.

Once we understand medieval atonement theory in its larger context—and this is my third point—we see that its increasing fixation on blood is not owing simply to a concept of penal substitution that would be easy to excise. Obsession with blood and suffering is lodged squarely at the heart of theology (both scholastic and vernacular), even where its outpourings carry no implications of exchange, substitution, or punishment. Despite the palpable increase in joyful, even erotic and ecstatic, response to God,[15] we might well

---

[14] Bernard McGinn, *The Flowering of Mysticism: Men and Women in the New Mysticism, 1200–1350* (New York: Crossroad, 1998), 19–24; Barbara Newman, 'On the Threshold of the Dead: Purgatory, Hell, and Religious Women', in *From Virile Woman to WomanChrist: Studies in Medieval Religion and Literature* (Philadelphia: University of Pennsylvania Press, 1995), 108–36; Nicolas Watson, 'Visions of Inclusion: Universal Salvation and Vernacular Theology in Pre-Reformation England', *Journal of Medieval and Early Modern Studies*, 27/2 (1997), 145–87. What I am suggesting generally in this section has some affinities to the interpretation of John C. Hirsh, *The Boundaries of Faith: The Development and Transmission of Medieval Spirituality* (Leiden: Brill, 1996), 91–110.

[15] The passages I quote at nn. 17, 18 and 44 make it clear that neither theology nor devotion in the later Middle Ages emphasizes suffering to the exclusion of joy. On this, see Erich Auerbach, 'Excursus: Gloria Passionis', in idem, *Literary Language and its*

call the piety of the fourteenth and fifteenth centuries 'blood piety' so prominent did themes of bloodletting, pain, sacrifice, and self-immolation become. I give four brief examples.

In the late twelfth century, a monk of Evesham abbey in England appeared to die on Easter weekend and his soul was carried afar off; when he returned to life, he recounted what he had seen in heaven:

> In the middle of endless thousands of blessed spirits who stood round, . . . the pious redeemer of the human race appeared. It was as if he were hanging on the cross with his whole body bloody from scourgings, insulted by spitting, crowned with thorns, with nails driven into him, pierced with the lance; while streams of blood flowed over his hands and feet, and blood and water dropped from his holy side!

Modern readers are surprised not only by Christ's graphic tortures in heaven but also by the final line of the chronicler's description: 'Near him stood his mother . . . rejoicing'.[16] Bleeding and pain—and the joy they engender—are lodged at the heart of heaven. When the fourteenth-century mystic and hermit Richard Rolle wrote—not as the monk's chronicler did in Latin but in the vernacular and for a wider audience—he explained:

> Sweet Jesus, your body is like a net, for as a net is full of holes so is your body full of wounds. Here, sweet Jesus, I beseech you, catch me up in this net of your scourging so that all my heart and my love be turned to you. . . .
> Second, sweet Jesus, your body is like a dovecote. For a dovecote is full of holes, and so is your body full of wounds. And as a dove, pursued by a hawk, is fully safe if she can reach a hole of her house, so, sweet Jesus, may your wounds be the best refuge to us in our temptation. . . .[17]

Ecstasy lies here in a net of scourging; redemption is wallowing in gore.

Public in Late Latin Antiquity and in the Middle Ages, trans. R. Manheim (New York: Routledge & Kegan Paul, 1965), 67–81, and Frederick C. Bauerschmidt, *Julian of Norwich and the Mystical Body Politic of Christ* (Studies in Spirituality and Theology 5; Notre Dame, Ind.: University of Notre Dame Press, 1999), 50–124.

[16] 'The Monk of Evesham's Vision', in Eileen Gardiner (ed.), *Visions of Heaven and Hell Before Dante* (New York: Italica Press, 1989), 214.

[17] Hope Emily Allen (ed.), *English Writings of Richard Rolle, Hermit of Hampole* (Oxford: Clarendon Press, 1931; repr. 1988), 35. And see René Tixier, 'Richard Rolle: La Mémoire des Plaies', in Marcel Faure (ed.), *Le Sang au moyen âge: Actes du quatrième colloque international de Montpellier, Université Paul-Valéry (27–29 novembre 1997)* (Montpellier: Association CRISMA, 1999), 377–90.

The Italian tertiary, Angela of Foligno (d. 1309), expressed to her scribe a graphic performance of the same piety. Standing before a crucifix, Angela bared her flesh (as Francis had done before her) and ritualistically pointed to each member, enacting less a renunciation of her body than a fusion with the saving and exuding bodiliness of Christ:

[I]n this understanding of the cross there was given to me such a great fire that standing next to the cross I stripped myself of all my clothing, and I offered myself to him completely. . . . I promised . . . not to offend him with any of my members, accusing all my members one by one. . . .
[And] he called me and said I should put my mouth to the wound in his side. And it seemed to me that I saw and drank his blood flowing freely from his side.[18]

A commonplace book from the same period expresses the joy of the blood in a simple anonymous jingle:

> I wolde ben clad in cristes skyn
> That ran so longe on blode
> & gon t'is herte & taken myn In.[19]

Redemption is climbing into the flayed skin of Christ, drinking from his side, merging one's own heart and blood with the blood of the crucified.

In these four passages, we find the enkindling of which Abelard, Peter Lombard, Aquinas, and Gabriel Biel spoke; there is no reference to punishment. Yet this piety grooves on horror. The art of the fourteenth and fifteenth centuries increasingly depicted Christ tortured in a winepress or pouring red globules from hundreds of wounds. Flagellants opened their own bodies to spill blood. Laypeople and ecclesiastics followed convicted criminals to the scaffold in the hope of being sprayed with, or of scooping up, the blood of the executed if they repented at the end and called on Jesus. Jews were lynched because stories spread of strange cries behind closed doors and of wells running with blood where tortured hosts declared the presence of Christ. Pilgrims who set out across Europe to shrines such as Andechs and Wilsnack, which boasted miraculous hosts,

[18] Trans. Elizabeth A. Petroff in *Body and Soul: Essays on Medieval Women and Mysticism* (New York and Oxford: Oxford University Press, 1994), 223 nn. 22 and 25, and see pp. 204–19.
[19] Douglas Gray, 'The Five Wounds of Our Lord', *Notes and Queries*, 208 (1963), 129.

interpreted the *corpus Christi* as *sanguis* or *cruor*. 'Blut, Blut!' they cried when the priest or monastic attendant elevated a monstrance filled with what appeared to be rust particles or crumbs of bread.[20] However we evaluate it, I do not think the blood piety of late medieval Europe can be reduced to (and hence expunged along with) a particular theology of the atonement any more than we can reduce to a single soteriological formula the powerful and ghastly hymn with which I was raised: 'There is power, power, power, wonder-working power, in the blood of the Lamb . . .'

With this as background, I turn now to a fuller picture of the theology of redemption in the later Middle Ages.

II ATONEMENT, EUCHARIST, AND PURGATORY

Resurrection continued sometimes to be implicit in crucifixion. The bleeding, almost comatose Man of Sorrows depicted on altarpiece after altarpiece often stood upright in a sarcophagus, evoking his resurrection, and even the hideous *transi* tombs in which skeletal and worm-eaten corpses appear below effigies of the well-clad elite of Europe suggested the simultaneity of our resurrected and glorified bodies with the ones that rot in the grave. Nonetheless the focus of piety was increasingly on the cross, and as Caesarius of Heisterbach (thirteenth-century author of a popular collection of moral tales) pointed out, in the sort of etymological analysis his readers loved, *crux* comes from *crucio* (to torture).[21] Even the mass was allegorized as the process of dying and the host sometimes treated ritually as a dead body.[22]

---

[20] Johannes Heuser, ' "Heilig-Blut" in Kult und Brauchtum des deutschen Kulturraumes. Ein Beitrag zur religiösen Volkskunde', dissertation, Universität Bonn, 1948; Mitchell B. Merback, *The Thief, the Cross and the Wheel: Pain and the Spectacle of Punishment in Medieval and Renaissance Europe* (Chicago: University of Chicago Press, 1999); Miri Rubin, *Gentile Tales: The Narrative Assault on Late Medieval Jews* (New Haven, Conn.: Yale University Press, 1999); Bynum, 'Violent Images'; Niklaus Largier, *Lob der Peitsche: Eine Kulturgeschichte der Erregung* (Munich: Beck, 2001).

[21] Caesarius of Heisterbach, *The Dialogue on Miracles*, trans. H. von E. Scott and C. C. S. Bland, ii (London: Routledge, 1929), 21.

[22] Yrjö Hirn, *The Sacred Shrine: A Study of the Poetry and Art of the Catholic Church* (Boston: Beacon, 1912), 79–80, 136, and 162–6; Colin Eisler, 'The Golden Christ of Cortona and the Man of Sorrows in Italy', *The Art Bulletin*, 51/2 (June 1969), 238; Fitzpatrick, 'On Eucharistic Sacrifice', 129–56.

All three of the themes to which Gustav Aulén famously called attention are clearly present: Christ's death is victory, satisfaction (appeasement, vicarious punishment, and payment), and enkindling of response (both *compassio* and *imitatio*). The monk of Evesham wrote: 'the devil [is]...conquered by this reproach, and hell... defeated and robbed of its weapons and spoils, the lost one...recovered, and the prey of devils...snatched from their infernal prison-house and placed in heaven among the choir of angels'.[23] The author of the *Ancrene Wisee* (*c.*1220) claimed that Christ interposed his body between us and God 'as a compassionate mother puts herself between her child and the angry, stern father, when he is about to beat it...[taking] the death-blow himself to shield us from it'. But Jesus, victorious or compassionate, could be seen to turn his weapons not to defence but to attack. Guibert of Nogent (d. *c.*1125) told of a crucified Christ who came down from the altar, all five wounds bleeding, and went through the church crying: 'If you will not confess, you will die'. Caesarius not only accused Jews and Saracens of martyring God but wrote as well: 'Christ is daily pierced and scourged by Christians through injuries done to his poor'.[24] The crucifix is accusation as well as appeasement. It is also soaring, passionate love. Abelard, for example, wrote to his discarded lover Héloïse, who though a nun still grieved for him:

[Christ] bought you not with his wealth but with himself. He bought and redeemed you with his own blood.... The Creator of the world himself became the price for you.... He is the true friend who desires yourself... who said when he was about to die for you: 'There is no greater love than this, that a man should lay down his life for his friends.' [John 15: 13]

It was he who truly loved you, not I.... You say I suffered for you, and perhaps that is true, but it was to bring you not salvation but sorrow. But he suffered truly for your salvation, on your behalf of his own free will, and by his suffering he cures all sickness....[25]

---

[23] 'Evesham's Vision', 214. For another example, see Peter Damian's 'Sermon 66', *De sancta Columba virgine et martyre*, PL 144. 884A. And see Gustav Aulén, *Christus Victor: An Historical Study of the Three Main Types of the Idea of the Atonement*, abridged trans. A. G. Hebert (New York: Macmillan, 1931).

[24] *Ancrene Wisse*, pt. 6, in *Anchoritic Spirituality: Ancrene Wisse and Associated Works*, trans. A. Savage and N. Watson (New York: Paulist, 1991), 182; Guibert, *A Monk's Confession: The Memoirs of Guibert of Nogent*, trans. Paul J. Archambault, ii (University Park, Pa.: Pennsylvania State University Press, 1996), 83; Caesarius, *Dialogue* 2. 28–9.

[25] *The Letters of Abelard and Héloïse*, trans. Betty Radice (Harmondsworth: Penguin, 1974), 152–3.

The thirteenth-century Flemish mystic Hadewijch wrote that we must join with the cross not by carrying it for only a short while, as Simon did, hoping for reward, but by abiding in suffering love. And such love is 'a heavy burden...terrible and implacable, devouring and burning'. Caught up in human nature which is caught up in God, we become one (says Hadewijch) with a love sweet 'in tempestuousness':

> [Love's] deepest abyss is her most beautiful form;
>
> . . . . . .
>
> Her despair is assurance;
> Her sorest wounding is all curing;
>
> . . . . . .
>
> Her tender care enlarges our wounds;
>
> . . . . . .
>
> Her table is hunger.[26]

An English preaching manual from the thirteenth century admonished: 'As the nails of the cross were warmed by the blood of Christ, so ought sinners to be inflamed in charity to the service of Christ by the blood of Christ'.[27]

It is perhaps ironic that the clearest theoretical statement of this conception of redemption as the enkindling of response—a theory usually thought of as Abelardian—should come from Bernard of Clairvaux, who attacked Abelard as 'Pelagian'. In the opening chapters of his *Steps of Humility and Pride*, Bernard explores Hebrews 5: 8 ('Yet learned he obedience by the things which he suffered') and explains that Christ as Wisdom could not learn but that he 'appeared to learn' in order to give us an example.[28] More, however, than an echo of Abelard's and Peter Lombard's idea that Christ enkindles our

---

[26] Poems in Couplets, poem 13, *Hadewijch: The Complete Works*, trans. Columba Hart (London: SPCK, 1980), 344.

[27] In R. Röhricht (ed.), *Quinti belli sacri scriptores minores* (Geneva: J. G. Fick, 1879), 15, quoted in Nicholas Vincent, *The Holy Blood: King Henry III and the Westminster Blood Relic* (Cambridge: Cambridge University Press, 2001), 37.

[28] Bernard of Clairvaux, *The Steps of Humility*, trans. George B. Burch (Cambridge, Mass.: Harvard University Press, 1950), 123–71; also Bernard, 'On Loving God', trans. G. R. Evans, in *Bernard of Clairvaux: Selected Works* (New York and Mahwah, NJ: Paulist, 1987), 192–7. And see Robert Javelet, *Image et ressemblance au douzième siècle de saint Anselme à Alain de Lille*, 2 vols. (Paris: Letouzey & Ané, 1967), and Caroline Walker Bynum, 'Monsters, Medians, and Marvelous Mixtures: Hybrids in the Spirituality of Bernard of Clairvaux', in *Metamorphosis and Identity* (New York: Zone Books, 2001), 113–62.

love by providing an example of the man who dies for his neighbour, Bernard's exegesis is embedded in an exploration of the individual's return to God, which he expresses as the restoration of *similitudo* (likeness) to the *imago* in which we were created (Gen. 1: 26). Bernard explores the process of return, the repairing of similitude, in a number of texts, which have significant variations. Only some versions involve love of neighbour. But the general argument is that the human person, lost in narcissism (sin), is turned from self-love to love of God through the intermediate step of encounter with the suffering Christ. The recognition that Christ's suffering is at least as terrible as ours and that it is offered *pro nobis* wrenches us from self to other and moves us into a process of return that outlasts life itself and carries us to union. Although Bernard clearly assumes (as did Abelard) that grace is necessary for such empathetic reorientation, what Christ offers here is a suffering self that inflames co-suffering (*compassio*) in us. For Bernard, we are able to return to similitude, to co-suffer, because we are created in the image of God, just as, like the great vernacular theologian of the fourteenth century, Julian of Norwich, we experience ecstasy in the blood because of our 'godly will', which is never separated from God.[29] Optimism about the human person is thus embedded in medieval redemption theology along with obsessive guilt and heightened attention to pain.

A brief look at the motif, both iconographical and literary, of the *arma Christi* ('arms' in the sense both of 'weapons' and of 'insignia', or 'coats of arms') makes the complexity of redemption theology clear. The *arma*—the instruments of Christ's torture and execution obsessively depicted and discussed in representations of the Man of Sorrows—are understood as signs of victory and shields defending sinners. They are also offensive weapons, accusing us for the death of God necessitated by our sin and failure. James of Voragine, the thirteenth-century author of the immensely popular *Golden Legend*, warned: '[The *arma Christi*] show Christ's mercy and justify his anger, for we remember that not all men are willing to accept his sacrifice'. James turns the weapons outwards, against scapegoats and enemies. The author of the *Speculum humanae salvationis* turned the weapons back against us. We are, after all, the ones who incurred the unpayable debt: 'All Christ's weapons are aimed against

---

[29] On Julian, see below nn. 45–6.

sinners'.[30] But the *arma* are also the tools of transformative love. In the odd motif of Christ crucified by the virtues, we find the suggestion that the bleeding and death of the Saviour are executed by the spears of *caritas* and *humilitas* in order that we may be saved.[31] The weapon of auto-sacrifice is love.

This sense of salvific suffering that appeases and expiates, triumphs, arouses, and lifts to heaven was at the heart of eucharistic theology as well. It is true that, from the eleventh century on, the discussions of university theologians concentrated increasingly on the exact mode of Christ's presence in the elements on the altar. The focus even of visions narrowed. Whereas in early medieval stories bystanders sometimes saw a child on the altar during mass or even in eucharistic procession, by the high Middle Ages the showings came at the moment of consecration as if to validate the real presence.[32] And what was seen was more and more often a bleeding or dismembered man.[33] Nonetheless both speculation and practice ranged far beyond a focus simply on the nature of the eucharistic elements. Whether the mass was understood to repeat the moment of Calvary or to manifest and mirror its eternal presence (and these matters were defined only in the sixteenth century), the blood in the cup was shed *pro nobis*. The mass was a sacrifice, one in which we might participate by seeing (*Augenkommunion*) as well as by eating. Moreover, even in the frenzy for absorbing a bleeding and fragmented Christ, mystics, theologians, and ordinary believers never forgot that the power in the blood was to lift them into an immutable God. We become Christ in the eucharist, he does not become us.[34] As the

---

[30] Gertrud Schiller, *The Iconography of Christian Art*, ii. *The Passion of Jesus Christ*, trans. Janet Seligman (Greenwich, Conn.: New York Graphic Society, 1972), 189.

[31] Jeffrey Hamburger, *The Visual and the Visionary: Art and Female Spirituality in Late Medieval Germany* (New York: Zone Books, 1998), 121–4.

[32] Fitzpatrick, 'On Eucharistic Sacrifice'.

[33] Peter Browe, *Die Eucharistischen Wunder des Mittelalters*, (Breslauer Studien zur historischen Theologie, NF 4; Breslau: Verlag Müller & Seiffert, 1938), and Caroline Walker Bynum, *Holy Feast and Holy Fast: The Religious Significance of Food to Medieval Women* (Berkeley, Calif.: University of California Press, 1987).

[34] Among the flood of recent works on eucharistic devotion in the later Middle Ages, see especially Pelikan, *Christian Tradition*, iii. *Growth*, 146, 184–204; Charles M. A. Caspers, '*Meum summum desiderium est te habere*: L'Eucharistie comme sacrement de la rencontre avec Dieu pour tous les croyants (ca. 1200–ca. 1500)', in André Haquin (ed.), *Fête-Dieu (1246–1996)*, i. *Actes du Colloque de Liège, 12–14 Septembre 1996* (Louvain-la-Neuve: Institut d'études médiévales de l'Université catholique de Louvain, 1999), 127–51; idem, 'The Western Church during the Late Middle Ages: *Augenkommunion* or Popular Mysticism', in Charles Caspers, Gerard Lukken, and Gerard

fourteenth-century German mystic Adelheid Langmann wrote: 'We eat God not so that he changes into us but so that we change into him.'[35] Hence, as the poems of Hadewijch suggest, the Eucharist was hymned in images of fecundity, pregnancy, and sexual union, of eating, admixture, and liquification. In the bodily sacrifice of the altar, the worshipper ascended into God through the pain of Christ.

There are clearly elements of substitution here. Discussions of the eucharist as sacrifice even suggest that the New Testament offering is a substitute for the Old; Alger of Liège, connecting sacrifice to the inevitable discussion of mode of presence, argued that Christ's giving of himself in the mass replaces and improves the sacrifices of the old covenant exactly because the bloody offering is unseen.[36] And in the mass Christ pays—and dies—in our stead and on our behalf: 'The Creator of the world himself became the price for you.'[37] But the substitution at the heart of the mass is also a substitution in which individual is subsumed into—*is*—species; part *is* whole. And despite the individualism of a piety that increasingly stressed interior responsibility and private prayer, this subsuming, this incorporation, joined Christians into a wider community. 'The precious blood, which is shed for many for the remission of sins, avails not only for the salvation of the living but even for the salvation of the dead.'[38] Thus it is impossible to understand the medieval theology of redemption without considering purgatory.

Historians have been interested in purgatory of late, stimulated by Jacques Le Goff's brilliant and controversial study, which argues that the notion of a third place between heaven and hell was the creation of the twelfth century. And there is a sense in which the emergence (whenever exactly it comes) of the notion of a place and time for

Rouwhorst (eds.), *Bread of Heaven: Customs and Practices Surrounding Holy Communion: Essays in the History of Liturgy and Culture* (Kampen: Kok Pharos, 1995), 83–97; and André Goossens, 'Résonances eucharistiques à la fin du moyen âge', in Haquin (ed.), *Fête-Dieu*, 173–91.

[35] See Leonard P. Hindsley, *The Mystics of Engelthal: Writings from a Medieval Monastery* (New York: St Martin's Press, 1998), 27–8. For another example, see the passage from William of St Thierry cited in Caspers, '*Meum summum desiderium*', 137.

[36] Alger of Liège, *De Sacramentis*, bk 2, c. 3, PL 180. 815.

[37] See n. 25 above.

[38] Remigius of Auxerre, *De celebratione missae et ejus significatione* (incorporated as ch. 40 of pseudo-Alcuin's *De divinis officiis*), PL 101. 1263C. And see Peter the Venerable, *Contra Petrobrusianos hereticos*, in James Fearns (ed.), *Corpus christianorum: Continuatio medievalis*, 10 (Turnhout: Brepolis 1994), paras. 215 and 265, pp. 128 and 156.

improvement after death reoriented understandings of person, history, and society. There is also a sense in which purgatory was, as both Lester Little and Jacques Le Goff have argued, a reflection of the new bourgeois world: as conceptualized by medieval theologians, although elaborated fully only at Trent in response to Protestant attacks, purgatory was in part a system of exchange.[39] Christ's sufferings on the cross, because innocent, earned merits greater than any payment humans could ever owe for original or personal sin; even the sufferings of the saints and martyrs, in *imitatio Christi*, could exceed punishments they might deserve or satisfaction they might owe. Hence such merits could be drawn on to remit or expiate the Christian's own punishment, a punishment he or she might have paid only partly by the time of death; they could also be drawn on, in intercessory prayer or through indulgences, to benefit loved ones who had died.

What is important for my purposes here, however, is the way in which purgatory was neither a place nor a system of exchange but rather a vast pool of suffering which joined the living and the dead. Purgatory could not, of course, abrogate the judgement of personal death, at which moment the decision was made forever whether the individual went to hell or (probably via purgatory) to heaven. (Indeed purgatory was a third place only temporarily, so to speak; ultimately the universe would resolve itself into the binaries of heaven and hell, good and evil.) But purgatory introduced development of self, fundamental change, into the realm beyond death; and it introduced such change for one's neighbour as well as for oneself. Not only did the self grow beyond the borders of death, punished by but also cleansed and aroused by love; the self could, even before death, participate in and contribute to the pool from which suffering—for self and for others—would be drawn. Especially in the piety of mystical women (as Barbara Newman, Jo Ann McNamara, and Thomas Sweetman have shown), personal suffering came to be seen less as payment for others than as experiential union with them. Saints and pious Christians did not simply pay a penalty owed by others. Rather they suffered their suffering, becoming a part of

---

[39] Jacques Le Goff, *The Birth of Purgatory*, trans. Arthur Goldhammer (London: Scolar Press, 1984), and Lester K. Little, *Religious Poverty and the Profit Economy in Medieval Europe* (Ithaca, NY: Cornell University Press, 1979). See also Takami Matsuda, *Death and Purgatory in Middle English Didactic Poetry* (Woodbridge, Suffolk, and Rochester, NY: Boydell & Brewer, 1997).

it.[40] The point was not so much the punishment or the substitution as the pain itself. Soul joined with soul in a communion of suffering and distress.

Even in women's piety there were quantitative elements; the later Middle Ages was a period of immense enthusiasm for calculations and measurings. Alice of Schaerbeke (d. 1250) felt, for example, that each limb she lost to leprosy won more souls, and her contemporary *Christina Mirabilis* jumped into ovens and icy ponds to enact pre-emptively exactly the pains of purgatory. But if we look closely at this 'purgatorial piety', we see that suffering is not primarily an exchange nor is it primarily a substitute for punishment. Nor indeed is it limited to purgatory, for it traverses the boundary between this life and the next. When Lutgard of Aywières (d. 1246), for example, offered her fasting for the conversion of heretics in this life, her suffering (like the *com-passio* of Mary at the foot of the cross) became one with, was subsumed into, the redemptive pain of Christ. Catherine of Genoa (d. 1510), the great theorist of purgatory, wrote:

If by taking my blood and giving it to man to drink, I could make known to him this truth [about love], I would give it all for love of him. I cannot endure the thought that man, created for the good that I see and know, should lose it. . . . If I knew how, I would leave nothing undone to make known how dreadful a thing is this privation of the love of God.[41]

To Catherine, purging (both in this life and beyond) is a suffering so vast that in it fuse one's own cleansing, one's neighbour's expiation, and the death agonies of Christ. However audacious it may seem, there is something here beyond penal substitution. The pain women offer to God yearns to subsume, represent, incorporate the pain of others and to become the pain of Christ himself.

Hence behind medieval ideas of redemption (whether atonement theory, eucharistic theology, or purgatorial piety) lies a curious

---

[40] Jo Ann McNamara, 'The Need to Give: Suffering and Female Sanctity in the Middle Ages', in R. Blumenfeld-Kosinski and Timea Szell (eds.), *Images of Sainthood in Medieval Europe* (Ithaca, NY: Cornell University Press, 1991), 199–221; Newman, 'On the Threshold'; Robert Sweetman, 'Thomas of Cantimpré, *Mulieres Religiosae*, and Purgatorial Piety: Hagiographical *Vitae* and the Beguine "Voice"', in Jacqueline Brown and W. P. Stoneman (eds.), *A Distinct Voice: Medieval Studies in Honor of Leonard E. Boyle, O.P.* (Notre Dame, Ind.: University of Notre Dame Press, 1997), 606–28.

[41] For these examples, see Bynum, *Holy Feast and Holy Fast*, 117–21, 185, and 351 n. 34. On the enthusiasm for calculation in the later Middle Ages, see Joel Kaye, *Economy and Nature in the Fourteenth Century: Money, Market Exchange and the Emergence of Scientific Thought* (New York: Cambridge University Press, 1998).

understanding of what is sometimes called 'representation'—an idea towards which modern theologians (and writers of what Freeman Dyson calls 'theofiction') gesture but which they find difficult to explain.[42] It is a dangerous notion, the idea that one person's suffering can become another's and the idea that we can become the suffering of God. It led to the death of Simone Weil.[43] But without it we cannot understand medieval theology and devotion. For medieval understandings of redemption assumed Christ redeems us not just because he substitutes for us or arouses our empathy but also because we are *in* Christ on the cross. He represents us because he incorporates us, lifting our distress and our guilt into God. And because he incorporates us, we can incorporate each other.

It is this idea that lies behind the wonderful parable of the servant in the long text of Julian of Norwich's *Showings*, one of the greatest works of late medieval vernacular theology. Julian struggled for years to understand the meaning of her vision of a servant who, flying to do the will of his Lord, fell into a ditch in his eagerness but was, in the end, rewarded by the Lord because of his suffering. How could failure and pain lead to God's reassurance that 'all will be well'? The answer to which Julian finally came was that the servant was not only Adam but also Christ—an answer she understood not didactically (as an allegory deciphered or a doctrine illustrated) but experientially. Just as she had, at age 33, experienced in acute illness a oneness with the agony of Christ's love for humankind, so she now saw that all humanity was forever represented, subsumed, incorporated in the pain and glory of Christ.

The lord is God the Father, the servant is the Son, Jesus Christ, the Holy Spirit is the equal love which is in them both. When Adam fell, God's Son fell; because of the true union which was made in heaven, God's Son could not be separated from Adam, *for by Adam, I understand all mankind*. Adam fell from life to death, into the valley of this wretched world, and after that into hell. God's Son fell with Adam, into the valley of the womb of the maiden who was the fairest daughter of Adam, and that was to excuse Adam from blame in

[42] On 'theofiction', see Freeman J. Dyson, 'Science and Religion: No Ends in Sight', *New York Review of Books* (28 Mar. 2002), 4–6. For an example, see Barbara Newman's use of the novels of Charles Williams in 'On the Threshold', 120. For some thoughts on modern notions of representation (which are very different from medieval ones), see Gerald O'Collins, Ch. 1 above.

[43] A. L. Loades, 'Eucharistic Sacrifice: The Problem of How to Use a Liturgical Metaphor, with Special Reference to Simone Weil', in *Sacrifice and Redemption*, 247–61. See n. 60 below.

heaven and on earth . . . For in all this *our good Lord showed his own Son and Adam as only one man.*

And so has our good Lord Jesus taken upon him all our blame; and therefore our Father may not, does not wish to assign more blame to us than to his own beloved Son Jesus Christ.

. . . His rushing away was the divinity, and his running was the humanity; for the divinity rushed from the Father into the maiden's womb, falling to accept our nature, and in this falling he took great hurt. The hurt he took was our flesh, in which at once he experienced mortal pains. . . . And . . . he could never with almighty power rise from the time that he fell into the maiden's womb until his body was slain and dead, and he yielded his soul into the Father's hand, with all mankind for whom he had been sent. . . .

And [on Easter morn] . . . our foul mortal flesh, which God's Son took upon him, which was Adam's old tunic, tight-fitting, threadbare and short, was then made lovely by our saviour, new, white and bright and forever clean, wide and ample. . . .

. . . Now the Son does not stand before the Father as a servant . . . but richly clothed in joyful amplitude, with a rich and precious crown upon his head. For it was revealed that we are his crown, which crown is the Father's joy, the Son's honour, the Holy Spirit's delight, and endless marvellous bliss to all who are in heaven.[44]

Julian is herself not merely enkindled by, she is incorporated in, this 'one man', this unity of 'his own Son and Adam'. Hence she not only, as Kate Greenspan suggests, claims a universal voice within the personal; she *is* one with all Christians, caught up in the 'one man' that is also God.

[W]e are all one in love. . . . If I pay special attention to myself, I am nothing at all; but in general I am . . . in the unity of love with all my fellow Christians. For it is in this unity that the life of all men consists who will be saved. . . . For in mankind which will be saved is comprehended all, that is to say all that is made and the maker of all. For God is in man and in God is all. And he who loves thus loves all.[45]

Julian's vision of the servant is more complicated than I am able to show here, and it begs (as does all redemption theory) the question of

---

[44] Julian of Norwich, *Showings*, trans. E. Colledge and J. Walsh (New York: Paulist, 1978), long text, c. 51, pp. 274–8; emphasis added. On Julian see the recent study by Bauerschmidt, *Julian of Norwich.*

[45] Julian, *Showings*, long text, c. 9, pp. 191–2. And see Kate Greenspan, 'Autohagiography and Medieval Women's Spiritual Autobiography', in Jane Chance (ed.), *Gender and Text in the Later Middle Ages* (Gainesville, Fla.: University Press of Florida, 1996), 220–2.

theodicy. My point in quoting it is not to explore it fully but only to give a sense of the strangeness of this notion of representation. It is of course Pauline: 'For as by the disobedience of one man many were made sinners, so also by the obedience of one many shall be made just' (Rom. 5: 19). Yet many modern theologians would argue that the notion of the incorporation of all in Adam is based in false science,[46] and rejection of Adam as *humanitas* in which we are contained makes it harder to grasp what it means to say that we are *in* the *humanitas* Jesus unites with *divinitas*. We will not understand medieval soteriology, however, unless we ask exactly what such representation, such participation, such incorporation, really means.

The notion had roots in earlier ideas. In so far as it is a notion of the representing of a group or body by its head, it has origins in corporate images (both biblical and antique) for society—images much explored in late medieval political theory and canon law.[47] In so far as it is the idea that an individual instance is explained ontologically—that is, accounted for in its nature—by an exemplar, its roots are Platonic. (Medieval theologians and philosophers had little Plato directly but absorbed his basic ideas through the Fathers, Latin and Greek, and later through Arab Neoplatonic commentaries on Aristotle). Both these ideas—that is, that the head *is* the body and that the instance *is* (has being) because it participates in the exemplar—are in a sense conceptions of representation. (They are also distant ancestors of Bernard's notion of the *imago* that must return to *similitudo*.) Even more central to the notion of representation as we find it in late medieval understandings of redemption is, however, what I have elsewhere called the habit of concomitance or metonymy—the tendency to think that part *is* whole. Worked out in the eleventh century in the context of eucharistic debate to explain how Christ is totally present in every celebration of the mass and every particle of the fragmented host, concomitance in a technical sense was later used to justify withholding of the cup from the laity and to explain how Christ's blood could be simultaneously preserved on earth in reliquaries and joined with his glorified body in heaven.

---

[46] Fitzpatrick, 'On Eucharistic Sacrifice', 131–3, 150. See n. 601 below.

[47] See Brian Tierney, *Foundations of Conciliar Theory: The Contribution of the Medieval Canonists from Gratian to the Great Schism* (Cambridge: Cambridge University Press, 1955).

Beyond such technical argumentation, the tendency to see whole in part, part in whole, became the characteristic response to the saints, who were understood to be fully present in their every bodily fragment (this was the great period of relic division and distribution) and yet fully present before the throne of God in heaven. (The bodies of kings and cardinals, similarly divided and distributed, were understood to be *pars pro toto* as well.)[48]

My point is this. The late medieval habit of understanding part to be whole, instance to be *in* exemplar, made it possible to think not only of humans subsumed in the *humanitas* of Christ but also of relatives, neighbours, even heretics as subsumed into one's own suffering in a union that was more participation than substitution. It is a problematic assumption—one Aquinas himself questioned when he argued that a person can substitute for his or her neighbour's punishment but not for that neighbour's contrition.[49] Even pious women such as Hadewijch and Catherine of Genoa were not sure how far they could spread their own participatory suffering to others. Our modern struggles show the difficulties with even a quite denatured concept of representation. In these days of identity politics, we have trouble thinking anyone can represent anyone else, so specific and particular have our ideas of 'standing in for' become. But we will not understand what Anselm, Bernard, Abelard, Bonaventure, Thomas à Kempis, Julian of Norwich, Catherine of Siena, or Gabriel Biel meant by redemption unless we understand that, to them, substitution, participation, and representation fuse: we are saved by, because we are *in*, the pouring blood of the Lamb.

III LEGACIES OF MEDIEVAL IDEAS

I shall not propose a theology of the redemption myself. I leave that to the theologians. But my reading convinces me that much modern discussion draws, perhaps without fully understanding them, on

[48] On concomitance, see James J. Megivern, *Concomitance and Communion: A Study in Eucharistic Doctrine and Practice* (Fribourg and New York: University Press and Herder Book Center, 1963), and Bynum, 'Violent Imagery', 20–3. As Bauerschmidt, *Julian*, 220 n. 72, points out, the idea was widespread and regularly included in instruction for the laity. On saints as synecdoche for community, see Monika Otter, *Inventiones: Fiction and Referentiality in Twelfth-Century English Historical Writing* (Chapel Hill, NC: University of North Carolina Press, 1996), 34.

[49] *ST* 3. 48, art. 2, reply obj. 1.

notions that are late medieval. Hence it seems to me useful to close by underlining what have been, for better or for worse, some of the lasting consequences of the late medieval reorientation of soteriology.

The first is a placing of suffering and pain at the heart of human experience. As a number of scholars have noticed, people before the late medieval period wrote relatively rarely of their own pain or that of others as *experienced*. Suffering was described as a physical event; expressionistic and exalted bearing of pain was admired; but how it *felt* was not elaborated. Of the early martyrs it was said, for example, that the pains of the arena were blocked by union with the glory of Christ. Theologians claimed that Mary felt neither birthpangs nor menstrual cramps. Epic and romance reported again and again the cleaving of bodies and spilling of gore; they did not say it hurt. By the later Middle Ages, however, both Aquinas and Bonaventure argued that Christ on the cross felt more exquisite pain than any other human being ever experienced because his body was more perfect. The word for suffering (*passio*) became in exactly this period the word for erotic love. Although we must wait until Erasmus and Montaigne for tales of the agony of kidney stones and gout, we find in the blood piety of the later Middle Ages a sense that suffering is not only redemptive but also experienced, and a sense as well that it is (as Catherine of Genoa wrote) *my* personal expression and *my* personal responsibility.[50] Esther Cohen has argued that medieval theorists located pain in the soul; I think it is more accurate to say that pain was located in the self, which was understood as a psychosomatic unity. The important point, however, as Cohen's analysis suggests, is that the centrality of suffering in modern religious sensibility—both redemption *by* suffering and redemption *of* suffering—has its roots in the later Middle Ages.[51]

---

[50] Auerbach, 'Excursus: Gloria Passionis'; Charles T. Wood, 'The Doctors' Dilemma: Sin, Salvation and the Menstrual Cycle in Medieval Thought', *Speculum*, 56 (1981), 710–27; Paulette L'Hermite-Leclercq, 'Le Sang et le lait de la Vierge', in *Le Sang au moyen âge*, 145–62; Caroline Walker Bynum, 'Why All the Fuss about the Body? A Medievalist's Perspective', *Critical Inquiry*, 22 (Autumn 1995), 1–33; Ellen M. Ross, *The Grief of God: Images of the Suffering Jesus in Late Medieval England* (New York: Oxford University Press, 1997); and Esther Cohen, 'The Animated Pain of the Body', *American Historical Review*, 105/5 (2000), 36–68.

[51] Cohen is certainly right that pain was not located in the body. But she makes too much out of passages in which theologians locate pain in the separated soul; such separation was, to these theologians, an abnormal situation. The paradigmatic person was the psychosomatic unity before death or after resurrection. And much medieval

As does the importance of the body, that currently fashionable topic of study.[52] We are often told in older scholarship that medieval theorists and ordinary believers were dualists, hating the body, desiring to escape its coils.[53] Recent interpretation, however, is agreed that medieval theologians and devotional writers understood the self as a body–soul unity, so inextricably bound together that the separated soul in the period between death and resurrection was imaged in vernacular literature as somatomorphic (i.e. body-shaped) and was said by university theologians to yearn for its body in order to experience the fullness of heavenly glory. Although Patristic theologians had already argued that what are saved are not unisex souls but specific persons whose to-be-resurrected bodies carried forever the physical markers of sex, race, height, etc., it was in the later Middle Ages that body became not only partner in the preservation of personal identity but also instrument of religious experience. Both Bernard of Clairvaux and the hagiographer of *Christina Mirabilis* expressed this. In his *On Conversion*, Bernard has body address soul, which is castigating it: 'I am your body, your very self'. The thirteenth-century author of Christina's life constructs a little soul–body dialogue that echoes Bernard's earlier one.

Then, taking her feet with both hands, she would kiss the soles of her feet . . . and say: 'O most beloved body! Why have I beaten you? Why have I reviled you? Did you not obey me in every good deed I undertook to do with God's help? You have endured the torment . . . most generously. . . . Now, O best and sweetest body, . . . is the end of your hardship, now you will rest in the dust . . . and then, at the last, when the trumpet blows, you will rise again purified of all corruptibility and you will be joined in eternal happiness with the soul you have had as a companion in the present sadness.'[54]

psychology was devoted to the nexus of body and soul—to finding the place (in upper body or lower soul) where sensation was experienced. See Bernard McGinn (ed.), *Three Treatises on Man: A Cistercian Anthropology* (Kalamazoo, Mich.: Cistercian Publications, 1977).

[52] See William R. LaFleur, 'Body', in Mark C. Taylor (ed.), *Critical Terms for Religious Studies* (Chicago: University of Chicago Press, 1998), 36–54.

[53] See Jacques Le Goff, 'Body and Ideology in the Medieval West', in *The Medieval Imagination*, trans. Arthur Goldhammer (Chicago: University of Chicago Press, 1988), 83–5, and idem, 'The Repudiation of Pleasure', in ibid. 93–103.

[54] Bernard, *On Conversion* 3. 4–4. 5, in *Bernard of Clairvaux: Selected Works*, trans. G. R. Evans (New York: Paulist Press, 1987), 69–70, and Thomas of Cantimpré, *The Life of Christina Mirabilis*, c. 5. 36, trans. Margot H. King, *Matrologia latina*, 2 (Saskatoon: Peregrina, 1986), 27–8.

As Thomas of Cantimpré's picture of Christina's enraptured conversation suggests, the new emphasis on the body as locus of religious significance enhanced and was enhanced by a flowering of women's piety.[55]

We can see ecclesiastical authorities contributing to the new emphasis on body through what recent historians call their 'construction of otherness'—that is, their interpretation of various positions and movements as heterodox. When theologians and polemicists wrote against heretics in the twelfth to fifteenth centuries, they charged again and again that groups as different as Waldensians, Cathars, and Lollards denied the embodiment of the self and its salvation by the cross. Behind their litany of charges (heretics supposedly denied the resurrection of the body, the proper burial of the dead, the goodness of procreation and property, the real presence of body and blood in the eucharist, the reality of Christ's body at the crucifixion) lay an obsession with vindicating embodiment as a place of encounter with God.[56] Church leaders labelled opposition to crosses, church buildings, sacraments, and eucharistic presence not so much anti-clericalism as docetism (denial of Christ's body as real) or Manicheanism (rejection of the goodness of matter and flesh). Moreover, fear of Jewish mockery of the God-man (of the idea of an atoning death or of a real presence in bread and wine) was a motive in persecution and pogrom. Ecclesiastical authorities sometimes opposed but frequently fomented anti-Judaism; charges both of ritual murder and of host violation were twisted and became hideous defences of the embodied God against perceived denial and desecration.

But anxiety about embodiment permeated the culture as well. There is evidence that popular religious movements did attack

---

[55] See Caroline Walker Bynum, 'The Female Body and Religious Practice in the Later Middle Ages', in *Fragmentation and Redemption: Essays on Gender and the Human Body in Medieval Religion* (New York: Zone Books, 1991), 181–238. And see Sarah Beckwith, 'A Very Material Mysticism: The Medieval Mysticism of Margery Kempe', in *Gender and Text*, 195–215.

[56] I cannot elaborate this point fully here. But see e.g. Walter L. Wakefield and Austin P. Evans, *Heresies of the High Middle Ages: Selected Sources* (New York: Columbia University Press, 1969), 204–8, for the details concerning the reality of the body added to the profession of faith required of Waldes, and 118–21, and 234 for similar elements in anti-Petrobruysian, anti-Cathar, and anti-Waldensian polemic. See also Peter Biller, 'Cathars and Material Women', in Peter Biller and A. J. Minnis (eds.), *Medieval Theology and the Natural Body: York Studies in Medieval Theology*, i (Rochester, NY: York Medieval Press, 1997), 61–107.

worship of the cross as worship of torture. Theologians (Anselm was one) took seriously Jewish criticisms of the incarnation as insult to omnipotence and, exactly in exaggerating such criticism, revealed their own inner hesitations about the emphases of affective piety. Authorities opposed as well as fomented the devotion of Christian pilgrims to blood miracles that reduced Christ to holy matter.[57] Moreover, new ascetic practices—extreme fasting, sleep deprivation, flagellation, and bodily mutilation—testify to a religious use of the flesh that was both punitive and liberating. In the theology (both Latin and vernacular) of the later Middle Ages, body was contested and valorized as never before, a site of terrifying significance.

The third consequential refocusing of redemption theory is the well-known emphasis on substitution, which sometimes became, as I explained above, a notion of representation. It is clear, as many scholars stress, that sacrifice and satisfaction are at the heart of late medieval theology; both assume substitution. Salvation comes *per sanguinem; sanguis Christi* is poured out *pro nobis*. Christ's sacrifice on the cross substitutes for earlier and incomplete sacrifices. His life pays in our stead and on our behalf; in some formulations, it suffers our punishment as well. Moreover, the suffering of the saints not only substitutes for our penalties in purgatory but can also be offered up in a kind of exchange for the evil deeds of heretics, Jews, blaspheming artisans, thieving servant girls, etc., who crucify Christ. (Anti-Judaism, misogyny, and scapegoating of the lower classes echo palpably in the litanies of those responsible for injury to God.[58]) Even the radical self-denial of ordinary Christians—the bodies whipped in flagellant processions, starved in convents, or torn apart on the scaffold—can be offered in the place of payment and punishment. And, as I explained, such substitution is often not so much exchange or replacement of one by another as representation in a metonymic sense. As we are all in the humanity subsumed in Christ, so we are all in each other. Alice of Schaerbeke and Catherine of Genoa not only offered their pain *for* others; they felt that, through it, they were caught up with others into the salvific pain of God.

---

[57] I discuss this in 'Seeing and Seeing Beyond: The Mass of St. Gregory in the Fifteenth Century', in Anne-Marie Bouché and Jeffrey Hamburger (eds.), *The Mind's Eye: Art and Theology in the Middle Ages* (Princeton: Princeton University Press, to appear).

[58] For more on this, see 'Violent Imagery', 26–32.

Unattractive as is the penal substitution implicit in some of this piety, there is thus another aspect to which Barbara Newman has called our attention. It is implicit in Bernard's idea that we are created as *imago* or *in imagine Dei* (hence *capax Dei*—i.e. God-capable), or in Julian's notion of the 'godly will' which never departs from God. To Julian and Bernard, as to Abelard, Anselm, Catherine of Siena and Gabriel Biel, we are selves that can be turned on by evidence of God's self-sacrificing love for us because we see ourselves in the suffering servant. Indeed not only do we see ourselves there; we have our existence in (i.e. are incorporated in, are ontologically accounted for by) his *humanitas*. Thus there are hints (although only hints) of universalism, especially in the form this piety takes with late medieval women. Hadewijch wanted her sufferings to remove souls from hell itself, although she admitted that the request was 'a fault'. Julian struggled against (although she ultimately accepted) what she understood to be the church's requirement that some remain in hell.[59] For all the guilt-tripping and scapegoating implicit in the late medieval obsession with human responsibility for the death of Christ, there are optimistic and universalist implications in the understanding that that death is representative. If it is *humanitas* that suffers, if *pars* is really *totum*, then *all* are in the suffering body lifted to God and *all* are in every self that joins with, that performs, the *humanitas* of Christ.[60]

It is, I would suggest, almost impossible for today's theologians to think back behind the emphases introduced into Christianity by late medieval thought and praxis. For better and for worse, we seem stuck with a medieval sense that suffering is redemptive, that an embodied self is the locus of religious experience and the guarantee of personal identity, that salvation involves substitution for and repre-

---

[59] Newman, 'On the Threshold', esp. 124–6, 130–3.

[60] If the traditional Western understandings of redemption are to make any sense, some reformulation of 'representation' along these lines must, it seems to me, be found. Modern meanings of the word do not work. After all, Christians do not elect Christ their representative, even when they respond with faith and love. Nor can Christ's work simply be the providing of an image or picture of a life, for his life is, if exemplary, nonetheless quite particular (male, Jewish, 1st-cent. CE, etc.) Something of the medieval sense of incorporation and concomitance, the Platonic sense of participation, must be retained, yet we in the Anglo-American tradition are not, by instinct, Platonists, nor is metonymy our natural mode of thinking. If we could recuperate what medieval representation really means, we might recuperate its universalism as well. To say this leaves, of course, untouched the question of why the salvific act in which we are incorporated is bloodshed.

sentation of the many by the one.[61] The emphases of late medieval redemption theology have thus fed, by a process I cannot trace here, the individualism, the universalism, and the violence of modern Western attitudes. Stimulating masochism, self-blaming, scapegoating, persecution, and a problematic rhetoric of self-sacrifice, they have also engendered a fascination with body as carrier of personal identity as well as a determination to include, value, and account for the full range of human difference.

IV CONCLUSION

Medieval redemption theory was a piety and theology of blood. It is far too simple, I think, to attribute the violence of Christian society in the later Middle Ages to the theology; nor should we see some essential violence in human persons as the cause of theological formulations. Both ideas and persons are, in my historian's view, too complicated for such analyses.[62]

---

[61] A perfect example of the modern expression of these attitudes (or the modern assumption that they are characteristically Christian attitudes) is Graham Greene's novel, *The End of the Affair* (1951; New York and London: Penguin Putnam, 1975). The heroine writes in her diary (109–12): 'I hated the statues, the crucifix, all the emphasis on the human body. I was trying to escape from the human body. . . . I thought I could believe in some kind of a God that bore no relation to ourselves, something vague, amorphous, cosmic. . . . And then I came into that dark church in Park Road and saw the bodies standing around me on all the altars—the hideous plaster statues with their complacent faces, and I remembered that they believed in the resurrection of the body, the body I wanted destroyed forever. . . . And of course on the altar there was a body too—such a familiar body, more familiar than Maurice's, that it had never struck me before as a body with all the parts of a body, even the parts the loin-cloth concealed. I remembered one in a Spanish church I had visited with Henry, where the blood ran down in scarlet paint from the eyes and the hands. It sickened me. . . . I thought, these people love cruelty. A vapour couldn't shock you with blood and cries. . . . So today I looked at that material body on that material cross, and I wondered, how could the world have nailed a vapour there? A vapour of course felt no pain and no pleasure. . . . I said I hate you, but can one hate a vapour? I could hate that figure on the Cross with its claim to my gratitude—"I've suffered this for you" but a vapour. . . . [ellipses in original] . . . Am I a materialist after all, I wondered? . . . Suppose God did exist, suppose he was a body like that, what's wrong in believing that his body existed as much as mine? Could anybody love him or hate him if he hadn't got a body? . . . I walked out of the church in a flaming rage, and in defiance of Henry and all the reasonable and detached I did what I had seen people do in Spanish churches: I dipped my finger in the so-called holy water and made a kind of cross on my forehead.'

[62] I personally am not attracted to either Girard's idea of sacrifice, which seems to me a priori and grounded in an outdated Freudianism, or to an 'exemplarism', 'abyssal theology', or theology of response that valorizes love located in suffering and death.

But the power in the blood was, for Europeans in the twelfth to the sixteenth centuries, a trigger of violence, confidence, shame, repentance, self-sacrifice, and trust in God. The blood excited and expiated, substituted and incorporated, accused and freed. I find it hard to see how the Anselmian and Abelardian aspects can be separated from each other either theologically or historically; I also find it hard to claim that the horror we sometimes feel at such piety results only from the theory of penal substitution. There is nothing penal or even substitutional in the idea that comfort lies in creeping into the flayed skin of the Saviour or drinking the blood of God. But the horror remains.

The cry 'Blut! Blut!' echoed in a world where people inflicted unspeakable cruelties on self and other, as they do today, and, as they do today, tried to do the best they could with what they had. 'Why by blood when he could have done it by word'?[63] Like Bernard, they were puzzled. But the power in the blood was what they had. That it was so they knew; like many of us, they were not certain why.

Fitzpatrick may, however, have a point when he says that the very crudeness in redemption theology keeps our attention focused on 'the reality of sin and evil in the world, and . . . the "costingness," if I may use von Hügel's word, of our release from it' ('On Eucharistic Sacrifice', 153).

[63] Bernard of Clairvaux, *Contra quaedam capitula errorum Abelardi epistola CXC seu tractatus ad Innocentium pontificem*, c. 8, in PL 182. 1069. Fuller quotation in the epigraph to this chapter.

Foundational and Systematic Issues

9

Narrative and the Problem of Evil: Suffering and Redemption

ELEONORE STUMP

INTRODUCTION

In this chapter, I am going to examine one form of the problem of evil, namely, that having to do with horrendous evil; I will consider whether there is anything that can redeem the suffering even of those whose lives include the perpetration of great evil. But I want to explore this question in a way unusual for a philosopher, and so I need to begin by explaining and providing some justification for the methodology I mean to use.

The contemporary philosophical debate over the problem of evil is becoming complicated and technical; questions of probability, for example, are playing an increasing role. In its focus on such philosophical technicalities, the discussion sometimes seems simply to side-step much that has been at the heart of the problem of evil for reflective thinkers. And so to many people there has also been something heartily unsatisfying about the direction of the contemporary debate.

In his recent book *The Empirical Stance*, Bas van Fraassen, who is a paradigmatic analytic philosopher, frames a related charge that he levels against a part of his own discipline, namely, analytic metaphysics. He says, '[analytic] metaphysicians interpret what we initially understand into something hardly anyone understands, and then insist that we cannot do without that. To any incredulous listener they'll say: Construct a better alternative! But that just signals their invincible presumption that [analytic] metaphysics is the sine qua non of understanding.'[1] And he goes on to say, 'The

---

[1] Bas van Fraassen, *The Empirical Stance* (New Haven: Yale University Press, 2001), 3.

metaphysical enterprise [of analytic philosophy]...subverts our understanding both of our own humanity and of the divine—be it real or unreal—by its development of a detailed intricate understanding of simulacra under the same names.'[2]

I would put the point, or my version of what I take his point to be, in this way. Left to itself, because it values intricate, technically expert argument, the analytic approach has a tendency to focus more and more on less and less; and so, at its worst, it can become plodding, pedestrian, sterile, and inadequate to its task. In particular, philosophy in the Anglo-American tradition has tended to leave to one side the messy and complicated issues involved in relations among persons. When analytic philosophers need to think about human interactions, they tend to make up short, thin stories of their own, involving the philosophical crash-dummies Smith and Jones.

Expertise regarding persons and personal interrelations can be found with psychologists and anthropologists, among others, but it seems to me to manifest itself most plainly among the creators of literature, especially the storytellers. One idea, then, for addressing the shortcomings of analytic philosophy while preserving its characteristic excellences is to marry it to the study of narrative. I am hardly the first philosopher to whom it has occurred that analytic philosophy would benefit by some attention to literature. Others, including Bernard Williams and Martha Nussbaum, have also advocated this approach. (The acidulous complaints by critics that some of Nussbaum's work isn't really philosophy seem to me more an indictment of analytic philosophy, revealing the very defects I have just canvassed, than a criticism of the methods Nussbaum employs.[3]) My reasons for turning to literature are somewhat different from those that have been given by others;[4] for present purposes, however, I want not so much to argue for the methodology as to try to allay some concerns about it which are bound to crop up.

---

[2] Bas van Fraassen, *The Empirical Stance* (New Haven: Yale University Press, 2001), 4.

[3] For an example of such criticism, see Jenny Teichman, 'Henry James Among the Philosophers', *New York Times Book Review* (10 Feb. 1999), 24.

[4] e.g. Nussbaum tends to talk in terms of knowing through emotion and imagination, and she argues that there are some kinds of knowledge which can't be grasped by the intellect. See e.g. *The Fragility of Goodness: Luck and Ethics in Greek Tragedy and Philosophy* (Cambridge: Cambridge University Press, 1986), 45–7.

One general concern stemming just from the inclusion of narrative in philosophical discussion has to do with order and structure. Philosophical work in the analytic tradition commonly has a certain sort of tight order to it because it is structured around arguments. There is a thesis that is the conclusion of an argument, and that argument consists of premisses, which themselves might need to be argued for or at least elucidated. And so the discussion proceeds in an orderly way designed to compel agreement. For philosophers, the structure of the argument is a kind of exoskeleton for the discussion, immediately visible and effective for defence.

Now one might suppose that this sort of structure can be preserved even with the inclusion of narrative in the discussion. One just has to let a narrative be brought in at the appropriate point where it supports or illustrates a premiss. But to weave narrative into philosophy in this way is to demean the role of narrative, so that the narrative becomes little more than a picture put next to the text for those who find books without pictures boring. If we use literary texts in this way, just to support premisses in a philosophical argument, we are in effect dragging the literature in gratuitously, like anecdotes in an after-dinner speech, added to give entertainment to the proceedings without advancing the thought.

But a real story cannot be reduced to a premiss or two. Unless the literary texts in question are like Aesop's fables, designed on purpose to teach one philosophical lesson, what is philosophically interesting about a text will illustrate or illuminate philosophical reflection in a much messier way. In fact, a real story cannot be captured even in a set of expository propositions designed to summarize the plot. That is why Cliff's Notes are no substitute for the literary work the Notes attempt to summarize; a plot summary of *Middlemarch* loses what is best in the book.

In this choice of methodology, there is therefore a sacrifice of tough and visible orderliness. By comparison with a philosophical work which moves in a disciplined way through argument to the demonstration of a thesis, discussion including narratives will look—will be—soft and rambling, with the bones of the thought beneath the surface.

Biblical Narratives: Methodological Concerns

A different set of problems arises because of the nature of the narratives I want to use. Those philosophers willing to engage narratives have tended to consider literary works devised by single authors who were the creators of that literature. But narrative comes in many forms, from the highly self-conscious artistry of Aeschylean tragedy to the communally produced narratives of folklore. I am going to consider a part of the spectrum different from that typically focused on so far by philosophers looking at literature. The narrative I want to think about in connection with the problem of evil is biblical. To my mind, there is a certain commonsensical obviousness about the choice to use biblical stories. Biblical narratives embody the reflections of communities signally concerned with both the insights and the problems of religion, and the narratives are also at least partially constitutive of the religions under attack in arguments from evil.[5] So it seems clearly appropriate to incorporate biblical narratives in any attempt to meld literature and philosophy in reflection on the problem of evil.

Nonetheless, my choice of narratives from biblical texts will raise questions. One concern regarding this choice of narratives arises because the method I intend to employ in examining the biblical texts is not a historical method. But the sort of biblical exegesis which has been dominant for a long time now is historical. Historical biblical scholarship is an attempt to understand biblical texts by exploring and reconstructing the circumstances within which those texts were generated. In so far as the point of my examination of the biblical texts is not to elucidate a period in history or a historical culture, but rather to shed light on a philosophical position, the historical approach is manifestly not germane to my project. Nonetheless, because of the prominent place historical biblical scholarship has had in academic institutions, it is probably necessary to say something in defence of my failure to employ it here.

Some proponents of the historical approach to biblical studies are inclined to think that their discipline has demonstrated the inadvisability or even the impossibility of employing on biblical texts

---

[5] This is true even for Islam, part of whose self-understanding depends on certain interpretations of narratives in the Hebrew Bible.

anything other than historical methods, and in particular the inadvisability of approaching the texts as literature. Literary examination of texts, they object, might be suitable for a novel or some other product of an individual mind operating at a high level of artistry.[6] But the biblical texts, in the view of historical scholars, tend to be a *mélange* of smaller bits put together by anonymous editors for various religious or polemical purposes.[7] It makes no sense, on this view, to ask philosophical and literary questions suitable to a single artist's work when the text being examined is a crazyquilt of bits and pieces stitched together at various times by various people whose governing concerns were religious or political, not artistic or philosophical.

But even if we assume for the sake of argument that the picture the historical approach paints of biblical texts is altogether correct and that biblical texts do tend to be composites of simpler bits assembled by editors with varying concerns and interests, it will not follow that we cannot treat a biblical text as a unified whole. On the historical approach, a text will have the form it does because there was a *last* redactor who brought the earlier sources or stories together into that final form. There is no reason for rejecting a priori the supposition that such a redactor may have had literary or philosophical skills which were employed in his compilation of the final form of the text, even if his primary motivation was political or ideological, rather than literary and philosophical. And, of course, one way for us to decide whether a final redactor was artistically or philosophically competent is to see if the text can be read as the product of such a mind.

So, I think there is nothing in the results of historical research on biblical texts which rules out approaching a biblical text as a unity or using on it the methods that have proved fruitful in other philosophical examinations of literature.

---

[6] For an example of this sort of complaint, see Mark Zvi Brettler, *The Book of Judges* (London and New York: Routledge, 2002). Brettler says that calling the Bible literature is 'anachronistic, and often suggests inappropriately that the Bible is "Literature." . . . I am deeply sympathetic to a point made by Robert P. Carroll, that reading the Bible as literature is a "misreading of the text" ' (p. 9).

[7] See e.g. Marvin Pope, *Job* (The Anchor Bible, Garden City, NY: Doubleday, 1973), pp. xl–xli: 'It is scarcely possible to speak of the author of any biblical book in the modern sense of the word, for virtually all biblical books are composite in some degree.'

THEODICY AND DEFENCE

Finally, I need to say a word about how my project relates to more common approaches to the problem of evil.

A theodicy and a rejection of theodicy each offer or presuppose a view about what the world is like. The picture theodicy paints is meant to show us God and human beings in such a light that we can begin to see how God and human suffering coexist in our world. The picture offered by opponents of theodicy, on the other hand, presents the world in such a way that some defect of mind or character would be required to believe that it included God as well as suffering. Sometimes the thing to do with such divergence of views is to try to adjudicate the truth or falsity of claims particularly important to it. But another thing we could do would be simply to consider a story which helps us see the world in one or another of the relevant ways, and then re-evaluate the divergence of views in light of the story. It is the second sort of strategy that I will pursue here, for the reasons I have given.

Strictly speaking, this puts my project in the realm of a defence, rather than a theodicy, as these terms have come to be used.[8] A defence provides just a *possible* morally sufficient reason why an omniscient, omnipotent, perfectly good God might allow evil, unlike a theodicy which is an attempt to explain God's allowing evil in the actual world. That is, defence considers possible worlds which contain God and suffering and which are similar to the actual world, at least in the sense that they contain rational creatures, natural laws, and evils much like those in our world; and then the defence proposes a morally sufficient reason for God's allowing evil in such worlds. What distinguishes a defence from a theodicy is that a defence does not claim that the morally sufficient reason it presents is the one which in fact justifies God's actions in the actual world. It might be, for all we know, but a defence does not require it. A defence, then, makes no claims about God's actual intentions and reasons for allowing evil, but it does give us one way to understand the coexistence of God and suffering.

---

[8] For Plantinga's explanation of this distinction, see James Tomberlin and Peter van Inwagen (eds.), *Alvin Plantinga* (Dordrecht: Reidel, 1985), 42, 242.

The biblical narrative I am going to examine constitutes a story of a world that contains both God and suffering and that can nonetheless evoke in us gladness rather than dismay. Because my project is defence and not theodicy, I will not claim that that story gives us God's actual morally sufficient reason for causing or allowing evil; that is, I will not argue for the truth of the world-view of the story. My aim is the more modest one of using the story to show a possible morally sufficient reason for God's action or inaction. Furthermore, my aim is limited in yet another way because I am not claiming that this defence is successful with regard to all evils. It is entirely possible that there is no single defence which is suitable for the whole panoply of human evil. Nonetheless, if the defence is successful in the extreme case I explore in this paper, it at least opens up new ways of thinking about the redemption of suffering in other cases as well.

With this much background explanation of the methodology at issue in this chapter, then, I want to turn to the problem of evil and the biblical narrative that I mean to examine in connection with that problem.

HORRENDOUS EVIL

In a recent excellent book on the problem of evil, Marilyn Adams defines horrendous evils as 'evils the participation in which (that is, the doing or suffering of which) constitutes prima facie reason to doubt whether the participant's life could (given their inclusion in it) be a great good' to the sufferer.[9] A large part of her book is given over to considering whether there are benefits to such unwilling innocent sufferers that could possibly redeem the suffering and turn the sufferer's life into a good for the sufferer. Many reflective people looking at cases of horrendous evil feel strongly that there is nothing, there could be nothing, which defeats the evil in such cases. No benefit is brought about by the suffering which could not be got without the suffering and which is worth the suffering. The efforts of theodicy to find such benefits strike them as shallow at best and obscene at worst. It must follow on such a view that a person whose life manifests horrendous evil is a person whose life was not a good for

---

[9] Marilyn McCord Adams, *Horrendous Evils and the Goodness of God* (Ithaca, NY: Cornell University Press, 1999), 26.

him; such a person would have been better off if he had died at birth or had never lived.

I think it is indisputable that sometimes the suffering a person endures breaks that person past healing. Sometimes a person's life is irremediably ruined, in the sense that it can no longer be made whole; its initial promise can no longer be fulfilled. The paradigm of such a person in the Greek world is Oedipus. Sophocles has Oedipus claim to be among the worst of the afflicted,[10] and it is not hard to see why. By the time he appears in *Oedipus at Colonus*, he is a homeless, blind beggar, disfigured, bedevilled by fear, tormented by self-loathing, and shunned with horror by all who meet him. What is broken and ruined in Oedipus could not conceivably be restored to wholeness. Surely this is horrendous evil if anything is.

And yet Sophocles' Oedipus is pitiably anxious to make clear that his dreadful acts were in some important sense involuntary. 'There is more of suffering than of violence in my deeds', he tells the Chorus.[11] It is not hard to see why this claim matters to him. Oedipus suffers horrendously, but at least he suffers as a victim of destiny; and so there remains this much beauty in him and in his life: he is innocent. It is also possible, however, to be broken and ruined and to know that one has brought the horror on oneself by one's own wrong acts.[12]

---

[10] *Oedipus at Colonus*, ll. 104–5.

[11] Hugh Lloyd-Jones (trans.), *Oedipus at Colonus* (Loeb Classical Library, 21; Cambridge, Mass.: Harvard University Press, 1994–6), 170.

[12] Because I am focusing on the brokenness and ruin of the life of a perpetrator of great evil, I am concerned with a somewhat different problem from that discussed by Ian Boyd in his excellent paper, 'The Problem of Self-Destroying Sin in John Milton's *Samson Agonistes*', *Faith and Philosophy*, 13 (1996), 487–507: 'Self-destroying sin is evil, the doing of which gives a Christian *prima facie* reason to doubt whether her life could be counted a great good on the whole. That is, most people would agree that her doing this sort of evil constitutes a *prima facie* reason to doubt whether, given the inclusion of such evil action, her life can be a great good to her on the whole' (p. 489). I am concerned not with the way a serious sin by itself mars a life, but with the life felt as broken and ruined by the sufferer, where the culpability for the suffering lies with the sufferer. My evaluation of Samson's case now differs from Boyd's, which I at one time shared. Boyd says, 'it would, of course, have been better if Samson could have attained all of the goods he did and fulfilled God's promise without sinning. But, given the choices Samson made, his suffering at his sin (and God's response to it) is sufficient for the attainment of the goods that defeat his evil' (p. 498). On Boyd's evaluation, although the combination of the evil of Samson's sinning and the subsequent good of Samson's heroism constitute a good life for Samson, it is not clear that there wouldn't have been a better life for Samson if God had brought about Samson's death before he began the process of wrecking his life by sinning. And so the problem that concerns me

ANOTHER VERSION OF THE PROBLEM OF EVIL

There is therefore another version of the problem of evil that also bears consideration, namely, that which focuses on the horrendous suffering of the lives of perpetrators, rather than victims, of great evil. This version of the problem has been largely left to one side, I think, because we tend to react without pity to the perpetrators. We take them to get what they deserve. And yet imagine that Joseph Goebbels failed to kill himself, after his wife had killed their six children and herself at his instigation; imagine that in the final fall of Berlin he had finally seen himself just as we see him today. It is not hard to imagine his lamenting that it would have been so much better for him if God had let him die at birth. And if that line is true, as it seems at first glance to be, then the problem of evil can surely also be raised about the horrendous evil of being a perpetrator, as well as a victim. Even if it were true that the suffering of the perpetrator were deserved, if both the evil and the deserved suffering could have been prevented, if the perpetrator would have been much better off dying young rather than living to perpetrate the evil, then why wouldn't an omniscient, omnipotent, perfectly good God provide for the death of the perpetrator before he does the evil?

The case of the perpetrators of horrendous evil is thus the hardest case for theodicy. If it can be shown that even a person whose own culpable acts have broken him and left him in horrendous suffering can have a life which is a good for him, then there is an a fortiori argument to other less disturbing cases. So, for these reasons, I want to explore one case of horrendous evil in which it is the sufferer's own doing that his life was wrecked as it is. I want to look carefully at the story of Samson.

It should be said here that I am not the only person to think that the case of Samson shows us the problem of evil in a particularly disconcerting form but that it also gives us deep insights useful for theodicy. Milton thought so, too, and wrote a play incorporating his

---

here remains. Why would an omniscient, omnipotent, perfectly good God allow Samson to live long enough to engage in the serious sins that ruin his life? Can there be some good for Samson which would not have been attainable without the sinning and the ruined life? That is, there has to be some Christian analogue to the view of the Greek tragedians that there is some great good which cannot be got without suffering.

understanding of the story of Samson. It is clear that Milton saw his own case as analogous to Samson's in many respects, and rightly so. When the Puritans fell from power, Milton, who had given so much of himself to their cause, was left blind, impoverished, and vilified and imperilled by his enemies. At that time, he was also a failure at what he himself saw as his vocation to poetry. Up to that time, his great gifts for literature had been prodigally spent on political pamphlets, and his announced plan to produce a great English epic poem looked more like bombast than promise.[13] So Milton's interest in the story of Samson was not abstract, but personal and anguished. He thought about the horrendous evil of Samson's life out of the ruin of his own life. And the thought is very good. In considering the biblical story of Samson, then, I will also be guided by Milton's understanding of it.[14]

SAMSON IN CAPTIVITY

In introducing Milton's *Samson Agonistes*, Douglas Bush picks out *Oedipus at Colonus* as one of the earlier works of literature Milton's play most resembles[15] and it is not hard to see why he thinks so. Milton's view of Samson is in many respects similar to Sophocles' view of Oedipus. Like *Oedipus at Colonus*, *Samson Agonistes* begins by calling attention to the panoply of the protagonist's sufferings, and there is considerable similarity between the two characters on this score. To begin with, like Oedipus, Samson is blind. The lament over the loss of sight that blind Milton puts in blind Samson's mouth is heart-rending, and it reminds us not to gloss over blindness as a small evil:

> Light, the prime work of God, to me is extinct,
> And all her various objects of delight
> Annulled, which might in part my grief have eased,
> Inferior to the vilest now become
> Of man or worm; the vilest here excel me,

---

[13] Horace, *Ars Poetica*, ed. Edward Henry Blakeney, trans. Ben Jonsen (Freeport, NY: Books for Libraries Press, 1970), ll. 137–9: 'parturient montes, nascetur ridiculus mus'. I am grateful to James Alexander Arieti for helping me with this reference.

[14] For an excellent study of this work of Milton's and its relevance to theodicy, see Boyd, 'Problem of Self-Destroying Sin'.

They creep, yet see; I, dark...
...exiled from light,
As in the land of darkness, yet in light,

.   .   .   .

Myself my sepulchre, a moving grave,
Buried, not yet exempt
By privilege of death and burial
From worst of other evils, pains and wrongs... (11. 70–105)

For Samson, there are indeed many other evils. Oedipus is at least free to wander among his countrymen with his daughters. Samson is exiled, imprisoned, and set to work at hard and demeaning labour, grinding grain like a beast for his enemies. Like Oedipus, Samson is a pariah to the communities around him. But there is an extra measure of humiliation for Samson, because he is forced to use his strength, which was meant to be employed in the liberation of his people, to give food to their enemies; and his enemies exult over him in this condition.

For both Oedipus and Samson, the pain of their condition is made more bitter by the memory of the state from which they have fallen. But for Samson the reversal in fortunes is considerably more complicated than it is for Oedipus, however tangled Oedipus' story is.

To begin with, Samson was called to the state from which he fell. Rescuing his people from their oppressors was his vocation; it was, quite literally, what he was born for. The angel who announces Samson's birth to the hitherto barren woman who becomes his mother tells her to avoid wine, strong spirits, and unclean food and to make sure that no razor ever comes on the child's head, because the child to be born will be a Nazarite from the womb.[16] This special son, the angel tells the woman, is destined to begin to deliver Israel from the Philistines (Judg. 13: 2–5).[17] Samson's downfall is thus not just a personal catastrophe; his failure to fulfil his vocation is also a national disaster. And this disaster is Samson's fault.

Milton sums up Samson's state succinctly by having Samson say,

---

[15] *The Complete Poetical Works of John Milton*, ed. Douglas Bush (Boston: Houghton Mifflin Co., 1965), 513.

[16] For the biblical rules regarding Nazarites, see Num. 6: 1–21.

[17] There is, of course, also a prophecy in Oedipus' story, namely, that Oedipus will kill his father and marry his mother. But although this prophecy could be interpreted as an indication that the gods have ordained Oedipus for the course his life takes, it

'Now blind, disheartened, shamed, dishonored, quelled,
To what can I be useful, wherein serve
My nation, and the work from Heaven imposed . . . ?'   (11. 563–5)

SAMSON'S RELATION TO GOD

Heaven is, of course, the other problem for Samson. There is the
problem of intolerable guilt, which Milton unaccountably left off the
list of Samson's troubles in the preceding lines and which I will
address a little later. But there is also Samson's relationship to God.

That there was such a relationship, that it was direct and powerful, and that Samson trusted in it as a regular part of his life is shown
by the episode of the battle at Lehi. There, the story says, Samson
single-handedly slaughtered a thousand of the enemy, and the Philistines were soundly defeated in the battle. But afterwards Samson
was very thirsty. And so, the text says, 'Samson called to Yahweh
and said, "It is you who gave this great deliverance by the hand of
your servant. And now I am dying of thirst, and I will fall into the
hands of the uncircumcised." ' And God provided water for Samson
by breaking open a place in Lehi, from which water then flowed
(Judg. 15: 14–19).

It is notable that Samson not only thought to call on God when he
needed a drink but that he called on him in such a familiar way.
There is not only no reverent address in Samson's prayer; there is in
fact no address at all. Samson simply turns to God to speak to him
directly, as if invocation of the deity, to get his attention and call him
to listen, were unnecessary for Samson.

None of the other common elements of prayer are present in
Samson's speech either. There is no plea for God's help, not even a
single 'please'. As far as that goes, Samson appears not to think it
necessary even to make a petition. He asks nothing of God. He simply
presents himself to God as thirsty and in want of water. The closest
he comes to making a plea or a petition is to point to a danger to
himself: unrelieved, the condition in which he is will lead to his being
captured by his enemies. Samson points to this possible outcome as a
sort of *reductio ad absurdum* of the idea that God could leave him
thirsty. As the prayer shows, then, Samson expects that his want of
water and the unquestioned unacceptability of his falling to the
Philistines will be enough for God to provide, immediately and on

the spot, what Samson needs. It is equally notable that in this story God seems to agree, at least to this extent: without comment, God provides the water.

The episodes recounting Samson's deeds and experiences also suggest some wild, strong connection between Samson and God. The story of Samson's exploits begins in this way: 'the boy grew, and Yahweh blessed him; and the spirit of Yahweh began to move him in the camp of Dan' (Judg. 13: 24–5). Subsequently, when Samson engages in some feat of great strength, the story often (but not always) says that the spirit of the Lord came down on him—or rushed into him, as the evocative Hebrew has it.[18] But in the catastrophe at the end, the text explains, not only is Yahweh's spirit not coming on Samson, but in fact Yahweh has departed from Samson.[19]

What would it be like to find that the God who had only to see your need to satisfy it, who rushed into you and made you triumphant, was gone from you? Among the things Samson must long for—light, freedom, home—the absent love of the God who rushed into him, with whose strength he was great, must prompt the most painful pining. If horrendous evils can be ranked, if they are not simply incommensurable, then, taken all in all, Samson's sufferings seem to me among the worst. However great Oedipus' misery, it lacks the torment of being abandoned for cause by a deity once intimately, gloriously, with you.

ABANDONED FOR CAUSE

And it is indisputable that Samson was abandoned for cause; his fall is his fault. But what exactly is Samson culpable of? Milton, like very many interpreters of the story, thinks that Samson's fault consists in having told Delilah his secret.[20] But here, I think, Milton has to have it wrong. To see that this is so, consider how we would have to read the story about Samson's capture if Milton were right.

would take a particularly tendentious person to consider a destiny to parricide and matricide as a vocation.

[18] See Judg. 14: 5–6; 14: 19; 15: 14–15.

[19] Judg. 16: 20 says of Samson that he did not know that the Lord had departed from him.

[20] Contemporary interpreters tend also to read the story in this way. So e.g. R. G. Boling, *Judges* (Anchor Bible, GA; Garden City, NY: Doubleday, 1975), 249:

Delilah wants Samson to tell her the secret of his strength (Judg. 16: 4–17). Now Samson has some practice at the suffering of having his secrets betrayed by a woman he loves. Samson's marriage to the Philistine woman at Timnath ended abruptly at the wedding when his bride treacherously revealed the secret she had wheedled out of him (Judg. 14: 10–20). And so Samson, who is as capable of drawing inferences from bitter experience as other people, does not tell Delilah his secret but rather lies to her instead. The wisdom of his decision to lie is immediately apparent—to him as well as to us—because Delilah loses no time in betraying him by passing his lie on to the Philistines, who use what Delilah tells them to try to capture Samson.

One might suppose that Samson would react to Delilah's betrayal in the same way that he reacted to the betrayal of the woman of Timnath, by exploding into fury, leaving her, and killing Philistines. But, in fact, nothing of the sort happens: no fury, no leaving, no attacks on the Philistines. On the contrary, we simply get a repetition of the same scenario. How are we to account for the fact that hot-tempered Samson not only does not explode against her and the Philistines in league with her but instead tamely gives into Delilah's whining and wheedling a second time and pretends again to tell her his secret?

The answer to this question lies in effect in Samson's answer to Delilah's first request for his secret. Why is his response to her initial request a lie? Surely, because he does not trust her not to betray him to his enemies to be put to death. So he believes that the woman he loves, with whom he is sexually intimate, cannot be trusted not to want him dead. That is a fairly stunning failure to trust, on his part.

And that is why Samson is not angry when he finds that Delilah is in league with his enemies. She does not betray his trust as his bride of Timnath did—he does not give her any trust to betray. He is prepared to take her and enjoy her; he is not prepared to give any of himself to her. And so he does not get angry when she tries to betray him to death. Because he has lied to her, she cannot in fact harm him; and because he has not invested himself in her, he does not mind when she tries to do him in. She is like a cat one has carefully declawed; her attempts at attack may be occasions for amusement or annoyance, but they cannot cause any serious reaction.

Now, on Milton's view, how will we have to read the story of Delilah's fourth and final attempt to betray Samson? After three occasions on *each* of which it has to be obvious even to the most obtuse that Delilah has betrayed him to his enemies, on Milton's reading of the fourth occasion Samson is so wearied by the endless importunities of the woman he is besotted with that he tells her the truth about the way in which his enemies can do him in.

But it cannot be that Samson now believes Delilah is trustworthy,[21] and it is equally absurd to suppose that he tells Delilah his secret because he now desires to surrender to his enemies. It is true that the story says Delilah has vexed him practically to death, so that in the end he tells her all his heart. And he does in fact this time, for the first time, tell Delilah something which is true: he has been a Nazarite from the womb, and he has never been shaven. But the question remains whether in telling her this truth, Samson is telling her what he believes is the key to his capture by the Philistines. If he did believe it, then it is evident that he would have to think Delilah would not use the information to do him in or that he would not care much if she did.

If it is not sufficiently clear that neither of these states for Samson is psychologically credible, the rest of the episode shows decisively that such an interpretation of the story is wrong. If Samson had resolved to let Delilah in on the way in which the Philistines could capture him, then when the Philistines did surround him, Samson would realize he was lost. Even if he had somehow supposed that after three attempts at betraying him to his destruction, Delilah had somehow turned trustworthy, he would know how wrong he had been when he found the Philistines around him. Or if he had anticipated such a result but did not care, then he would simply surrender tamely—or at least despairingly—when the Philistines attack him. But none of these things happens in the narrative. On the contrary, in the story, when Delilah wakes him with the cry that the Philistines are upon him, he responds by saying, 'I will go out this time as before and shake myself free' (Judg. 16: 20). To suppose that Samson has this reaction after having given the manifestly treacherous Delilah what he himself believes is the key to his destruction is to make psychological gibberish of the story.

'[Samson's] treason is the betrayal of state secrets and the tragic squandering of his great strength'.

So although very many people read the narrative as Milton does here, Milton cannot be reading the story correctly at this crucial point. But, then, how are we to understand this last episode with Delilah? What is it that Samson is culpable of?

SAMSON AS LIBERATOR OF HIS PEOPLE

To see the answer to this question, it is helpful to look at the episodes in which Samson demonstrates his great strength (Judg. 14: 5–16: 3). Yahweh's spirit is said to come on Samson in only half of these episodes. In the interest of brevity, I want to look at just one of these.

In that episode, Samson seeks out a prostitute who is in Gaza, the Philistine territory to which he is taken when the Philistines finally capture him. Surely, there is a kind of complacency, if not arrogance, in Samson's taking the risk of visiting a prostitute in enemy territory; and, of course, in the story Samson's enemies do get wind of his presence, alone and unprotected, in their midst. Their plan for capturing him depends on the fact that the city's gates are barred at night; they feel sure that they have got him penned up in their city till the morning, when they mean to try to kill him. But the story suggests that Samson also has a plan and that it also involves the city's gates. The story says that Samson got up at midnight to leave through the barred gates. There is no suggestion that Samson knows his presence has been revealed to his enemies. As far as that goes, there is no suggestion that Samson is or needs to be worried about the Philistines even if they were to surround him in the morning. He has, after all, single-handedly defeated a small army of Philistines in the preceding battle. Nonetheless, Samson gets up in the night to leave the barred and gated town—and to make sure the Philistines know that the great Samson was in it.

Samson could leave the town in some simple way, by using his strength to get through the gates somehow. But getting away is not what Samson wants, or at least not all he wants. And so he removes the gates themselves, to flaunt his strength and to manifest his disdain of his enemies to them. Samson will have the whore he wants when he wants her, without hindrance from the contemptible Philistines, just because he is the mighty Samson. If there is any doubt about this reading, it ought to be dispelled by what Samson does with those gates. It would have been a sufficient thumbing of his nose at the Philistines for Samson to uproot the gates and throw them down outside the city wall. What Samson actually does is to put them on his shoulders and lug them all the way up to the top of a hillside, to deposit them there, in view of the surrounding country. There is more than a little hubris in this. And Yahweh's spirit does not come on Samson for this stunt (Judg. 16: 1–3).

It is worth keeping this last episode in mind as we look at the part of the story involving Delilah (Judg. 16: 4–20). The episode involving Delilah occurs near the end of Samson's two decades of serving as judge of Israel. And what does the story suggest about this time? Certainly not that Samson has succeeded in liberating his people from the Philistines. The Philistines are still at least a force to be reckoned with seriously, as their capture of Samson himself makes plain. But there is also no sign that Samson is planning any great public exploits designed for the liberation of his people. On the contrary, the only thing recorded of him at this stage of his career is that he is busy dallying with Delilah. His miraculous birth, his earlier victories over the enemies of his people, his intimacy with God have come to this: after twenty years, his people are not liberated from the Philistines, and his strength is going into preserving a liaison with a woman from whom he knows he has to keep a careful psychic distance.

Furthermore, consider the way in which his great strength comes into play in the episode with Delilah. With the Gaza prostitute, Samson used his power as a means of evading and scorning his enemies. With Delilah, he no longer cares to evade the Philistines, and he even seems bored with scorning them. He knows that they cannot beat him, and he no longer has much interest, apparently, in beating them. He is content just to let them surround him when they will and to brush them off like flies, as a nuisance not worth much notice, when they do. How glorious a flowering of his life and mission is this? The great gift of strength God gave him for the liberation of his people he is now using as a private means to keep his shabby and inadequate love life going. Yahweh's spirit does not come on him when he does.

But this petty self-absorption is not the worst of the episode with Delilah. On each of the first three times when Delilah presses Samson for his secret and he tells her a lie, the Philistines immediately afterwards do to Samson what Samson's lie leads them to expect will defeat Samson. At least after the first occasion, Samson cannot be surprised at what happens; he must expect it. So, at least after the first time, when Samson tells Delilah a lie about what will defeat him, he must expect that the Philistines will do to him whatever he himself puts into their heads with his lie. It is clear, too, that he expects to shake free of their devices, as he himself puts it in the story. This is also what he expects when, on the fourth time of being betrayed, he finds himself surrounded by the Philistines and shaven. When he sees the Philistines around him after he has told Delilah about his Nazarite status, he supposes that he is going to experience nothing more than the fourth repeat of the same farce. And so he tells himself that he will shake himself free this time as before. It cannot be, then, that he himself really believed what he told Delilah, namely, that if he were shaven, he would be weak like other men.

And why would Samson believe a thing of that sort? It is so clearly false. Both from the narrator's point of view and from Samson's, there is just one correct explanation of the source of Samson's strength: it comes from God. The narrative drives home the point that Samson's strength comes from God by its comment on Samson's mistaken belief that he can shake the Philistines off this fourth time as on the preceding three occasions. The text explains Samson's mistake *not* by saying that Samson did not know he was shaven. The text says Samson did not know that Yahweh had departed from him.

So the right way to understand Samson's fourth explanation to Delilah of the secret of his strength is as a mixture of truth and lies. Samson believes and says truly that he has never been shaven because he has been a Nazarite of God's from birth. But the next part of his speech is not true and he does not believe it: it is not the case that simply shaving him will destroy his strength. The lazy complacency that keeps him by Delilah lying and brushing off the Philistine attacks when they come leads to his revealing some deep and important truth to her; but it does not give her the secret of his strength, and Samson does not expect that it will. When he tells Delilah that cutting his hair will make him weak, he is again lying to her, at least in the sense that he is telling her as true what he himself believes to be false.

It is important to see one other implication of Samson's fourth explanation to Delilah of the secret of his strength. After the first three attacks by the Philistines, Samson has to know that his telling

Delilah about his Nazarite status is tantamount to giving it up. If Delilah and the Philistines believe that Samson's strength is in his hair, then Delilah and the Philistines will shave him, and Samson must understand that they will.

In this light, consider the attitude that has to underlie Samson's telling Delilah about his Nazarite status. That status was given to him together with the mission to which his life is supposed to be dedicated. But Samson is not taking that mission seriously here. In the episode with Delilah, Samson is fighting with the Philistines not for the sake of freeing his people but just as a way of continuing to sleep with Delilah. That in these circumstances Samson elects to tell Delilah about his Nazarite status is evidence that it does not mean much to him. Samson does not suppose that his strength depends on his hair. It depends on God, as Samson knows, and it is God's gift to Samson. But if strength is God's gift to Samson, Nazarite status is God's demand of Samson. To rely on having the gift and to be willing to dispense oneself from the demand is to treat God as if he were in Samson's service. Explaining his Nazarite status to Delilah as a means of placating his Philistine concubine and continuing to hang around in enemy territory enjoying her is thus a little like a Dominican's using his habit as a make-shift sheet for his mistress. The purpose for which the symbol is being used shows a disdain for the thing symbolized. It therefore also shows a disdain for God, to whom respect for the symbol and what it symbolizes is owed.

The worrisome element in Samson's attitude towards God after the battle at Lehi thus finds its full-blown awfulness here. Here, with Delilah, Samson takes it for granted that since he is the champion of his people, God will have to continue to bestow the gift of strength on him, but that it does not matter much what Samson himself does or how he treats God. As Samson sees it, dispensing himself from his Nazarite status as a means of mollifying his mistress carries no cost for him, the mighty Samson. With unreflective complacency, he simply assumes that God will keep him mighty when the Philistines surround him after shaving his hair.

And so, in an odd sort of way, by his attitude towards his Nazarite status and by lying about it, Samson makes true what was false before he lied about it: cutting his hair deprives him of his strength. Samson's strength departs from him when his hair is cut, not because his strength is in his hair but because Yahweh departs from him when Samson does not care that his hair is cut. If Samson was contumelious towards the Philistines in the episode with the Gaza prostitute, he is contumelious towards God in this episode with Delilah. This, then, is what Samson is culpable of.

THE END OF THE STORY

The part of the narrative that, in effect, constitutes the end of Samson's story begins with the text's comment that Samson did not know the Lord had departed from him (Judg. 16: 20). Samson is culpable for the contumely that prompts God to depart from him; but God's departing is responsible for the catastrophe that follows, and it is worth noticing this fact. If God had stayed with Samson till after the Philistine attack, then Samson would not have been captured by the Philistines. He is captured, blinded, imprisoned, subjected to hard labour, and paraded as a trophy to an alien god because God chooses to leave Samson when he does. And so, as it turns out on my reading of this narrative, God has not only the sort of indirect responsibility for horrendous evil which I discussed at the outset of this lecture; he also has direct responsibility for the suffering Samson undergoes at the hands of the Philistines. God could have waited till Samson was safe before leaving him, and at that point he could have let Samson know that he was bereft of the strength God gave him, so that Samson kept himself out of danger in consequence. Instead, in the story, God leaves just then when Samson must have his strength to avoid ruin. Although Samson brings the disaster on himself in the sense that his contumelious acts are responsible for God's leaving him, it is God's leaving Samson at that very time that lands Samson in the catastrophic condition he is in at the end. Why does God do this?

This question in effect returns us to the question with which this chapter began the examination of this narrative, namely, whether the life of a person suffering horrendous evil brought on himself by his own evil actions can somehow be a good for that person. We will have an answer to the question about God's reason for leaving Samson when he does, if we can see something that redeems the horrendous evil of Samson's life and makes it a good for Samson. But if there is anything of that sort in this narrative, it will have to come in the very last acts of Samson's life, when he is a captive among the Philistines.

In his captivity among the Philistines, Samson is plunged into the horrendous suffering I described at the start of this chapter, and the mission for which he was born looks like a decisive failure. The victorious Philistines are having a celebration to thank their god for letting them capture Samson, and Samson is the main entertainment for the celebration. By the time of this celebration, Samson has been a Philistine prisoner long enough for his hair to have begun to grow back, and also long enough for some change to have taken place in him.

The nature of the change can be seen in the prayer he makes to God in the Philistine temple. The regrowth of his hair is not the return of his strength; the restoration of his strength requires the return of his God to him, and Samson knows it. And so he prays to God for strength. But this prayer is significantly different from that other recorded prayer of his, after his victory at Lehi when he needed water.

When he was dying of thirst, he prayed to God in this way: 'It was you who gave this great deliverance by the hand of your servant. And now I am dying of thirst, and I will fall into the hands of the uncircumcised'. What he says now, standing between the pillars, is this: 'Oh Lord Yahweh, remember me, please, and give me strength, please, just this once, O God; let me be avenged on the Philistines with revenge for my two eyes' (Judg. 16: 28). The elements notably lacking in the earlier prayer are here now. There is not just one invocation of God in this prayer; there are two. And although the prayer is very short, just a sentence in effect, 'please' also occurs twice in it. There is a plea in it, too, of the sort that was lacking in the earlier prayer. Someone who says 'please, just this once' to another person thereby conveys the power of his need or desire and his awareness of his dependence on the other to give him what he wants.

The implicit repentance in Samson's later prayer of his earlier contumely towards God is by itself a huge change for the better in Samson. In this later prayer, Samson's need, his vulnerability, his recognition that his own will is not enough to save him, are all manifest; and Samson is willing to let them be evident both to himself and to God. In this prayer, Samson is present to God, and for that reason God can also be present to him.

That in the narrative God shares this view is made evident by the fact that God grants Samson's prayer. God, who departed from him when Samson was distant from him and contumelious towards him, returns to Samson after this prayer. God fills Samson with enough strength to bring down the entire Philistine temple.

For my purposes, it is also important to see that the turn to God represented by Samson's prayer coexists with much of Samson's old spirit. Although Samson's suffering turns him to God, it does not tame him. In addition to the absence of any explicit request for forgiveness or direction in his last prayer for strength, there is also the fact that in Samson's last plan he is still confusing his private concerns with his public role as the liberator of his people. In his prayer, he asks God for strength not in order to fulfil his mission, but in order to get personal revenge; he wants his strength back in order, as he says, to be avenged on the Philistines for his eyes. And then there is his last recorded line: 'Let my soul perish with the Philistines' (Judg. 16: 30). This is a prayer, too, but one which is more nearly in the style of Samson's earlier prayer at Lehi. True, it is not a prayer based on a desire that God provide miraculously for him so that he might succeed in triumphing over his enemies. On the contrary, it is a prayer that God might not let him survive the general destruction of the temple's collapse. It is a complete giving up on triumphing. In this sense, the line shows the change from the old Samson. But the style of the prayer is reminiscent of the earlier prayer; and the wilfulness of it, the intransigent refusal to accept life on terms other than his own, has a lot of the old Samson in it. God returns to Samson when Samson's turning to God is far from full and finished.

Samson's death in the temple's collapse gives us the final complication of Samson's turning again to God and his mission; it is the final part of the story of Samson's life. What are we to say here? Is Samson triumphant at the end of his life or not? On the one hand, of course, the answer has to be 'no'. Samson dies, and he dies as a blinded Philistine captive among his enemies, a ruined wreck of what he has wanted to be. Where is the triumph in this? This is rather the culmination of the ruining of his life. On the other hand, the text says that the Philistines who die in the temple's fall are many more than those Samson has killed in all his earlier battles taken together. Furthermore, it is worth noticing that Samson's family come to get his body. If his family are able to retrieve his body from a Philistine temple in Philistine territory when Samson is responsible for the destruction of that temple and the people in it, then we can reasonably assume that the collapse of the temple seriously undermines Philistine rule in that place at least for a time. And so, in his death,

Samson fulfils his mission, finally, as he has not managed to do in his life. And he does so because in his suffering he turns to God and is present to God as he has not been before, so that God is also present to him. Surely, this is not defeat.

This odd and complicated mix, of conversion to God coupled to the old sin-prone character, of defeat that nonetheless effects the fulfilment of a mission, of the most broken of lives which is somehow still glorious—this is what Milton also saw in Samson's story, and maybe in his own story as well. Milton sums it up this way:

> Samson hath quit himself
> Like Samson, and heroicly hath finished
> A life heroic...
> ...To Israel
> Honour hath left, and freedom...
> To himself and his father's house eternal fame;
> And, which is best and happiest yet, all this
> With God not parted from him, as was feared,
> But favoring and assisting to the end.   (ll. 1709–20)

Milton's own dreadful suffering entitles him to the next lines in the play. Lines that would be intolerable coming from those at ease are a kind of testimony from the world of horrendous evil when they are written by Milton:

> Nothing is here for tears, nothing to wail
> Or knock the breast, no weakness, no contempt,
> Dispraise, or blame; nothing but well and fair,
> And what may quiet us in a death so noble.   (ll. 1721–4)

GLORIOUSNESS

The answer to the question about God's withdrawing from Samson and the answer to the questions with which this chapter began are implicit in Milton's view.

It will help us understand this view if we reflect on the standard of good for human lives which Milton relies on in his reading of the story of Samson. What is the worst thing that can happen to a human being? Bone cancer? Leprosy? These are indeed dreadful; but a person suffers the depredations of disease as an innocent, and therefore even the terrible suffering of disease is not the worst that can happen to a person. What then is the worst? Is it betraying the woman you love to save yourself, as Winston does in George Orwell's *Nineteen Eighty-four*? Is it standing in the dock at Nuremberg, reviled by all the world for unspeakable crimes against a whole people? Even this is not the worst, because it is possible to live to be broken-hearted in contrition even for such crimes, as Franz Stangl, the commandant of Treblinka, seems to have done.[22] But for Christian doctrine, the worst thing that can happen to a person is to die unrepentant in evil. And that is because to die unrepentant is to be at a permanent distance from a perfectly good God; it is to be endlessly isolated from God's redemptive goodness in self-willed, self-protective loneliness, the full-blown horror only hinted at in Samson's sort of distance from Delilah. *This* is the worst thing that can happen to a human being, on the Christian view.

If that is the worst, then what is the best? The best, we might think, is to have no evil to repent of. But, on the Christian view, there are no human beings without evil to repent of. There is a moral cancer that has infected every human will. On this view, then, the best state for human beings—best because it wards off the worst state for human beings—is repentance.

This is not, of course, our ordinary view of the good life for human beings. But the story of Samson prompts a more considered view of the nature of human flourishing. What is it for a human person to flower into glory? On the Christian view, it is not winning your battles and building monuments to your victories. It is drawing near to God and letting him draw near to you. The general idea here is not uniquely Christian; something roughly similar to it can be found in pagan Greece as well. *It is what Achilles was thinking about, when he sat, grieved and angry, in his tent, refusing to join in the battles where Greek warriors got glory and died young.* There are two sorts of honour, he explains to the embassy which has come to try to persuade him to fight again. There is honour from men, and that is worthless; and there is honour from Zeus, which is everything—but that can be had even by a person who dies in obscure old age, without any battlefield glories.[23]

---

[21] Though this is how some contemporary interpreters read the story at this point. According to Boling, ibid.: '[Samson] could not believe, as in the wedding story, that the woman would betray him'.

[22] Gita Sereny, *Into that Darkness: An Examination of Conscience* (New York: Vintage Books, 1983).

So although Samson may look as if his life is a great good to him when he wins at Lehi or when he toys with Delilah and disdains his Nazarite status, it is not. Physical strength and health, political power and honour, are not enough for a good life if they are coupled with the proud, self-protective loneliness with which Samson keeps Delilah and God at bay. On Achilles' view, on Milton's view, and on mine, Samson is most glorious not after his victory at Lehi or in his established Superman status with Delilah. His flowering comes in his worst suffering, in his praying to God as he does and in the drawing near to God that the prayer represents. He is most glorious in the expectant repentance with which he makes his prayer and waits for God to flood him with strength. His glorious flowering comes in his turning to God and God's returning to him.

But what moves Samson from the corrupt and jaded state in which he is before God departs from him, when his mission is forgotten and his divinely given gift of strength is subservient to his concubine, to this turning to God at the end? Surely, it is his suffering. What else would do it? Ethics lectures from the deity? A divine display of displeasure in thunder and lightning? If we were going to rewrite the story of Samson, to get him from the episode with Delilah to some condition in which he makes that last petitioning prayer in which he turns to God, could we credibly write scenes moving him from the first condition to the last without including serious suffering for Samson? Anything other than 'no' does not seem to me a credible answer to this question.

And that is why in the narrative God leaves Samson when he does.

CONCLUSION

Nothing in this reading of Samson's story diminishes one iota the horrendous suffering of Samson's life. The laments Milton writes for Samson are moving testimony to Milton's raw sensibility to the

---

[23] Homer, *Iliad*, book 9, trans. Richard Lattimore (Chicago: Phoenix Books, 1967), 432, 600–10: 'at long last Phoinix the aged horseman spoke out…"Listen then; do not have such a thought in your mind; let not | the spirit within you turn you that way, dear friend. It would be worse | to defend the ships after they are burning. No, with gifts promised | go forth. The Achaians will honour you as they would an immortal. | But if without gifts you go into the fighting where men perish, | your honour will no longer be as great, though you drive back the battle." | Then in answer to him spoke Achilleus of the swift feet: | "Phoinix my father, aged, illustrious, such

horrendous suffering of his own life as well as that of the protagonist in his poem. And yet Milton bears witness, for himself and for the Samson of the story, that it is possible for even a life of horrendous suffering to be a great good to the sufferer. On Milton's way of reading the narrative of Samson, it is possible for there to be glorious flowering for the sufferer not in spite of the suffering but because of it. The suffering is not decreased by the flourishing; it is redeemed by it. And so it would not have been better if God had let Samson die before Samson fell into contumely against God. If Samson had died earlier, say because he had no water after the battle at Lehi, or because he had a heart attack in bed, Samson would have been the poorer for it.[24] It is possible, then, for a person to be irremediably broken and glorious nonetheless.

The gloriousness of Oedipus at Colonus, as Sophocles portrays him, consists of being specially beloved of the gods; but Oedipus' relationship to the gods is manifest largely in his ability to know things ordinary mortals don't know, including the precise time and place of his death, because the gods reveal these things to him. So for Sophocles Oedipus' suffering is redeemed by some extraordinary excellence of mind. But what redeems Samson's suffering and what constitutes his gloriousness is more nearly an excellence of will than an excellence of mind. It consists in his repentance—in his letting go of his willed self-protective isolation, in his willingness to be open to God, in his drawing near to God. In this condition, he accepts what God gives him as a gift, and in using that gift for the purpose for which God gave it, he in effect accepts the giver with the gift. And so his suffering is redeemed in relationship with God, in his being present to God and God's being present to him.

This answer applied to a fictional character in a fictional case is a possible solution for the problem of evil, as the rich detail of the story makes clear. The narrative thus gives us a defence, a possible morally sufficient reason for God's allowing evil.

---

honour is a thing | I need not. I think I am honoured already in Zeus' ordinance | which will hold me here beside my curved ships as long as life's wind | stays in my breast, as long as my knees have their spring beneath me." '

[24] There are many other people whose lives are impacted by Samson's, of course, and so it will occur to someone to wonder whether or not other lives would have been better if Samson had died before the episode with Delilah. As the narrative in question is about Samson primarily, the story doesn't give us the information needed to

It is, on the face of it, a limited defence, at least in part because it relies on a complex set of psychological states had by a normally functioning adult human being in close relations with another person. In my view, however, a limited defence is sufficient here. There is no a priori reason for thinking that a solution to the problem of evil has to be based on only one benefit, or only one kind of benefit, for defeating the whole panoply of human suffering; and it is enough for my purposes to have argued, through the examination of this narrative, for one limited defence. On the other hand, it is not immediately apparent that the sort of defence I have argued for cannot be adapted to cases other than those of adult human beings with fully functional psychological capacities. I am not arguing here that the defence I have presented *should* be extended in this way. I am pointing out only that it would be hasty to suppose that it could not be.

At any rate, the examination of the biblical narrative should give us increased imagination for the sorts of benefits which can be considered as redeeming human suffering. It should also give us an increased awareness that the details of the stories of the sufferers are important in any assessment of the suffering. Our assessment of the suffering in the biblical story would be skewed and wrong-headed without the insight the story provides about the inner life and relationships of the sufferer. Part of the problem in thinking about suffering and what might redeem it is precisely that so much of the inner life of the sufferers is opaque to us. Their stories are largely hidden from us.[25]

---

evaluate the impact of Samson's story on them. But in so far as Samson's story includes his being glorious in some sense, then all those who care about Samson or whose welfare depends on him are also the beneficiaries of the good that comes to Samson. I am grateful to Fr Michael Barber for calling my attention to this point.

[25] As the suffering of a child or an animal is presented in philosophical literature, or even in philosophical discussions in such works as Dostoevsky's *Brothers Karamazov*, the inner life of the sufferer is either not presented at all or else presented as if there were nothing but suffering in that inner life. It seems to me that we do not have enough evidence about the inner life of such a sufferer to warrant presentations of this sort. Even if an adult reports the sufferings he had as a child, so that we have adult insight coupled to the first-person experience of the child, the memories that the adult is using to make the report are the memories laid down as a child. But the memories that a child lays down about her experiences as a leukaemia patient, say, and the memories that her mother has of her in those same experiences may be highly discrepant. Furthermore, not everything that makes a contribution to the inner life of a person is consciously perceived by that person as making that sort of contribution. Anxiety, for example, can be aroused by an unconscious association between some-

Finally, in this chapter, I have also granted that a human being can be irrevocably broken. I have argued that it is possible for a broken person to flower in that very brokenness and to fulfil the promise of his life, in one way or another. But in so far as that person has his heart set on having whole something which is irremediably shattered in him or in his life, then, barring miracles, he will not have the desires of his heart in this life. To that extent, he will live his life in the pain of heartbreak. What the story of Samson shows is that even such a life can be glorious, and that the pain of it can be enveloped in close, loving relations with God.

10

Karma or Grace

STEPHEN T. DAVIS

I

Those whose conduct here has been good will quickly attain a
good birth (literally womb), the birth of a Brahmin, the birth of a
Ksatriya or the birth of a Vaisya. But those whose conduct here
has been evil, will quickly attain an evil birth, the birth of a dog,
the birth of a hog or the birth of a Candala [outcast].[1]

The predominating sense of grace in the New Testament is that
which the word bears in the writings of Saint Paul, who thinks
of the Divine salvation primarily as a 'boon' flowing from the
generous, unmerited graciousness of God to sinful, lost humanity, as expressed supremely on the cross of Christ. For Saint Paul
the free outgoing and self-imparting of the redeeming love of
God to man in Christ is constitutive of the whole of salvation.
God deals with men in Christ purely on the basis of infinite,
undeserved mercy.[2]

All religions contain both a description and a diagnosis of the human
predicament. People are unhappy because they are avaricious and
striving. The gods are angry with us. The world is a terrible place
because people care about themselves more than they do about
others. People suffer because they have sinned against God.

Each religion also typically offers a solution to the problem. The
gods must be placated by proper ritual. People can escape ignorance
and achieve liberation. People should engage in proper practices of
meditation, and so achieve self-realization. People need to obey God's
laws. People must accept God's mercy and be forgiven.

---

[1] Cited in Bruce R. Reichenbach, *The Law of Karma: A Philosophical Study* (Honolulu:
University of Hawaii Press, 1990), 194 (*Chandogya Upanishad*, V. 10. 7).

[2] William Manson, 'Grace in the New Testament', in William T. Whitley (ed.), *The
Doctrine of Grace* (New York: Macmillan, 1932), 59.

Let us say that human beings at the diagnostic stage of the problem are at 'Stage 1'. And let us say that saved, transformed, redeemed, liberated, enlightened (or whatever term is preferred) human beings are at 'Stage 2'. The point is that every religion has a proposed way of moving people from Stage 1 to Stage 2. They offer both a diagnosis and a cure of the human condition. Let us call any religious method of achieving this a *system of salvation*.[3]

In this chapter I will contrast two quite different systems of salvation. Let me call them Karma and Grace.[4] I want to stress that my intent is to talk about these two concepts almost entirely theoretically or in the abstract. Although I do think that these terms, as I will define them, broadly fit some of the religions of the world, I will make little reference to actual religions or religious teachings. There are two reasons for this. First, I am not a historian of religion, and my knowledge of religious traditions apart from my own is limited. Second, I want to treat Karma and Grace as if they were entirely opposed or irreconcilable systems of salvation, whereas in fact the notions of karma and grace are mixed in many religious traditions in complex and fascinating ways.[5]

Indeed, it might be more historically accurate to distinguish among *three* systems of salvation: (*a*) grace-oriented systems that involve one lifetime only and no karma (e.g. Judaism and Christianity); (*b*) grace-oriented religious systems that include reincarnation and karma (e.g. the Ramajuna and Madhva schools of Hinduism or Pure Land Buddhism); and (*c*) reincarnational and karmic religious traditions in which one reaches Stage 2 not via the grace of a higher being but by one's own efforts—through meditation, for example, or ethical action (e.g. Advaita Vedanta Hinduism or Zen Buddhism).[6] But in the interest of simplicity, I will instead simply posit two

---

[3] The very word 'salvation' has connotations that make it more appropriate to grace-oriented than to karma-oriented religious systems. Still, I will try to use the term as a neutral reference to what I am calling 'Stage 2'.

[4] I will capitalize these two terms only when referring to them as systems of salvation.

[5] Some Western scholars even try to synthesize them. See e.g. three works by Geddes MacGregor: *Reincarnation in Christianity* (Wheaton, Ill.: Theosophical Publishing House, 1978); *Reincarnation as a Christian Hope* (London: Macmillan, 1982); and *The Christening of Karma* (Wheaton, Ill.: Theosophical Publishing House, 1984).

[6] There are also schemes in Western philosophy (e.g. those of Spinoza or Hegel or McTaggart) in which reality is intelligible, pervaded by thought, and even purposive, but not personal. I will not consider those fascinating options in the present chapter.

abstract systems of salvation, Karma and Grace, and will compare them. In other words, I will ignore systems of salvation like those falling in category (*b*) and concentrate on two abstract ones that are like (*a*) and (*c*). Although in the end I will not be able to give a definitive answer, my aim in this chapter is to ask, on philosophical grounds, which system of salvation shows more promise of moving people from Stage 1 to Stage 2.[7]

I do not pretend to write from a neutral, detached perspective. I myself am a believer in a religion of grace, and so it is not surprising that I will end up defending that system of salvation. Indeed, I will argue that it is subject to fewer serious difficulties than is karma. But I also hope to be fair to the concept of karma.

Before contrasting the two systems of salvation, I will also note that there are crucial points of agreement between Karma and Grace. First, both systems of salvation agree that the deepest human problems are spiritual in nature. This point is important, because some people suppose that the deepest human problems are economic in nature, or perhaps political, or perhaps medical. Karma and Grace agree that what is wrong in human life is, at its deepest level, spiritual in nature.

Second, Karma and Grace agree that moral right and wrong are 'objective'—they are facts about the nature of reality itself.[8] Moral relativism is false; what is right and wrong does not depend on who you are or what you happen to believe. This is a controversial point in our day. Many people hold that right and wrong have nothing to do with the way things are. There are brute facts and there are

---

[7] It is technically incorrect to consider karma a system of salvation. Karma simply means action, and the law of karma (an extension of karma as action) states that what happens to us later in a given life or in later lives results from our own actions in this life. So the law of karma may in some sense explain why things happen to us, but it does not, by itself, recommend any spiritual or moral conduct. Those recommendations—the eightfold path, renunciation, etc.—come from particular karmic religious traditions. So it is important to note that in the present chapter I am offering a technical definition of the word 'Karma'. I mean it to include both (1) the law of karma and (2) particular religious or moral ways of achieving Stage 2 as found, say, in typical karmic religious traditions.

[8] This point needs to be nuanced in relation to some Asian karmic systems. In some such systems, evil appears to have no logical place or seems a muddled category. It is either illusory (as in Sankara); or the good–evil opposition is ultimately transcended and ethical levels are merely transitional (as in Aurobindo Ghose); or the world is considered a kind of 'body' for God (as in Ramanuja), in which case evil is essential to this ultimate reality.

evaluative opinions, and the two are in totally different realms. Both Karma and Grace, in contrast, reject any rigid distinction between facts and values. Followers of both Karma and Grace hold that certain things are morally right and certain other things are morally wrong. Intentions and actions can be objectively judged to be right or wrong.

Third, Karma and Grace agree that justice lies behind the real or apparent injustices and inequities that we see in the world. The traditional problem of evil may be a more serious intellectual difficulty for the advocate of Grace than for the advocate of Karma, but both theories suggest that evil will be punished and virtue rewarded in some future life. Both hold that the universe is essentially moral. It is not true that the world operates with complete indifference to morality, like the movements of a planet or the operation of a machine. Morality is at the heart of reality.

II

It is time for me to describe the two systems of salvation. There are of course many different karmic theories and many different theologies of grace. So let me again note that I am abstracting from the teachings of any particular religion. It is possible that no actual religious tradition will precisely recognize itself in every aspect of either of the accounts that I will give.

Karma

Karma denies that any personal God exists; it posits instead an impersonal absolute that might be called Reality Itself.[9] People are born, and then die, and then are reborn in another body. Their new stations in life are karmic consequences ('fruits') of the sorts of moral lives that they lived in previous lives.[10] Not everything that happens

---

[9] The law of karma, by itself, neither affirms nor denies that a personal God exists. And there are religious traditions that are both theistic and karmic. But since the law of karma is usually associated with non-theistic religious systems, I am simply positing that my technically defined system of salvation called 'Karma' is non-theistic.

[10] I recognize that certain Buddhists, Hindus, and other advocates of karmic religions interpret karma symbolically or non-realistically. They do not literally believe that after death they will be reborn elsewhere with karmic consequences intact; they

to a person is due to karma: some things that occur are consequences of one's genetic inheritance, some of one's own choices, some of the choices of others or of natural events. Nor does Karma hold that everything karmic is ineluctably determined or fated. Those who are hungry should try to find food; those who are sick should try to be cured. Karma is an impersonal law, like gravity or thermodynamics, which says that all actions for which one can be held morally responsible have consequences, good or bad, in this and subsequent incarnations.

The karmic theory stresses cause and effect: you get just what you deserve, no more and no less. Nothing happens that is unjust. Actions that are due to craving, greed, hatred, or ignorance will produce bad karma. Moral acts will produce good karma. This aspect of karma is not a matter of retribution. Good karma is conducive to spiritual growth; bad karma is less conducive. One important thing that karma can do is move us along the path of spiritual growth. By hard spiritual and moral effort it is possible to grow spiritually and eventually to escape from the cycle of reincarnation. A liberated, enlightened state is possible for human beings. Achieving it means reaching the ultimate spiritual goal, which is oneness with Reality Itself.

Grace

Human beings were created by a holy and personal creator. We are required to obey the creator's laws. When we fail to do so, we sin and accordingly separate ourselves from God. Sin must be punished. The punishment for sin is permanent separation from God. Human beings—who live but one life on this earth—are lost in self-centredness, violence, pride, greed, and lust. They are in bondage; that is, they are quite unable, on their own strength, to overcome the pervasive effects of sin in their lives. They can do nothing to save themselves; no matter how hard they try, they fail. So, although they do not morally deserve it, God reveals himself to them and offers to forgive them of their sins and reconcile them to him. This offer is a free gift of grace. People do not deserve it—indeed, they deserve to be

rather interpret the karma doctrines of their religions as emphasizing certain ethical imperatives. In the present chapter, however, I will interpret the system of salvation that I am calling 'Karma' as entailing a realist understanding of the doctrine.

separated from God. Grace means that God treats us better than we morally deserve to be treated. Still, there is something that humans must do in order to be recipients of grace, namely, sincerely ask for it and sincerely receive it. But the main effort in achieving salvation, so to speak, is God's not ours. Those who accept the gift of grace live eternally with God in heaven. Accordingly, whereas Karma presents salvation as ultimately within human control, in Grace salvation depends on the grace of God.[11]

There are many differences between these two systems of salvation. Probably the most important is the presence of higher personal agency—the agency of God—in Grace. (As noted, there are theistic karmic religions, but the abstract theory called 'Karma' that I am considering in this chapter is non-theistic.) A second is that Karma affirms and Grace denies that one gets only what one deserves in this life, that perfect justice rules here and now. Grace affirms that many things that happen to people are undeserved, including the gift of grace itself. A third difference, to which I will return later, is that Karma attributes the human predicament primarily to what we might call false consciousness or spiritual blindness, while Grace attributes it to guilt.

III

At this point, I want to raise several criticisms of each system of salvation, objections that advocates of one system would or might raise against the other. Let me begin with five criticisms of Grace.

(i) Who Gets the Grace?

Why is it that some people receive the grace of God and are forgiven while others do not receive it and are condemned? Is this not unfair? Some advocates of Grace respond to this charge by arguing that we all deserve condemnation, and so those who do not receive grace (and stay condemned at Stage 1) have no right to object. But that is a

---

[11] On the Christian theology of grace, see Henri Rondet, *The Grace of Christ* (Philadelphia: Westminster Press, 1966), and Piet Fransen, *The New Life of Grace* (New York: Seabury, 1969).

feeble argument. Suppose a certain parent has two children, John and Jane, who are both equally guilty of some fault. Let us say they both intentionally trample on some prized geraniums in the flower-bed, and so both equally deserve punishment. Then suppose the parent says to them, 'You are both equally guilty and both deserve to be grounded for a week. John, you are grounded to your room for a week. But as a free gift of grace, Jane, you are forgiven. You will not be punished in any way.' Is it not obvious that this scenario is radically unfair?

(ii) Why Doesn't God Intervene More Often?

The problem of evil is a pervasive intellectual problem for all theistic systems of salvation that presuppose the ability of God graciously to intervene in human affairs from time to time. Why doesn't God do so more often? Why didn't God intervene to prevent the Holocaust, for example? The fact that God allows so much human suffering entails either that God is not strong enough to prevent it, or that God is not morally good enough to want to prevent it, or that God does not exist. Whichever is true—so the criticism runs—the system of salvation called Grace collapses.

(iii) Grace can be Morally Corrupting

Some argue that followers of religions of grace can easily lapse into moral listlessness or even moral turpitude because of their conviction that 'grace covers everything'. In other words, it is easy for grace to become cheap and morally worthless if it leads people to evade their moral responsibilities out of the belief that no matter how much moral wrong they do, God's grace will overcome it and they will be forgiven.

(iv) Not Enough Time

One aspect of the system of salvation called Grace is that human beings live only one life on this earth and then are judged on the basis of that life. But surely one lifetime is not enough to achieve salvation. This claim is substantiated by the simple observation that most people die at far less than an optimal or perfect spiritual state. Obviously, for the vast majority of people, many more lives than one are needed to reach the spiritual end-state. A loving God will make that possible; a God who does not is a moral monster.[12]

(v) Grace is Immoral

Even if the first criticism (about the unfairness of grace for some people and not others) is waived, it can still be argued that the very idea of grace is inherently unjust and unfair. Morality requires that people should be treated exactly as they deserve. Just as it is unfair to treat people *worse* than they deserve (e.g. by sentencing someone to twenty years in prison for failing to put a stamp on an envelope), so it is unfair to treat people *better* than they deserve. Justice must be upheld at all times, and it is radically unjust to forgive people who do not merit forgiveness. Moving from Stage 1 to Stage 2 must be achieved by the moral agents themselves. If it comes as a free and undeserved gift from someone else, it will not be appreciated. Human beings must work hard spiritually and morally, and if they do they can move themselves to Stage 2. That is the far better way.

IV

How might advocates of Grace criticize Karma? I will now consider five objections that can be raised. The first, in my opinion, is a serious point but can be answered; the cogency of the second depends on theological considerations that are beyond the scope of the present chapter; but the final three, in my opinion, create serious difficulties for karmic systems of salvation.

(i) Karmic Explanations are Unfalsifiable

Karma is said to be an impersonal law that prevents injustice in the world. Whatever happens to a person, whether it is good or bad, is an entirely just consequence of that person's actions in the present or in previous incarnations. It follows from this claim that here is no such thing as undeserved human suffering. But one conceptual difficulty with this system of salvation is that karmic explanations—for

---

[12] See MacGregor, *Reincarnation as a Christian Hope*, 11. John Hick has also used this argument. See e.g. his *Death and Eternal Life* (New York: Harper & Row, 1976), 408.

example, 'Sally is suffering from arthritis as a consequence of her unforgiving, condemning spirit in previous incarnations'—are completely unfalsifiable. As Paul Edwards argues, no matter what happens to a person, some plausible-sounding karmic explanation or other can be generated. There is no way that any karmic explanation could be tested against alternative karmic explanations.[13]

One way of understanding this criticism is to point out that even if the basic claims of Karma as a system of salvation were true, there would be no way that the law of Karma could accurately predict future events. Karma is empty and unfalsifiable because it is compatible with anything that could possibly occur. Accordingly, Karma cannot be convincingly used to show that everything is just and that there is no undeserved suffering.

But it seems that Karma can be defended at this point. Even if karmic explanations of events are strictly unfalsifiable, what follows is that the law of Karma cannot be used to show *empirically* that everything that happens is just. However, there may be other, non-empirical, grounds for accepting the law of Karma, and thus other grounds for holding that nothing unjust occurs. Edwards may believe that it is always wrong to accept religious doctrines that are not empirically falsifiable, but few religious people, including advocates of Grace, will agree with him.

Moreover, it may be that predictability is too narrow a criterion to use for the purpose of judging the acceptability of religious or non-religious claims. As Bruce Reichenbach has argued,[14] the law of Karma may be like the theory of evolution in this way: neither can be used to make predictions and hence are strictly unfalsifiable; both are instead postdictive (that is, they have to do with explaining past events rather than predicting future ones), so that criteria relevant to postdiction can be brought to bear. Both theories claim to provide (Darwinian or karmic) histories of events leading up to the present—histories that are said to be helpful and powerful in explaining the present situation, more so than alternate theories. In other words, non-predictive theories, whether scientific or religious, can in

---

[13] See Paul Edwards, 'Karmic Tribulations', in Paul Edwards (ed.), *Immortality* (New York: Macmillan, 1992), 200–12.

[14] Bruce Reichenbach, 'Justifying In-Principle Nonpredictive Theories: The Case of Evolution', *Christian Scholars Review*, 24/4 (May 1995), 397–422.

principle be justified on the basis of how well they explain existing facts.

Finally, while Karma certainly implies that nothing morally significant happens 'accidentally', it may be that the present objection misrepresents Karma. Perhaps Karma does not produce predictable consequences in future lives but rather sets contexts for and limitations on future events. Presumably, what actually will occur in a future life will be a function of many factors, not just Karma, with karmic laws acting as setters of conditions or contexts, much as a card-player is dealt a certain hand and then can make free choices how to play the hand.[15]

(ii) Can we Save Ourselves?

An important criticism that defenders of Grace will make of karmic religious systems is that human beings are quite unable to save themselves and need the help of God's grace if they are to progress from Stage 1 to Stage 2. This, indeed, is perhaps the deepest issue that divides the two systems of salvation. Are human beings able to save themselves, or not?

Obviously, some facts about myself are such that I have it within my power to change them. I can make a decision to change the fact that I am now sitting at my computer; I can change the fact that I have not yet replied to a certain letter; maybe I can even change the fact that I have never been to Thailand. Some people have even changed more embedded facts about themselves—cured themselves of the need to smoke cigarettes, for example. Equally obviously, there are some facts about myself that I cannot change, no matter what I do. I cannot change the fact that I was born in Nebraska, for example, or the fact that I am not a horse. So the crucial question is this: is it or is it not within my power to bring it about that I achieve the spiritual state of salvation or liberation?

That will depend in part on what exactly is meant by salvation or liberation (which of course can only be answered in the context of specific religious traditions) and in part on one's view as to the

---

[15] I will not discuss the often-repeated criticism that karmic theories are sometimes used to rationalize suffering and injustice (on the grounds that the suffering people are justly being punished for actions in past lives), and thus to discourage efforts to alleviate suffering or correct injustice. This is because the criticism does not speak to the *truth* of Karma.

spiritual powers and abilities of human beings. Some religions stress the inability of human beings by themselves to bring about the necessary spiritual changes (and most of the religions of grace fit here). Others hold that human beings can actually effect the required changes, difficult as it might be to do so (and most of the karmic religions fit here). I will return to this point below.

(iii) Can Karma be Impersonal?

As already noted, Karma posits no godlike personal judge or administrator who decides, say, that the past lives of some person cause her to suffer terribly in this life. The idea is rather that Karma works impersonally, just like gravity. No person or agent decides that unsupported things that are heavier than air tend to fall toward the centre of the earth—this is just how things always behave. Now perhaps some karmic consequences can be explained impersonally, especially those that operate within a given lifespan. Suppose for years I live a life of hostility and selfishness, and thus do moral harm to myself later in the same lifetime—say, make myself into a bitter and hateful person. That scenario seems quite plausible.

But what about a situation where Karma says that a given individual who suffers for years from a terrible and painful disease does so because of that person's misdeeds in previous lives? Here the connection is much more difficult to discern, and it is not easy to see how the system is supposed to work.[16] What exactly is the impersonal causal connection between this person's misdeeds in past lives and the pain of this life? How is it 'decided' that the just karmic consequence in this case is suffering from the painful disease rather than, say, living as a poor beggar? If the pain is indeed due to misdeeds in past lives, then without some sort of personal administrator or supervisor of Karma, it is not easy to see how karmic 'decisions' as to what are the just and proper consequences are to be made.[17] The upshot is that Karma needs a personal judge or administrator who makes karmic decisions.

[16] This point is discussed skilfully in Bruce Reichenbach, *The Law of Karma: A Philosophical Study* (Honolulu: University of Hawaii Press, 1990), 96–100, 121–2, 159, 189–90.

[17] Perhaps the self—if it continues as a conscious agent between incarnations—can make decisions about which station in the next life will best serve its own karmic interests. But I am unaware of any karmic systems of salvation that affirm that this in fact occurs.

(iv) Does Karma Really Solve the Problem of Unjust Suffering?

Believers in karmic religious systems typically aver that the strongest argument in favour of their theory is that it solves the problem of why there is so much undeserved suffering and inequality of human birth and circumstance. As already noted, the argument is that there is no injustice; those who suffer are actually paying the price of bad karma accumulated in previous lives. But suppose the question is put in this way: how did suffering begin? That is, how did it become part of the world that we experience?

If the defender of Karma believes that there was a first incarnation, that is, a beginning of human or sentient life before there was any karma or reincarnation, then the question is whether suffering and inequality existed then. If they did, then Karma obviously cannot explain why there is suffering. But the opposite claim—the claim that at time in the past history of human or sentient life perfect justice and equality existed—seems implausible in the extreme.

But many karmic systems deny that there was ever a first life; reincarnation and Karma—so it is said—have always existed. There was no beginning. But if that is the case, then of course no explanation of unjust suffering is given. Every event of suffering is explained in terms of things that occurred in previous lives. Accordingly, the explanation of apparently unjust suffering is never in fact given, but is only indefinitely postponed.[18] There would be an explanation for any particular evil event, but not for why there is any evil at all.

(v) Me and my Karmic Heir

The system of salvation I am calling Karma presupposes that every human being will have karmic heirs—that is, future persons who are the reincarnations of those human beings and who inherit their karma. Suppose that a person, Bill, dies, and then has a karmic heir, Tom, who is born soon after Bill's death. Notice that Karma only seems just—and that this system of salvation is entirely just is one of the most important claims made by its defenders—if Tom *is* (the reincarnation of) Bill. That is, Tom must be a continuation of

---

[18] This point has been argued by John Hick. See his *Death and Eternal Life* (New York: Harper & Row, 1976), 308–9.

the life of Bill. Otherwise it will hardly be fair that Tom experiences the karmic consequences of Bill's deeds. But the conceptual difficulty here is that on philosophical grounds it seems that Tom *cannot* be Bill.

Notice first that Tom will share nothing of Bill's body. Reincarnational theories insist on this much; Tom's body will be totally different from Bill's.[19] Furthermore, apart from the possibility of a few yoga memories (which only a tiny minority of human beings claim to experience), Tom will share precisely none of Bill's memories and need not share any of his personality, likes, dislikes, or opinions. What is there, then, that, so to speak, holds Bill and Tom together? What makes it the case that they are two different temporal episodes of one and the same person?

In some reincarnational theories the only connecting thread is the putative fact that Bill and Tom possess the same soul or *jiva* (or some sort of immaterial essence), together with its karmic imprints and latent memories. Of course defenders of Karma might just insist that sameness of immaterial essence entails sameness of the person. And if they are right, that solves the metaphysical problem. But an epistemological issue remains: in the absence of other bodily or memory similarities, there seems to be no good reason to accept such a strong claim. Suppose it is true that some immaterial aspect of the person passes from one incarnation to the next. This would perhaps be enough to make us consider that there are similarities and maybe even causal connections between Bill and Tom. However, it would hardly seem sufficient to establish a claim of identity between them. So it is a serious problem for defenders of Karma to explain—even if it is true that all human beings have karmic heirs— why I should believe that my karmic heir is me.

Some karmic systems explain the connection this way: it is in principle possible for Tom to recover all or many of Bill's memories; and it is similarly in principle possible for Bill to have many of Tom's character traits—temperament, taste, outlook, etc. But I would argue that the second point is not nearly enough to establish identity—presumably there will be many people of Tom's generation

---

[19] Grace-oriented religions that stress resurrection rather than reincarnation also wrestle with the problem of identity in the next life. See Stephen T. Davis, *Making Sense of the Resurrection* (Grand Rapids, Mich.: Eerdmans, 1993), 85–146. But their emphasis on bodily continuity makes the problem much easier to solve.

who will roughly possess Bill's character traits. And as for memory, the mere *possibility* of Tom recovering Bill's memories is not enough. What will go a long way towards establishing identity is Tom *actually having* Bill's memories. And that kind of thing rarely happens in actual fact, as even defenders of Karma admit. Yoga memory claims are rare, and exceedingly difficult to verify when they do occur.

I do not claim that this and other difficulties make Karma logically impossible or incoherent. I do claim that they create serious problems for the theory.

V

My own view is that each of the five criticisms of Grace mentioned above can be answered. Let me now set out to do so.

(i) Who Gets the Grace?

The moral problem that supposedly exists is greatly mitigated by the claim of most grace-oriented systems of salvation that divine grace is offered freely to all people, and that those who freely choose to receive it benefit from grace. Moral problems remain—I do not say they cannot be solved—for predestinarian theological systems that stress election, reprobation, and other such notions that entail that the choice of who receives grace and who does not is God's and God's alone. But it seems that grace-oriented theologies in which human beings freely choose whether to receive the grace of God can answer the present criticism fairly readily.

Of course the critic of Grace might reply in this way: clearly, not everyone has an equal access to grace, or an equal grasp of it, and that is surely unfair. Given their cultural and religious backgrounds, most of the people who have ever lived or will live will find it difficult to accept a grace-oriented religious system; that is simply not a realistic option for them. And this much certainly seems to be true. But while this point does constitute a difficulty for Grace, it does not seem to constitute a reason to prefer Karma to Grace, for karmic systems of salvation are doubtless hidden from most people as well. Presumably the law of Karma, if it is true, operates equally for all people, whether or not they have ever heard of it. Moreover, the specific moral or religious actions that typical karmic systems of salvation recommend are also known to but a few. Most people have never heard of the Eightfold Path, for example.

(ii) Why Doesn't God Graciously Intervene More Often?

This question is of course an aspect of the traditional problem of evil, which is by nearly universal consent the most serious intellectual difficulty that theists face. I will not try to solve the problem here.[20] Let me simply suggest that theists hold: (1) that God has good moral reasons for graciously intervening in human history on some occasions and not others; (2) that we do not always know those reasons and are asked to trust in God's goodness nonetheless; (3) that God will triumph in the end over all evil, pain, and injustice, and will bring about a supremely good eschaton; and (4) that the most optimal way for God to achieve this conclusion is to create a world like this one, with its natural laws and regularities (including human moral freedom).

Moreover, if it is God's desire that human beings be morally free, this fact places stringent limits on the frequency of divine interventions. Suppose we say that God is morally obligated to remove the most bothersome evils (which seems to be the main concern of many who use the problem of evil to criticize theism). But virtually all evils can be considered horrendous by those who are aware of no worse ones. Accordingly, consistent application of that principle would eliminate virtually all evils. This in turn would also eliminate human moral freedom, that is, freedom to do either good or evil. The conclusion seems to be that God has no such moral obligation.

(iii) Can Grace be Morally Corrupting?

Yes, Grace can indeed be morally corrupting in the indicated ways. The sense that one will be forgiven by God no matter what, that forgiveness depends not on one's own performance or dispositions but on the free and undeserved grace of God, such convictions may well lead certain persons to succumb to temptation. If that happens,

---

[20] I have addressed the problem on other occasions. See my essay 'Free Will and Evil' in Stephen T. Davis (ed.), *Encountering Evil: Live Options in Theodicy* (2nd edn Louisville, Ky.: Westminster John Knox, 2001), 73–107.

however, it is taken by grace-oriented systems of salvation as a moral failure and as a mistaken interpretation of Grace.[21]

The proper way to understand Grace is to see it as costly and as requiring effort and risk. Grace involves, on our part, genuine contrition, confession, repentance, renunciation, obligation, and discipline. It involves a sense of gratitude to God so strong that it entails a sincere desire to follow God's path. Our wanting to follow God is not what saves us—that is one of the basic implications of Grace; only God's work achieves that. But those who use Grace as an excuse for moral laxity or moral turpitude are not genuine recipients of Grace.

(iv) What about the 'Not Enough Time' Criticism?

The defender of Grace can happily grant that the vast majority of people die without having achieved spiritual or moral sainthood, and that this would be a better world if many more people *did* achieve such a state before dying. But since the core idea is that by God's Grace one has been forgiven and cleansed of sin, the problem is not fatal to the theory. The point is not that we all achieve sainthood, but that we are graciously forgiven—in this, the one and only, life—for *not* achieving it. According to Grace, forgiveness is attainable by anyone in this life.[22]

(v) Is Grace Immoral?

What about the claim of defenders of Karma that Grace is wrong, that people ought to be treated only as they deserve? Let us take it as an established moral principle that *people ought not be treated worse than they deserve*. Determining precisely which punishments 'fit' which crimes is not always easy, of course, but in extreme cases—like sentencing someone to twenty years in prison for failing to put a stamp on an envelope—every morally sensitive person can see that I am talking about something that is morally wrong.

---

[21] Certain Christian theologians have noticed this problem, e.g. see Dietrich Bonhoeffer, *The Cost of Discipleship* (New York: Macmillan, 1958), 37–49.

[22] Grace-oriented religious systems have other options for dealing with the 'not enough time' problem, e.g., the Roman Catholic notion of purgatory, or the notion of degrees of reward in heaven.

Defenders of Karma also seem to be on firm moral ground when they extend the principle that people should not be treated worse than they deserve and insist on the wider principle that *normally people ought to be treated precisely as they deserve*. For moral as well as pedagogical reasons, this principle seems acceptable. I mention pedagogy because clearly excessive leniency and gift-giving is no way to train someone morally. It is often said that children who are allowed to do anything at all with impunity and who are spoilt with excessive gifts often grow up to become the kinds of people whom we do not morally admire.

But the defender of Grace will respond to this argument as follows: yes, normally we should treat people just as they deserve, but for two important reasons this admission does not rule out Grace as a system of salvation. First, although it is never *required*, at times it is morally *allowable* to treat someone better than he or she deserves. There are, in morality, recognized acts of supererogation, where people do more than what is strictly morally required. We would not charge with immorality the soldier who sacrifices his life for his buddies by jumping on a hand grenade. Now defenders of Karma could rightly point out that this act in itself does no moral harm to his buddies, while excessively lenient acts of Grace might well harm the people at whom they are directed. But the defender of Grace will argue that we are not talking about 'excessively lenient' acts of Grace, but rather gracious divine acts that make our salvation possible.

This leads directly to the second point. The defender of Grace will explain that the rightness or wrongness of Grace cannot be settled by pointing to examples of moral behaviour in the natural or human realm. What we are talking about is the rightness of *God's* graciously forgiving our sins in situations where, apart from the Grace, no one at all would be saved. If it is morally desirable that human beings be saved, and if no one can be saved apart from God's Grace, then it is not only morally allowable, but also morally praiseworthy, that God act graciously towards us.

Again we see that the deepest issue in relation to the Karma–Grace dispute centres on whether we have it within our power to save ourselves. If we *can* move ourselves by our own efforts from Stage 1 to Stage 2, Grace seems superfluous and excessively lenient. If we *cannot* do so, and if God wants us to be saved, then God's treating us graciously is not only morally allowable, but also morally praiseworthy.

VI

It is time to conclude. I will mention a caveat that has been implicit throughout the discussion. It is possible that my argument is empty of much real-world reference because the categories I have created called 'Karma' and 'Grace' do not fit any actual religious traditions. I myself do not admit as much—indeed, I think they do in a rough and broad way fit certain extant religious traditions—but the point must be noted nonetheless.

I have tried to answer the criticisms of Grace that were introduced earlier. I will also express the opinion that defenders of Karma have serious work to do in defending their theory against some of the criticisms of that theory that I also introduced, especially the third, fourth, and fifth.[23]

It would be desirable to reach a definitive decision as to which system of salvation is preferable or even true (if indeed one is true). For three reasons it is probably not possible to do so. First, the issue cannot be decided apart from metaphysical considerations that are outside the purview of this chapter. The central questions would be as follows. What sort of world do we live in? Do we live in a world that was created by a personal God who cares about us and works for our salvation, or not? Is the putative natural law that we call Karma true, or not?

Second, perhaps the notions of salvation, of Stage 2, in the two systems of salvation are so different as to be incommensurate. That is, what religions of Grace mean by 'salvation' differs markedly from what religions of Karma mean by such terms as 'liberation', 'emptiness', 'enlightenment', etc. If so, this incommensurability will make it impossible to answer, at least on the basis of philosophical considerations alone, what appears to be the crucial question that has emerged from our discussion. That question is, is it possible for human beings to save themselves, to progress from Stage 1 to Stage 2 on their own initiative and by their own effort?

---

[23] It should be noted that defenders of certain karmic religious traditions have tried to address some of the objections to Karma raised above. I leave open the possibility that some of the problems that I have pointed out are answerable from the perspective of actual religious traditions, even if they are not answerable from the perspective of the abstract system of salvation that I am calling Karma.

The third point relates closely to the second. Is the central spiritual problem for human beings false consciousness or guilt? Most religions of Karma seem to teach that the central human problem grows out of our clinging to a false view of reality and that what we most deeply need is enlightenment. Most religions of grace teach that the human predicament develops out of our guilt for wrongdoing and that what we most deeply need is forgiveness or redemption. It may be difficult to decide whether human sinfulness is due to false consciousness or whether false consciousness is due to human sinfulness.

As we have seen, defenders of Grace insist that we cannot reach Stage 2 by our own efforts. They hold that only a full revelation of the gracious love of God can break down and overcome hardened human hearts. Indeed—so they claim—since suffering and injustice fall in this life on the innocent as well as the guilty, Grace is necessary to bring about the ultimate justice of the Kingdom of God.

Let me conclude with two thoughts. First, I have made a case, based entirely on philosophical considerations (i.e. not on any particular revealed theology), that Grace should be preferred to Karma. This conclusion follows because, as I have argued, Karma is subject to telling objections, while Grace is not. In the very nature of the case, this is admittedly a weak sort of argument. (Perhaps Karma can be defended after all; perhaps the objections to Grace are stronger than I have recognized.). Still, the argument of the present chapter does constitute at least a prima-facie case for preferring Grace to Karma.

Second, suppose it is true (as defenders of Grace claim) that human beings are *not* able to save themselves. Then if the law of Karma holds (you get precisely what you deserve), that would seem to lead to nothing but pessimism and despair. Indeed, it might be taken to lead to the spiritual ruin of the human race. If on the other hand Grace is true (despite our inabilities, we can still be saved by God's Grace), that would seem to lead to an attitude of profound religious gratitude. Grace could then correctly be seen as offering relief and even escape from Karma.[24]

---

[24] I would like to thank Robin Collins, Paul Copan, Douglas Geivett, William Hasker, Gerald O'Collins, SJ, Susan Peppers-Bates, Bruce Reichenbach, Charles Taliaferro, William Wainwright, and Ellen Zhang for their helpful comments on earlier drafts of this chapter. They are not responsible for any errors that I have made.

11

Catholic–Protestant Views of Justification: How Should Christians View Theological Disagreements?

C. STEPHEN EVANS

One of the more promising developments within the contemporary Christian world has been the dialogue between Protestants and Catholics over key Christian doctrines, particularly the doctrine of justification. The exciting aspect of these discussions is that they have clearly reduced misunderstandings on both sides and led to a greater appreciation of the common ground that these two streams of Christian faith share.

PROTESTANT–CATHOLIC DIALOGUE ON JUSTIFICATION

Lutherans and Catholics have worked especially hard on these issues. The United States Lutheran–Catholic Dialogue published a statement in 1983 that included twelve important points of agreement, concluding with a 'Common Declaration' that sets forth 'a fundamental consensus on the gospel'. From 1986 until 1993 the Lutheran–Roman Catholic International Commission had intense discussions about this issue, and in *Church and Justification* supported the conclusions the Americans had reached.[1] This in turn led to a 'Joint Declaration' drafted in 1994 by representatives of the Vatican and the Lutheran World Federation. After lengthy consultation and criticism from Lutheran bodies, this Joint Declaration

---

[1] For a fine introduction to the European discussions see Karl Lehmann and Wolfhart Pannenberg (eds.), *The Condemnations of the Reformation Era: Do They Still Divide?* trans. Margaret Kohl (Minneapolis: Fortress Press, 1990).

was approved by the Lutheran World Federation in 1998. On the Catholic side, the process was more difficult; the Council for Promoting Christian Unity released a response that contained some severe criticisms of the document. (I will say more about some of these criticisms later.) This led to the attachment of an 'Official Common Statement', an 'Annex' and a 'Note on the Annex'. After these additions were made, the Joint Declaration was officially signed by representatives of both bodies on Sunday, 31 October 1999, in Augsburg.

On a different but complementary track, there have been encouraging discussions and a measure of agreement between a group of leading evangelical and Catholic scholars. In the spring of 1994 a statement was issued entitled 'Evangelicals and Catholics Together: The Christian Mission in the Third Millennium'. Discussions arising out of this document focused, as was the case in the Lutheran–Catholic dialogue, on the doctrine of justification, and in turn led to a new document, 'The Gift of Salvation', agreed to in October 1997.[2] In this chapter, for the sake of specificity and clarity I shall focus on the way these issues have been raised in the context of Lutheran–Catholic dialogue, and I shall not say anything about the 'Evangelicals and Catholics Together' documents, or other arenas where Catholics and Protestants have sought agreement. However, I believe that what I have to say is of relevance for Protestant–Catholic discussions more generally, and I shall signal this more general significance by speaking of 'Protestant' views rather than merely 'Lutheran' ones.[3] It goes without saying that in using typically Lutheran expressions to represent Protestant tendencies in general there is some oversimplification. I realize that on some issues, some Protestants, such as Methodists, for example, might actually be closer to Catholic than Lutheran views. Nevertheless I believe that most Protestants who are not Lutherans will be broadly sympathetic to the views I here describe as 'Protestant'.

---

[2] Published jointly by *First Things*, 79 (Jan. 1998), 20–3; and *Christianity Today*, 41 (8 Dec. 1997), 35–8.

[3] An important book dealing with the evangelical–Catholic dialogue is Thomas P. Rausch (ed.), *Catholics and Evangelicals: Do they Share a Common Future?* (New York: Paulist Press, 2000). See also Anthony N. S. Lane's *Justification by Faith in Catholic–Protestant Dialogue: An Evangelical Assessment* (Edinburgh: T. & T. Clark, 2002).

UNRESOLVED AREAS OF DISAGREEMENT

I personally rejoice to see the various branches of the Christian faith focusing on what unites them rather than what divides them. In the Western intellectual world, where aggressive secularism is still an important force, whether represented by a Richard Dawkins or a Richard Rorty, it is important to see that the differences between Christians are dwarfed in significance when compared with the differences between Christian perspectives and those of non-Christians. Nevertheless, differences between Christians remain, and remain important, a fact that is acknowledged by all sides in the discussions.

An important illustration of this point is given by the thoughtful analysis Avery Dulles has provided in *First Things* of the Lutheran–Catholic discussions.[4] Cardinal Dulles affirms the historic importance of the agreement embodied in the document, particularly a sentence in paragraph 15, which states 'Together we confess: By grace alone, in faith in Christ's saving work and not because of any merit on our part, we are accepted by God and receive the Holy Spirit, who renews our hearts while equipping and calling us to good works.' This part of the statement, says Dulles, 'dispels some false stereotypes inherited from the past'. It recognizes that Catholics accept that God's justification is not earned by human merit, and that Lutherans understand the importance of good works.

This shared agreement, however, does not mean that serious disagreements do not remain between the two groups. One of the major purposes of the Joint Declaration is to make it possible for both Catholics and Lutherans to regard past mutual condemnations, such as those embedded in the Council of Trent or various Protestant confessions, as no longer applicable to the other church. In commenting on the 'Official Response' of the Holy See to the initial draft of the Joint Declaration, Dulles discusses a number of contentious points.

One area of serious disagreement concerns 'human cooperation in the preparation for and reception of justification'. Dulles says that Trent 'taught under anathema that the recipients of justification

---

[4] 98 (Dec. 1999), 25–30.

cooperate freely in their own justification and do not receive it purely passively as if they were puppets'. Dulles interprets the Joint Declaration as denying these claims, implicitly assuming an understanding of 'justification as a divine decree, prior to any human act of faith or love'.

A second area of disagreement consists in the question as to whether or not justification consists 'in an imputation of Christ's righteousness, as Lutherans generally hold, or in an interior renewal and sanctification, as the Council of Trent taught'. Dulles interprets the Joint Declaration as favouring a 'theory of alien righteousness that was rejected at Trent'.

The third area discussed is whether or not justification totally removes the sin of the person (the Catholic view), or rather whether the justified individual remains a sinner and is *simul justus et peccator*—at once righteous and a sinner, as Lutherans contend. Finally, Dulles raises the issue of merit. Though both sides agree that 'nothing preceding justification merits justification', Catholics affirm and Lutherans deny that a person can, after justification, 'merit the increase of grace and the reward of eternal life'.

Obviously, much more could be said about all of these issues and many others. However, I think I have said enough to show that though common ground is recognized between Protestants and Catholics, serious disagreements remain. For Dulles these disagreements are significant enough to call into question whether or not the mutual anathemas of the Reformation can really be regarded as no longer applicable. Yet, in the end, despite his doubts, Dulles does want to affirm that the churches were right to proceed as they did, which was in effect to agree that their disagreements, while not currently resolvable, are 'tolerable'. Catholics and Lutherans have come to respect one another as Christian believers, who have much in common and 'precisely because of our different perspectives . . . can learn from one another'. Dulles would like to be able to 'establish that Lutheran proclamation and Catholic speculation are both legitimate derivatives of the same gospel, and therefore compatible', though he clearly thinks this is a goal to work towards, rather than an accomplishment. As things stand, disagreements remain, as does the question as to how those disagreements should be viewed.

CAN THEOLOGICAL DISAGREEMENTS, EVEN IF NOT GOOD OVERALL, SERVE GOOD ENDS?

Though I am a Protestant and I would probably incline towards Protestant views on most of the issues Dulles discusses, I share his fundamental view of the nature of these disagreements. I should like in this chapter to explore, in a tentative but hopefully suggestive way, the implications of this view of theological disagreement. I shall not undertake in a sustained or systematic way the task of attempting to reconcile the divergent views or at least narrow the differences, though I strongly support that project, and I shall make a few suggestions towards that end. For thorough work along these lines more expertise in theology is required than I possess. Instead, I shall deal with the question as to how unresolved issues should be viewed. I shall argue that there are principled reasons why Christians might not only tolerate, but respect and appreciate the views of other Christians, even when they find those views to be at least partially mistaken. Christians can, even while regretting their divisions, see the providence of God as present through their divisions, bringing good of what is not in itself good. I believe that these attitudes are especially appropriate when the disagreements concern the doctrine of justification.

Let me begin by removing some possible misunderstandings. Since I shall be arguing that disagreements between Christians can produce good, I want to make it clear that I am not saying that it is a good thing overall for the church to be divided or for disagreements to exist. Rather, I regard the division of Christ's body into various denominations with the accompanying doctrinal disagreements to be a sad and even tragic consequence of human sinfulness. But the claim that it is a bad thing for the church to be divided does not imply that no good things can come from that division. God is the One for whom all things are possible, and he is quite capable of making the actions of humans which go against his commands serve his purposes. As Joseph said to his brothers after the death of their father Jacob, when they feared he might retaliate against them for selling him into slavery, 'You intended to harm me, but God intended it for good to accomplish what is now being done, the saving of many lives' (Gen. 50: 20).

I think that we can in fact recognize some of the good which God has drawn and is drawing from Christian divisions. If I am right, what practical attitude should Christians take towards those divisions? The right attitude is not, I would urge, a complacent acceptance of the divided status quo. Rather, Christians should earnestly work to overcome their divisions and realize their unity. However, while doing so, and while the divisions remain, Christians should learn to cultivate an attitude of thankfulness for the good that God can draw from those divisions. Specifically, Christians of one persuasion should be thankful for what God can teach them through the convictions and the lives of Christians from other persuasions.

Can we hope to make progress in resolving Catholic–Protestant disputes over justification? I see no reason why this is not possible, though, as I said above, it is not the primary goal of this chapter. A good example of an attempt at reconciliation can be found in Richard Swinburne's treatment of the issue in his book *Faith and Reason*.[5] At least part of the dispute between Lutherans and Catholics about justification by faith, on Swinburne's view, rests on a crucial semantic difference. Catholics affirmed that faith without works is insufficient for salvation, while Lutherans affirmed that faith alone is sufficient. The two views appear to contradict one another, but Swinburne argues that the apparent contradiction is at least partially resolved if we recognize that the two parties understood different things by 'faith'. Catholics understood by 'faith' intellectual assent, and thus the claim that faith alone is insufficient for salvation is a claim that mere intellectual belief is not sufficient. Protestants, however, had a more expansive conception of faith, but this more expansive notion actually corresponds closely with the 'faith formed by love' which Catholics see as the faith which is actually meritorious.[6]

I am not competent enough as an historian to say whether Swinburne's attempted reconciliation here actually works, though it certainly seems plausible to me that at least some of the apparent disagreement at the time of the Reformation may indeed be due to mutual lack of understanding concerning the meanings of key terms. What I want to affirm is that I at least applaud this kind of effort; nothing in what follows should be taken as implying that Catholics

---

[5] Oxford and New York: Clarendon Press and Oxford University Press, 1981, 104–24.
[6] Ibid. 108–10.

and Protestants should not vigorously seek to narrow their differences and reach a common understanding on key issues. Until the millennium arrives and full understanding is reached, however, the question still remains as to how Christians should view their remaining disagreements. For reasons that will, I hope, be clear later, I shall not focus on any type of disagreement, but only on disagreements between those committed to historic Christian doctrines, such as are embodied in the Nicene Creed. My comments would not be applicable to a disagreement between two individuals, one who affirmed and one who denied that Jesus was raised from the dead or was God incarnate.

WOLTERSTORFF AND THE CONCEPT OF AUTHENTIC CHRISTIAN COMMITMENT

I would like to begin with a concept employed by Nicholas Wolterstorff, that of a person's 'authentic Christian commitment'.[7] Wolterstorff begins with the notion of a person's *actual* Christian commitment, which is simply 'the complex of action and belief in which his fundamental commitment [to Christ] is *in fact* realized'. A person's authentic Christian commitment is the normative counterpart to this reality, 'the complex of action and belief' that the person's commitment to Christ 'ought in fact to assume'.[8] Wolterstorff makes it clear that there are fundamental elements of authentic Christian commitment that hold for all Christians: 'One's following of Christ, then, ought to be actualized by taking up in decisively ultimate fashion God's call to share in the task of being witness, agent, and evidence of the coming of his kingdom'.[9] Despite this commonality, however, the concept of authentic Christian commitment is an individual one, and what it entails 'varies not only from person to person but also from time to time within a given person's life', both with respect to beliefs and actions.[10] On this account, then, what God expects and desires from me as a follower of Christ may differ from what is expected and desired from some other individual, or even from what God expected and desired of me when I was 15 years old.

---

[7] Nicholas Wolterstorff, *Reason Within the Bounds of Religion* (Grand Rapids, Mich.: Eerdmans, 1976), 67–72.
[8] Ibid. 68.   [9] Ibid. 69.   [10] Ibid. 70

One of the factors that might shape a person's authentic Christian commitment would be the particular Christian community that has brought an individual to faith and/or nourished that faith. It seems plausible, to me at any rate, that someone raised in a devout Mennonite home ought to express his or her commitment to Christ differently than someone who is raised a Presbyterian or a Lutheran. Those Mennonite convictions might require such an individual who wishes to be faithful to Christ to refrain from killing other humans, even in a war that other Christians might rightly view as just.

It is clear that Mennonites and members of other Anabaptist churches hold different convictions about the relations of the Christian to the state than do members of the Catholic church and many Protestant churches. It seems to me that such disagreements are not likely to be resolved in the immediate future, and that one or more parties to the disagreements must be mistaken on some points. The claim that it is permissible for Christians to take up arms in a conflict where certain specified conditions are met is one that must be either true or false. Nevertheless, I think that Christians on one side of such an issue can understand and affirm the convictions of those on the other side, and even see God's providential hand in the division, bringing good out of a situation that is not in itself good.

For the purpose of illustrating this point, let me assume that the advocates of a just war position are right about the particular issue in dispute. (Even though this is in fact my view, for the purposes of the present chapter this is just an assumption; the point could be made just as well by making the opposite assumption.) Even the advocates of a just war theory can and should recognize how easily such a theory can be used to justify wars that are by no means just, and how often this has in fact occurred. In such a situation the just war theorist can be glad that the historic 'peace' churches continue to witness to the fundamental importance of non-violence for the Christian church. Given the fallenness of the human race, and even the way sinfulness infects the visible church, it may well be that the total message of the gospel is better seen when one of the components of that gospel is stressed in a pure and unadulterated way by a community of the faithful than would be possible otherwise, even if this emphasis taken by itself leads to a one-sided view. If this is so, then even someone who believes that pacifism is theologically mistaken may be thankful to God for its existence within the church, given the fallen world which we occupy.

Interestingly, Wolterstorff himself seems to allow for the possibility that God may desire that some or even all segments of the church believe something that is not true, strictly speaking: 'not all of what belongs to the belief-content of one's authentic commitment may be true. Some of what God wishes us to believe may be fit and proper for us as his "children" to believe, yet strictly speaking, false.'[11] Why might this be so? Wolterstorff does not say, but we may speculate as to some possible reasons.

First of all, some of what is strictly true may be beyond our capacity to grasp. Merold Westphal has given the example of a parent who wishes to teach a toddler not to put into his or her mouth things such as coins found on dirty floors.[12] In such a situation the parent may tell the child, 'Don't put that into your mouth; it has tiny little bugs on it.' Strictly speaking, what the parent says is false. However, the young child is not capable of understanding germ theory, and cannot really grasp what bacteria are. The practical import of the parent's advice is served well enough by the parent's rough and ready explanation of the admonition. In a similar way, truths about the character and actions of an infinite God may not be understandable by finite humans, and God might well wish us humans to believe rough and ready approximations that are as close as our minds allow.

The second reason that God may allow and even desire his children to believe what is, strictly speaking, false is also implicit in the Westphal analogy. The truths of Christian faith are not, by and large, offered to us simply to satisfy our intellectual curiosity. They are intensely practical. We are to know God so that we can love God and serve God. It seems likely then that God is fully justified in giving us rough and ready approximations to the truth in cases where our practical response to those approximations is all-important. And we can even go beyond this point. It seems possible that there might be cases where we would be capable intellectually of grasping the truth, or at least something that is closer to the truth, but because of our fallenness be prone to draw the wrong practical conclusions from that truth. In such a situation we might be better served by a view

[11] Nicholas Wolterstorff, *Reason Within the Bounds of Religion* (Grand Rapids, Mich.: Eerdmans, 1976), 95.

[12] I first heard Westphal develop this analogy in a lecture at Calvin College in the summer of 1996. It can be found in print in his *Overcoming Onto-Theology* (New York: Fordham University Press, 2001), 80.

that is less close as a theoretical approximation, but whose adoption is more likely to lead to beneficial results on our lives. Another possibility in such a case is that we might be better served if some hold to the view that is theoretically closer to the truth, while others hold to the more pragmatically beneficial approximation, because in that case those who hold to the theoretically superior view might be somewhat protected against the possible bad pragmatic implications of their view by the example of the other party. For example, advocates of pacifism might, in theory at least, help those who advocate a just war theory become more sensitive to the ways just war theory can be abused to justify injustice.

Humans have a positive genius for justifying and rationalizing sinful forms of behaviour by appealing to principles and ideals which are in themselves true and noble. Of course we cannot in general take this as a reason not to embrace the truth; the fact that a true ethical theory can be misused, while a sad fact about human nature, does not mean we should not accept the theory. However, God in his wisdom might realize that there are some truths which we humans would be especially prone to misuse; in our sinfulness perhaps such a misuse would be nearly inevitable, and the consequences to our character disastrous. In such a situation, since we cannot assume that God's purpose for humans is solely to maximize true beliefs and minimize false beliefs, God might have good reason for wanting us humans to believe what is false, strictly speaking. Or, and this is the case most relevant to my discussion of theological disagreements, God might wish the truer view to be preserved in certain segments of the church, while allowing other segments to represent a view which, though in itself strictly mistaken, engenders a practical witness that serves as a corrective to the ways the truth is generally misused.

If Wolterstorff and Westphal are right in their contentions, and I am right in thinking through some of the implications of those contentions, then this provides us with a principled reason why a Christian might hold that some other Christian is mistaken in a conviction, and yet hold that the other Christian would be less faithful to Christ, at least at that particular time and in that particular situation, were he or she to give up the belief. I can recognize that the authentic Christian commitment of another person (or myself) may require the acceptance of a belief that is, strictly speaking, false. Of course I cannot myself believe a proposition which I know or believe to be false, so it is easier to apply this principle to others with whom we disagree, or to beliefs that we held in the past but no longer hold, than to ourselves and our current beliefs. However, we can recognize the applicability of the principle in a general and abstract way to our present convictions as well, and the result will likely be a healthy intellectual humility. Wolterstorff himself affirms that his principle implies that '[f]or all we know' the false theories that Christians are led to embrace by virtue of their authentic Christian commitments are 'fully satisfactory for our human purposes'.[13]

CRITICAL REALISM

Wolterstorff's claim does not, as I understand it, imply that one must take an 'anti-realist' view of theological propositions, or view such propositions solely in terms of their pragmatic function. A robust epistemological realism is rather being presupposed. It is only because truth is objective and independent of human knowers that it makes sense to suppose that a theory which is 'fully satisfactory for human purposes' is nevertheless false. The view I am endorsing fits best, I believe, with what is usually termed 'critical realism', a term first developed in the early twentieth century by Roy Wood Sellars, A. O. Lovejoy, and others, but which has been increasingly applied in theology as well.[14] On a critical realist model of how theology gets done, humans have genuine access to the reality that theology attempts to characterize, but the insights that we can acquire, even with the help of special revelation, are not final and comprehensive. Rather, we should think of our theories as capturing important aspects and dimensions of God and God's actions and purposes. Such theories are, however, neither final nor complete, but open to revision and supplementation. We can recognize the pragmatic

---

[13] Ibid, 95.
[14] For a brief summary of what critical realism might mean in theology and biblical studies, see N. T. Wright, *The New Testament and the People of God* (Minneapolis: Fortress Press, 1992), 32–50. Wright himself cites Thomas Torrance, *Space, Time, and Resurrection* (Grand Rapids, Mich., Eerdmans, 1976), and Colin Gunton, *Enlightenment and Alienation: An Essay Towards a Trinitarian Theology* (Grand Rapids, Mich.: Eerdmans, 1985), among others, as explicating the notion of critical realism in theology in more depth.

function of religious convictions on such an account without seeing those convictions as simply 'true' in some purely pragmatic sense. Rather, it is because they are approximately true in a realistic sense that they have the pragmatic value that they do have. However, since the truths grasped are approximative in character, it is possible that in some cases there will be more than one account that approximates the truth. In some cases these might be roughly equal in what might be termed their approximative adequacy, but differ somewhat with respect to pragmatic value. Such an account does imply, I think, that views that are regarded as mistaken but nevertheless divinely intended cannot be *completely* mistaken. They must embody some truth in a partial manner. Perhaps they are only false *strictly* speaking.

Another way of making the point would be to say that we should not expect a high degree of theoretical precision in theology, given the fact that God so greatly transcends our human capacities. The matter is further complicated by our sinfulness. Not only does sinfulness further impair our cognitive faculties. It also damages the way we put the truths we are able to understand to work in our lives. All of this may be understood as helping us to see how it is possible for those we recognize as faithful Christians to be partially mistaken on important theological issues, and yet recognize that those mistaken Christians may be entirely faithful to their calling as Christians, at least with respect to the issues in dispute between us.

Is God a Deceiver?

I should now like to pose some possible objections to this way of thinking and see what can be said in response to those objections. The objections will require certain qualifications to Wolterstorff's suggestion, but the qualifications are, I think, already present in the view as I have developed it, either implicitly or explicitly. The cluster of objections centres on the supposition that God desires humans to believe what is false. Does this make God a deceiver? If God reveals claims which are false, then why should God be trusted? Furthermore, if we adopt such a principle, can it be restricted to propositions that do not contravene the claims of the ecumenical Christian creeds? Why should we not suppose that, though God has revealed to us that Jesus is divine and that he rose from the dead, these claims are really false?

Let me deal first with this last worry. We are looking at whether or not a person's authentic Christian commitment might require that person to believe what is strictly false. The notion of authentic Christian commitment is defined in terms of faithfulness to Jesus the Christ. To ask about one's authentic Christian commitment is to ask how one's commitment to Christ as Lord should be actualized in one's life. It is hard, therefore, to see how views that are incompatible with seeing Christ as Lord, the one who has complete authority over one's life, could be part of a person's authentic Christian commitment. I cannot be faithful to Christ as Lord by believing that he is not Lord. At the very least, any argument that this is so would require a subtle exploration of such issues as whether an objectively mistaken or wrong course could nonetheless be subjectively obligatory because of the individual's obligation to follow conscience.

If one believes, as I do, that the obligation to be a follower of Christ is always at the same time an obligation to be a member of Christ's body, the church, then this will put yet more restrictions on the application of the principle that God may will that some believe what is strictly false. It seems unlikely to me that beliefs that deny the central convictions expressed in the ecumenical creeds and held in common by all the major branches of Christendom could be part of an individual's authentic Christian commitment. (Subject to the same qualification made in the last paragraph about the possibility of such a belief being obligatory even though objectively wrong because of reasons of conscience.) For denying the central tenets of Christian faith would be a way of separating oneself from the church. At least in the normal course of things, one cannot be a faithful follower of Christ without also being part of the community that professes faith in Christ. Hence, I think that the restriction of my discussion to disagreements between those committed to the ecumenical creeds is not arbitrary in character.

Is a God who reveals claims that are false or desires humans to believe claims that are false deceptive? I do not believe that what we may call the 'Wolterstorff–Westphal view' I have developed implies that God is deceptive. The reason this is so is that, as I have developed the view, it does not imply that God reveals to us claims that are completely or simply false. If God revealed propositional claims that led us diametrically away from the truth, then perhaps one could argue that he would be deceiving us. However, on the view as I have developed it, God reveals to us something that approximates the truth, something that embodies at least an aspect of the truth. God does not reveal the precise truth to all of us, either because we are incapable of grasping that truth, or incapable of truly drawing from that truth the right practical implications. God does not deceive us because he wants to draw us towards the truth, as closely as is possible given our finitude and sinfulness and God's own purpose of making us holy.

Another objection that could be raised concerns the alleged benefits of theological disagreements. The critic might argue that, while in theory disagreements could have the beneficial results I am discussing, in reality, religious disputes have often led to wars and persecution. The reply to this objection is a reminder that I am not claiming that theological disagreements are, on the whole, a good thing. They are rather one of the bitter consequences of human fallenness. All the tragic consequences of such disagreements can be honestly acknowledged. My claim is only that Christians today, who live in the midst of such disagreements, can see God's faithful providence at work in and amidst the brokenness. The question is not whether or not it would have been better had the church never divided, but whether or not faithful Christians today can recognize that Christians who disagree with them can be genuinely faithful to their calling as Christians.

APPLYING THE PRINCIPLE TO DISPUTES ABOUT JUSTIFICATION

I wish now to try to apply this general principle to the issue of disputed understandings of justification. I shall try to do so in an irenic manner, without assuming anything about which party to a given dispute is more nearly correct, though of course I will not be able to be completely even-handed since I do have convictions with respect to many issues. I want to comment on several of the issues that Avery Dulles has highlighted as serious bones of contention. For some issues I shall look for further points of convergence, in the spirit of Swinburne, by trying to remove misunderstandings of positions. Where that does not seem possible, I shall try to apply the principle developed above, in which Christians who disagree can understand

and appreciate the views of those whom they see as mistaken, recognizing those mistaken views as embodying partial truths and as perhaps serving some good purposes of God.

The first issue concerns 'human cooperation in the preparation for and reception of justification'. As we have seen, Dulles interprets the Joint Declaration as tilting towards a Protestant view of this matter, implicitly assuming an understanding of 'justification as a divine decree, prior to any human act of faith or love'. The problem, from the Catholic side, is that we must understand the recipients of justification as beings who 'cooperate freely in their justification and do not receive it purely passively as if they were puppets'. Some progress might be made here, I suspect, by questioning whether or not it follows from an understanding of justification as a divine decree that its human recipients are passive puppets. Following Swinburne's lead with respect to the concept of faith, one might ask whether or not the parties have precisely the same thing in mind by the term 'justification'. Dulles himself accepts the view that Catholics do not think that humans do anything to earn God's justification, and so he must think that as part of this process God does something that is not simply a response to some human action. And Protestants will surely reject the claim that humans are simply passive puppets throughout the process, even if Protestants wish to say that human actions are not part of that particular reality they wish to designate as 'justification'.

However, suppose that rapprochement along these lines (or some other) cannot be achieved? Can we see these differing views as each having valuable pragmatic functions? I think that we can. Protestant views on this matter emphasize that God's gift of justification is indeed a free gift; they thus minimize a human tendency to see ourselves as in some way responsible for our own salvation, and seek to curb the sin of pride. Catholic views have other pragmatic virtues; they emphasize the fact that humans are responsible moral agents and not puppets or robots. They thus push us away from a tendency towards quietism or fatalism, and help us recognize that God requires a response from us as part of his salvific plan. Each view thus emphasizes and highlights a desirable pragmatic implication that, while perhaps not completely absent from the other view, is at least present in a less evident manner.

Someone might object here that it would be better to have a complete theory that embodies both of these pragmatic functions.

And indeed it would be better. Such a theory would be one that enables Catholics and Protestants to resolve their differences, and I have already said that this would be a more desirable result. However, if this result cannot yet be achieved, we can still recognize the beneficial aspects of a view that we may think partially mistaken.

The second area of disagreement I wish to touch upon concerns the question of whether justification consists in 'an imputation of Christ's righteousness' (the Protestant view) or in 'an interior renewal and sanctification'. Once again we might make the move of seeing whether this dispute is partly semantic. Could it be that one party is simply calling one part of the process by which God saves humans 'justification', describing other parts by different terms such as 'sanctification', while the other party uses the one term 'justification' for the entire process?

One might think that the inner transformation that the Catholic position emphasizes as vital is one that is made possible precisely by the remarkable gift of forgiveness that God freely offers. In that case the 'alien righteousness' that Protestants speak of would not be so alien after all, in so far as an understanding that God sees me not as a guilty individual who bears the responsibility of my sin but rather as a person who is joined to Christ and for whom Christ's atoning work suffices may be an understanding that transforms me. God sees me not simply as I am but as I am and will become as I am united to Christ. The liberating recognition that God sees me this way even now may be precisely what revolutionizes my character. Whether we call the resulting transformation a part of justification or a natural consequence of justification, both aspects are present and are tightly linked. Given a critical realist understanding of theology and a recognition of the lack of precision in the referential application of theological terms, it is not always easy to determine how to parse the various elements of the salvific process.

However, if we once more assume that full agreement cannot be reached, what desirable pragmatic functions might the two views embody? It seems to me that Protestant views here highlight and emphasize the way in which God's attitude towards the sinner can be seen as one of loving forgiveness. The Protestant view offers the comfort that this attitude of God towards the sinner is not one that the sinner must or can do anything to earn; it is completely grounded in God's action. Not only are we blocked from taking any credit for our salvation; we are firmly freed from anxiety as to whether we have done enough to assure it. The Catholic position, as I see it, highlights the fact that God's purpose in salvation is not simply a juridical exchange, as if the major goal is to accomplish a bit of cosmic bookkeeping. Rather, God's purpose is the transformation of the individual, so as to make the person capable of sharing in the life of God himself and the life of the community of the people of God.

Note that I am not saying that the positive pragmatic functions are present solely in only one of the two positions. It is not that Protestants have nothing to say about the acquisition of a righteous character or that Catholics have nothing to say about the free grace God extends to humans. It is rather that each view magnifies a particular characteristic in such a way that it becomes easier for fallen humans to grasp it and see its practical implications in the right way. Conversely, each view protects against a certain understanding that, while not genuinely implied in the other view, may easily be derived from that view by fallen humans. It is, I suspect, historically true that Protestants have been more likely than Catholics to misunderstand justification as a juridical ruling that has no implications for a person's transformation, and that Catholics have been more likely than Protestants to misunderstand justification as something that humans must merit. At the very least this has been true in my own experience of discussions with Christian friends from various communions, going all the way back to my teenage years. And this is true even though in both cases these understandings are indeed misunderstandings.

The last issue I shall discuss concerns whether or not justification totally removes the sin of the person, as Catholics maintain, or whether the justified individual remains a sinner. Once more it appears that there are possibilities for narrowing the area of disagreement, and a suspicion arises that semantic differences may be partly responsible for the divergence. In affirming that justified humans remain sinners, Protestants do not necessarily mean that such humans continue to rightly be judged to bear the guilt of offences against God. Perhaps they mean rather that justified humans continue to possess many of their sinful habits and tendencies, such that it is likely that they will continue to sin and require God's grace and forgiveness. However, this state in which an individual possesses sinful habits and tendencies seems close to what Catholic theologians have usually meant by 'sinfulness'. Theologians who distinguish between sin and sinfulness could affirm that justified humans who are no longer 'sinners' in one sense (they no longer are rightly judged guilty of offences by God) continue to possess the quality of sinfulness, and thus must battle against impulses that push them towards sin. In another sense they thus remain 'sinners', people who sometimes sin and must constantly struggle against sin.

I think that prospects for eventual agreement with respect to this issue are fairly bright. However, once more we can ask the question as to what purposes the disagreements serve so long as they exist (or did serve when they existed if they could be overcome). And I think a plausible answer can be given. The Protestant view on this issue protects against triumphalism; it warns the forgiven sinner to be on guard, since the old sinful habits and tendencies have not yet been completely eradicated. He or she should therefore expect the Christian life to be a battle in which the assistance of the Spirit must be sought. The Catholic view, on the other hand, protects against several ills. The good news that my sin has been completely forgiven tends to protect against the despair that can accompany an excessive consciousness of guilt, and an understanding that God's act of justification has begun the process of transformation protects against the pessimistic assumption that progress in the spiritual life is impossible. This pessimism can also lead to despair; the justified individual who falls into sin can be tempted to think that such failures are inevitable.

These thoughts on the pragmatic value of differing Catholic–Protestant views of justification are of course only an initial stab. A careful, knowledgeable theologian can doubtless go much further, towards both narrowing the differences and understanding in a nuanced way the possible pragmatic goods that any remaining differences can serve. Much more could be said, for example, about the ways in which the church's theological understanding, like human understanding in general, has been advanced by controversies of various sorts. This of course mirrors the very structure of theological inquiry as it was developed in the great medieval 'Summas', with their careful dialectical development of arguments. It was thought then, and still to many seems true today, that the pursuit of truth is best advanced by a disputational context. At the very least we can see what goods, intellectual and non-intellectual, were made possible by differences in the past. I want to claim that besides the very real goods that past disputes have fostered, there are benefits to our continued disagreements.

To repeat my earlier qualification, the recognition of such goods by no means relieves us of the task of seeking a unified Christian understanding. We can and should seek, in a spirit of charity, to incorporate the truths from our neighbours while rooting out the one-sidedness and error in our own perspectives. However, we can also understand how some of our disagreements can be ascribed, not to hard-heartedness and stubbornness, but to faithfulness to God's call to us in a fallen world.

The Redemption Practised and Proclaimed

12

'Graven with an Iron Pen': The Persistence of Redemption as a Theme in Literature

ROBERT KIELY

Why do ye persecute me as God, and are not satisfied with my flesh? O that my words were now written! O that they were printed in a book! That they were graven with an iron pen and lead in the rock forever! For I know that my Redeemer liveth, and that he shall stand at the latter day upon the earth; And though after my skin worms destroy this body, yet in my flesh I shall see God.

(Job 19: 22–6, KJV)

And it was the third hour when they crucified him. And the inscription of the charge against him read, 'The King of the Jews.' ... And those who passed by derided him, wagging their heads and saying, 'Aha! You who would destroy the temple and build it in three days, save yourself and come down from the cross!' So also the chief priests mocked him.. saying, 'He saved others; he cannot save himself. Let the Christ, the King of Israel, come down now from the cross, that we may see and believe.'

(Mark 15: 24–32, NRSV)

Job's declamatory speech and the silence of Jesus are striking moments in two great scriptural narratives about redemption or, more precisely, about the promise of redemption scorned by sceptics who doubt that it can occur. Both episodes represent the suffering of an innocent victim mocked by observers who taunt them for being unable to save themselves. Both suggest on the part of the mockers a relatively simple understanding of redemption or salvation as release from present suffering. However, Job's hope for a future Redeemer and Mark's reference to 'building the temple in three days' hint powerfully at the possibility of a more complex and radical salvation by means of which time itself will be redeemed, Job justified, and Jesus resurrected. The suffering of both victims is 'on the record', written down in narrative form, yet the details of both episodes defy common readerly expectations about stories with clear beginnings and conclusive endings. From a conventional literary point of view, a 'redemption narrative' is a contradiction in terms, a rejection of starting and stopping points, an unending effort to extend the boundaries of stories, to abolish the limits of time-bound narration. In some realm seemingly beyond telling Job will see God and know that he is on his side, and Jesus will rebuild the ruined temple.

These two crucial and paradigmatic moments in the lives of Job and Jesus, with elements of hope and despair, faith and doubt, solemnity and mockery, contain a dynamic tension that has been present with surprising frequency in English and American literature when the idea of salvation or the terms 'redeem', 'redemption', 'Redeemer' have occurred. Whatever the genre, a narrative is explicitly provided or implied. Some person is in an undesirable situation (of pain, bondage, or debt) from which he or she hopes, against all odds, to be released. Against the hope of the victim is the hatred and mockery of an enemy who does not believe release is possible and, in any case, does not want it to take place. Often even the seemingly most straightforward versions of a redemption story contain complications and ambiguities of definition. Is the nature of the release exclusively material? Are the wounds to be healed, debts to be paid, chains to be broken literal? Or are there moral and spiritual components of the release which may or may not coincide with the physical evidence? Who pays the debt and at what price? Can victims redeem themselves or, as Job suggests, do they need an advocate?

Before looking into these questions as they pertain to four works in the American literary canon, it will be useful to look briefly at some common deployments of 'redemption' language in post-Reformation English literature since English usage and, in many cases, particular English texts have strongly influenced American practice. I choose Shakespeare because all of the American writers I wish to discuss knew Shakespearian diction and the plays almost as well as they knew scripture. I want also to spend a moment reflecting on John Donne, not because of direct influence, but because he represents an early modern religious sensibility in contrast to Shakespeare's secularity.

In an early speech in Act I Shakespeare's Othello narrates episodes from his life before coming to Venice: 'Of being taken by the insolent foe, And sold to slavery, of my redemption thence.'[1] Shakespeare puts into play a common secular understanding of redemption as 'release from bondage' and, at the same time, foreshadows with tragic irony the last scene in which after murdering Desdemona, Othello realizes that he has lost his love and his soul: 'Speak of me as I am; nothing extenuate;...of one whose hand, Like the base Indian, threw a pearl away, Richer than all his tribe.[2]

For Shakespeare's Christian audience, the pearl that Othello has thrown away was clearly Desdemona, but just as clearly 'the pearl of great price', the kingdom of heaven, and therefore his own salvation. As always in Shakespeare, as indeed in most literature, terms draw their meanings from a combination of popular usage, allusion to well-known texts and common traditions, and to their placement in a particular narrative. The irony of Othello's story intensifies as his release from one kind of captivity cannot prevent him from being caught in Iago's net and in the destructive passion of his own jealousy. The nature of redemption, its physical and spiritual connotations, its alternation between permanence and impermanence, are all touched on with deepening and darkening variations as the play proceeds.

An even more concentrated mixing of the secular and religious connotations of 'redemption' occurs in *Measure for Measure*. The virginal novice Isabella has been told by the wicked Angelo that her brother will be released from prison only if she agrees to spend a night with Angelo. When she refuses, Angelo warns that her brother then must die. Isabella responds angrily:

> And 'twere the cheaper way:
> Better it were a brother died at once,
> Than that a sister, by redeeming him,
> Should die forever.[3]

As with the 'pearl' image, redemption here is associated with comparative value, life on earth or life everlasting, and with the necessity of exchange. One way or another, a price must be paid: Isabella's virginity for her brother's life or her brother's life for what she

---

[1] *Othello*, I. 3, in *The Complete Works of Wlliam Shakespeare: The Cambridge Edition*, ed. William Aldis Wright (Philadelphia: Blakiston Co., 1936), 942.
[2] *Othello*, 5. 2. 979.   [3] *Measure for Measure*, 2. 4. 914.

perceives as her eternal damnation if she gives in to Angelo's demand. Once again, the audience must recognize the secular and spiritual economics of redemption in order to understand Isabella's dilemma. The play's plot is inextricably bound to the common human experience of barter and to conflicting interpretations of the masterplot of Christian salvation.

As long as writers could assume that they were addressing a largely Christian audience, they could also assume a general know-ledge of the spiritual ramifications of redemption as a release from eternal misery purchased for humankind by Christ. But throughout Christian history and especially after the Reformation, many import-ant details of this masterplot were subjects of disagreement. How exactly did Christ pay the debt for all? To what extent must human beings participate with Jesus in the process of their own redemption? Is it so hard to be redeemed that only a few make it?

John Donne, the great preacher-lawyer-poet of the seventeenth century, often railed against Calvinist pessimism about salvation. In a sermon on Christian hope preached in 1612, he concluded as if addressing the Puritans of his day: 'But even in this inordinate dejection thou exaltest thyself above God, and makest thy worst better than his best, thy sins larger than his mercy.'[4]

Donne is an interesting case because his orthodox optimism was often in conflict with his melancholy temperament, especially after the death of his wife and his prolonged and nearly fatal illness. Donne's sermons, unlike Shakespeare's plays, do not have fictional plots, but they are no less dramatic, specific to their time, and bound to narratives. While rebuking the morose Calvinists, Donne is also rebuking himself for a preoccupation with his own sins and doubts about the mercy of God. In doing so, he endows his language with enormous power precisely because he is able to fuse narratives of scriptural, historical, and personal reference into one dynamic discourse.

In one of his great, morbid meditations on death delivered in a sermon at Whitehall on the first Friday of Lent, 1621, Donne seems almost to take pleasure in terrifying his congregation of courtiers with repeated images of dust, decay, and silence: 'The dust of great

---

[4] John Donne, *Sermon Preached at Lincoln's Inn, Sunday after Trinity, 1612*, in *The Complete Poetry and Selected Prose of John Donne*, ed. Charles M. Coffin (New York: The Modern Library, 1994), 480.

persons' graves is speechlesse too, it says nothing.'[5] But since he, like many in his congregation, is a 'great person', a famous divine, he is, as usual, talking to himself. After all, who could be more depressed by the prospect of speechlessness than a preacher renowned for his eloquence? Nonetheless, like Job, as long as he has breath, Donne will not stop talking, even to the point of imagining his own death at the hands of a personified Death that sounds very much like a personified God: 'And when he hath sported himself with my misery upon that stage, my deathbed, shall shift the scene, and throw me from that bed, into the grave, and there triumph over me, God knows, how many generations, till the Redeemer, my Redeemer, the Redeemer of all of me, body as well as soule, come againe.'[6] As the sermon draws towards its conclusion, it is increasingly dramatic as Donne's generalized portrait of death becomes more particular, more personal, and more scriptural. Emotion builds through the development of the long periodic sentence evoking Donne, the learned rhetorician, simultaneously with Donne, the frail mortal, hopeful Christian, and soulmate of Job. The shift from 'the' to 'my' Redeemer conveys in a highly compressed form not only Donne's daringly intimate tonal modulation, but a theology based on faith in a personal Saviour who, despite a very long absence, will not forget to 'come again', as promised, and deliver this particular poet-preacher from death.

It is clear that in both Shakespeare's 'worldly' plays and Donne's 'unworldly' sermons, religious—and specifically biblical and Christian—associations lend dimensions of meaning to the idea of redemption that take it beyond the literal level of fictitious plot or autobiography. As we turn to two American works of the nineteenth century and two of the twentieth century, it is worth asking whether the religious associations can still be discerned. And if so, in what form? One might expect certain distinctive characteristics to emerge because of the influence of Puritanism, the founding of the American republic after a war of independence, and the great conflict caused by the existence of slavery. Three expectations, even assumptions, stand out. First, that the American emphasis

---

[5] Donne, *Sermon Preached at Whitehall, First Friday in Lent, 1621* in *Poetry and Prose*, 486.
[6] Ibid. 487–8.

in a redemption story would be on the actual establishment of a 'promised land' of freedom and equality, a political more than a spiritual realm. Second, that the American emphasis would be on the individual's ability to redeem himself or herself without depending on an advocate or mediator. And third, that Americans would understand the 'redeeming of time' not as a return but as progress into a future in which the past would no longer matter.

In the nineteenth century, Henry David Thoreau and Herman Melville provide fascinating and instructive examples of peculiarly American tales about redemption because of the deeply philosophical nature of their writing. Thoreau's *A Week on the Concord and Merrimack Rivers* is ostensibly nothing more than a journal of a camping trip taken by the author and his brother in the late summer of 1839. But, like everything Thoreau wrote, it is also a journey filled with political, moral, and spiritual meanderings. Indeed, digression is key to Thoreau's writing, a stylistic habit but also a habit of a mind that perceives greatness and beauty in minor unexpected side-trips rather than in the supposedly major events and concerns of the times. In the Sunday entry Thoreau makes a particular point of saying that, unlike most of his countrymen, he is not attending church and therefore not following the Christian calendar or Christian patterns of behaviour in undertaking this trip, but instead following the twists and turns of the rivers and his own imagination. Throughout the journal, Thoreau not only takes leave of Concord and Christian observance, but of the particular journey itself as his mind wanders off to books he has read or other trips he has taken. At three in the morning on Tuesday, he and his brother are unable to sleep because of the wind, so they set off before sunrise: 'So, shaking the clay from our feet, we pushed into the fog. Though we were enveloped in mist as usual, we trusted that there was a bright day behind it.'[7]

---

[7] Henry David Thoreau, *A Week on the Concord and Merrimac Rivers* (Orleans, Mass.: Parnassus, 1987), 220. Further references will appear in the text as *Week*. Recent critical works of particular interest include Michael Berger, *Thoreau's Late Career and the Dispersion of Seeds* (Rochester, NY: Camden House, 2000); David R. Foster, *Thoreau's Country: Journey through a Transformed Landscape* (Cambridge, Mass.: Harvard University Press, 1999); Linck C. Johnson, *Thoreau's Complex Weave: The Writing of A Week on the Concord and Merrimac Rivers* (Charlottesville, Va.: University Press of Virginia, 1986); and Daniel H. Peck, *Thoreau's Morning Work: Memory and Perception in A Week on the Concord and Merrimac Rivers, The Journal, and Walden* (New Haven: Yale University Press, 1990).

The two sentences seem simple and merely descriptive except for the fact that they lead Thoreau into a twelve-page digression about climbing a mountain alone and coming face to face with 'the gracious god'. With careful attention to every detail, Thoreau takes the reader back with him to North Adams, Massachusetts, to the hay-fields and meadows he crossed on his way to Saddle-back Mountain. As he leaves civilization behind and approaches the woods, the tone and even some of the details take on an allegorical note. He passes a beautiful young woman in 'dishabille' combing her hair and a pedlar who warns him that there is no path to the summit, that it is too steep to climb, and nobody 'ever went this way'. All this only encourages Thoreau to press on and to meditate on the supposed difficulties of travel and fear of getting lost:

So far as my experience goes, travellers generally exaggerate the difficulties of the way. Like most evil, the difficulty is imaginary. For what's the hurry? If a person lost would conclude that after all he is not lost, he is not beside himself, but standing in his own old shoes on the very spot where he is, and for the time being he will live there; but the places that have known him, *they* are lost,—how much anxiety and danger would vanish. I am not alone if I stand by myself.   (*Week*, 226)

This is a wonderful piece of American self-reliance. Thoreau proceeds to explain how he forged on, drinking water from clear puddles in the granite, collecting dry sticks for a fire, and whittling a spoon with which to eat his small portion of rice. Yet by comparing the supposed hazards of mountain climbing with imaginary 'evil' and through his repetition of 'way' and 'lost', he subtly begins to weave another larger narrative into his Massachusetts adventure. With no direct allusion to *The Divine Comedy* or *Pilgrim's Progress*, he gradually aligns his digression with two great Christian narratives about life's journey through and around the obstacles that separate humankind from paradise. Having left 'earth' behind and reached the summit, he reads old newspapers by firelight and thinks with godlike detachment of their editorial opinions as 'flimsy' and the commodities being advertised as words in a poem. When it comes time to sleep, he is so cold that he covers himself in old boards left behind by campers, enclosing himself in a kind of coffin: 'I at length encased myself in boards, managing even to put a board on top of me, with a large stone on it to keep it down, and so slept comfortably' (*Week*, 230).

Though he 'entombs' himself and there is no mention of Christ or crucifixion, there is little doubt that his allegorical pilgrimage has taken him beyond Dante and Bunyan to scripture itself. When he awakens in early morning and comes to what he calls the 'pith' of his digression, he imagines or really experiences his own resurrection into new life:

As the light in the east steadily increased, it revealed to me more clearly the new world into which I had risen in the night, the new terra-firma perchance of my future life. There was not a crevice left through which the trivial places we name Massachusetts, or Vermont, or New York, could be seen.... All around beneath me was spread for a hundred miles on every side, as far as the eye could reach, an undulating country of clouds... It was such a country as we might see in dreams, with all the delights of paradise. (*Week*, 232)

As he attempts to express his feelings of awe, Thoreau's language becomes less that of the naturalist and more that of a mystic: 'It was a favor for which to be forever silent to be shown this vision' (*Week*, 232). He goes on to speak of reaching 'the region of eternal day', and when the sun begins to rise, he proclaims, 'I saw the gracious god' (*Week*, 233). Yet despite the implicit identification with Moses on Mount Sinai and the risen Jesus, Thoreau's moment of redemption is just that, a moment. As he prepares to return to the valley below and a gray, drizzly New England day, he detects 'some unworthiness in myself', an inability to sustain the purity of his experience. He concludes the digression with a poem that ends: 'O, raise thou from his corse thy now entombed exile!' (*Week*, 234).

The note of despondency is surprising, almost shocking, after the optimistic enthusiasm of the climb, the rejection of evil as imaginary, the denial that human beings are ever really 'lost' as long as they are self-possessed, and the ecstatic rising with the new day. Up to a point, Thoreau's digression on redemption seems to fit all the expected American criteria. His salvation consists in reaching a clearly defined and earthly goal, the top of the mountain. He does not require a redeemer or even a guide or companion since he is perfectly capable of finding his own way. And he never looks back on his past. One might well argue that the parallels to Dante, Bunyan, and scripture—unmistakable, yet unacknowledged—are never brought into consistent focus because Thoreau rejects their overarching assumptions about sin and salvation. He is ready to make use of suggestive fragments but not to rely on the exemplary structures.

In many ways, this reading is accurate but not complete. It does not fully explain the otherworldliness of so much of Thoreau's language and, most of all, it does not explain why, since he rejects evil as imaginary, he feels unworthy of the beauty he has witnessed. Perhaps, as in the case of John Donne's sermons on death, one needs to inquire into a personal narrative, hinted at, but not fully told, that weaves in and between the lines with the various journeys that compose this digression. Thoreau did not publish his journal until 1849, ten years after the trip. In 1842, his brother John cut his finger, contracted lockjaw, and died in Henry's arms eleven days later. In the remaining years before publication, Henry revised and rewrote large sections of the journal turning it, in part, into an elegy for his brother and a meditation on mortality.

The self-reliant New Englander is never, in fact, alone on this journey. Indeed his brother is so much with him that his elisions from 'I' to 'we' become so familiar in the text as to seem almost invisible. The cocky mountain climber can pull himself out of his own home-made coffin after a good night's sleep, but he cannot bring his beloved brother back to life except in his memory and his prose. After seeing what he calls 'the gracious god', he still must return to earth, to his own mortality, and life without his brother. With this in mind, we find that the last line of his poem makes new sense: 'O, raise thou from his corse thy now entombed exile!' The ambiguity of the third person 'his' can refer to the author and to his dead brother and to anyone for whom redemption from death remains an unrealized dream rather than a religious conviction. On the way down the mountain the redemptive epiphany gives way to a recognition of mortality and impotence. Yet paradoxically, it is precisely when Thoreau departs from his optimistic self-reliance and retreats into self-doubt that he sounds most like a person at prayer, like Job, or the psalmist, or Martha and Mary at the tomb of Lazarus.

Perhaps the most famous nineteenth-century American text about the need for redemption is Herman Melville's *Billy Budd*. Like Thoreau's journal, the narrative is part naturalistic detail and part moral allegory. Billy, the handsome sailor, seems the perfection of innocence, Adam before the Fall, loved and trusted by all the crew except John Claggart, the master-at-arms, a personification of envy and hatred. When Claggart falsely accuses Billy of fomenting mutiny,

Billy, whose only physical flaw is a stutter, cannot speak in his defence but strikes out at his accuser who falls to the deck and dies. In the symbolic, neo-Calvinistic scheme of things, Billy needs no redemption because he is already saved by his unimpeachable innocence. Similarly, Claggart is beyond redemption because in this book, unlike Thoreau's, evil is real and unredeemable. It is the ship's captain, Edward Vere, a thoughtful, modest, moderate Englishman, who considers it his duty to convene a drumhead court and sentence Billy to be hanged, who is most ordinary, most human, and most in need of redemption.

Much has been made of the parallels between Christ's passion and the execution of Billy. The expression on his face when he is falsely accused 'was as a crucifixion to behold'.[8] He approaches death with no fear. As he stands beneath the cross-shaped mainyard, 'the rare personal beauty of the sailor' is seen by the onlookers to be 'spiritualized' by his ordeal. The moment of Billy's death is described as seemingly miraculous partly because there is no sign of the usual bodily spasm and because the sky appears to bless the victim: 'At the same moment it chanced that the vapory fleece hanging low in the East was shot through with a soft glory as of the fleece of the Lamb of God seen in a mystical vision, and simultaneously therewith, watched by the wedged mass of upturned faces, Billy ascended; and, ascending, took the full rose of the dawn' (*BB* 376). If Thoreau weaves scriptural allusions almost imperceptibly into his naturalistic prose, Melville here makes absolutely certain that his reader will not miss his biblical borrowings. It is important to note that he conflates the crucifixion with the ascension of Jesus, skipping, as it were, the resurrection. Billy, it would seem, goes straight to heaven, no three days in the tomb, no harrowing of hell.

But what of Captain Vere, the Pontius Pilate of the story? Billy's last words before the assembled crew are, 'God bless Captain Vere!' which elicits a sympathetic response from the other sailors who repeat as in an echo, 'God bless Captain Vere!' Here again there is a parallel, this time with Jesus' words on the cross in Luke 23: 34:

[8] Herman Melville, *Billy Budd and Other Stories* (New York: Penguin Books, 1986), 350. Further references will appear in the text as *BB*. Among the large number of critical studies of Melville, the most useful for the purposes of this chapter are Robert Milder (ed.), *Critical Essays on Melville's Billy Budd* (Boston: G. K. Hall, 1971); Hershel Parker, *Reading Billy Budd* (Evanston, Ill.: Northwestern University Press, 1990); and Howard Paton Vincent (ed.), *Twentieth Century Interpretations of Billy Budd* (Englewood Cliffs, NJ: Prentice Hall, 1971).

'Father, forgive them for they know not what they do.' According to the gospels, Jesus' words of forgiveness are efficacious, but can the same be said of Billy Budd's blessing? Vere, we are led to believe, is sympathetic towards Billy, but believes that military justice and order must be maintained, that, as he says, 'forms, measured forms, are everything' (*BB* 380).

When Vere is later wounded in battle and lies dying, he is over-heard to murmur, 'Billy Budd, Billy Budd', but the attendant reports that 'these were not the accents of remorse' (*BB* 382). What were they the accents of then? Frustration? Despair? Anger? Love? We are not told. Innocence remains a problem and redemption an uncer-tainty. Though the events of the story involve Englishmen aboard an English vessel, this too is an American story. Some of the expected secular American ingredients are present. Redemption may be thought of as nothing more than dying with a clear conscience, which Billy quite obviously does and Captain Vere may or may not do. Billy requires no redeemer and indeed when the chaplain visits him before his execution, he listens politely but does not 'appropriate' or need religion to be saved. Like Thoreau climbing the mountain, Billy has never been lost. As to the redemption of time, Billy's story is preserved in the ballad, 'Billy in the Darbies', which gives him a voice perpetually caught between life and death, waiting in chains or sleeping forever among the 'oozy weeds' of the sea.

Once again, the language associated with Christ as Redeemer may be borrowed to reveal its inadequacy. But in this legend which undermines some of its own seemingly clearest signals, that too may be far simpler and easier a conclusion than the narrative allows. Billy may be beautiful, but the association of innocence with physical beauty can be a misleading clue. The suffering servant is not comely and he certainly does not strike out and kill his enemies for lack of words. Claggart may also not be all evil. There are rumours that he may have been French, an outsider, one who does not understand the ways of an English crew. Vere may be moderate and upright, but he is the captain of a warship that has taken Billy aboard against his will. In short, the clear Calvinist allegory is only one frame for a complex event. The biblical allusions, perhaps more than anything, show that Billy is not Jesus, Claggart not Satan, and Vere not Pontius Pilate. Rather they are human beings of mixed motives and emotions who cannot save themselves from ambivalence and death. The Lamb of God might be merely a 'vapory fleece hanging low in the East', pie in the sky, but it may also be the only sign left of undiminished innocence.

In Toni Morrison's novel *Beloved* (1987) the idea of redemption has a double meaning from the start. As a novel about slavery in the pre-Civil War South and its consequences after the war, it touches repeatedly on the monetary value placed on slaves as property: how much each one costs in the slave trade and what the purchase price is to gain freedom. One former slave reflects on that 'redemption' market: 'Remembering his own price, down to the cent, . . . he wondered what Sethe's would have been. What had Baby Suggs' been? How much did Halle owe, still, besides his labor? What did Mrs Garner get for Paul F? More than nine hundred dollars? How much more? Ten dollars? Twenty?'[9] All the calculations are heavily weighted with the cruel irony of attempting to assign economic value to a human being and the necessity of paying an arbitrary price to someone who had no right to ownership in the first place. This kind of 'redemption' is corrupt and wildly unbalanced, an exchange based on an unjust social system that recognizes material but not moral or spiritual worth in an entire group of people. Even when the price is paid for others by former slaves, the generosity of the act is tainted by its cooperation with an evil system. Just as Thoreau says that he does not believe he has ever been 'lost', the black slaves in Morrison's novel do not believe that they have ever been truly owned. In so far as their bondage is fraudulent, so in a sense is the price paid for their 'redemption'. The desire for freedom is genuine, but the process by means of which it is obtained is riddled with iniquity. Harriet Jacobs, in her narrative, *Incidents in the Life of a Slave Girl*, writes with bitterness about her own purchase of freedom:

'The bill of sale!' Those words struck me like a blow. So I was *sold* at last! . . . I well know the value of that bit of paper; but much as I love freedom, I do not like to look upon it. I am deeply grateful to the generous friend who procured it, but I despise the miscreant who demanded payment for what never rightly belonged to him or his.[10]

---

[9] Toni Morrison, *Beloved* (New York: Penguin, 1987), 228. Further references will appear in the text as B. Helpful discussions of Morrison's fiction can be found in Lucille P. Fultz, *Toni Morrison: Playing with Difference* (Urbana, Ill.: University of Illinois Press, 2003); Terry Otten, *The Crime of Innocence in the Fiction of Toni Morrison* (Columbia: University of Missouri Press, 1989); Linden Peach, *Toni Morrison* (New York: St Martin's Press, 1995); and Barbara H. Solomon (ed.), *Critical Essays on Toni Morrison's Beloved* (New York: G. K. Hall, 1998).

[10] Harriet Jacobs, *Incidents in the Life of a Slave Girl Written by Herself* (Cambridge, Mass.: Harvard University Press, 1987), 200.

If one shifts the reference point to the Christian narrative of redemption, it is not difficult to see how a troubling ambivalence can creep into a believer's faith. Emotionally and logically, it seems natural to love Jesus and resent or even hate the Father who demands suffering and death from the innocent. There is a spiritual connotation of 'redemption' in *Beloved* that does indeed reflect this ambivalence in the heart of the main character Sethe. When in flight from her owners, she is cornered by an agent who has been sent to take her and her children back to the plantation. In a moment of panic and dread, she decides to kill her children rather than allow them to suffer what she has endured, but she only succeeds with one before she is taken. That one, she comes to believe, returns to haunt her after the war when she is legally 'free' and living with her daughter Denver in Ohio. Whether the strange young woman, Beloved, is merely another freed slave wandering lost out of the Reconstruction South or the ghost of Sethe's murdered daughter matters less than the fact that Sethe becomes so obsessed by her that she seems to enter into another form of slavery from which she desperately needs to be freed.

It might at first seem strange that an American novel about slavery would focus on the guilt of a former slave rather than that of a former slave owner. Yet it has often been true historically as well as in fiction that oppression breeds guilt and shame in the oppressed who feel that they may have deserved their suffering or, as in Sethe's case, been cornered into committing one atrocity in order to avoid another. The central concern of *Beloved* is the condition of Sethe's soul once her body has been freed from bondage. Can she be forgiven for killing her baby daughter? Is she, in fact, guilty of a sin or crime when her intention was to 'save' her children? Does she need help or is this a matter of forgiving and saving herself? How will she know?

The apparent moral centre of the novel is Baby Suggs, an old former slave, who goes about preaching in any church that will have her, 'to AME's and Baptists, Holinesses and Sanctifieds, the Church of the Redeemer and the Redeemed' (*B* 87). Christian orthodoxy is neither her manner nor her message. She is 'uncalled, unrobed, unanointed' (*B* 87). When summer comes and the churches are too hot, she preaches in a clearing in the woods. The narration makes a point that her homilies are not like the Sermon on the Mount: 'She did not tell them to clean up their lives or to go and sin no more. She did not tell them they were the blessed of the earth, its inheriting meek or its glorybound pure.... [She told them], "We flesh...Love it" ' (*B* 88).

After going through all the parts of the body that should be loved, she ends with the heart. 'Love your heart. For this is the prize' (*B* 89). Once again, we are on familiar American 'redemption theory' territory. The message is to love and save yourself. For the black slave, this seems particularly important since their bodies have been despised and abused by those who assumed they had no self, no soul or heart, capable of love or salvation, independence or initiative. As in the case of Thoreau's Sunday excursion and Billy Budd's prelapsarian innocence, Christianity seems to be evoked only to be rejected as unnecessary or irrelevant. The message is not, 'Love one another', but 'Love yourself'. Yet, by privileging the heart, Baby Suggs reopens a scriptural door. How far is she from the teaching of Jesus when she asks her congregations to love what in themselves is the organ traditionally associated with the capacity to love others?

In the course of the constantly circling narrative, we learn that Baby Suggs has spent her life helping others, even purchasing the freedom of fellow slaves. We also learn that Sethe is loved and encouraged by Paul D and, most of all, by her live flesh-and-blood daughter Denver who stays with her mother through all the best and worst times. If one applies the Christian masterplot of salvation to a reading of the novel, the central figure is neither Beloved nor Sethe but Denver, whose unselfish love for her mother overcomes every obstacle of poverty, neglect, and humiliation. At the same time, it is also reasonable to argue that the novel follows a familiar American pattern of secular redemption: Sethe goes to Ohio not to heaven; she may need a little help from others to stay alive, but she alone can forgive and save herself; and her full redemption depends on her ability to put the ghosts of the past behind her.

Though both readings have merit, neither seems completely satisfying. As with Thoreau and Melville, Morrison leaves the reader on a threshold of longing, somewhere between a secure Christian faith in redemption and an American confidence in the future of democracy. As the novel draws to a close, the story becomes a lyrical meditation on lost souls—unnamed slaves, children dead before their time, daughters torn from their mothers—gathered together and personified in the ghost-child Beloved: 'Everybody knew what she was called, but nobody anywhere knew her name. Disremembered and unaccounted for, she cannot be lost because no one is looking for her, and even if they were, how can they call her if they don't know her name? Although she has claim, she is not claimed' (B 274). Like Thoreau's brother and Billy Budd, Beloved is a haunting figure of innocence snatched from life at an enormous cost to the survivors. There is no doubt that in some universal economy, a price has been paid. But to whom and toward what end? Each text provides possible answers that borrow heavily from scripture and from American political ideology without resting securely in either.

As a coda to this enquiry into some versions of the redemption narrative in American literature, we might look very briefly at a short story by Flannery O'Connor, a Southerner and a Catholic, whose work explores large metaphysical questions within the limits of a unique region of the country. Her characters are typically zealous Protestant fundamentalists or godless tricksters, bums, outcasts, and criminals who collide whenever their worldly and otherworldly selves come into contact. For the outcasts, redemption usually means getting the better of someone else in order to survive; for the religious believers, redemption is a heavenly reward granted to the righteous few by a severe God. In short, O'Connor places the tension between the secular and religious attitudes of Americans under a fierce light that exposes the folly and sometimes the cruelty of both.

In 'Parker's Back', a handyman given to heavy drinking and getting tattoos on every available space on his body marries a plain God-fearing woman named Sarah Ruth. The more Parker tries to please his wife by displaying his tattoos, the angrier she becomes: '"At the judgment seat of God, Jesus is going to say to you, 'What you been doing all your life besides have pictures drawn all over you?'"'[11]

One day while driving a tractor and contemplating his next tattoo, Parker loses concentration, crashes, and, as he is flying through the air, the unbeliever calls out, 'GOD ABOVE!' ('PB' 520). Having

---

[11] Flannery O'Connor, 'Parker's Back', *The Complete Short Stories* (New York: Farrar, Straus & Giroux, 1978), 519. Further references will appear in the text as 'PB'. For critical commentary on the fiction of Flannery O'Connor, see Kathleen Feeley, *Flannery O'Connor: Voice of the Peacock* (New York: Fordham University Press, 1982); Richard Giannone, *Flannery O'Connor and the Mystery of Love* (New York: Fordham University Press, 1999); George A. Kilcourse, Jr., *Flannery O'Connor's Religious Imagination* (New York: Paulist Press, 2001); and Sura P. Rath and May Neff Shaw (eds.), *Flannery O'Connor; New Perspectives* (Athens, Ga.: University of Georgia Press, 1996).

survived the accident and sensing that 'there had been a great change in his life', Parker drives to town determined to have a picture of God tattooed on his back. From the artist's book, he chooses a Byzantine Christ with 'demanding eyes', but when asked if he has suddenly got religion, he replies in characteristic American self-reliant fashion: ' "Naw," he said, "I ain't got no use for none of that. [If] a man can't save his self from whatever it is he don't deserve none of my sympathy" ' ('PB', 524–5).

After a few days, Parker returns home to show off his tattoo to Sarah Ruth. Already angry because of his absence, she becomes incensed when he tells her the design on his back is a picture of God: ' "God? God don't look like that!" ' ('PB', 529). She begins beating Parker with a broom, screaming, 'Idolatry!' 'Parker was too stunned to resist. He sat there and let her beat him until she had nearly knocked him senseless and large welts had formed on the face of the tattooed Christ' ('PB', 529).

The story ends with Parker leaning against a pecan tree in the garden 'crying like a baby'. Despite what we know of O'Connor's religious convictions, we are left with disparate interpretative possi-bilities. A Christian reading might go as follows. Having called on God for help in a moment of danger and having taken Jesus onto his back, Parker, whether he fully comprehends it or not, has been redeemed from his drunken, meaningless existence. Suffering from the lashes of his wife is part of the price he must pay, but that suffering is now united with that of Jesus whose welts he shares. A secular and pragmatic American reading might be that both husband and wife are pitiful losers, superstitious, ignorant, and incapable of improvement, never mind redemption. They are the underbelly of the American dream, prisoners of a democracy that has failed to educate them and carry them with it. They are stuck in the prejudices and habits of their past, unable to lift themselves or one another into a new and better life.

O'Connor's story, like the others I have examined, illustrates dra-matically the extraordinary persistence and power of the scriptural redemption narratives in literary works of different periods and distinctive regional colouration. The fact that each of the American texts leaves the door open to doubts about the possibility of redemp-tion of any kind—physical, moral, or spiritual—aligns them with the tradition of the great religious narratives with which I began. Job's defiant declaration and the silence of Jesus confronted by mockers must forever be read as part of a dialectic between redemptive suffering and scepticism, faith and unbelief.

While four American texts can hardly be considered fully representative of the rich array of possibilities in the American canon, they are not merely a random sample either. Two are from the nineteenth century, two from the twentieth; two have their origins in the North, two in the South; two are by women, two by men; two are by sceptics, two by religious believers. Not surprisingly, the most striking and instructive contrast is between the works of the two authors with the strongest, most nearly dogmatic attitudes towards matters metaphysical, Thoreau and O'Connor. Few American writers have been more adamant and unrelenting in rejecting 'established' Christianity than Thoreau; and few have been more orthodox in their Christianity than Flannery O'Connor. It is particularly noteworthy, then, to find Thoreau ending his mountain sojourn with a prayer-like poem in which he asks that the 'entombed exile' be 'raised from his corse'. The play on 'corpse'/'course' is part of an unexpected plea from the self-reliant wanderer who begins his climb up the mountain with a reflection on the folly of feeling 'lost'. Ever protective of his individuality and his right to question all doctrine, Thoreau comes down the mountain uttering a prayer to whatever divinity may be listening. Orthodox in her Roman Catholicism and fascinated by the possibility of miracles in the most hopeless of lives, Flannery O'Connor gives her reader the freedom to take Parker's story as a moment of redemption or a grotesque farce. In both narratives, the faith in self-reliance has been badly shaken.

In its democratic impulse, the American emphasis on 'saving yourself' may never have been intended to echo the mockers passing before Christ on the cross, 'Save yourself and come down from the cross' (Matt. 27: 40). However, given the continual interweaving of secular and scriptural texts, the resonance is hard to ignore. But who finally is being mocked in these American works? Is it Jesus or the self-reliant American confronted with the limits of his singular power? 'With the exercise of self-trust, new powers shall appear', wrote Emerson in his hugely influential essay of 1840, 'Self-Reliance'.[12] Emerson's American requires no mediator since *he* 'is the word made flesh, born to shed healing to the nations'. And just in

---

[12] Ralph Waldo Emerson, 'Self-Reliance', in Stephen E. Whicher (ed.), *Selections from Ralph Waldo Emerson* (Boston: Houghton Mifflin Co., 1960), 162.

case the point is not clear, the Concord sage concludes, 'Nothing can bring you peace but yourself.' Such sentiments still sound familiar and benign to American ears and indeed have been adopted by therapists who may never have read Emerson. Emerson's words can be justified as innocuous variants on the idea that the Kingdom of God is 'within', but taken to the extreme they can also lead to an arrogant egocentricity—individual and collective—at complete odds with the teachings of Christ in the gospels.

Emerson crystallized a new American creed of redemption which had—and still has—enormous appeal, influence, and durability in the young country. But what sounded like inspiration, hope, and courage in nineteenth-century America can sound like blind hubris in the twenty-first. It is perhaps not surprising, then, that in each of the American works I have examined, there comes a prophetic moment when a character confronts the limits of self-reliance, yet again leaving the way open for a diminished but not entirely extinguished hope for a helping hand from a friend, a neighbour, a sister, or brother, perhaps even a Redeemer who will come down from the cross of innocent suffering and 'stand at the latter day upon the earth'.

13

Images of Redemption in Art and Music

DAVID BROWN

In this chapter I want to explore how the Christian doctrine of redemption has been understood through an examination of some key images by means of which it has been appropriated. Hopefully, this will avoid merely repeating the standard accounts of which particular theories of atonement came to prominence when and also any suggestion that we are dealing simply with theory rather than a lived reality within the Christian's life.[1] I do not pretend that the examples I have chosen are the most central or significant, only that they are illuminating. The examples in question are the lamb of God, the descent into hell, and the prodigal son. Although all three play a role in the church's liturgical life, the meaning extracted from them is far from being as uniform or constant as this might initially suggest. There is a richness in the biblical imagery that defies too narrowly defined interpretations. Readers familiar with the role of the first image in the Agnus Dei and of the second in the Apostles' Creed may still be surprised to discover the third labelled as liturgical. In this I reveal my own identity as an Anglican, as one of the most popular innovations in the modern Church of England has been the introduction of a concluding prayer that takes the prodigal son as its theme. Representative applications in art and music will be used to draw some tentative conclusions.

THE LAMB OF GOD

Liturgical use in the Agnus Dei and Gloria of course derives from John's Gospel but initially at least it seems that it was the version of

---

[1] For a simple survey, L. W. Grensted, *A Short History of the Doctrine of the Atonement* (Manchester: Manchester University Press, 1920); for a more controversial account, G. Aulén, *Christus Victor* (London: SPCK, 1970).

the image in the Book of Revelation that had the greater influence.[2] Although the author of the latter repeatedly returns to the Lamb, the stress is less on taking away the sins of the world or even on crucifixion, and much more on the Lamb as now victorious and reigning in heaven.[3] It is this focus that one finds reflected, for instance, at Ravenna in the sixth-century roof mosaics of S. Vitale.[4] However, in Syrian practice the term had a more explicit sacrificial sense, as the phrase was used to refer to Christ's presence in the eucharist, and it is in this sense that it is first introduced into the Western liturgy by the Syrian pope, Sergius I.[5] Even then, though, its meaning did not remain entirely constant, as its closeness to the exchange of the Peace eventually led in the tenth century to the final petition being modified from *miserere nobis* to *dona nobis pacem*. As the Latin verb *tollere* can mean both 'bear' and 'take away' there was in any case some latitude of interpretation: the focus could be either on the burden imposed on Christ by our sins or on the joy of having that burden removed. It is an ambiguity taken up in the alternative form of the Agnus Dei allowed in modern versions of the liturgy of the Church of England: 'Jesus, lamb of God, have mercy on us. Jesus, bearer of our sins, have mercy on us. Jesus, redeemer of the world, grant us peace.'[6] Meantime in the East, although an icon with the Christ-child on the eucharistic paten is still known as an *Amnos*, ironically any symbolic representation of Christ as a 'lamb' was prohibited as early as the Council of Trullo in 692.[7]

I want now to explore the potential impact of these different sorts of emphasis in both Bible and liturgy by considering some significant examples from art and music. In the case of the former, perhaps the

---

[2] The liturgical use is drawn from John the Baptist's words about Christ, John 1: 29, 36.

[3] Particularly obvious in Rev. 5, despite the allusion to the crucifixion in v. 6.

[4] For illustration and wider context, G. Bovini, *Ravenna* (Ravenna: Longo, 1991), 25–48, esp. 27, 39. Angels with arms uplifted adore a lamb (with no signs of suffering) set against stars and fruit.

[5] Sergius was pope from 687 to 701; the attribution is made by the *Liber Pontificalis*. It had already entered the Liturgy of St James in the 5th cent. for use by the priest after the fraction.

[6] Composed by the liturgical scholar, G. J. Cuming, it is also an approved ICET text (International Consultation on English Texts).

[7] L. Ouspensky, *Theology of the Icon*, i (Crestwood, NY: St Vladimir's Seminary Press, 1992), 92–4. Pope Sergius by introducing the Agnus Dei seems in part to have been responding to this prohibition.

two best-known paintings are the van Eycks' *Adoration of the Lamb* and Zurburán's *Agnus Dei*. Painted in the early fifteenth century jointly by the two brothers Hubert and Jan, *The Adoration of the Lamb* is part of a larger and more complex polyptych consisting of no less than twelve panels painted on both sides and now housed in a special exhibition area in St Bavo's cathedral in Ghent.[8] One art historian describes the work as scholastic and rigidly hierarchical, 'an exaggerated relic of the past' which would have required the advice of 'a learned theologian'.[9] Perhaps the prior of the church, Olivier de Langhe, did help, but I do want to challenge the view that its basic conception would only have been intelligible to the learned and thus that it excludes a more personal piety.

When the polyptych is closed, what one sees on the lower register is the wealthy donor (Joos Vyd) and his wife framing John the Baptist and John the Evangelist and on the upper the prophets Zechariah and Micah bracketing the Erythrean and Cumean sibyl, while the central register has the Annunciation with the angel and Mary on the outside, leaving the two central panels to display an open window and a recessed arch. There are quite a number of Latin inscriptions to advance more learned folk's understanding, but even without their benefit it is not too difficult to comprehend what is going on.[10] The Annunciation is self-explanatory. Its anticipatory quality is underlined by the prominence given to the open window and arch between, which seem inevitably to invite further exploration, suggesting as they do a looking beyond, or in this case within, as the polyptych is opened. The recessed arch contains a kettle, water basin, and towel. To my mind this hints at the appropriate route into the greater mystery that lies within, a need for personal purity and commitment to service.[11] The readily identifiable figure of John the

---

[8] For illustrations and some commentary, G. T. Faggin, *The Complete Paintings of the Van Eycks* (New York: Abrams, 1968), plates II–XXVIII and 89–93. See also Pl. 1 and 2 in this volume. An inscription attributes the greater role to Hubert: 89.

[9] C. Harbison, *Jan van Eyck: The Play of Realism* (London: Reaktion, 1991), 193–7, esp. 195.

[10] Apart from the obvious ones for the Annunciation, the biblical quotations are from Mic. 5. 2 and Zech. 9.9. The Erythrean sibyl is assigned Virgil's *Aeneid* 6. 50: 'nec mortale sonans, adflata est numine' (she is infused by divine power as she utters immortal thoughts). The Cumaean sibyl paraphrases Augustine's *City of God* (18. 23) which talks of a future king coming in judgement.

[11] Panofsky prefers a reference to the Virgin's purity. But, while in theory the niche is part of her room, its positioning on a separate panel and next to the open window makes my suggested account, I believe, the more natural reading.

Evangelist immediately beneath would remind the alert observer of
the foot-washing incident, while John the Baptist to his left would
speak of baptism and its call to purification.[12] The four figures on the
top register are all made to look either definitely Jewish or else
antique and so alike anticipatory of the Christian dispensation. The
quotations from Zechariah, Micah, Virgil, and Augustine merely
reinforce the sense of expectation rather than provide clues without
which the painting would be unintelligible.

Open the window as it were, and we now find two registers giving
an account of redemption. The upper level has on its outside fallen
Adam and Eve covering their genitals and the story of Cain and Abel
is in the background. Further in are angels singing and playing
music, while two representative saints (the Virgin Mary and John
the Baptist) sit enthroned on either side of God. Although the figure
could be God the Father, the inclusion of christological symbolism
suggests that no more specific reference is intended,[13] and that what
we thus have above is the problem of sin exposed on the outside edge
and its happy resolution in the middle; the panels below are where
we must turn to discover the means of its resolution. Here the church
is being led towards Christ by just judges and warriors on the left and
by holy hermits and pilgrims on the right, all drawing our eye into
the central panel. Yet more groupings—of prophets, patriarchs, and
confessors on one side and of apostles, martyrs, and virgin saints on
the other—continue that drawing inwards, and so lead our eyes
onwards to the great denouement of the Lamb on the altar. For
those who could read, the words of the Agnus Dei are embroidered
on the altar frontal but they are quite unnecessary since the symbols
of Christ's passion are already there in the hands of angels who stand
around the altar.[14] To complete the story of appropriation, the two
principal sacraments of the Christian church are both represented:
blood from the Lamb flowing into a chalice and a fountain for
baptism in the foreground.

Certainly the connection with St John the Evangelist as the pre-
sumed author of the Book of Revelation is even now unlikely to have

---

[12] John the Baptist holds a lamb towards which he is pointing, John the Evangelist
the traditional symbols of his testing (a chalice with snakes emerging from it).

[13] On the brocade behind there is the image of the pelican feeding its young with its
own blood. On the other hand, the presence of the Spirit and the Son in the panel below
might be thought to argue in favour of the Father.

[14] Included are cross, crown of thorns, and pillar of flagellation.

been made by the illiterate: both allusions could be justified from that work.[15] However, that is surely incidental to the clarity of the overall message: the redemption wrought on the cross can be appropriated sacramentally through baptism and the eucharist. It was a mystery anticipated by prophet and pagan seer alike (outer panels) and this is the means whereby we will be brought to the worship of angels and saints in heaven (upper register). Nor is this to speak of a reality remote from our own world. Through the Annunciation window the houses of Ghent were to be seen, and behind the Lamb's altar one now observes St Bavo's church and the tower of Utrecht cathedral, as well as other familiar landmarks of the day. So I want to reject any suggestion that it is an intellectual piece, not readily intelligible to the ordinary Christian. Nonetheless, objections could come from other sources. The complaint could, for instance, be made that the presentation is altogether too triumphalist, with little suggestion of pain or penitence. Certainly the aureole of the Holy Spirit at the top floods the scene with light, flowers are blooming everywhere, and the Lamb himself stands triumphant on the altar. But the symbols of the passion are there too, as are implicitly the cost to the Christian of following Christ. For example, at top right Agnes, Barbara, and Dorothy all carry the symbols of their martyrdom, while below there is a particularly gruesome depiction of Lieven, patron saint of Ghent, holding his tongue in a pair of pincers.

Contrast this now with what turned out to be perhaps the most popular image from the 'Seeing Salvation' exhibition which took London by storm in 2000, Zurburán's *Agnus Dei* from the Prado in Madrid.[16] The image could scarcely be simpler, consisting as it does of a lamb tied at its feet and lying on a butcher's slab. Zurburán painted no less than six versions. While some add an explanatory title, no Christian could be unaware of the first meaning, given the ubiquity of the image in liturgy and scripture alike.[17] It would be a mistake, though, to think that the painting derives its power from

[15] Rev. 7: 13–14 connects the blood of the Lamb with Christian martyrdom, but since being made 'white in the blood of the lamb' seems a precondition for heaven, the eucharistic reference would seem a natural extension of such thinking. For 'the water of life' coming from the throne of the Lamb, Rev. 22: 1.

[16] Illustrated in the exhibition catalogue, N. MacGregor (ed.), *The Image of Christ* (London: National Gallery, 2000), 37. For black and white illustration, Pl. 3 in this volume.

[17] 'Tanquam agnus' is found on two versions. The key biblical verses in addition to John 1: 29, 36, are Isa. 53: 7–8, Acts 8: 32, and 1 Pet. 1: 18–19.

allusion alone. Certainly, elsewhere the lamb does perform precisely that role. In an *Adoration of the Shepherds* Zurburán placed a tied lamb and a basket of eggs near the front of the canvas, precisely in order to complement the nativity with references to crucifixion and resurrection.[18] Here, however, he is trying to get us to engage with the image as such, and so adopts the simplicity of focus that is such a recurring feature of so many of his canvases. Turn to some of his versions of the crucifixion, and one sees the point. All further detail is precluded, and Christ is left alone on his cross.[19] The result is that his body assumes an almost statuesque or realist quality, with the play of light and dark allowed to speak simultaneously of human death and its accompaniment by divine light and presence.[20]

In those paintings there is no stress on the horror of the deed. Indeed, the fineness of the body's physique is only slightly modified. What concerns Zurburán is that we should be drawn in to reflect on the essentials of what has occurred: divinity associated with human pain and transforming it. Similarly his technique for emphasizing the burden of sin that Christ carries on our behalf is to simplify the carrying of the cross. In a painting lacking other details a Christ bent double by the cross fills the frame and looks out questioningly at us.[21] In a similar vein then here the lamb is made to stand out alone from a dark background with 'its moist face, delicate eyebrows, tactile wool, thick fuzzy hair, and rough, hard horns'.[22] The empirical details accentuate the creature's vulnerability. But for us, we are being told, it could get up and walk away. With that reflection comes the realization of what our sins have done to Christ. The power in such simplicity is well illustrated by contrast with a related painting of half a century later by the Portuguese artist and nun, Josefa d'Óbidos, *Cordero Pascal*.[23] The image is in effect sentimentalized by

---

[18] For illustration and commentary, A. Moreno, *Zurburán* (Madrid: Electa, 1998), 94–5.

[19] For perhaps the most effective, now in Chicago, J. Brown, *Zurburán* (London: Thames & Hudson, 1991), 54–5. For discussion of one version still in Seville, N. MacGregor, *Seeing Salvation* (London: BBC, 2000), 118–21.

[20] In the Chicago work his left side is in shade, his right bathed in light.

[21] Illustrated in Brown, *Zurburán*, 116–17.

[22] My trans. of the Spanish: Moreno, *Zurburán*, 92–3. The horns are an interesting detail. Absent from the *Adoration*, they are presumably included here to allude to Gen. 22: 13.

[23] Illustrated in A. L. da Silva, *Josefa d'Óbidos* (Lisbon: Fundaçâio Calouste Gulbenkian, 1984), no. 23.

the introduction of flowers, and complicated by grapes, presumably introduced to allude to the lamb of the eucharist.

Turn now to the music of the liturgy and one finds rather different contrasts, with some interesting questions posed about its appropriate role. In medieval plainsong or sixteenth-century polyphony, the changes of style and mood between the various parts of the ordinary of the mass seem subtle and undramatic to our modern ears; the effect is to generate an atmosphere and to provide space for reflection on the text and liturgical action. The styles that subsequently develop are often characterized as a decline, but the introduction in the seventeenth century of instrumental accompaniment and solo singing did allow the possibility of a story to be told, and so for redemption to be presented as something appropriated rather than simply achieved. If this is most obviously so in the various movements in settings of the Creed, particularly with the *incarnatus*, the Agnus Dei was also now commonly seen as consisting of two acts, the appeal for mercy and the achievement of peace.[24]

In Mozart's Coronation Mass the Agnus Dei is a single movement but with three clear sections suggesting a three-stage progression: the soprano's calm and lyrical assertion of Christ's status combined with a gentle but pressing petitioning for mercy (intensified by the low notes of the accompanying muted violins) is followed by increasing confidence in the gift of peace as the tempo and key change and other soloists enter, all seeming to lead naturally into an even faster section for chorus and full orchestra as trumpets and drums reinforce the climax. A gentle *andante sostenuto* has thus gradually given place to an *andante con moto* first heard in the earlier Kyries (its cheerful music surely seeming more appropriate here), and to a rousing *allegro con spirito*. Intriguingly, Barth and Küng agree in praising highly this mass.[25]

Earlier in the same century Bach in his B minor mass had started in the same way with a soloist (an alto), but the contrast with his clearly differentiated second movement is much more dramatic. Not only is the chorus substituted immediately, whereas in Mozart it

---

[24] A good example of how elaborate the *incarnatus* could become is the beautiful but liturgically impractical coloratura soprano aria used in Mozart's unfinished Great Mass in C minor.

[25] Küng, *Mozart: Traces of Transcendence* (London: SCM, 1992), 37–69, esp. 67–9. Barth requested that a performance should open the WCC meeting at Evanston in 1948.

emerges gradually via the introduction of further soloists, there is also a striking change of key, from G minor to D major. The effect is to move from an almost tragic pleading to a mood that is consoling and affirming. The quite different application to which soloists and chorus are put by both composers could be taken to reflect the need for personal penitence (*miserere*) that is then transmuted into a corporate peace (*dona pacem*), a church that is at one with its God. It is probably no accident that the key is the same as for 'gratias agimus tibi' in the Gloria, for that way we are led to experience the peace as gratitude for divine assurance of forgiveness.

In the early nineteenth century Schubert in his Mass in E flat major provides an example of an Agnus without soloists, but there are other differences as well. The *miserere* virtually disappears, and so the Agnus is in effect transformed into a personal prayer of peace. But there is still development, for in a twice repeated movement towards *dona nobis pacem* the adjectival clause *qui tollis peccata mundi* now seems to function as a distinct action: Christ removing the sins that prevent peace. Partly under the influence of Palestrina later in the nineteenth century Bruckner was to go back to a more meditative, less narrative style, and such an approach also came to be encouraged by church authorities.[26] However, rather than pursue that history here, I want to address the use of the Agnus Dei in war settings, for these would seem to offer an obvious impetus to exploration of the theme of reconciliation, and so of how the Lamb might bring peace out of conflict.

In Haydn's *Paukenmesse* or *Missa in tempore belli* a kettledrum is used very effectively to remind the congregation of Napoleon's invasion of Austria. The section opens with *Agnus Dei* sung quietly but confidently, only to be interrupted by the increasing sound of the drum and *miserere nobis* given pleadingly in response. Gradually *Agnus Dei* and *pacem* then take over: the Lamb has won its victory. A drum roll evocative of the Napoleonic wars also appears in Beethoven's *Missa Solemnis* but at a juncture where one might have least expected it. A long exchange between male and female soloists of anxiety-laden pleas appears to reach its climax and resolution in *dona nobis pacem*, only for that peace to shattered by the sound of the drum.[27] It is also at this point that any remaining pretence of

---

[26] Note esp. Bruckner's Mass no. 2 in E minor.

[27] As well as by the sudden, unexpected key change and military-sounding trumpets.

liturgical structure is finally abandoned.[28] Yet peace is the final message as the last solitary drum-beat fades away. Beethoven himself described the piece as a 'prayer for inner and outer peace', and that seems right.[29] The long exploration of struggle had in effect broken the connection with eucharist and crucifixion, and so, however superior musically Beethoven may be to Haydn, it is Haydn alone who retains a specifically christological rather than general religious content. Indeed, the beautiful violin solo of the preceding Benedictus might be said to be more obviously evocative of the Lamb.[30]

Such exploration continued into the twentieth century. Perhaps the best-known example is Benjamin Britten's War Requiem, written for the consecration of Coventry cathedral in 1961, but there are other examples. Britten's juxtaposition of nine of Wilfred Owen's poems against the traditional Latin words of the Requiem might so easily have come across as simply yet another critique of Christianity that it is fascinating to observe how exactly Britten succeeds in deepening both. His skilled hand, for example, is evident in the way in which he makes Owen's best-known poem on the sacrifice of Isaac immediately follow the Latin words of promise: 'quam olim Abrahae promisisti, et semini eius . . . so Abram rose . . . ' The result is that the conclusion of the poem becomes all the more shocking, as this time Abraham refuses to obey the angel

> But slew his son,—
> And half the seed of Europe, one by one . . .

And were that not enough, the Latin that immediately follows talks of the offering of *hostias* ('sacrifices' or 'victims'). But it is of course the music as such that carries the main burden in evoking both war and its horrors and the possibility of reconciliation. So the march-like music of the opening movement, 'Requiem aeternam', can speak at one and the same time of solemn funerals, advancing troops and fleeing refugees, while in the concluding 'Libera me' the moving baritone solo, expressively accompanied for the most part by

---

[28] Though Beethoven did originally intend one: the mass was meant for the enthronement of his former pupil, Archduke Rudolph, as archbishop of Olmütz, but expanded subsequently. For a defence of its religious content: M. M. Scott, *Beethoven* (London: Dent, 1934), 223–9.

[29] He inscribed the manuscript: 'Bitte um innern und äussern Frieden.'

[30] Coming 'humbly and mounted on an ass': Matt. 21: 5 and 9, the context for the Benedictus.

the chamber orchestra with a wealth of graphic instrumental detail, reaches its emotional climax as the voice alone sings the words, 'I am the enemy you killed, my friend'. But it is the treatment of the Agnus Dei just before this which especially concerns us here. The choral setting is interlaced with a tenor singing the words of an Owen poem that tells of a war-damaged wayside crucifix which has seen many a Christian betrayal as chaplains urge on the soldiers to war. Yet the final lines remind us:

> ... they who love the greater love
> Lay down their life; they do not hate.

It is at this point, with what seems a quite brilliant stroke of genius, that Britten does something quite revolutionary with his text. Hitherto roles had been clear: the soloists always sing Owen's words, the choir the liturgy. Now, however, the tenor takes over, and responds to the choir's traditional requiem plea (*dona eis requiem*) with his own *dona nobis pacem*. The liturgy has ceased to be alien to the soldiers' world and in phrasing of extraordinary but simple beauty reconciliation is achieved. One might contrast Britten's approach here with his roughly contemporary Missa Brevis in D. Whereas there the phrases the choirboys are expected to sing are separated by insistent dissonances with an edgy rhythm from the organ that powerfully evoke their fears (and ours), in this case the inexorable tread of the five-note falling and rising motif which undergirds the tenor solo and is then taken up by the choir is enough to inject solemn reflection and noble sorrow into the words.

Written for the same cathedral as Britten's Missa Brevis, the Scottish composer James Macmillan's Westminster Mass (2000) sets the modern vernacular liturgy, including the consecration prayer. A progression of moods is observable both in the mass as a whole and in particular elements, including the Agnus Dei. Here rather anguished cries to the Lamb alternate with the movement in parallel thirds of 'have mercy on us' and 'grant us peace'. Although there is resolution, it does seem somewhat uneasy, not least because of low rumblings on the organ that perhaps conjure up the sound of distant explosions. In this, despite his own devout Roman Catholicism, Macmillan reflects our own less confident world. A decade earlier in *Búsqueda* (1988), however, where the issue is more explicitly addressed, in the 'searching' of Argentinian mothers for the 'disappeared', Macmillan does appear prepared to offer a more positive message. The piece opens and closes with sounds of breathing, but whereas on opening it seems rather troubled as if shortly to be interrupted, by the end the same sound exudes acceptance and hope. What has made the difference in the interim is the effect of some of the mothers' poems being juxtaposed and interspersed with excerpts from the ordinary of the mass. Harps and strings are rudely interrupted by staccato outbursts from brass and percussion suggestive of gunfire that jar with recitation of the christological sections of the creed (here kept in its original Latin). But such conflict is eventually overcome during the concluding Agnus Dei, with the actors' last words being, 'I will not have waited in vain'.[31]

What these musical and artistic examples propose, I would suggest is that appropriation of Christ as Agnus Dei comes not by simple assertion, but through invitation to further exploration, the very complexity of the works I have analysed being their strength rather than a weakness. The Ghent altarpiece moves the viewer by complex paths from anticipation to the achievement of salvation to its personal appropriation. If Britten and Macmillan insist on a meandering struggle towards resolution, even Mozart and Bach allow corporate peace only to emerge gradually out of individual penitence.

DESCENT INTO HELL

What is intriguing about this phrase from the Apostles' Creed is the way in which it has been subject to two quite different interpretations across the centuries, interpretations which pose deep questions about how the appropriation of redemption should be presented. In modern writing the tendency is very much to gloss the phrase as speaking of the depths of suffering and alienation into which Christ entered. Calvin had described the cross in this way, and in this he is followed by Barth.[32] If Balthasar wants to give Holy Saturday its own

---

[31] An unusual variant on the Agnus Dei of war and peace must be Samuel Barber's *Adagio for Strings*. Originally written for orchestra only (in 1938), the composer added the words in 1967. Its role as the theme music for Oliver Stone's Vietnam movie *Platoon* (1986), however, means that for many the dialectic of war and peace has now come to be associated with it.

[32] Calvin, *Institutes of the Christian Religion*, II. xvi. 8–12, tr. F. L. Battles (Philadelphia: Westminster Press, 1975), 512–20; K. Barth, *Credo* (London: Hodder & Stoughton, 1964 edn.), 88–94.

distinctive form of alienation, the basic strategy remains the same.[33] But different sorts of emphases remain possible. At times Balthasar seems to treat death as itself a form of punishment and that might be taken to recall penal theories of atonement.[34] That is one possibility, but another is that the phrase could be used to speak of Christ's maximal identification with the human condition.

Either option, though, is quite different from the earlier, more mythological understanding of the phrase.[35] The second-century *Gospel of Nicodemus'* hugely popular expansion of a couple of obscure New Testament verses ensured that, whatever may have been the intention of the original authors of the Apostles' Creed, it was normally taken to imply Christ's release of the holy dead from the place of their interim imprisonment pending Christ's redeeming sacrifice.[36] Indeed, so dominant did this interpretation become that it looks as though the Breviary's version of the Latin was a modification solely intended to make that meaning more clear: instead of descending to 'the depths', Christ goes to 'those below'.[37]

Here my intention is not to arbitrate between the two approaches, but rather to explore what further implications they did and might have for the presentation of the Christian faith. In the more conservative East, although the Apostles' Creed plays no role, the earlier understanding of the descent continues to dominate, and indeed in the traditional twelve icons for the feasts of Orthodoxy it is this image that is used to indicate Easter Sunday: Christ overcoming death by bringing redemption to the dead.[38] Such images were also once common in the West, but progressively from the late Middle Ages onwards began to give way to more explicit representations of the resurrection. At the same time the West had been moving throughout the Gothic period to more and more explicit images of Christ's suffering on the cross, forms of representation that would have been

---

[33] H. U. von Balthasar, *Mysterium Paschale* (Edinburgh: T. & T. Clark, 1990), 148–88.

[34] For some problematic examples, ibid. 164, 166–7, 173.

[35] For an attempt nonetheless to combine both approaches, W. Pannenberg, *The Apostles' Creed* (London: SCM, 1972), 90–5.

[36] Matt. 27: 52; 1 Pet. 3: 19. For some further background and reflection on the imagery, see my *Discipleship and Imagination* (Oxford: Oxford University Press, 2000), 111–15.

[37] 'Descendit ad inferos' replaced 'descendit ad inferna'.

[38] For a 14th-century Byzantine example of the twelve feasts, K. Weitzmann, *The Icon* (London: Studio Editions, 1982), 74–5.

anathema even in the West in the first millennium and remain so to this day in the East. It is worth exploring further how these different histories worked out in practice in both art and music.

As the Eastern pattern can be dealt with more briefly, I shall consider that approach first. The usual convention in icons is for the earth to be portrayed opening up before Christ with its gates laid aside, as he stretches forth his hand to draw some individuals from the depths. Adam and Eve are invariably present somewhere, but often other Old Testament figures also make an appearance.[39] The devil, if present, tends to be less conspicuous than in Western versions.[40] Two relatively late Western examples come from Dürer and Mantegna. If Mantegna's *Descent into Limbo* of 1492 is remarkably undramatic, Dürer's woodcut of *Christ in Limbo* of 1510 is more typical in being mythological to its core.[41] It may have been the Western obsession with ogres that made the image in the end both less accessible and less acceptable.[42] Certainly, there is a transcendent dimension to the icons that Western portrayals lack. However, the problem goes deeper than this, as the substitute image also often fails in this regard. At one level the placing of Adam's skull at the foot of the cross could be used to make the same point. It is not just that Golgotha was 'the place of the skull'; we are also being told that through the cross the old Adam can become the new, death transformed into life. More commonly, however, it is Christ rising from the tomb that comes to be seen as the appropriate substitution. Yet few images of resurrection seem to work. So many look merely pedestrian. Significantly among the most successful are those that modify the story, as in the case of Michelangelo or van Dyck, or else continue to be allusive, as with Titian's *Noli me tangere*.[43] This perhaps raises the question of whether the resurrection is one area where matters

---

[39] David and Solomon are often recognizable with their crowns.

[40] For a 15th-cent. example of devils being dealt with by angels, K. Onasch, *Russian Icons* (Oxford: Phaidon, 1977), no. 23.

[41] For illustrations, N. Bätzner, *Mantegna* (Cologne: Könemann, 1998), 91; W. Kurth *The Complete Woodcuts of Albrecht Dürer* (New York: Dover, 1963), 217. For latter see also Pl. 4.

[42] Not that the image ever entirely died out in the West. Catholics still experience elements in e.g. the Exsultet of Holy Saturday, while Grundtvig even secured some surviving imagery in 19th-cent. Protestant Denmark: A. M. Allchin, *N. F. S. Grundtvig* (Aarhus: Aarhus University Press, 1998), 80–1.

[43] Michelangelo presents Christ naked and stretching heavenwards. Van Dyck, in common with a number of other artists such as Tintoretto and Titian goes one stage further, and has him actually ascending into the sky: for illustration, A. Moir, *Van Dyck*

can only be put other than directly, and so in this respect at least the intuitions of Orthodoxy were right. One wonders, though, whether its own imagery is still not allusive enough. Certainly, Sir John Tavener's attempt to turn the icons into music raises the possibility that here at least music has the edge.[44]

Yet that is not to concede that right is wholly on the side of Orthodoxy. The Western focus on the amount of suffering involved in the crucifixion gave not only a more dramatic contrast with the following resurrection but also some real sense of Christ's involvement in human suffering. Conventional wisdom on the history of atonement theology likes to differentiate sharply between successive theories, but actual life is seldom quite so neat. Although the analogy was criticized by both Gregory Nazianzen and Anselm, Augustine's mousetrap image is still there a millennium later in Robert Campin's 1430 Annunciation Triptych.[45] Again, the way in which Dante places exposition of Anselm's theory in his *Paradiso* suggests that he thought that it had more in common with the earlier victory theories than most commentators would allow, while both Caroline Walker Bynum and I are united in wanting to see more complementarity than conflict between Anselm and Abelard.[46] In a similar way, then, suffering as penalty and suffering as empathy should not necessarily be seen as wholly opposed. Admittedly, for Anselm the penalty lay essentially in death itself, but there is no shortage of illustrative examples where the two aspects subsequently become

(London: Thames & Hudson, 1994), 93. Titian's well-known painting in the National Gallery in London keeps the gardener, but uses the angle of Mary's body merging into a tree behind Christ to suggest a heavenly reality as both figures' ultimate destiny.

[44] In the final two sections of his *Lamentations and Praises* of 2000: 'Procession into Hades' and 'Resurrection in Hades'. Intriguingly, despite the fierceness of his attacks elsewhere on external influences on Western religious music, here he is prepared to employ a Tibetan temple bowl, while in the piece as a whole one is sometimes reminded of Greek secular music. The bowl is struck along with a monastery bell every twenty beats to give some sense of the continuing eternal divine presence.

[45] Augustine, *Sermons* 130. 2: 'ad pretium nostrum tetendit muscipulam crucem suam; posuit ibi quasi escam sanguinem suam' (for our ransom he set a mousetrap, his cross; as bait he placed there his blood). Campin's painting (in the Metropolitan Museum, New York) has as one of its side panels Joseph busily making mousetraps.

[46] Anselm's theory is expounded by Beatrice in *Paradiso*, 7; divine love is also made one of its themes, e.g. ll. 31–3, 73–5. For C. W. Bynum, her chapter above; for my views, see my essay 'Anselm on Atonement' in B. Davies and B. Leftow (eds.), *Companion to Anselm* (Cambridge: Cambridge University Press, 2004).

fused.[47] Bach's two major Passions are an obvious case in point, but first I want to consider a rather different example of this more confused situation, the way in which presentations of the cross as victory and as extreme suffering occurred side by side in art.

The common way of reading Grünewald and Raphael is to say that, despite being contemporaries, they are products of different cultures, Northern High Gothic in the one case and the Italian Renaissance in the other. That cannot of course be denied, but a closer look at their characteristic crucifixions suggests rather more in common than may initially meet the eye. If Raphael's Christ of 1502 shows few obvious signs of suffering, empathy is clearly there in the angels beneath the cross's arms gathering his blood for our benefit at communion.[48] Some may find offensive the way in which they seem almost to dance, but of course, if the death is really to our benefit, such an attitude is surely not wholly inappropriate, while that this is not all that is required is effectively indicated by the two saints who join the Virgin Mary and the Beloved Disciple at the foot of the cross, namely the two penitents Mary Magdalene and St Jerome.[49] None of this is to claim that this is among the most effective of Raphael's works and indeed in my view his former teacher Perugino still surpasses him at this point, but it is to suggest that Renaissance crucifixions are not nearly as unqualified in their stress on the transcendence of suffering as is often suggested.[50]

Turn now to Grünewald's famous Isenheim altarpiece of 1515. It is perhaps today the best known crucifixion scene in the West, and indeed in the twentieth century it has acquired some famous imitators, among them Francis Bacon, Pablo Picasso, and Graham Sutherland.[51] What attracted them was the intensity of the pain that Grünewald had succeeded in capturing, and which these artists

[47] Already in Dante, Anselm's theory is made to anticipate Calvin, e.g. *Paradiso*, 7. 40–4; taken up in Dorothy L. Sayers's 1946 play, *The Just Vengeance*.

[48] Now in the National Gallery, London; illustrated in J. H. Beck, *Raphael* (New York: Abrams, 1976), 83. See also Pl. 5.

[49] Jerome's penitence is indicated in the traditional way, with him holding a stone with which to beat his breast.

[50] Compare Perugino's Galitzin triptych, now in the National Gallery, Washington. This was Michael Ramsey's favourite painting. I attempt a detailed exposition in 'God in the Landscape: Michael Ramsey's Vision', *Anglican Theological Review*, 83 (2001), 775–92, esp. 780–2.

[51] With Bacon it became almost an obsession. Sutherland's best-known version is in St Matthew's church, Northampton; Picasso's at the Centre Pompidou in Paris. For illustration see Pl. 6.

thought could also be used to say something in response to all the suffering that has occurred in their own age. Nonetheless, there are dangers in isolating the crucifixion scene, as Grünewald intended the painting to function in relation to a much wider programme. Painted for a hospital of the Antonite order, the crucifixion is in fact only the final stage of three possible levels of display. When fully closed, there are wooden statues of Anthony, Augustine, and Jerome by another artist to which Grünewald has added painted side-panels reflecting Anthony's life. Open this up and one then encounters a complex nativity scene with angels and church adoring the Christ-child, while annunciation and resurrection appear on its two side-panels. Finally, fully opened and we see the famous crucifixion flanked by St Sebastian and St Anthony. The hospital cared for patients suffering from St Anthony's fire or ergotism, a bread deficiency that produced gangrene, boils, and blackened skin, and there seems little doubt that the total ensemble is addressed to them.[52] So, for instance, the figure in the bottom left in the outer panel showing St Antony's temptations looks very like one of the patients affected by this condition, while St Sebastian's arrows were often used to refer to diseases that pocked the skin. The saints' battles with adversity could thus be seen as their own, but more importantly so could Christ's suffering, and thus his overcoming of death become part of a promise to them as well. It is one of the few paintings to which Barth ever refers in his theology, but I seriously doubt whether his emphasis is right. For him the key lies in a pointing away from humanity and towards Christ.[53] But for me there is more of God drawing close, to identify with us in our pain. Yet, however intense that suffering, the message of Raphael is not subverted. Admittedly, there is more of sequence than of simultaneity, more of the Synoptics than of John, but the resurrection promise is there even in the crucifixion scene. For, as one German commentator observes, 'at Christ's death John the Baptist is raised once more. Through him becoming again enfleshed, he gives visual expression in advance to the triumph of

---

[52] Well explored by A. Hayum in *The Isenheim Altarpiece: God's Medicine and the Painter's Vision* (Princeton: Princeton University Press, 1989), esp. 13–52.

[53] K. Barth, *Church Dogmatics* (Edinburgh: T. & T. Clark, 1936), 1/1, 126, 301; 1/2, 125. At one point (125) he seems to imagine something that is not so: 'Only the little child ... sees ... the Father.' In fact, the infant appears to be looking into the eyes of his mother.

the resurrection.'[54] That would seem confirmed by the Lamb's blood flowing into the chalice below.

Among his possessions when he died it is reported that Grünewald possessed 'much Lutheran trash'.[55] Certainly, the Reformation did seem to entail that he spent more of his time earning his living as an engineer and, although there were some further paintings, none was to reach the profundity of Isenheim. Indeed, one suggests that he now accepted the Protestant view of the superiority of word over vision.[56] There are large questions about meaning here, in particular whether word or vision is more constrictive in meaning and thus whether in consequence one or other might better engage the believer in pursuing a deeper appropriation of redemption. There is not the space to explore matters here, but it is important to challenge any notion that the answers are obvious. The way in which Barth and I have given significantly different interpretations to Grünewald demonstrates that a painting is not necessarily more idolatrous than words in the sense of being more restrictive and limited in its ability to point beyond itself. Nonetheless, that is the way Protestants commonly thought in the past, and so found music easier to appreciate than art. It is therefore fortunate that we have Paul Hindemith's musical recreation of Grünewald's work, to effect some comparisons. Here there is quite a degree of latitude in interpretation. Even so it seems a strength in Hindemith when he almost compels us to hear threatening brass transformed into an assuring regularity as marvellously suggestive of the triumph of good over evil.[57] So convinced was the Swiss Calvinist, Frank Martin, that any attempt to represent God publicly in music must ultimately be blasphemous that he held back his own eucharistic setting for forty years.[58] Yet his musical portrait of the incarnation in the Credo must surely rank among the

[54] My trans. of the German: W. Fraenger, *Grünewald* (Dresden: Verlag der Kunst, 1995 edn.), 13.

[55] E. Ruhmer, *Grünewald: The Paintings* (London: Phaidon, 1958), 29 (quoting comments on his Frankfurt estate, which also included twenty-seven of Luther's sermons).

[56] Two years before he died (in 1528), he painted *The Carrying of the Cross* (now in Karlsruhe), where a quotation in German of Isa. 53: 5 is made to dominate the scene.

[57] Hindemith's opera *Mathis der Maler* was banned by the Nazis but delivered as a symphony under Furtwängler in Berlin in 1934, and it is in this form that it is now usually performed. Its third movements is what is referred to in the text, and corresponds to the Temptations of Anthony in Grünewald's painting.

[58] From 1922 to 1963: Mass for Double Choir. His *et resurrexit* is particularly delightful.

most carefully nuanced, detailed, and profound of the twentieth century. It would seem a mistake to suppose any of the three media (word, art, and music) automatically more liable to corruption or distortion than the others because necessarily more constrictive in meaning.

Martin greatly admired Bach, and it is to Bach and his two great Passions that we may turn to illustrate how music also, like art, wrestled with two quite different ways of presenting the significance of the crucifixion. In part, this was of course a function of the different narrative content of the two gospels in question (Matthew and John), but, as we shall see, by no means wholly so. In an influential book Jaroslav Pelikan found Anselm in the *St Matthew Passion* and the Christus Victor approach in the *St John*.[59] Nonetheless there are more surprises than this contrast might lead one to expect. In the *John Passion* no sound of victory is given to Christ's final words.[60] Instead 'it is finished' quietly concludes a recitative and although the beautiful alto aria that follows has one triumphant section, it opens and concludes with the same quiet falling melody for the words 'it is finished' as was heard in the recitative.[61] Only at the third time of its occurrence in the next (bass) aria and chorus has it more positive resonances as we hear: 'As thou hast now the cross endured | And thyself hast said, It is finished ... Shall all the world redemption see?'[62] Even so cosmic significance is finally given not through John's own words but through importing Matthew 27: 51–2 into a recitative and then expanding on this in the following arioso. Although musically clearly not in the same league, it is fascinating to compare this with a nineteenth-century work like Sir John Stainer's *Crucifixion*, where congregational involvement continues to be expected, unlike the normal conventions now with Bach. Although using a composite text, Stainer is, I think, in fact much nearer to the theology of John. 'It is finished' is given a more robust feel partly through the addition of Luke's 'Into thy hands I commend my spirit'

[59] J. Pelikan, *Bach among the Theologians* (Philadelphia: Fortress, 1986), 89–115.

[60] The Greek perfect tense at 19: 30 might be better translated: 'all has now been accomplished'.

[61] Even then speed and number of instruments can also affect mood. John Elliot Gardiner makes the aria much sadder than Sir David Willcocks. The joyful line is: 'Victorious Judah's hero comes, and ends the fight.' This and the lines quoted in the main text follow the Peter Pears's translation.

[62] Rhythm, harmony, and melody all inviting the response 'Yes'.

and partly through more extensive use of a major key, while there are also frequent returns to the theme of divinity throughout the story. Thus, for example, sandwiched between Gethsemane and Golgotha is the great organ solo and chorus 'processional', 'Fling wide the gates', the bass recitative 'He made himself of no reputation' leads into the tenor aria 'King ever glorious', while the final stages of the crucifixion are preceded by another fine chorus, 'From the throne of his cross'.

By contrast the actual moment of death is not treated all that differently in the *St Matthew Passion* from what takes in the *St John*, and there is also a very similar approach to the earthquake. Quite different, though, is what happens with the cry of dereliction which is conveyed with an anguished assertiveness quite unlike the quiet Johannine 'It is finished.'[63] It is really in the sung commentaries on the action that the difference is most marked. The Anselmian strand could scarcely be more noticeable than in the chorale verse which Bach chooses to follow the crowd's call for Christ's crucifixion: 'How extraordinary is this punishment! The good shepherd suffers for the sheep; the master pays the penalty, the justified for his vassals.'[64] Indeed, the greater emphasis on sacrificial atonement is obvious from the outset, where the first use of such imagery occurs through the depiction of Christ (in the chorale which soars above the opening chorus), as the Lamb, 'guiltless but butchered on the mast of the cross'.

So, in short, the difference in approach is reflected less in the actual words of the two gospels than in the accompanying commentary and its music. Might this have something to do with the necessarily sequential character of music? With Raphael and Grünewald, and indeed the words of the gospels themselves, there is always time to explore beyond, say, the primary joy of Raphael or the corresponding sadness of Grünewald. But with music one must go on, and the danger in presenting John's 'it is finished' as unalloyed victory would be a death that appeared ultimately shallow. In a similar way, visual artists inevitably fail if they try to offer too immediate an answer, which is no doubt why Western resurrections all too

---

[63] Made more dramatic still by suspension of the string 'halo' that otherwise accompanies Christ's words.

[64] My trans. Note esp.: 'Die Schuld bezahlt der Herre, der Gerechte | Für seine Knechte.'

often appear shallow rather than evocative of a deep mystery worthy of further contemplation. That is to say, music, perhaps more than any other art form, inevitably compels our thoughts in one direction rather than another, and so Bach was surely right in allowing time for more extended sorrow at Christ's death before full weight was given to John's words.

THE PRODIGAL SON

Although earlier images of the parable do occur, it became particularly popular among artists in post-Reformation times.[65] If Dürer provides an interesting example on the eve of the Reformation with the son kneeling penitentially in the midst of a herd of pigs, Rembrandt's famous painting helps provide an explanation of one major reason why the theme became so frequent in the Protestant homes of the Netherlands.[66] Painted towards the end of his life in 1669, it portrays the moment of reconciliation of father and son, modifying a framework that Rembrandt had already employed in a copper engraving of 1636.[67] In the earlier one it is easy to become distracted by the busy servants in the background and, although there is clearly a reconciliation of father and son, the anxieties and concerns of both still remain prominent, particularly on their faces. In 1669 Rembrandt resolves these two difficulties by making the four figures in the background mere observers, while father and son are no longer presented to us side-on.[68] Instead the kneeling son buries his shaven head in the father's bosom, while the father closes his eyes as he rests his hands on his son's shoulders. The net effect is that there is now a simple, unmuddied declaration of a gospel of pure

---

[65] Luke 15: 11–32. The earliest surviving examples are from the 12th cent. at St Nectaire, Puy-de-Dôme in France.

[66] For illustration of Dürer's engraving, *Albrecht Dürer: The Complete Engravings* (Bristol: Artline, 1967), no. 15. For some statistics on popularity and the general background, W. H. Halewood, *Six Subjects of Reformation Art* (Toronto: University of Toronto Press, 1982), 52–63, esp. 52.

[67] For the engraving, Halewood, *Six Subjects*, 57, or for more detail, A. Blankert, *Rembrandt: A Genius and his Impact* (Melbourne: National Gallery of Victoria, 1997), 396–7.

[68] For illustration, S. Schama *Rembrandt's Eyes* (London: Penguin, 1999), 683; see also Pl. 7. Schama prefers a different explanation for the closed eyes: that touch can sometimes convey what the eyes cannot (685).

grace. One can almost feel the father lifting the burden of sin from the son's shoulders, while the closed eyes may speak of a vision that no longer sees the rags and weary feet. As neither the son's face nor what his hands are doing is visible, it becomes easy to read the painting as laying all its stress on divine grace, with even the prodigal's penitence essentially God's act rather than his. So Calvin would have been pleased, as indeed also Barth who waxes eloquently on this parable in his *Church Dogmatics*.[69]

This is scarcely the place to arbitrate between competing theories of grace, but intriguingly almost exactly contemporary with Rembrandt's painting are two Catholic presentations of the denouement of the story where the emphasis is quite different. Both the Dutchmen Jan Steen and the Spaniard Bartolomé Esteban Murillo chose to interpret the conclusion of the parable in much more synergistic, cooperative terms. Steen is perhaps best known now for his satirical works, but he was a practising Roman Catholic and his *Return of the Prodigal Son* does come across as an expression of genuine commitment. He draws on Rembrandt's early engraving, but reverses it so that the door now appears on the left. Most important is the way in which the son's hands are made to draw together in prayerful petition, and the father to endorse this action by grasping them in his own.[70] Murillo attempted more than one series on the story.[71] It is, though, his painting of 1668 that is best known.[72] In it the father embraces the penitent son but as in Steen the son has his hands clasped in prayer and is looking expectantly into the father's eyes. This could be taken to imply an arrogant

---

[69] Calvin, *Commentary on a Harmony of the Evangelists*, ii (Grand Rapids. Mich.: Eerdmans, 1949), 344–8; Barth, *Church Dogmatics* (Edinburgh: T. & T. Clark, 1958), iv/2, 20–154, esp. 21–5. Although Barth devotes only four pages to the parable, it does really provide the framework for the longer section as a whole, 'The Homecoming of the Son of Man'. Barth treats the parable christologically in terms of the humiliation and exaltation of humanity in Christ.

[70] For illustration and history, H. P. Chapman, W. T. Kloek, and A. K. Wheelock (eds.), *Jan Steen: Painter and Storyteller* (Washington, DC: National Gallery of Art, 3rd edn., 1996), 225–7.

[71] For eleven examples, J. Martineau (ed.), *Murillo* (London: Royal Academy of Arts, 1983), 119, 123–9. It is sometimes suggested that Rembrandt's *Polish Rider* was once part of such a series (the prodigal riding off to enjoy his inheritance). For some other suggestions, C. Ryskamp, B. Davidson, E. Munhall, and N. Tscherny, *Paintings from the Frick Collection* (New York: Abrams, 1990), s.v.

[72] Martineau, *Murillo*, 119; see also Pl. 8. Painted for the Hospital de la Caridad in Seville, it is now in the National Gallery of Art, Washington. An earlier, less impressive version of the *Return* can be seen at ibid. 129.

presumption of forgiveness once penance had been shown. It is perhaps to eliminate any such reading that both artists include a dog, for dogs were conventionally used to evoke humble trust, and that is therefore the more charitable interpretation here.

I mentioned at the beginning of this chapter that the parable has now made its way into the liturgy of the Church of England. It forms the basis of a post-communion prayer that begins as follows: 'Father of all, we give you thanks and praise that when we were still far off you met us in your Son and brought us home.' 'Far off' probably alludes to the father running to meet the son, an image that would be hard to capture in paint without undermining the Father's dignity.[73] The prayer was written by a Cambridge English scholar, David Frost by name. Intriguingly, the old debates about grace continue. General Synod rejected one line of the original version of Frost's prayer that had requested, 'Anchor us in this hope that we have grasped', substituting in its place: 'Keep us firm in the hope that you have set before us'.[74] Whatever the rights or wrongs of the two theologies, the imagery has undoubtedly become much weaker.

Although there was an occasional musical anticipation before the twentieth century, none has survived the test of time, and so it is exclusively to that century's adaptations that we must turn for presentations in music.[75] Four are significant, and all quite different. Undoubtedly, the best known is Prokofiev's ballet of the same name, the most loyal to the biblical text Benjamin Britten's third *Church Parable*,[76] while the other two are intriguing variants though pulling in opposed directions, Debussy's *L'Enfant prodigue* and the Swedish composer, Hugo Alfvén's *Den Förlorade sonen*.[77]

If Prokofiev's ballet music for *Romeo and Juliet* and *Cinderella* is perhaps now better known, *The Prodigal Son* does continue to enjoy periodic revivals, not least because of Balanchine's original choreography. First performed in Paris in 1929, it also had had scenery designed by the devout Roman Catholic painter, Georges Rouault.

---

[73] Luke 15: 20. Gentle hints of movement are inserted into a number of such paintings, including Rembrandt's earlier etching, but not in my view with any degree of success.

[74] Frost was developing Heb. 6: 19 at this point.

[75] Sir Arthur Sullivan produced an oratorio on the subject in 1869.

[76] The earlier two were *Curlew River* and *The Burning Fiery Furnace*.

[77] Strictly speaking, Debussy's work could be regarded as a 19th-cent. product since the cantata was first performed in 1884, but the final version dates from 1908.

The music is firmly anti-Romantic and is given a decidedly bombastic quality by what are sometimes described as Prokofiev's 'motor rhythms'. Where they aid is through the force of contrast. So, for instance, in the opening scene a dramatic difference is observable between the dancing, high-spirited rhythms that represent the prodigal's intended departure and the more lyrical melody which accompanies the family at prayer and which the prodigal reluctantly and briefly joins before going off on his own. Scenes of seduction and drunkenness follow. Swift and disturbing clarinet phrases then vividly introduce and paint the image of the young man being stripped of all his possessions, and so render all the more solemn the viola melody that follows during which themes of penitence and an awakening conscience are first encountered.[78] If the heavy tread of the son returning home is what one might expect from scripture, intriguingly it is his sisters who first act on his behalf and summon the father. A beautiful flute melody indicates the father's forgiveness and blessing, symbolized on stage by the father throwing his cloak over his son who remains kneeling at his feet.[79]

If there is no mention in Prokofiev of the elder brother and his dilemma, matters are quite otherwise in Britten's version which ends with the elder son also reconciled. As with his other two *Church Parables*, Britten deliberately gives the story a ritualistic context, of a play within a play, in this case with an abbot turning into the tempter and the whole performance beginning and ending with monks singing a plainsong hymn. He draws on the traditions of medieval liturgical drama and Japanese Noh plays, not to suggest events remote from daily life, but rather in order to induce spiritual reflection. Solo instruments are used to particularly good effect in creating atmosphere. As with Prokofiev the flute is used to suggest the Father as gentle, forgiving and kind.[80] It is Britten's use of the trumpet, though, which is most memorable, in its evocation of the sensuousness of temptation.[81] Britten turns to the viola to represent

---

[78] Contrast the episodes from Scene II entitled *Pillage* and *Réveil et remords*. In both cases the melodic material is subsequently taken up by other instruments.

[79] So a performance I saw by Birmingham Royal Ballet in 2001. The melody is in C major and so recalls the more positive aspects of the opening scene.

[80] As in the father's opening speech, 'I am father to you all.' It occurs again during the dialogue between the Father and the Younger Son before his departure, and quite marvellously at the point of reconciliation with its simple but profound words, 'My son'.

[81] Especially in the central section set in the city.

the son and his longings.[82] If these consist initially of a desire to be
elsewhere than at home, intriguingly it is the same instrument that is
used to suggest his desire for return. The viola takes up the melody
sung to the words 'I will arise and go', and is then joined in counter-
point by the trumpet and horn playing the same melody at various
pitches, their entries growing closer and closer together while above
them the flute develops the melody of the plainsong hymn which
frames the whole work.[83] The section thus brings together the
instrumental colours associated with the prodigal, with temptations,
with the servants (the horn), and with the Father. Integration is thus
certainly the theme. So striking, though, is the viola and trumpet
now as one that Britten may possibly be hinting that the son's
disintegration was simply one stage through which he had to go in
order to achieve a more profound integration. That seems confirmed
by some of the Abbot–Tempter's own words.[84]

The pieces by Debussy and Alfvén are less well known, and indeed
are now usually only performed in part; in Alfvén's case as an
orchestral concert suite, while all that is heard from Debussy's cantata nowadays is its opening beautiful soprano solo.[85] Alfvén's original ballet score was a work of his old age, based on folk music and
paintings (the latter on the walls of farmhouses in Dalarna in his
native Sweden). The ballet had a richness of contrast which the
present arrangement now lacks. The son's departure and his wel-
come by the Queen of Arabia are both positive in tone, and indeed it
is only the reconciliation with his father that now hints at a more
complicated reality. The joy of the father is indicated by a delightful
polka that initially contrasts with the heavy tread of the son only to
absorb that sound in turn.[86] Yet, despite the absence of other significant oppositions, the impact of the achieved reconciliation is still a
powerful one. By contrast, Debussy's music is much more sombre,
with the cantata opening with the son (Azaël) already fled his home

---

[82] In the first dialogue between the Younger Son and the Tempter the son's viola is
made initially to respond to the tempter's harp, but as he gradually succumbs we hear
a trumpet's clarion call.

[83] The musical structure of the Younger Son's soliloquy and the instrumental
interlude as he returns home.

[84] When the Tempter first meets the Younger Son he declares: 'I am no stranger to
you | you know me very well. | I am your inner voice, | your very self'.

[85] There is a particularly fine recording of Lia's recitative and aria by the American
soprano, Eileen Farrell.

[86] In the penultimate section of the 1957 arrangement, the Polka.

by the lake of Genezareth and his mother, Lia, lamenting their loss. While there is due stress on remorse and repentance, it is the mother's intercessions that ensure the father's forgiveness.[87]

It would be all too easy for theologians to complain about such departures from Luke's text, but I seriously doubt whether this is the best way to approach such matters. By their alterations to the parable, each of these musical works helps raise important questions about salvation. Prokofiev's ballet and Debussy's cantata, for instance, put to us the question of whether salvation is ever purely an individual matter, of whether we are not always dependent on others' prayers and aid (in Prokofiev's case, that of the sisters, in Debussy's the mother's). Again, Britten poses the old issue of *felix culpa*, whether God may not sometimes use our falls to deepen and enrich our characters.

In all of this some salient themes of my two earlier sections recur. Art and music function at their best when they move beyond a purely illustrative role to one in which they invite viewer or listener to further exploration of how redemption works and may be appropriated. The resultant theology may not always be to our personal taste, but whether it inspires or grates that is surely better than that it leaves us unmoved, our faith neither challenged nor deepened.[88]

---

[87] 'Ne garde pas un front sévère. A qui t'implore à deux genoux. Pardonne au fils! Songe à la mère': C. Debussy, *L'Enfant prodigue* (Paris: Durand, 1908), 41–2.

[88] I am extremely grateful to Anne Harrison for her detailed and careful reflections on the first draft of all my comments on the music.

1. Jan and Hubert van Eyck (1432). Exterior of *Ghent Altarpiece*,
St Bavo's Cathedral, Ghent

Note the centrality given to the open window with its invitation to proceed beyond, and so implicitly to the interior of the polyptych. The towel, kettle and basin in the adjoining embrasure, while
no doubt in part alluding to the Virgin's purity, also seem to request a corresponding purity from
us for that further move within, not least when set in the context of the two Johns immediately
below, one associated with baptism (John the Baptist with lamb on the left) and the other with
Christ's washing of his disciples' feet at the Last Supper (unique to Gospel of John, portrayed as
youth with chalice and snake).

2. Van Eyck, Adoration of the Lamb from the interior of the *Ghent Altarpiece* (1432),
St Bavo's Cathedral, Ghent

In the midst of adoring angels and saints, the golden rays of the Holy Spirit and a blossoming meadow, the Lamb stands enthroned on the altar. Engagement on the part of the viewer is sought not only through familiar landmarks from Ghent and Utrecht in the background but also, more importantly, by the centrality given to the two principal Christian sacraments. The Lamb's blood flows into a chalice on the altar, while nearer to us is the fountain of life with its allusion to baptism.

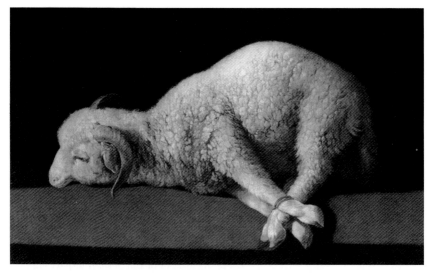

3. Zurburán, *Agnus Dei* (1640). Prado, Madrid

The simplicity of the image gives it its power. The animal's tactility underlines not only its accessibility but also its vulnerability. It is almost as though the viewer is being told: if only you made the effort, its legs could be free. The somewhat surprising addition of the horns recalls Genesis 22. 13, and the deeper meaning in the Father's love.

4. Albrecht Dürer. *Christ in Limbo* (1510) Woodcut from the Great Passion

Dürer well illustrates the strength and weakness of western depictions of the descent into hell. On the positive side there is the clear affirmation that Christ's resurrection is also relevant to humanity in general. A muscular Adam and buxom Eve are already released, while others are being given a helping hand. The negative side is the riot of imagery of devils, largely lacking in eastern depictions.

5. Raphael, *Crucifixion* (1503). National Gallery, London

The dancing angels and sun and moon looking on may appear to make the message of this painting overwhelming optimistic. But it is as well to remember that this was once part of an altarpiece,
and so the eye would first have alighted on what is happening below, where the two kneeling figures emphasise the need for penitence before any possibility of eucharistic joy. Mary Magdalene is
on the right, and Jerome on the left (holding the stone with which he used to beat his breast).

6. Matthias Grünewald (1516), crucifixion scene from the *Isenheim Altarpiece*.
Isenheim Museum, Colmar

Twentieth century imitators of Grünewald have almost wholly focused on this scene with its depiction of the intensity of Christ's pain. While not discounting that aspect, two factors pulling the other way should be noted. First, there is the way in which it is part of a larger programme that includes joyful depictions of the nativity and resurrection. Secondly, even in this scene itself, there are some signs of hope—the Lamb receiving blood in the chalice to feed us, John the Baptist resurrected to tell us who Christ is, and the upward thrust of Christ's arms pointing heavenwards.

7. Rembrandt, *Return of the Prodigal Son* (1669). Hermitage, St Petersburg

The son throws himself entirely upon his father's mercy, not so much as raising his eyes from his father's breast, while the father seems almost to absorb the burden and pain through his own closed eyes. It is only gradually that we become aware that the angle of our vision of the scene must be from the right, and so the two male figures on our far left are intended to exercise a more central role. It looks as though they provide some sort of commentary on the interaction between father and son, the resistant clenched hands of the standing elder brother contrasting with the seating man's penitent hand at his breast. A movement between the two responses is thus also sought from us as viewers.

8. Murillo, *Return of the Prodigal Son* (1668). National Gallery, Washington

The parable was put to a number of different uses in the seventeenth century. Here it was intended to illustrate 'clothing the naked' as part of series on the seven corporal acts of mercy that were derived from Matthew 25. Tenderness is conveyed in the father's eyes, joy in the boy bringing the fatted calf and suspicion in the elder brother's querying of the offer of a ring. The dog exhibits the faithfulness that the prodigal had lacked.

14

The Redemption of the Created Order: Sermons on Romans 8: 18–25

MARGUERITE SHUSTER

INTRODUCTION

As Gerald O'Collins suggests in several different ways in his introduction to this volume, the hope of redemption may rightly be extended beyond humankind to the created order as a whole. Not only are creation and redemption tied together in so far as they occur through the mediation of Christ, but God's promise is of a new earth as well as a new heaven—a whole redeemed universe. Not only human beings suffer the effects of human sin and thus stand in need of redemption, but also the rest of creation struggles, suffers, fails to reach its proper end, and deteriorates or dies. And scripture is explicit both that this futility seen in creation is on humankind's account, and that creation's deliverance is linked to that of humankind (Rom. 8: 19–23).

It is true that redemption of the created order, along with humankind, is not as such a major theme of scripture. As Käsemann notes when commenting on Romans 8, even for Paul, concern for 'nature' in itself plays a small role: his main emphasis is on creation as a historical phenomenon, creation as the stage of human history.[1] Still, one can hardly deny the basic sympathy involved in speaking of creation's groans and its eager expectation. We might also refer to Colossians 1: 20 (reconciliation of 'all things') and perhaps Acts 3: 21 ('universal restoration'), as well as to 2 Peter 3: 13 and Revelation 21: 1 ('new heavens and a new earth'), along with the various OT eschatological images of peaceable beasts in a restored creation (especially Isa. 11: 6–9; 65: 17–25) and of humans sitting securely, not on an ethereal cloud, but under their own vines and fig trees

---

[1] Ernst Käsemann, *Commentary on Romans*, trans. and ed. G. W. Bromiley (Grand Rapids, Mich.: Eerdmans, 1980), 233.

(Mic. 4: 4; Zech. 3: 10). Even the story of Noah involves the preservation not just of humans but of animals both clean and unclean, desirable and apparently undesirable: Noah was not saved alone or along with only the creatures he might have counted useful. And the covenant made with Noah was explicitly with the animals as well (Gen. 9: 10, 15, 16). Human bodily life has a broad material context without which it is not now, or perhaps ever, truly human life.

The importance of this broad material context for our life on this earth has of course come home to us in recent times in increasingly pressing ways, as we seek to come to terms with our massive destructiveness to other creatures and our greediness in consuming resources that are not, as least on the scale of human history, renewable. Furthermore, various scientific scenarios promising an eventual hot or cold death for our planetary system, along with the relentless increase in randomness posited by the Second Law of Thermodynamics, scarcely sound promising for the long term. But that religious conviction matters—a lot—in how we regard this devastation and our final end comes home when we consider attitudes like that of former United States Secretary of the Interior James Watt, an evangelical Christian infamous for his remark that he was not too worried about ecological matters, since he did not know when the Lord would return and the earth be destroyed. If we do not see the creation as having a future, or if we see our and our Christian loved ones' future as unrelated to the creation's future, then we will have little motive apart from sheer sentimentality to care for it. Thus, that our future does indeed appear in some sense to be tied theologically to that of the earth may be seen as having no small consequence for our present behaviour.

The purpose of this chapter is to explore in what ways and to what extent such consequences appear in sermons on Romans 8: 18–25. This particular text commended itself both because in it the 'revealing of the children of God' and the redemption of the (human) body are directly connected to creation being freed from its bondage to decay; and because it is included as a reading in both the Revised Common Lectionary and the Roman Catholic Lectionary, thus increasing the likelihood that contemporary sermons and homilies might be found on it. (It is true that an old exegetical debate, going back to the time of the church Fathers, revolves around whether κτισις should be taken as referring to the non-human creation only, or whether it refers only to humans, or involves at least some humans. But the argument in favour of the non-human creation surely appears to have prevailed and to be the common-sense reading of the passage.) Naturally, with respect to so rich a passage, one would expect to find sermons on various themes that touch lightly if at all on the question I have in mind; but to see how these matters play out is part of the purpose of this chapter.

My method for this chapter was primarily to search the internet, supplemented by a small number of written sources, for sermons and homilies on Romans 8: 18–25, or on longer passages overlapping at least vv. 19–23. I hoped to tap both classic sermons and a significant sampling of preaching that modern congregations are getting from day to day.[2] I found, as anticipated, both a few older sermons (from the nineteenth century or earlier) and a rather large number of pieces from the last ten to fifteen years. I threw out pieces that were nothing but outlines or that were about nothing discernible, leaving me with a total of fifty sermons, including those by the handful of preachers represented twice, and two *Christian Century* articles of sermonic style and tone. I shall proceed by looking first at four classic sermons, then at sermons explicitly on an ecological theme, then at other primarily topical sermons, and finally at more or less expository sermons, dealing at least generally, and not in a strongly topical way, with the text itself.

One additional preliminary matter requires comment, and that is the extreme difficulty of finding substantive Roman Catholic homilies on this passage. A search of all 161 sites, with their associated links—surely a thousand or more in all—referenced at *www.catholiclinks.org/homiliaseng.htm* (in addition to more general homiletical sites) produced *not one* homily on or including Romans 8: 18–25 (there was a link to the Chrysostom sermon commented upon below; and I found one homily in a volume by Karl Rahner). Indeed, it may be significant that the excellent Roman Catholic Deacon Sil site[3] provided links to dozens of Protestant sermons on the text, but not to any Roman Catholic ones. Part of the reason, naturally, is that Roman Catholic homilies are overwhelmingly on the Gospel

---

[2] The key bias here is in favour of the 'internet enabled' congregation, which turns out in Protestant circles, at least, to be a negligibly slight bias in favour of very conservative churches (the old evangelical penchant for 'new methods' comes through once again: theological and methodological conservatism must not be assumed to be linked). The appendix listing the sermons gives the denomination of the preacher, when discernible.

[3] http://www.deaconsil.com/

reading, with occasionally a sentence or two referring to other readings, but nothing sufficient for the purposes of this study. Another reason may be the extreme brevity of most of these homilies, hinted at by the names of certain links: one was to 'Father Joe Horn's Seven Minute Killer Homilies' (dead link!); another, to 'Longer Homilies based on Scripture Passages', had no listings at all. From a Protestant perspective, one could wish that the resources of excellent Roman Catholic biblical scholarship on the whole of scripture might find fuller expression in the church's homiletical reflection.

In looking at the sermons I found, I will keep five fundamental questions in mind. (1) Does the sermon treat the natural order at all; and if so, does it comment on current ecological issues? (2) Is the current state of things linked to Genesis 3 and the Fall, as is generally understood to be implied by the text? (3) Is there explicit or at least strongly implicit mention of redemption; and if so, is it linked specifically to human bodiliness? (4) Is the text's emphasis on future hope clear; and if so, is that hope extended to the natural world? (5) Are humans and the natural order tied together in terms of their futures as well as in terms of their past? Briefly to state my own bias upfront, I do consider this text, like the creation narratives themselves, to be fundamentally but not exclusively anthropocentric. That is to say, not only are humankind the crown of creation, but they are the ultimate as well as a self-evidently proximate source of its trouble—not automatically or inevitably, but because God so determined it to be (the latter determination being an act of judgement). But even to speak of the creation as subjected to futility and of having a hope suggests that it has a proper end not to be identified with its current state; and thus some sort of future for the created order is implied.[4] That future is integrally related to human hope, a hope that depends not on 'progress' or on mere elapsed time, but on God's own redemptive activity.

---

[4] The point is widely granted. See e.g. John Murray, *The Epistle to the Romans* (Grand Rapids, Mich.: Eerdmans, 1965), in loc. Similarly C. E. B. Cranfield, *The Epistle to the Romans*, 2 vols. (Edinburgh: T. & T. Clark, 1975); Joseph A. Fitzmyer, *Romans* (New York: Doubleday, 1992); Martin Luther, *Commentary on the Epistle to the Romans*, trans. J. T. Mueller (Grand Rapids, Mich.: Kregel, 1954 (reprint 1967)); Anders Nygren, *Commentary on Romans* (Philadelphia: Fortress, 1949); William Sanday and Arthur C. Headlam, *The Epistle to the Romans* (5th edn., Edinburgh: T. & T. Clark, 1902).

CLASSIC SERMONS

Fortuitously and instructively, the four classic sermons I discovered—by John Chrysostom (*c.*347–407) (8),[5] William Huntington (1745–1813) (23), John Wesley (1703–93) (48), and Charles Spurgeon (1834–92) (41)—take greatly different approaches to the text. Chrysostom's Homily 14 on Romans is primarily a verse-by-verse commentary on Romans 8: 12–27. Huntington, preaching on vv. 19–21, refers the text to humans only. Spurgeon, referencing only vv. 22–3, gives a broad-based treatment, but one focused primarily on human hope. Wesley alone, reflecting on vv. 19–22, gives prominence to the non-human creation.

Chrysostom's sermon is remarkable not least for an unapologetic anthropocentrism that nonetheless gives a certain weight to the rest of creation. His purpose, derived from vv. 12–13, is that his hearers should not live according to the flesh. In service of this goal he emphasizes the glory awaiting them, which must not be bartered for the attractions of this life. Creation, in both its corruptibility and its hope, provides instruction and impetus. On the one hand, its current condition can move us to contempt for the present and a desire for things to come. On the other hand, Paul personifies its expectation, 'that we may learn the greatness of the blessings, so great as to reach even the things without sense also'. In every respect the non-human creation is tied to humanity's fate, with humankind taking the lead: it 'received a curse and brought forth thorns and thistles', because humankind became mortal and liable to suffering; it will be freed and become incorruptible similarly on humankind's account. For the latter, Chrysostom uses the striking figure of the nurse bringing up a king's child who shares in his good things when he comes to power. Chrysostom's concern, however, is so exclusively with humankind that it moves far from Paul's apparent sympathy. He does not consider creation to be wrongly treated in the present, since it was made to begin with for the sake of human beings and now suffers for their correction. Besides, it will finally be restored:

---

[5] For the sake of convenience, I will generally refer to sermons discussed by their number in the alphabetical source list at the end of this chapter. It is not useful to indicate page numbers, as these are contingent upon font size and printer conventions, given that the sermons are found on web pages (though I have for my own convenience used NPNF for Chrysostom).

texts like Isaiah 51: 6 and 2 Peter 3: 13 should not be taken as
implying an utter perishing, but should rather be read along the
lines of 1 Corinthians 15: 53. Chrysostom in any case doubts that
right and wrong apply to things without soul and feeling—a seemingly odd ignoring of the sentience of animals. That creation is
subjected 'not of its own will' emphasizes not its agency but rather
that everything is brought about by Christ's care rather than by any
achievement of creation itself. Its groanings of unfulfilment should
shame humankind, should they become content with their present
state. Hope—and a clearly future hope—is thus paramount, and
applies both to redeemed human beings and to the natural world
tied to them. This hope is not ethereal but in some sense bodily:
Chrysostom explains that it is not the body as such but the deeds of
the flesh that are the problem. The redemption of the body, involving
freedom from death and ailments and passions, will constitute 'perfect glory'; and along with the change of the body will come 'the
change of the whole creation'.

   In this sermon, then, Chrysostom treats affirmatively all of my
questions, except for the ecological issues. These, of course, would
not have arisen even as a conceivable issue at the time that he
preached; although one suspects, from the wholly anthropocentric
focus of the sermon, that he would have seen such issues as for
humankind's instruction, and not as having a claim in their own
right. He did not, however, shy away from drawing conclusions
about proper care for the physical needs of the poor, which is a
way of respecting not just human beings abstractly, but their bodies
as temples of God. In all, this sermon powerfully affirms the eventual
redemption of the natural order, but not in a way that promotes
hearers' duty of responsibility, sympathy, or care for the subhuman
world.

   William Huntington, by contrast, insists in a somewhat flat-footed
manner that, since beasts and irrational creatures are incapable of
hope, the passage from Romans 8 as a whole can have no reference
to them. After heaping scorn on the hope of Bishop John Jewell
(1522–71) that he might see 'an old favourite mare of his in some
large field, in the millennium', he proceeds to eliminate from consideration fallen angels, those who have not heard the gospel, those
who have heard but not believed the gospel, and even those who
have made a profession of faith but are now hypocritical or asleep. He
concludes that 'the expectation of the creature' applies only to real

believers in Jesus Christ. These alone shall be delivered from bondage to corruption. The vanity to which they are now subject is not to be identified with any of their futile passions or attachments, for they pursue these willingly enough; rather, it is death, imposed as a penalty for Adam's sin. Hope, too, is referred first to the protevangelion of Genesis 3, and then to the resurrection of Christ, which promises the resurrection of those who belong to him. 'To the full and eternal enjoyment of this glory, God hath subjected this creature in hope. Christ's flesh rested in hope, because it was not to see corruption; and ours shall rest in hope also.' Huntington is clear that our future hope involves the redemption of the body, but he scorns our present bodies as 'nothing else but corruption'. And while he cannot deny that vv. 22–3 involve more than just human believers, he dismisses them as a digression that simply affirms that the present misery afflicts all, more or less. His whole positive focus is on the prospects of true believers only.

Huntington refers to the natural order only to dismiss its significance, at least in the context of this passage. He does link the passage to Genesis 3, but with surprising neglect to take into account the fact that Genesis 3 shows the Fall as affecting more than just humankind. And while he is orthodox enough explicitly to affirm bodily resurrection, he does so in a way that impugns present bodiliness. He presents a powerful future hope for true believers, but one without positive consequences for anyone or anything else.

In the introductory portion of his sermon, Charles Spurgeon shows a palpable enjoyment and affirmation of the natural world, a world he understands as built to be a temple of God, even though now 'the slime of the serpent is on it all'. Now it is a sad world; and after referring to natural evils and human misery, Spurgeon concludes, 'If there were no future to this world as well as to ourselves, we might be glad to escape from it, counting it to be nothing better than a huge penal colony from which it would be a thousand mercies for both body and soul to be emancipated.' One might expect from this introduction a treatment that unfolded these thoughts, but in fact Spurgeon proceeds in a rather different direction—to an exposition of his text in terms of what the saints have attained, wherein they are deficient, and what their state of mind should be. His subject is almost entirely our human condition and hope. He nonetheless touches on matters relevant to my theme when he speaks of the promised deliverance of the body—referred to not, with Huntington, in disparaging terms, but as a 'poor friend'. Subject to sickness and pain, the body can now depress the spirit and may lead into sin; yet we are made to be body and spirit, and that the body shall be set free 'is the Christian's brightest hope'. Not a disembodied heavenly existence, but bodies set free from the last vestiges of the Fall, will bring perfect contentment. Furthermore, in our present lack of liberty, we are linked to the creation. Whereas Adam was in full harmony with his world, now 'everything is contrary to us'. But one day (referencing Isa. 11; 2 Pet. 3; Rev. 21—a world renewed after fire, not annihilated), 'God will...change our bodies and make them fit for our souls, and then he will change the world itself'. Matter 'will be as immortal as spirit, this very world will become the place of an eternal jubilee'. All of this is adumbrated when we see the groaning of ourselves and of creation as that which precedes birth rather than that which points to coming death. Let us then not groan after anything that does not lead towards the coming perfection.

Obviously Spurgeon holds a bright future hope for both humankind and the natural world, tied firmly together. He touches upon the current state of creation only in passing, though he clearly refers to Genesis 3. His strongest affirmations on issues related to the concerns of this chapter have to do with the basic goodness of our bodily existence, later played out in terms of renewed bodies having a suitable, renewed environment. While he refrains from elaboration on the grounds that it would be merely speculative, his obvious assumption is that bodily creatures are properly to be found in a material setting, however transformed it may be. One finds in this sermon a refreshing balance of appreciation and caution with respect to our earthly circumstances, a stance neither dismissive nor complacent, but one confidently expecting God to bring the harvest promised by the first fruits.

Wesley, as suggested by his title, 'The General Deliverance', preaches on the restoration of the whole creation, though with special attention to animals, which he treats with tender concern and with reference to many texts affirming God's care for the animal world. He assumes that they, along with our first parents, began by enjoying perfect happiness in Eden. Indeed, he gives much attention to Genesis 1–3 and expands upon the example of those early expositors who attributed vast excellencies to Adam and Eve in their original state, assuming that animals, too, were then swifter, smarter, and more beautiful than they are now. They differed from humankind fundamentally only in that humankind were capable of knowing and obeying God. Utilizing these capacities was humankind's perfection; and obeying humans, according to the dominion God gave to humans, was the perfection and source of blessing of the animals. The Fall meant that humankind could not exercise proper dominion or transmit these blessings, leading in due course to the disordered state of the animal kingdom we see today, with all preying upon all, suffering, and being enslaved to their appetites. Most animals fear humans, and humans abuse and torment unnecessarily even domestic animals that serve them. (In a curious bit of exegesis, Wesley suggests that those spoken of as dying even though they had not sinned 'after the similitude of Adam's transgression', Rom. 5: 14, were animals.) But God hears the creatures' groans and will deliver (not annihilate) them—applying Revelation 21: 1–4 to all creatures according to their capacity: 'The whole brute creation will then, undoubtedly, be restored, not only to the vigour, strength, and swiftness which they had at their creation, but to a far higher degree of each than they ever enjoyed.' Nothing will cause them uneasiness; and as Isaiah 11: 6–9 suggests, their irregular appetites will be gone. Wesley even offers the fond conjecture that if humans are to become like angels, then perhaps animals will become like humans and be themselves capable of relating to God. To potential objections that animals are of no use in the future state, Wesley responds that it is not necessary that they be of use: creation is far more abundant now than would seem to be strictly necessary. Furthermore, as we contemplate the animals' happiness, we may see illustrated that mercy of God that is over all his works, as well as think of his love for us humans, who are better than the animals. We may see that justice is finally granted creatures who have suffered unjustly. And finally, we may learn that we ought to imitate God's mercy.

Obviously, Wesley gives far more attention to the animal world than any of the other preachers treated above, and his regretting of the abuse people heap upon animals is a fitting counterpart in his day to broader ecological concerns in our own. He is clear that human sin brought down the whole creation, and he is clear that all will finally be restored; but he does not make that future restoration explicitly contingent upon humankind's redemption, though he surely sees these as taking place together. Curiously, he makes no direct reference to redemption; nor does he dwell on the human body, which he mentions only in passing. His argument for the importance of the restoration of the animal world is, however, well developed, with a clear moral conclusion with respect to our duty of mercy in the present moment. This sermon demonstrates that a fundamental anthropocentrism is not inconsistent with care for the natural world, but should be seen as entailing it.

These four sermons, all without exception strongly anthropocentric in their handling of a text that is, after all, itself strongly anthropocentric, provide notable illustration of the point that anthropocentrism does not determine where one falls on the scale of concern for the non-human creation. Anthropocentrism may lead one to dismiss it (Huntington), see it instrumentally (Chrysostom), think of it in terms of its fittingness for human life (Spurgeon), or give it intrinsic worth, albeit a lower worth than that of humans (Wesley). Blaming humans for the misery of non-humans does not, interestingly enough, appear to generate much sense of present responsibility except in so far as the creation is seen as vulnerable in ways that are specifically under human control (as Wesley alone observed in human mistreatment of animals). In no case did these preachers hint that restoration of the creation was a sort of project humans could and should undertake on their own: all obviously assumed, with the text, that we await an act of God.

Sermons on Ecological Themes

Out of my sample of fifty sermons, eight (nos. 7, 19, 20, 27, 31, 33, 47, 49) have explicitly or at least generally ecological themes and in that sense directly take on my first question. Perhaps unsurprisingly, all of these were written by preachers associated with mainline denominations; and both *Christian Century* articles (19, 27) fall in this category. About two of these, not much can be said (and they are only tangentially on the text in any case). For instance, one Earth Day (fourth Sunday in Easter) sermon sets in contrast to Romans 8: 19–22 the affirmation:

The Earth herself, taken for granted for millennia of abuse, shouts, 'You may have killed him but now he is ME! I will not die!' She shouts, 'I will not die, but live, and declare the works of the Lord!' She shouts in an orgy of pollen and mating rituals and spring fever. The planet refuses to die its winter death to acid rain, polluted rivers, mercury in the water, refuses to be gashed in strip mining and refuses to yield its rain forests to the arthritic desperate grasp of human greed. You and I are its refusal. You and I are its resurrection, its hope of life.   (31)

This scream into the wind does not even purport to be an exposition of Romans 8 or a presentation of the hope of redemption, but simply naturalizes and generalizes the idea of resurrection, and does so in a way that surely strains credulity. Another preacher (20) makes the exegetical leap of identifying the children of God in Romans. 8: 19 with the peacemakers of Matthew 5: 9 and then sets these over against various despoilers of the creation, using the refrain of Psalm 120: 7 (KJV), 'I am for peace: but . . . they are for war'. A poetic and moving plea to be peacemakers results, but one that ignores redemption altogether.

Of the six remaining pieces, two (47, 49) explicitly connect the Fall to the current state of things; one (7) speaks of Genesis 3 in terms of even the name 'Adam' coming from the earth and thus showing our connectedness to it; one (33) comments with somewhat vague hope on the 'growing awareness that we share a common destiny with our planet' (with some additional remarks about the striking continuities in the DNA of all living beings); while a sophisticated treatment (19) posits instead of earthly hope, 'the steel vise of evolution's law', by which progress 'is fueled by bloody competition and suffering'. But this latter piece is clearest of any on the interrelatedness of creation, redemption, bodiliness, and eschatological hope: 'The creation which presently is the ground of human suffering will one day be made the ground of human redemption! . . . Though our sinful deeds are indeed works of the "flesh," our ultimate hope lies in "the redemption of our bodies." ' The resurrection of Christ 'decisively shows the limits of decay'; and we must acknowledge that, 'For Paul, the world as we experience it is not the final expression of God's creative purpose. God's ultimate purpose in creation is, and always has been eschatological.'

Redemption for both humankind and the natural order, linked together, also appear, at least implicitly, in the other five sermons, though only one (47) mentions specifically the redemption of the body. All but one (7) emphasize future hope. All six sermons mention stewardship of the natural world, though on a spectrum from warning that we must not 'fool ourselves into thinking that the salvation of the world's ills will be brought about by mere human efforts', and that 'when the end does come for the old world it will be because it is time for the creation of the new earth. It won't be because of ecological crisis' (49); to the quite different warning that 'the Redemption of Creation through the "first born" redeemed ones cannot be achieved if the earth is destroyed' (7). The trick is holding eschatological hope, finally dependent upon God, for a renewed creation, together with human responsibility for this creation. One preacher, like Wesley, emphasizes re-establishment of proper human dominion as a means of blessing (49; see also, to a lesser extent, 27). Two counsel the Spirit's work (27) or God's honour (19) as motives. Another suggests we should defend creation to demonstrate that we are redeemed (7). We may seek to retrieve St Francis's sense of tender commonality with the rest of creation (27); we might even ask, 'if creation were in some way actually to suffer pain—not in a merely metaphorical sense—would this give at least some of us certain pause?' (19). Such questions move us away from crassly utilitarian and self-interested approaches, and closer to the tone of a text that takes the created order seriously.

MORE-OR-LESS TOPICAL SERMONS

Of eighteen more-or-less topical sermons presumably based on all or part of Romans 8: 18–25, the largest number, eight (13, 24, 28, 34, 39, 40, 43, 46), were understandably on hope, and especially hope in the face of suffering of some sort. Interestingly enough, however, this hope often appears not to have much of a Godward direction, but rather to be a human duty that spurs present effort. In a particularly crass example, in an Advent sermon tellingly entitled 'Pragmatic Hope', the preacher dismisses the biblical witness as 'not particularly persuasive for many people' and concludes that we should 'consider the possibility that God needs us to bring the light of hope into this world' (34). One counsels 'invisible hope', along with the Spirit's invisible energy, to buoy our determination not to give up in the face of adversity (like the trials of trying to learn to ride a bicycle!): 'grit, groaning and sweat' are required, we are told (46). Another (while admittedly making some references to God) informs us that, 'The Bible teaches us that hope is the heart-felt confidence that a person derives from the expectation that he will be able to accomplish something which he desires'; he continues: 'Hope is an exercise in the growth of our spirit. You have to stretch yourself to have hope'

(39). A couple of sermons treat death and our fear of it, one with vague counsel to anticipate glory (40); another assures us that we and not God have made earth as it is, but if we put aside our fear of death, we can live. This assurance is capped by a striking misquote of Romans 8: 39: 'We remember that neither death, nor life, nor tragedy, nor loss, nothing in all creation can separate us from the love and hope God has for us' (24; here hope has become *God's* task). Yet another preacher, while saying in passing that we must set our hope on eternal things, still preaches essentially solely on hope with respect to this life (13). To say that these sermons miss the text, and certainly miss both creation and redemption, understates the case.

A somewhat better long sermon that at least (barely) mentions creation's bondage, our bodies, and our future hope, so focuses on that hope as to dismiss the whole of this life and all its sufferings as 'just a school time that we Christians are going through, and here we have been placed to learn some lessons that are preparing us for the great day yet to come' (43). Nothing of comfort here for any part of creation but Christians themselves; and treating all suffering as an occasion for growth surely fails to take the depth of evil and the extent of grotesquely gratuitous suffering seriously. The last sermon of this hope-focused group briefly touches upon the Fall and the hope of liberation of creation in the course of what will sound to some like a chipper piece of cheer-leading with respect to hope (28). Obviously, I see these pieces as unsatisfactory in general, and as a serious cheapening of the text.

One of the remaining sermons (allegedly on Rom. 8: 18–39) simply asserts that God works for good (3); another that God is in charge, with particular reference to Romans 8: 20 (30); another that we cannot separate the spiritual and the physical (in a sermon on prayer, but with reference to Rom. 8: 19–23, incarnation, and bodily resurrection) (9); another that we have freedom in Christ (29, jumping off from, but not treating, Rom. 8: 21). Yet another treats waiting and patience, with Romans 8: 17–25 merely as a prooftext (26). A sermon entitled 'Labor Pains' (45) confidently proclaims that *we* are pregnant: we 'just have to bear down and keep on pushing.... That baby is your new life in him. A life of prosperity—your bills all paid'. A topical piece on frustration notes in passing the unremarkable point that the world is a mess and we all groan (22). A sermon on our longings tells us that Paul's message in Romans 8: 22–5 is that 'our inward dissatisfaction is a God implanted urge for improvements' (16). A rather disconnected sermon that emphasizes the continuity of life all the way back to creation, speaks of 'God's vision' of love for God and creation, for neighbour and for self, and a reversal of the decisions made in the Garden of Eden that produced 'the feeling' of a great distance between God and humans (17). To be fair, the sermon is clear that we need saving and that only God can do it, but in an especially odd turn references John 14, with the suggestion that 'God is looking to us to be one of his mansions or dwelling places'. The final sermon in this group, on 'Christ and Cancer' (35), is a full and responsible treatment of illness, naturally focused on humankind, but with brief comment on the Fall, the redemption of our bodies, and the hope of another age to come—a topic appropriately handled in the context of the text we are considering. It is gratifying to find one example of responsible topical preaching on this passage, but nothing short of alarming to find only one.

MORE-OR-LESS EXPOSITORY SERMONS

The final eighteen[6] sermons do not clearly demonstrate that studied attention to a text delivers one from absurdity in preaching. Still, in particular contrast to the last set, they suggest that this apparently commonsense supposition—that focussing on a text helps—holds. (Recall that all but one (no. 38, Rahner's) of the sermons I am treating appear on no other basis of selection than that I was able to obtain them on the internet: the sample was intended to be eclectic and representative of what God's people are actually hearing.) Unsurprisingly, preachers from very conservative churches cluster overwhelmingly in this category.

All of these sermons without exception treat the natural order at least briefly. Only a very few (10,[7] 18, 36) fail to make a connection to Genesis 3, or at least to human sin (though one, after linking the current state of creation to the Fall, continues, 'This is really a

---

[6] Two sermons (1 and 44) I shall put aside on the grounds that, while their listed text covers the verses I have selected, in actuality the sermons do not.

[7] This odd piece asserts, along with a few *very* vague references to sin and evil, 'It isn't our choice that we live in a frustrated world. Paul says that God has subjected the world to frustration. It was God's will to subject the creation to frustration.... Paul indicates that frustration can be the mother of liberty.'

fulfillment of a scientific law called the Second Law of Thermo-dynamics' (21), which would seem to put things exactly the wrong way around). Several give *very* brief mention to ecological concerns (2, 11, 18, 42, 50); but of these, only three (2, 11, 50) give a still briefer mention of the propriety of good stewardship; and two of these three (2, 50) caution against over-valuing the creation or our own efforts, as if afraid of being identified with environmental causes. It was surprising indeed that several preachers confidently asserted the condition of the created order and sometimes human suffering to be God's *plan* or 'built into' creation (10, 14, 36; similarly the assertion, '[Life] was never *meant* to be fair' (37, emphasis added)), failing altogether to make a distinction between plan and judgement, and undercutting motivation to protect the natural world.

Given the prominence of the theme of hope in the passage, one is not surprised that future hope for humankind, involving at least a vaguely implied redemption, appears in all of this set of sermons; but three (6, 10, 21) do not include hope for the rest of creation. These same three, plus two more, do not link the future of the created order to humankind's future (14, 18; a few others (2, 4, 15, 42) make only a vague temporal connection). This list as a whole overlaps almost completely with the list of those sermons that make no mention (apart from the appearance of the phrase in the text itself) of the resurrection of the body (4, 6, 10, 14, 18, 21, 38, 50)—an overlap that can hardly be merely by chance. Lack of attention to the material world is logically enough correlated with lack of attention to material bodies. Indeed, one preacher (6) combines the assertion that, after the Fall, creation becomes the enemy, with the hope that one day we will trade our bodies in: while he may possibly intend a redemptive metaphor, the dismissive tone prevails.

These sermons, with the sole exception of one that is explicitly on the Second Coming of Christ (15), are overwhelmingly anthropocen-tric, though generally not neglecting to comment on the absolute necessity of divine action. Some put primary emphasis on topics like human suffering now (2, 14, 18, 21, 37), frustration (10), waiting or longings (4, 32); others take up several thematic elements of the text. Two preachers see the eschatological hope for creation as conse-quent upon a re-established, proper dominion of humankind (5, 11 (and 12)). Several, along with Chrysostom and Spurgeon, counsel that hearers not settle for or cling to this world (21, 32, 37, 50); while one wants at least to caution that emphasizing hope does not mean

that we fail to deal responsibly with the present world and its pres-
sures (25). Even where these sermons treat the natural order responsibly, they do so as something of a sideline to more pressing
concerns.

While most of the material in these sermons is fairly predictable
and unremarkable, even when perfectly appropriate, a few preachers
offer something a little fresh or different. One lovely, coherent
piece entitled 'A Universe Made to Our Measure' picks up and elaborates the old, intriguing thought that God right from the beginning
made the world not only centred on humankind, but also, in view of
his sure knowledge that humankind would sin, subject to suffering
and bondage right from the start. We are now integrated with it in
futility but will one day be integrated with it in beatitude (38).[8]
Another sounds the strongly Reformed note that God created
the material universe and humans with physical bodies, 'in order
to create added possibilities for the ways in which the inexhaustible
wealth of his glory could be shown forth and enjoyed by his creatures'; and insists that, 'It is our old bodies that will be made new in
the resurrection, and it is our old earth that will be made new when
Jesus comes' (36). One preacher uses as illustrations such details as
the research on plants being sensitive to human attitudes, and the
observation someone made that the sounds of nature are overwhelmingly in a minor key (42). And a long (32 single-spaced
pages!), rather combative sermon by a preacher so conservative
that he relies upon Archbishop James Ussher's chronology, contains
thoughtful observations such as the idea that apart from revelation
we could never know of creation's universal anticipation and
longing, but (in a sort of echo of Chrysostom) it would be odd
indeed if God's children should have less expectation than does the
impersonal creation (5).

---

[8] This idea is found in Augustine (*Enchiridion* 104; and in a sense in Gregory of
Nyssa's thought that the two sexes were created in anticipation of the Fall (*On the
Making of Man*, 17, NPNF 2/5)). Aspects of it were picked up, in a somewhat different
way, by Franz Delitzsch (*A New Commentary on Genesis*, 2 vols., trans. Sophia Taylor
(Edinburgh: T. & T. Clark, 1899), i. 103); and later the full-blown thought was
developed, tentatively, by Emil Brunner (*Christian Doctrine of Creation and Redemption*,
trans. Olive Wyon (London: Lutterworth Press, 1952), 131). It gets around the problem
that nature as we know it has always, even prior to the advent of humankind and their
sin, been 'red in tooth and claw'.

Reflections

All too obviously, the vast variety in this sample of sermons on a single text is impressive—and sometimes depressing.[9] It is surely instructive, though, that in virtually no respect do twentieth-or twenty-first-century sermons break ground completely untilled by preachers centuries earlier;[10] nor do earlier possibilities of interpretation easily disappear from the scene. Interpreting this last observation by cheerfully invoking the perspicuity of scripture would seem to run aground on the sheer diversity of these sermons; though that diversity would appear for the most part to involve less a matter of substantive differences in understanding of the meaning of the passage than various flights away from the passage altogether, most particularly in the topical sermons. True, the current scholarly consensus about the non-human referent of 'creation' is formally reflected in modern sermons, as is the idea that the dissolving of the old order by fire (e.g. 2 Pet. 3: 12) does not entail its utter destruction; but the old practice of taking only humankind into account is not thereby done away. That the older sermons, being longer than most of the modern ones, had more time for deeper reflection may be worth noting; but in other qualitative respects one cannot fairly compare sermons that have borne the test of time to many that one can only trust will not survive that test.[11] It will not be news to regular church-goers that altogether too much preaching is unsatisfactory both exegetically and pastorally.

In past contributions to our 'summits', I have affirmed, and even pleaded for, sound doctrinal preaching on the topic of the summit. This time I would add to my plea the hope that preachers might give more care to the non-human world. It took a long time for many Christians to affirm that the social demands of the gospel were not made irrelevant by the hope of heaven (interestingly enough, Chrysostom's argument *for* caring for the poor was precisely that they do

---

[9] This variety is also represented in matters like length, and in homiletical style and sheer competence (some of the sermons are stunningly incoherent, or odd almost to the point of being bizarre); but such issues are beyond the scope of this chapter.

[10] Ronald Goetz (19) might seem to be something of an exception here, but his sharp and compelling examples and analysis are fresh more in their treatment of the contemporary scene than of the biblical text.

[11] As a sign that they will not, some of the URLs for these sermons are already dead links.

have a hope of heaven). It is high time that the same discovery be
made with respect to the groaning natural order, not only subjected
to futility by God's own act, but ravaged in an ongoing way by
human sin and greed. I find it sad that preachers, when apparently
trying to take Romans 8: 18–25 seriously at the exegetical level and
even preaching an explicitly ecological sermon, seem embarrassed to
come to really robust conclusions about the *worth* of the created
order that is destined one day to be set free by God. That the old
anxiety about material reality comes into play here is surely suggested by the correlation between preachers' neglect of the resurrection of the body and their failure to affirm a future for the material
world (or failure to affirm that such a future is connected directly to
our own future). None of this, of course, involves the slightest
suggestion that we can redeem the environment by our own
strength, any more than we can redeem ourselves. But as we have
a duty to care for and not destroy our physical bodies, so we have a
duty to care for and not destroy our world.

In so far as the divine image—in the NT perfectly manifested by
Jesus—involves human dominion over the creation, and in so far as
we understand the incarnation to be permanent, it is fitting that
redemption should involve restoration of right relationships with the
(transformed) natural order. Indeed, the more we learn of our closeness to that order—not just that chimpanzees and humans have 99
per cent of their DNA in common, but even that chlorophyll and
haemoglobin are strikingly similar chemically—the less plausible it
seems that a redeemed humanity would be as it were surgically
extracted from this whole fabric of life. The bond commentators[12]
have often noted in our text from Romans has been shown to run
deep in the physical structure of things. By affirming this essential
connectedness of humankind and the natural world, we do not deny
human priority but only human isolation and utter self-centredness.

Such affirmations do not answer the questions many parishioners
will bring to a subject of this kind, most especially regarding the
future hope of beloved pets and the like. If Bishop Jewell is to enjoy
observing the contentment of his favourite mare, what about the

---

[12] e.g. James Dunn: 'Paul's thought is clearly that creation itself must be redeemed
in order that redeemed man may have a fitting environment.... Just as the resurrection hope is hope of a resurrection body, so resurrection life is to be part of a complete
creation' (*Romans 1–8* (Word Biblical Commentary, 38; Dallas, Tex.: Word, 1988), in
loc.); similarly Käsemann, Murray, and Nygren.

gardener with a favourite plot of land or the ecologist with a favourite wild river? Hopes and speculations can obviously be extended to the point of absurdity, into areas about which scripture offers us no guidance.[13] But if value is conferred by love—fundamentally by God's own love, but perhaps secondarily by our love, in so far as it escapes mere selfishness—then perhaps there are possibilities wider and richer and deeper than we dare imagine. In the context of the sympathy and hope for creation we find in Romans 8: 18–25, we may find ourselves at least resonating with the charming words of Martin Luther, who, upon reading this passage, turned to his little dog and said, with respect to the world to come, 'and you, too, shall have a little golden tail'.[14]

APPENDIX: SERMONS CONSULTED

1. Allred, C. Robert, 'Papa! Papa!', http://www.atlantafumc.org/sermons/archive/990718.html (United Methodist).

2. Andrus, Michael P., 'The Agony and the Ecstasy', http://www.efree.org/sermons/romans/agony_and_the_ecstasy.htm (Evangelical Free).

3. Blackburn, Peter J., 'God Works for Good', http://www.peterjblackburn.com/sermons/pb941114.htm (Uniting Church, Australia).

4. Blackburn, Peter J., 'Waiting in Hope', http://www.peterjblackburn.com/sermons/pb991107.htm.

5. Blakely, Given, 'Suffering Is the Prelude to Glory', http://www.wotruth.com/rom-26.htm (Independent?).

6. Campbell, Phil, 'A Series of Sermons on Romans 1 to 8: Romans 8', http://members.ozemail.com.au/~philcam/Romans.html#Sermon%208 (Presbyterian).

7. Castuera, Ignacio, 'An Act of God', from SermonCentral.com, but link is now dead (Methodist).

8. Chrysostom, St John, 'The Epistle of St. Paul the Apostle to the Romans', Homily 14 (NPNF, 1/11, 439–52).

---

[13] Though if we purpose to eschew speculation, we perhaps should eschew it altogether and not have quite the confidence manifested by the preacher who dismisses all such hopes as absurd, on the grounds that, in the presence of the Creator, impersonal associations can hardly maintain importance; and anyway, 'the liberation of creation is nowhere associated with a resurrection' (5).

[14] Quoted without source by Wilkinson (49). Luther makes a similar comment, though in a different context, in *WA TR* i. 567–8, no. 1150.

9. Collins, Ken, 'Does It Matter Whether We Sit, Stand, or Kneel to Pray?', http://www.kencollins.com/pray-21.htm (Christian Church (Disciples of Christ)).

10. Davis, Jim, 'Creation Subjected to Futility in Hope', http://focusongod. com/Romans-12.htm (Church of Christ).

11. Deffinbaugh, Robert, 'From Agony to Ecstasy', http://www.bible.org/ docs/nt/books/rom/deffin2/rom2-10.htm (Independent?—Bible Chapel).

12. Deffinbaugh, Robert, 'From Groaning to Glory', http://www.bible. org/docs/nt/books/rom/deffin/ro-23.htm

13. Dudley, Scott, 'Standing in the Middle of Hope', http://www. mppc.org/e_sermons/esermon_1998/mar_98/3_7_98.html (Presbyterian (PCUSA)).

14. Duncan, J. Ligon III, 'Present Sufferings/Future Glory', http://www. fpcjackson.org/resources/sermons/romans/romansvol3to4/27bRomans8 _18to25.htm (Presbyterian Church in America).

15. Fayard, Cecil A., 'Three Groanings Pointing to the Second Coming', http://www.elliottbaptist.org/sermon-081901.html (Independent Baptist).

16. Fritz, Paul, 'What Can We Learn from the Dissatisfaction Implanted on Our Hearts?', http://www.SermonCentral.com/sermon.asp?Sermon ID=30515&Contributor ID=6170 (unknown; teaches at Trinity College, Fla.; Christian and Missionary Alliance institution).

17. Gamble, Robert, [no title], http://www.rrcnet.org/∼umcj/sermon611. htm (United Methodist).

18. Gehrels, Ken, 'The Way of Righteousness: Hope amidst Groaning', http://www.cyberus.ca/~calvincrc/Sermons/Dec06pm.htm (Christian Reformed).

19. Goetz, Ronald, 'Cosmic Groanings', http://www.religion-online.org/ cgi-bin/relsearchd.dll/showarticle?item_id-32 (unknown, teaches at UCC college).

20. Hoffman, Frank L., 'I am for Peace, But they are for War', http:// www.all-creatures.org/sermons98/s/0May98.html (Federated Church, United Methodist and American Baptist).

21. Hoke, David J., 'Groaning for Glory', http://www.horizonsnet.org/ sermons/rom27.html (Southern Baptist).

22. Holwick, David, 'Frustrated?', http://holwick.homestead.com/files/ chrmas/adv6.html (Baptist).

23. Huntington, William, 'The Expectation of the Creature, and its Certain Deliverance', http://www.users.wwd.net/user/RONT/WH00006.htm (Reformed).

24. Jong, Patricia de, 'Coming to Terms,' http://www.fccb.org/sermons/ s96/sr960721.html (United Church of Christ).

25. Kihyohiro, Takao, 'Living in Hope', trans. Mike Furey, http://www.j-e-s-u-s.org/e981108.htm (translator is Baptist; the two have a joint USA–Japan ministry).

26. Loughran, David, 'Waiting for Salvation', http://atschool.eduweb.co.uk/sbs777/snotes/note0606.html (unknown, Bible School).

27. Lueking, F. Dean, 'Pentecost for the World (Romans 8: 22–27)', http://www.religion-online.org/cgi-bin/relsearchd.dll/showarticle'' item_id =679 (Lutheran).

28. Mertz, Jim, 'It Will Be Worth It All', http://members.aol.com/dabeej/FWBaptist/sermons3.htm (Free Will Baptist).

29. Metcalfe, Russell, 'Freedom in Becoming', http://www.enc.edu/org/wollynaz/rmetcalfe/dad.freedom_in_becoming (Nazarene).

30. Morley, Patrick, 'Coming Back to God', http://www.SermonCentral.com/sermon.asp?Sermon ID=4276&Contributor ID=7154 (non-denominational ministry).

31. Oliver, Juan M. C., 'Earth Day', http://www.episcopalchurch.org/worship-that-works/970420sx.html (Episcopalian).

32. Ortland, Raymond C., Jr., 'Don't Lose Your Longings!', http://www.firstpresaugusta.org/firstpres/sermons/Romans08,22-25.htm (Presbyterian Church in America).

33. Pearce, Patricia, 'A Common Destiny', http://www.tabunited.org/sermons/01_06_17.html (United Church, Presbyterian and United Church of Christ).

34. Pearce, Patricia, 'Pragmatic Hope', http://www.tabunited.org/sermons/00_12_03.html.

35. Piper, John, 'Christ and Cancer', http://www.soundofgrace.com/piper80/081780m.htm (Baptist).

36. Piper, John, 'Our Hope: The Redemption of Our Bodies', http://www.soundofgrace.com/piper86/jp860020.htm.

37. Pounds, Wil, 'The Groan Before the Glory', http://www.abidein-christ.com/messages/rom8v18.html (Baptist).

38. Rahner, Karl, 'A Universe Made to our Measure', *Biblical Homilies* (New York: Herder & Herder, 1966), 91–8. (Roman Catholic).

39. Raymer, Doug, 'In Hope We Have Been Saved', http://www.slsoftware.com/study/html_outlines/In_Hope_We_Have_Been_Saved.html (Independent ministry?).

40. Scott, Janice, 'The Hope of Glory', http://www.sermons-stories.co.uk/matep21ent.htm (Church of England).

41. Spurgeon, Charles H., 'Creation's Groans and the Saints' Sighs', http://www.spurgeon.org/sermons/0788.htm (Baptist).

42. Stedman, Ray C., 'The Agony and the Ecstasy', http://pbc.org/dp/Stedman/romans2/3521.html (Independent).

43. Stedman, Ray C., 'The Joy of Being Grown Up', http://www.pbc.org/dp/Stedman/romans1/0018.html.

44. Strayhorn, Billy D., 'Heirs to the Greatest Promise', http://www.epulpit.net/billy117.htm (Methodist).

45. Torrence, Antonio, 'Labor Pains', http://www.SermonCentral.com/sermon.asp?Sermon ID=31670&Contributor ID=2298 (Lutheran).

46. Wagner, Keith, 'Invisible Hope', http://www.bright.net/~coth/invhope. htm (United Church of Christ).

47. Wehrfritz-Hanson, Garth, 'Labor Pains and Hope', http://members.tripod.com/wehrhan/47-index.html (Lutheran).

48. Wesley, John, 'The General Deliverance', http://gbgm-umc.org/umhistory/Wesley/sermons/serm-060.stm (Anglican).

49. Wilkinson, Dave, 'A Theology of Ecology', http://www.moorparkpres.org/Sermons/11898.htm (Presbyterian (PCUSA)).

50. Zeisler, Steve, 'Eager Anticipation', http://www.pbc.org/dp/zeisler/4347.html (Independent).

Index of Names